REA

D0205684

DO NOT REMOVE
CARDS FROM POCKET

Critical Essays on
LORD BYRON

CRITICAL ESSAYS
ON
BRITISH LITERATURE

Zack Bowen, General Editor
University of Miami

Critical Essays on

LORD BYRON

edited by

ROBERT F. GLECKNER

G. K. Hall & Co. / *New York*
Maxwell Macmillan Canada / *Toronto*
Maxwell Macmillan International / *New York   Oxford   Singapore   Sydney*

G. K. Hall & Co.
Macmillan Publishing Company
866 Third Avenue
New York, NY 10022

Maxwell Macmillan Canada, Inc.
1200 Eglinton Avenue East
Suite 200
Don Mills, Ontario M3C 3N1

Macmillan Publishing Company is part of the Maxwell Communication
Group of Companies.

Library of Congress Cataloging-in-Publication Data
Critical essays on Lord Byron / edited by Robert F. Gleckner.
      p.   cm.—(Critical essays on British literature)
   Includes index.
   ISBN 0-8161-8859-9
   1. Byron, George Gordon Byron, Baron, 1788–1824—Criticism and
interpretation.   I. Gleckner, Robert F.   II. Series.
PR4388.C75   1991
821'—dc20   91-21926
                                                                 CIP

The paper used in this publication meets the minimum requirements of
American National Standard for Information Sciences—Permanence of
Paper for Printed Library Materials, ANSI Z39.48-1984. ∞™

10 9 8 7 6 5 4 3 2 1

Printed in the United States of America

Contents

◆

General Editor's Note

◆

The Critical Essays on British Literature series provides a variety of approaches to both classical and contemporary writers of Britain and Ireland. The formats of the volumes in the series vary with the thematic designs of individual editors and with the number and nature of existing reviews, criticism, and scholarship. In general, the series represents the best in published criticism, augmented, where appropriate, by original essays by recognized authorities. It is hoped that each volume will be unique in developing a new overall perspective on its particular subject.

Robert Gleckner confines his discussion of Byron criticism and selection of essays to those that began in the great decade of Byron scholarship, the 1960s, and later essays that were heavily influenced by the criticism of that era. In his introduction, Gleckner describes earlier critical studies as saturated with discussion of the circumstances of Byron's life and its effect on his poetry, and the burgeoning of new and fruitful avenues of exploration in the 1960s and beyond. In a departure from the usual series format, Gleckner appends to each essay a brief bibliographical discussion of the critical history and importance of the selection.

ZACK BOWEN

University of Miami

Publisher's Note

◆

Producing a volume that contains both newly commissioned and reprinted material presents the publisher with the challenge of balancing the desire to achieve stylistic consistency with the need to preserve the integrity of works first published elsewhere. In the Critical Essays series, essays commissioned especially for a particular volume are edited to be consistent with G. K. Hall's house style; reprinted essays appear in the style in which they were first published. Consequently, shifts in style from one essay to another are the result of our efforts to be faithful to each text as it was originally published.

Introduction

◆

ROBERT F. GLECKNER

Since I have appended to each essay or book excerpt included in this volume an Editor's Bibliographical Note—some fairly extensive, others less so—and since they serve in toto as a kind of history of Byron criticism since roughly 1960, there is little need here to recapitulate the substance and scope, not to say the particularity, of those notes. What does call for some comment, however, is the basis (or bases) for my selection especially since, as two recent publications demonstrate, critical publications on Byron's work, both poetry and prose, are almost bewilderingly various in kind and quality—as befits any major author. The two books I have in mind are *George Gordon, Lord Byron: A Comprehensive Bibliography of Secondary Materials in English, 1807–1974,* compiled by Oscar José Santucho, with a 166-page "Critical Review of Research" by Clement Tyson Goode, Jr. (Metuchen, N.J.: Scarecrow Press, 1977), and John Clubbe's 127-page bibliographical essay on Byron in *The English Romantic Poets: A Review of Research and Criticism,* edited by Frank Jordan (New York: Modern Language Association, 1985). In addition, I should also note here the slim but helpful *Byron Criticism Since 1952: A Bibliography,* edited by Ronald B. Hearn et al. (Salzburg: University of Salzburg, 1979)—though it is to the first two that I owe major debts—not least the lesson (implicit in Clubbe's multisectioned and subsectioned essay) that any neat classification or grouping or clustering of kinds of Byron criticism is simply not possible except as a basic patterning from which almost immediately to diverge. In many ways it is fair to say that the following selections, all previously published, diverge and remerge, point in directions beyond their announced purview as well as speak to Byron's works other than their immediate textual focus, react against and interact with each other, and so on. Yet all draw their sustenance and critical efficacy, in one way or the other, from the extraordinary decade of the 1960s.

As both Goode and Clubbe have rightly indicated, prior to this time, with obvious exceptions (many of which are cited in my bibliographical notes), the Byron critical arena was saturated with commentary on Byron's life. Such criticism (in the strictest sense) that emerged out of that concentration falls into the category we somewhat lamely, and generously, call biographical criticism—not, I hasten to add, that sort of biographical-historical-textual criticism advocated and practiced so eloquently in recent years by Jerome J. McGann and a number of other modern critics and scholars, virtually all of whom are represented in this collection in the selections themselves or in the bibliographical notes. And, as again both Goode and Clubbe note, the decade of the 1960s inaugurated a "new" Byron criticism that laid the foundations for, though did not always specifically anticipate, the exciting and illuminating commentary on, discussions of, and debates over the entire range of Byron's poetry—and to a lesser extent his prose. Goode calls this era (1957 to 1972) "Balance Restored: Renaissance in Biography and Criticism," to which Santucho adds a bibliographical "Epilogue: 1973–1974"; and in his essay Clubbe extends the era in the section entitled "The 1980s."

It is with the sixties that this present collection begins, George M. Ridenour's "A Waste and Icy Clime" from *The Style of "Don Juan"* (1960). This book, although preceded by fine studies of *Don Juan* by Elizabeth Boyd (*Byron's "Don Juan": A Critical Study* [New Brunswick, N.J.: Rutgers University Press]) and Paul Graham Trueblood (*The Flowering of Byron's Genius: Studies in "Don Juan"* [Palo Alto, Calif.: Stanford University Press]), both in 1945, richly deserves, in my judgment, the pride of place I accord it—not merely for its original and ground-breaking analysis of *Don Juan* but for its enduring influence on the subsequent study of virtually all of Byron's poetry, nondramatic and dramatic. Its immediate progeny, or in several cases immediate contemporaries or successors rather than direct descendants, include the following stunning group of books—all preceded (as was Ridenour) by the equally stunning *Byron's "Don Juan": A Variorum Edition* in four volumes, edited by Truman Guy Steffan and Willis W. Pratt (Austin: University of Texas Press) and Leslie A. Marchand's three-volume *Byron: A Biography* (New York: Knopf), both in 1957, and the still insufficiently attended to two-volume *Lord Byron: Un Tempérament littéraire* by Robert Escarpit (Paris: Le Cercle du livre, 1955, 1957): in 1960 Paul West's erratic and idiosyncratic *Byron and the Spoiler's Art* (London: Chatto & Windus), in 1961 Andrew Rutherford's *Byron: A Critical Study* (Edinburgh: Oliver & Boyd) and Harold Bloom's 42-page section on Byron in *The Visionary Company: A Reading of English Romantic Poetry* (New York: Doubleday), in 1962 William H. Marshall's *The Structure of Byron's Major Poems* (Philadelphia: University of Pennsylvania Press) and Peter L. Thorslev's *The Byronic Hero: Types and Prototypes* (Minneapolis: University of Minnesota Press), in 1963 Edward E. Bostetter's 60-page section on Byron in *The Romantic Ventriloquists* (Seattle: University of Washington Press), in 1964 Michael K. Joseph's *Byron, the Poet* (London: V. Gollancz), in 1965 Alvin B. Kernan's 51-page section on *Don Juan* in *The Plot of Satire* (New Haven: Yale University Press) and Leslie A. Marchand's *Byron's Poetry: A Critical Introduction* (Boston: Houghton Mifflin), in 1966 G. Wilson Knight's *Byron and Shakespeare* (London: Routledge & Kegan

Paul), in 1967 Robert F. Gleckner's *Byron and the Ruins of Paradise* (Baltimore: Johns Hopkins University Press), in 1968 Jerome J. McGann's *Fiery Dust: Byron's Poetic Development* (Chicago and London: University of Chicago Press), W. Paul Elledge's *Byron and the Dynamics of Metaphor* (Nashville: Vanderbilt University Press) and Truman Guy Steffan's *Lord Byron's "Cain": Twelve Essays and a Text with Variants and Annotations* (Austin: University of Texas Press), and in 1969 Michael G. Cooke's *The Blind Man Traces the Circle: On the Patterns and Philosophy of Byron's Poetry* (Princeton: Princeton University Press). And to these must be added, though a bit later, Thomas L. Ashton's *Byron's "Hebrew Melodies"* (Austin: University of Texas Press, 1972).

Some brief comments on each may be in order here as a kind of shorthand guide to what these books cover and how—though what I have to say should certainly be compared to Goode's and Clubbe's differing judgments of their accomplishment. West's book, which Clubbe characterizes, accurately, as "flashy and superficial," shares with Philip W. Martin's 1982 *Byron: A Poet before His Public* (Cambridge: Cambridge University Press) the dubious distinction of being the most hostile critique of Byron's poetic achievement among major university press publications, although Martin's is redeemed somewhat by his efforts, though often abortive, to deal with Byron's audience—a subject that still calls for more serious and extensive research and discussion. With F. R. Leavis hovering subliminally in the background (see his "Byron's Satire" in *Revaluation: Tradition and Development in English Poetry* [London: Chatto & Windus, 1936]), Rutherford pays scant, and then generally denigrating, attention to the nonsatiric poems except for *Childe Harold, Manfred,* and *The Prisoner of Chillon.* The first of these, according to Rutherford, improves only in Canto IV, III being regarded as interesting but finally unsatisfactory, and I and II judged, for the most part, as forgettable as the Turkish Tales of 1812–1816; *Manfred* is important though seriously flawed; but *The Prisoner* is his finest nonsatiric work, matching the "aesthetically perfect" satiric achievement of *The Vision of Judgment.* The "real" Byron is that of *Beppo* and *Don Juan,* and Rutherford's discussion of both (in almost half the book's pages) is valuable. Bloom's *The Visionary Company,* published in the same year, is far more judicious despite its only relatively brief comments on a wide range of the poetry.

Marshall's book, in retrospect seemingly more modest than it appeared to be then, is still better than the above three, essaying a coherent view of Byron's poetic development from *English Bards and Scotch Reviewers* through *Childe Harold,* three of the so-called Turkish Tales (most notably *Parisina*), *Manfred, Mazeppa, Beppo,* and *Don Juan.* Thorslev's book usefully categorizes and defines the several antecedent literary components that constitute the genealogy of what we (I think misleadingly) refer to as the "Byronic Hero," and then sets most of Byron's "heroes," not always fully satisfactorily (or even accurately), in that context. Bostetter's *The Romantic Ventriloquists* deals with all the major romantic poets, and its treatment of Byron is notable for the excellent discussion of *Cain, The Vision of Judgment,* and *Don Juan.* M. K. Joseph's *Byron, the Poet* is, by contrast, the most capacious, thoroughgoing, and intelligent commentary up to 1964 on Byron's entire poetic corpus, with extensive attention to *Don Juan,* though with little or no attention to the lyrics, both early and late. Goode's judgment of it is sound: it "may remain for some time the standard introduction to Byron's poetry," although it must vie strenuously for that laurel with Marchand's *Byron's Poetry: A Critical Introduction,* which appeared a year later (and which does treat the "lyric" Byron), and with Bernard Beatty's 1987 *Byron: "Don Juan" and Other Poems: A Critical Study* (London: Penguin Books).

Similarly, the best introduction to the "satiric Byron," as well as a first-rate "reading" of *Don Juan* that contrapuntally compares well with Ridenour's (and indeed all previous major analyses of that work), is Kernan's *The Plot of Satire,* which appeared the same year as Marchand's far more wide-ranging "introduction." It also sets the stage expertly for all subsequent arguments with respect to the relative status of *Don Juan* as comic, epic, satiric, or some combination of these. Knight's *Byron and Shakespeare* is in many ways incomparable, stimulating and exciting even as it is irritating and often unreliable in its elevation of Byron to the status of modern Shakespeare. It is fun to read, more so than his 1952 *Lord Byron: Christian Virtues* (London: Routledge & Kegan Paul) or, the inception of his extraordinary multivolumed and multifaceted preoccupation with Byron's life and work, *The Starlit Dome: Studies in the Poetry of Vision* with its appendix "on Spiritualism and Poetry" (London: Oxford University Press, 1941). My own *Byron and the Ruins of Paradise* of 1967 is not fun to read. Indeed it has been accorded the dubious distinction of being the prime exhibit of an unrelentingly grim and pessimistic view of Byron's presentation of "the human condition." While it clearly reflects my admiration for, and the influence of, Ridenour's more graceful pursuit of the idea of the Fall in Byron—as well as my complicity, often unintentional, with other earlier books like Charles Du Bos's *Byron et le besoin de la fatalité* (1927), translated excellently by Ethel C. Mayne as *Byron and the Need for Fatality* (London: Putnam, 1932)—the grimness of my view is all my own. Whether grimness is precisely right or not, the book does deal, as Joseph's and Marchand's did earlier, with virtually all of Byron but with considerably less of *Beppo, The Vision of Judgment,* and *Don Juan* than I would have liked; and it does represent the first extensive treatment of *Hours of Idleness* and major attention to all of *Childe Harold* and the tales.

The essay of mine included in the present volume is my only attempt to moderate the thesis of the book, though a more extensive "moderation" is to be found in the "positive" analysis of Byron's development in Jerome J. McGann's excellent *Fiery Dust* in 1968. It is, as Clubbe rightly says, "one of the most important books about Byron to appear in the twentieth century"— albeit the fundamental view developed therein of Byron's poetic development has undergone major modification in McGann's many, many subsequent books and articles on Byron. The book contains what is still the best treatment of all of *Childe Harold's Pilgrimage* and certainly some of the best work to date on the early lyrics, *The Giaour, Mazeppa, The Island, The Prisoner of Chillon,* and no less than five of the plays. *Don Juan* he reserved for his next book, the splendid *"Don Juan" in Context* (Chicago: University of Chicago Press, 1976). In the same year as *Fiery Dust* W. Paul Elledge's book eschews all comment on the satires (and *Don Juan,* however it is classified) in favor of basically image-pattern analyses of *The Corsair, Lara, Parisina, The Prisoner, Manfred,* the third canto of *Childe Harold,* and three of the plays (*Marino Faliero, Sardanapalus,* and *Cain*)—part of the continuing correction of pre-1960s assumptions about, or indifference to, Byron's poetic artistry.

Steffan's exhaustive study of *Cain,* also published in 1968, is a kind of scholarly critical overkill, especially in its inclusion of the amazing eruption in England and on the continent of reactions to the play's publication. Nevertheless, all future critical attention to *Cain,* as well as to Byron's religious (and political) ideas, has benefited from Steffan's exhaustive research into the text's history, reception, and progressive criticism—and will continue to do so even though virtually all recent critical studies go considerably beyond, and in different directions from, Steffan's own. At the end of the decade, and thereby fortuitously providing a closing critical bracket fully worthy of matching Ridenour's opening one, is Michael Cooke's fine study of Byron's poetry with all its ambivalences, its fundamental philosophically skeptical bent, and its underlying "counter-heroism." While it does not have the scope of Joseph's earlier study, or even of mine, the fundamental importance of what he has to say about *Childe Harold, Manfred, Mazeppa, Cain,* and *Don Juan* (and to a lesser extent some of the lyrics and other shorter poems) will remain unquestioned. Some testimony to the enduring value of Cooke's interpretation of Byron's skepticism is evidenced in Donald Reiman's continued pursuit of full understanding of *Byronic* skepticism in his *Intervals of Inspiration* (1988), from which I have reprinted most of the Byron section in this collection.

Of these books from the sixties the reader will find excerpts from only three (Ridenour, McGann, and Cooke). In a much larger book, the decade would have been more exactly served by excerpts from virtually all of the above-listed books. Needless to say the tempo of journal publishing on Byron was also stepped up, fueled by the remarkable decade; but I think it fair to say that no comparable outpouring of Byron criticism, and certainly none of comparable overall quality, originality, and provocativeness, has occurred since—although the years 1987 to 1991 do rival the sixties in their inauguration of what has all the earmarks of still newer directions, fueled in large part by the work of such Byron scholar-critics as McGann, Frederick Garber, Peter J. Manning, Susan Wolfson, Bernard Beatty, and Jerome Christensen, all of whom are represented in this collection.

What is not represented is a wide variety of essays on specific poems.

Although in one way or another most of Byron's works *are* dealt with or referred to in this volume, *Don Juan* (I think properly) appears under scrutiny more than the other poems. There is little here on the plays, for example, although most of them figure prominently, if indirectly, in several of the bibliographical notes. They deserve better, and, as my citation in several bibliographical notes of a number of critical studies indicates, the last decade or so has experienced a most welcome increase of interest in all of Byron's plays—indeed one, I believe, well worth honoring with a separate volume of modern critical essays devoted entirely to the plays. *Manfred, The Prisoner of Chillon,* and *Cain* are perhaps the most conspicuously, and lamentably, absent except for Garber's pages on the former two, not because important, valuable criticism of these works is wanting, but rather because the most exciting recent critical directions have tended, to date, to deal less with these works than others, a relative neglect I anticipate being remedied in the near future. A number of other shorter poems are also generally absent from these pages: *English Bards and Scotch Reviewers, Beppo,* and *The Vision of Judgment* among the well-known satires; a few of the Turkish Tales (most notably *Parisina,* which is now generally thought of as Byron's best); "The Lament of Tasso" and "The Prophecy of Dante"; the 1816 lyrics addressed to Augusta; "Darkness" and "The Dream"; and most of Byron's lyrics and occasional verse (other than those few in the *Hours of Idleness* collection dealt with by Cooke and Heinzelman), including, much to my regret, the *Hebrew Melodies.*

In part to remedy the lack of material from these last two groups, I list here some representative critical work on both *Hours of Idleness* and *Hebrew Melodies.* There are remarkably few articles devoted to these poems, and of the sixties books cited above, only Gleckner, McGann, and Cooke provide substantial analyses of the former. Spurred by Thomas Ashton's edition and commentary on *Hebrew Melodies,* cited earlier, and following the early essay by Joseph Slater, "Byron's Hebrew Melodies" (*Studies in Philology* 49 [1952]: 75–94), there has been some excellent work done recently on those poems: Frederick Shilstone, "The Lyric Collection as Genre: Byron's *Hebrew Melodies,*" in *Concerning Poetry* 12 (1979): 45–52; Frederick Burwick, "Identity and Tradition in the *Hebrew Melodies,*" and Paul Douglass, "Isaac Nathan's Setting for *Hebrew Melodies,*" both in *English Romanticism: The Paderborn Symposium,* ed. R. Breur, W. Huber, R. Schowerling (Essen, Germany, 1985). Although on neither of the two book collections of lyrics, Jean H. Hagstrum's "Byron's Songs of Innocence: The Poems to 'Thyrza,'" in *Evidence in Literary Scholarship,* ed. René Wellek and Alveiro Ribeiro (Oxford: Clarendon Press, 1979): 380–93, is exemplary in its judicious dealing with those important early lyrics.

Byron criticism from 1970 to the present is relatively well represented in this collection, as well as in the brief commentaries on individual authors, books, and articles during this period included in the bibliographical notes. It is difficult to categorize precisely the nature of the new directions virtually all these essays represent, but one element in any such categorizing is clearly the far more intensive focus than before on the political, social, and economic backgrounds and dimensions of Byron's poetry and career, as well as the beginnings at least of feminist criticism. The essays by Heinzelman and Christensen included in this volume are at the center of the former focus—as are *Byron: Poetry and Politics,* edited by Erwin A. Stürzl and James Hogg (Salzburg: Salzburg Institut für Anglistik und Amerikanistik, 1981), and Malcolm Kelsall's far more penetrating *Byron's Politics* (Sussex: Harvester Press, 1987). Of the latter focus, the best to date is Susan Wolfson's essay reprinted here, but one hopes that Anne K. Mellor's collection of essays, *Romanticism and Feminism* (Bloomington: Indiana University Press, 1988), will galvanize others into action on behalf of all Byronists. Certainly Peter Vassallo's *Byron: The Italian Literary Influence* (New York: St. Martin's Press, 1984) has opened a number of (at least potentially) new doors into the post-1816 Byron, as have Marjorie Levinson's recent work on Wordsworth and Keats, and her Byron essays in *The Romantic Fragment Poem: A Critique of a Form* (Chapel Hill: University of North Carolina Press, 1986). And add to these Louis Crompton's *Byron and Greek Love: Homophobia in 19th-Century England* (London: Faber; Berkeley: University of California Press, 1985) and Jerome Christensen's more shrewdly and sophisticatedly critical "Setting Byron Straight: Class, Sexuality, and the Poet," in *Literature and the Body: Essays on Populations and Persons,* edited by Elaine Scarry (Baltimore: Johns Hopkins University Press, 1988).

What we need is more on Byron's stormy relationship with his readership, for none of the best we have on the subject has yet done the job: Andrew Rutherford, *Byron the Best-Seller* (Nottingham Lecture, 1964); Ian Jack, *The Poet and His Audience* (Cambridge: Cambridge University Press, 1984); Philip Martin's book mentioned earlier in this introduction; and, closer to the mark, Jon P. Klancher, *The Making of English Reading Audiences, 1790–1832* (Madison: University of Wisconsin Press, 1987). And we need more, *much* more, on the letters and journals, for themselves as well as for their intimate and complex interrelationships with the poetry. This is to say that with McGann's magnificent new seven-volume edition of *The Complete Poetical Works* (Oxford: Clarendon Press, 1980–) and Marchand's twelve-volume edition of *Byron's Letters and Journals* (Cambridge, Mass.: Harvard University Press, 1973–82), as well as his magisterial *Byron: A Biography* (New York: Knopf, 1957), together in hand, one can expect more of the "new" biographical critique in the broadest sense, historical, political, economic, social, textual, and so on.

A final note on the arrangement of the essays: they are generally organized in chronological order from 1960 through 1988 rather than on the basis of poems dealt with, or of similar or related critical approaches, or of possible pairings to illustrate sharply contrasting approaches. In fact, this simple temporal arrangement of contemporary or very nearly contemporary essays rather fortuitously recounts the progressive emergence of the varieties of approach and content this volume aspires to represent.

I conclude by offering no apology for the unusual practice of including more than one contribution from any individual critic—having committed this editorial frame-breaking for Jerome J. McGann who, as clearly one of the major doers and shakers in my "history" of Byron criticism, richly deserves that honor. My regrets about having to exclude a considerable range of fine essays and chapters of books are, I hope, adequately voiced, both implicitly, and on occasion explicitly, in virtually all the editor's bibliographical notes.

ARTICLES AND ESSAYS

◆

"A Waste and Icy Clime"

George M. Ridenour

One of the principal obstacles to an appreciation of *Don Juan* on the part of many serious readers of poetry in our day has been what seems to them the irresponsible nature of Byron's satire. They feel that, clever as the poem undoubtedly is in parts, taken as a whole it is immature, exhibitionistic, lacking in integrity. This has caused distress on both moral and aesthetic grounds. But though it is not prudery to refuse assent to the implications of the poet's vision, it would be unjust to deny due praise to the style of that vision—its special grace and swagger. Certain obvious faults in the manner of the poem may be frankly conceded. Byron is sometimes careless, and there are times when he is obviously showing off. Sometimes, though rarely in *Don Juan,* he is guilty of bad taste.

But it is not these things, I suspect, that constitute the real problem. It has more to do with the uncertainty of the satirist's point of view as compared, say, with Horace or Pope. Satirists are normally conservatives and are proceeding at least ostensibly on the basis of a generally accepted (or in any case familiar) system of norms, principles, and attitudes. That this is not true of Byron in the way in which it is true of Horace or Pope (though the consistency of both is liable to some criticism) is clear enough. Byron is notoriously a rebel, and rebels have not enjoyed high critical esteem lately.

But Byron is not a consistent rebel. There is, for example, his apparently snobbish insistence on Juan's birth and breeding. And his views on women would hardly commend themselves to emancipated spirits. But then what were Byron's views on women (or aristocrats)? They seem to undergo such remarkable shifts in the course of sixteen cantos that is not easy to say. The apparent lack of structure in terms of which these shifting points of view can be assimilated is, I gather, the basic problem of *Don Juan* for the modern reader. It is not so much "What does he stand for?" (that is not always self-evident in the most traditional of satires), as "How do his various professions fit together?" In short, is *Don Juan* a chaos or a unity?

The question is natural and not unanswerable. The answer, however, cannot be in terms of a system. . . . Even more than his Scriblerian predecessors, Byron had a temperamental aversion to system. He is not to be categorized either intellectually or poetically. But this is not to say that his vision is

From *The Style of* "Don Juan" (New Haven: Yale University Press, 1960). Reprinted by permission.

incoherent. It is, in fact, elaborately coherent. And it is with what seem to me the dominant modes of this coherence that I shall be largely concerned.

In the first place, Byron, rebel that he is, is perfectly willing to make use of traditional concepts for his own ends. Some elements of the Christian myth especially commended themselves to him both as man and as poet. Whether it was the result of the Calvinistic influences of Byron's Scottish childhood, whether it was temperamental, aesthetic, the product of his own experience, or any combination of these factors, Byron seems throughout his life to have had peculiar sympathy with the concept of natural depravity. Lovell has asserted that "Byron held consistently to a belief in the existence of sin and the humanistic ideal of virtue as self-discipline. The fall of man—however he resented the injustice of its consequences—is the all-shadowing fact for him."[1] Whatever one may think of this as a biographical generalization, it is clearly true of the imagination of the poet of *Don Juan*—with the reservation that in the poem the Christian doctrine of the Fall is a *metaphor* which Byron uses to express his own personal vision. In *Childe Harold,* as we shall see, he developed an original reading of the Prometheus myth for similar purposes.

The myth of the Fall, then, is an important means of organizing the apparently contradictory elements of *Don Juan*. In the context of Byron's reading of the myth, Helene Richter's and William J. Calvert's interpretation of Byron in terms of a classic-romantic paradox and Antonio Porta's very similar Rousseau-Voltaire split are seen as elements in a vision not readily to be categorized under any of these headings.[2]

Byron introduces Canto IV with a stanza on the perils of poetry:

> Nothing so difficult as a beginning
>   In poesy, unless perhaps the end;
> For oftentimes when Pegasus seems winning
>   The race, he sprains a wing, and down we tend,
> Like Lucifer when hurled from Heaven for sinning;
>   Our sin the same, and hard as his to mend,
> Being Pride, which leads the mind to soar too far,
> Till our own weakness shows us what we are. (IV. 1)

What one immediately notices is the connection between this stanza and the imagery of flight in the Dedication. One thinks particularly of Blackbird Southey "overstraining" himself and "tumbling downwards like the flying fish," or even more, perhaps, of the ominous reference to the Tower of Babel. Here again a fall results from the attempt at a flight beyond one's proper powers. And, indeed, the motif is recurrent throughout the poem. At the beginning of Canto XI, for example, Byron describes the "spirit," some of whose metaphysical flights he had been discussing, as a liquor (a "draught," "Heaven's brandy") which is a bit too heady for the "brain" (XI. 1). Metaphysical speculation is a kind of drunkenness, and the image is one of genial diminution. Then, with a characteristically Byronic modulation of the image of "indisposition," he adds: "For ever and anon comes Indigestion / (Not the most 'dainty Ariel'), and perplexes / Our soarings with another kind of question" (XI.3). Man's loftiest flights are subject to the unpredictable activities of the digestive system. (The further modulation of the image in stanzas 5 and 6, by which physical ills, just now seen as hazards to spiritual flight, become incentives to religious orthodoxy, strikes me as adroit.) The passage is only one of many emphasizing man's physical nature and the folly of forgetting it or trying to pretend that it is other than it is.

But both the stanza on poets and the lines on metaphysics differ in at least one important way from those passages in the Dedication which also make use of the image of flight. In the Dedication, while the satire is not merely personal, it does take the form of an attack on a real individual or group. This is a common device of satire, and one which Byron continues to use throughout the poem. But in *Don Juan* the satiric implications of the image are characteristically generalized. It is "we" who fall, and it is "*our* soarings" that are perplexed. Byron is making a comment on human beings in general, on human nature. And if the comment is not remarkably optimistic, neither is it broodingly grim.

The point is of particular importance with regard to the first passage ("Nothing so difficult, etc."). For what Byron is speaking of here is not merely a quality of bad poets; it is something that he sees as characteristic of *all* poets, including himself. A poet, to earn the name, *must* sometimes soar. How seriously he takes this may be seen from one of his most extended (and savage) attacks on Wordsworth. As usual, in order to appreciate properly a particular passage of *Don Juan,* it is necessary to see how it fits its context. The passage in question, stanzas 98–100 of Canto III, stands as the climax of a variation on one of the most important themes of the poem, the social significance of language (cf. the Dedication). The section has been initiated with the song of the island laureate, "The Isles of Greece." Here poetry is fulfilling its proper function (as it does not, we are told, in the case of Laureate Southey), serving the real interests of society rather than merely flattering its rulers. For ". . . words are things, and a small drop of ink, / Falling like dew, upon a thought, produces / That which makes thousands, perhaps millions, think" (III.88). Furthermore, in order to fulfill its social function poetry must be socially accessible. Hence the relevance of the attacks on Wordsworth's obscurity: "He there [in the *Excursion*] builds up a formidable dyke / Between his own and others' intellect" (III.95). These, then, are the most important considerations lying behind the stanzas on Wordsworth with which the section concludes:

> We learn from Horace, "Homer sometimes sleeps;"
>   We feel without him,—Wordsworth sometimes wakes,—
> To show with what complacency he creeps
>   With his dear "*Waggoners,*" around his lakes.

He wishes for "a boat" to sail the deeps.——
   Of Ocean?——No, of air, and then he makes
Another outcry for "a little boat,"
And drivels seas to set it well afloat.

If he must fain sweep o'er the ethereal plain,
   And Pegasus runs restive in his "Waggon,"
Could he not beg the loan of Charles's Wain?
   Or pray Medea for a single dragon?
Or if, too classic for his vulgar brain,
   He feared his neck to venture such a nag on,
And he must needs mount nearer to the moon,
Could not the blockhead ask for a balloon?

"Pedlars," and "Boats," and "Waggons!" Oh! ye shades
   Of Pope and Dryden, are we come to this?
That trash of such sort not alone evades
   Contempt, but from the bathos' vast abyss
Floats scumlike uppermost, and these Jack Cades
   Of sense and song above your graves may hiss——
The "little Boatman" and his *Peter Bell*
Can sneer at him who drew "Achitophel!" (III.98–100)

The first complaint made about Wordsworth is that he not only does not soar, he creeps. And he creeps around lakes, permitting Byron to emphasize his alleged provinciality and limitation by repeating the lake-ocean contrast of the Dedication. But this lake-ocean contrast is present only by implication in the explicit ocean-air contrast. While any flight is necessarily through the air, Byron is here taking advantage of its associations of triviality and bluff in order to discredit the flight of a poet whose characteristic motion is that of creeping around lakes. Byron's playing with the common Scriblerian notion of the proximity of the high and the low is brought out even more clearly by the highly Swiftian comments on the scum floating to the top "from the bathos' vast abyss."

But the satirist is also offended at the vehicle chosen for the poet's flight—"a little boat." There is something essentially improper, apparently, in a poet's soaring off in a boat, especially a little one. Perhaps he feels the symbol too private (cf. the final contrast between the fanciful *Peter Bell* and the public, socially relevant "Achitophel"), or, perhaps merely childish. It is not, at any rate, a proper bardic conveyance. Real poets ride the winged horse Pegasus (a persistent image in *Don Juan,* and an important one). Wordsworth's choice of a little boat, the satirist suggests, is a tacit admission of poetic inadequacy. Pegasus is far too spirited a steed for him: "He feared his neck to venture such a nag on."

In contrast to the creeping and floating of Wordsworth, the satirist bends and soars. The first refers to the natural gesture of the truthful muse, who is scrupulous in following her sources:

> A brave Tartar Khan—
> Or "Sultan," as the author (to whose nod
> In prose I bend my humble verse) doth call
> This chieftain—somehow would not yield at all. (VIII. 104)

And this is by no means the only time that we shall be reminded of the famous couplet from the "Epistle to Dr. Arbuthnot": "That not in Fancy's Maze he wander'd long, / But stoop'd to Truth, and moraliz'd his song" (ll. 340–1).

In contrast both with the creeping and floating Wordsworth and the bending of the satiric muse is the soaring poet of the beginning of Canto x:

> In the wind's eye I have sailed, and sail; but for
>   The stars, I own my telescope is dim;
> But at the least I have shunned the common shore,
>   And leaving land far out of sight, would skim
> The Ocean of Eternity: the roar
>   Of breakers has not daunted my slight, trim,
> But *still* sea-worthy skiff; and she may float
> Where ships have foundered, as doth many a boat. (x.4)

One notices first of all the elements common to this stanza and the section on Wordsworth. Here again there is flight described in terms of floating in a boat. But what were there images of contempt are here images expressive of a disarming modesty (an old rhetorical shift particularly valuable to the satirist, whose pose inevitably implies pretensions of personal merit). To be sure, he presents himself as an explorer of the Ocean (cf. the ocean-lake contrast) of Eternity, but then he owns that he has no very clear view of the stars, and that his "slight, trim, / But *still* sea-worthy skiff" merely "skims" the ocean, floating on its surface. It is important to notice that while he makes no very extravagant claims as to his discoveries on the "Ocean of Eternity," he does claim some credit for having undertaken the voyage. He even asserts that it is of social (or generally human) utility, a point to which we shall return.

We are now perhaps in a position to profit from another look at the passage from which we set out:

> Nothing so difficult as a beginning
>   In poesy, unless perhaps the end;
> For oftentimes when Pegasus seems winning
>   The race, he sprains a wing, and down we tend,
> Like Lucifer, when hurled from Heaven for sinning;
>   Our sin the same, and hard as his to mend,
> Being Pride, which leads the mind to soar too far,
> Till our own weakness shows us what we are. (IV. 1)

The passage is, as I shall try to show, a particularly clear statement of one version of the poem's central paradox. For the moment it is enough to see how Byron is complicating the traditional images of flight and fall. It is not merely that the satirist's attacks on particular kinds of poetry and particular literary figures are elements in a more general criticism of a particular state of society (as the island Laureate puts it: "The heroic lay is tuneless now— / The heroic bosom beats no more!"). But Byron has associated the poetic "flight" with diabolic pride, and he means it. Whatever may have been his own personal convictions regarding the myth of the war in heaven, it serves the poet as an indispensable metaphor for some concepts and attitudes which seem to have been very important to him and which are of central importance for a proper understanding of his greatest poem. The movement of the thought is roughly as follows: to be a poet is a fine and valuable thing; poets, to be worthy the name, must essay the grand manner (soar); but soaring is a manifestation of the prime sin. It is this kind of paradox that Byron's reading of the myth of the Fall is designed to sustain and justify.

Byron most commonly, however, plays with the notion of fall in terms of the Fall of Man:

> We have
> Souls to save, since Eve's slip and Adam's fall,
> Which tumbled all mankind into the grave,
> Besides fish, beasts, and birds. (IX.19)

We have here at the very least an admission of man's radical imperfection, presented in terms of the Christian myth. Eve slipped,[3] Adam fell, and mankind became subject to death. And—this is very important—not mankind alone. "Fish, beasts, and birds" shared the curse of death placed on our First Parents. Nature, too, fell.[4] We live in a fallen world.

This fact may help explain Byron's notoriously ambiguous attitude toward the arts of civilization. They are at one time emblems of man's degeneration from an original paradisal state; at another they embody high human values. We are told, for example, that Haidée

> . . . was one
> Fit for the model of a statuary
> (A race of mere imposters, when all's done—
> I've seen much finer women, ripe and real,
> Than all the nonsense of their stone ideal). (II.118)

And of the Sultana we learn that she was "so beautiful that Art could little mend her" (VI.89). Here, of course, there is the implication that whatever might be true of Gulbeyaz, there are women whom art might conceivably improve. But then we are told, with reference to Juan's dress uniform at the court of Catherine the Great, that "Nature's self turns paler, / Seeing how Art can make her work more grand" (IX.44). The statements, taken in themselves, are clearly contradictory. But again this is not indecision or confusion. Not only do both points of view have their validity, but Byron supplies us with a consistent metaphor in terms of which the fact may be contemplated. That basis is again the Christian myth of the Fall.

Four stanzas preceding the last passage quoted, Byron writes of the new Fall of Man that will occur when, according to Cuvier, the earth will next undergo one of its periodic convulsions and a new world is formed (Byron seems to think temptation integral to creation, and fall the inevitable consequence of temptation). He speaks with some compassion of

> . . . these young people, just thrust out
> From some fresh Paradise, and set to plough,
> And dig, and sweat, and turn themselves about,
> And plant, and reap, and spin, and grind, and sow,
> Till all the arts at length are brought about,
> Especially of War and taxing. (IX.40)

The development of the arts of civilization, of which the art of poetry is exemplary, is clearly a consequence of the Fall, part of the taint of Original Sin.

I have thus far been stressing the negative side of the paradox. It is time now to imitate the poet himself and shift the emphasis to the positive pole. This change in emphasis may conveniently be considered with regard to the four beautifully modulated octaves with which Byron opens Canto X. He is here making explicit the mythic presuppositions in terms of which he is proceeding:

> When Newton saw an apple fall, he found
> In that slight startle from his contemplation—
> 'Tis *said* (for I'll not answer above ground
> For any sage's creed or calculation)—
> A mode of proving that the Earth turned round
> In a most natural whirl, called "gravitation;"
> And this is the sole mortal who could grapple,
> Since Adam—with a fall—or with an apple.
>
> Man fell with apples, and with apples rose,
> If this be true; for we must deem the mode
> In which Sir Isaac Newton could disclose
> Through the then unpaved stars the turnpike road,
> A thing to counterbalance human woes:
> For ever since immortal man hath glowed
> With all kinds of mechanics, and full soon
> Steam-engines will conduct him to the moon. (X.1–2)

The concluding couplet of the first octave suggests that ever since the Fall of Adam man has suffered from a lack, a something wanting or a something wrong, with which Newton was the first successfully to contend. The reference is, of course, to the traditional notion of aberrations entering into a perfect creation with the Fall of Man, the crown of creation. Man, who in his paradisal state had ruled all things, now becomes subject to the vicissitudes of a fallen natural order. Byron sees a symbol of this state of subjection in natural man's helplessness before the law of gravity. The idea of fall, then, which we have already examined in connection with the Scriblerian concept of bathos, is here given much greater range by being associated with the force which in the physics of Byron's day was regarded as the governing principle of the natural order. As Byron sees it, since the Fall men naturally fall (morally and physically). The imaginative concept is very close to Simone Weil's notion of sin: "When . . . a man turns away from God, he simply gives himself up to the law of gravity."[5]

The second octave is most explicit: "Man fell with apples, and with apples rose." In a celebrated passage of his journal Baudelaire observes that true civilization "does not consist in gas or steam or turn-tables. It consists in the diminution of the traces of Original Sin."[6] But while Byron would probably not argue with this definition of civilization, his own views are rather more catholic. In his eyes gas and steam and turn-tables are legitimate and even important means for "the diminution of the traces of Original Sin." They are civilization's way of contending with and rising above a fallen nature. Scientific advance of the kind represented by Newton is "A thing to counterbalance human woes." And while there is mild irony in the picture of immortal man glowing over his gadgets and his steam engine to the moon, Byron's awareness of absurdity is clearly a complicating rather than a negating element.

Yet Byron is not merely (or even principally) interested in scientific advance. The art he is most concerned with is, as we have seen, the art of poetry:

> And wherefore this exordium?—Why, just now,
>   In taking up this paltry sheet of paper,
> My bosom underwent a glorious glow,
>   And my internal spirit cut a caper:
> And though so much inferior, as I know,
>   To those who, by the dint of glass and vapour,
> Discover stars, and sail in the wind's eye,
> I wish to do as much by Poesy.
>
> In the wind's eye I have sailed, and sail; but for
>   The stars, I own my telescope is dim;
> But at the least I have shunned the common shore,
>   And leaving land far out of sight, would skim

> The Ocean of Eternity: the roar
>> Of breakers has not daunted my slight, trim,
> But *still* sea-worthy skiff; and she may float
> Where ships have foundered, as doth many a boat. (x.3–4)

We have met this last stanza before. Here the poet, who has been discussing scientific investigation, applies the image of exploration to his own pursuit. If Newton was an explorer, so too in his modest way is he.[7] This is a corollary to what he has said about the necessity of poetic "flight," the social utility of poetry, and the importance of a poet's rising above provinciality. The poet, who has been speaking of how science helps repair the faults in nature that arose as a result of the Fall, announces that it is his aim "to do the same by Poesy." Poetry too, then, is being seen as not merely emotional relief (though it is that) or relief from ennui (though it is that too), but "A thing to counterbalance human woes," an agent of civilization in its struggle for "the diminution of the traces of Original Sin."

The point is made only slightly less explicitly in the first two stanzas of Canto VII:

> O Love! O Glory! what are ye who fly
>> Around us ever, rarely to alight?
> There's not a meteor in the polar sky
>> Of such transcendent and more fleeting flight.
> Chill, and chained to cold earth, we lift on high
>> Our eyes in search of either lovely light;
> A thousand and a thousand colours they
> Assume, then leave us on our freezing way.
>
> And such as they are, such my present tale is,
>> A nondescript and every-varying rhyme,
> A versified Aurora Borealis,
>> Which flashes o'er a waste and icy clime.
> When we know what all are, we must bewail us,
>> But ne'ertheless I hope it is no crime
> To laugh at *all* things—for I wish to know
> *What*, after *all*, are *all* things—but a *show?* (VII. 1–2)

The claims here are rather more modest, but the principle is the same. Byron's "wasteland" symbol is that of a frozen world. Since Byron sometimes believed in Cuvier's theory of periodic destruction and recreation of the earth, and since on at least one occasion he conceived the annihilation of life on our world as the result of freezing (in the fragment "Darkness"), he may be thinking of a kind of progressive chill leading to final annihilation. At any rate the "icy clime" is not a cultural wasteland. It is presented rather as a state natural to man, an inevitable symbol of a fallen world. Man is "chained to cold earth" (like Prometheus on "icy Caucasus")[8] and is able to alleviate his sufferings only by his own efforts—by love and glory and, as we learn in the second stanza, by poetry. This very poem is presented as an attempt to give color, form, warmth to a world naturally colorless, indefinite, and chill.

The poem, like the meteor, exercises a double function. First of all, it sheds light ("flashes o'er a waste and icy clime"), the light that reveals the rather grim truth about the state of man on earth ("when we know what all are, we must bewail us"). But the poem, even while revealing the melancholy state of man, helps him to come to terms with it. The act of exposing the sad reality exposes the absurdity of the pretense that it is otherwise, while providing through art a means of dealing with it without the hypocrisy and self-deception integral to Love and Glory:

> Dogs, or men!—for I flatter you in saying
>   That ye are dogs—your betters far—ye may
> Read, or read not, what I am now essaying
>   To show ye what ye are in every way.
> As little as the moon stops for the baying
>   Of wolves, will the bright Muse withdraw one ray
> From out her skies—then howl your idle wrath!
> While she still silvers o'er your gloomy path. (VII.7)

This I take to be the true rationale behind the alleged "cynicism" of Don Juan. It is thus a prime expression of the positive pole of the paradox whose negative aspects we have already examined.

The argument thus far, then, would run something as follows. Byron, in developing the world of Don Juan, makes use of the Christian concepts of sin, fall, and the fallen state. He is writing a poem in terms of such a world. The poem is presumably going to be of help with regard to man's fallen condition. But at the same time, like all products of civilization, the act of writing poetry holds in itself the danger of fall. It inevitably implies, for example, participation in the original sin of pride and revolt. Or, to reverse the emphasis (as Byron does), there is "evil" in art, but there is also a good which can help at least to overcome the evil. And this paradox is based on a still profounder one, a vision of the radically paradoxical nature of "the way things are"—that is, of nature itself. For, as we have seen, in the world of Don Juan nature is fallen and stands in need of redemption. And at the same time, nature is valuable both in itself and as a norm against which a corrupt civilization may be exposed. For the Christian, nature is fallen and must be redeemed. But though fallen, nature is God's creation and must of necessity retain the imprint of the Creator (hence the possibility of "natural theology").

The practical importance of close attention to this paradoxical nature of both art and nature is evident when one comes to consider an episode such as the banquet at Norman Abbey (xv.62–74). Even so useful a critic as Truman Guy Steffan, for example, has permitted himself to dismiss the episode as a kind of tour de force whose only function is "to make his point about fastidious elegance, conspicuous waste, and the sodden dullness of gormandizing."[9] That there is something in this I should not attempt to deny. But an adequate reading of this brilliant episode would reveal something rather more interesting. It is satire, of course, but it is not merely satire. And as satire it is more in the vein of *The Rape of the Lock* than of Juvenal's Fourth, which is what Steffan's rather grim description calls to mind.

The opening lines, in fact, seem almost like a deliberate reminiscence of Pope's mock epic—the Invocation, perhaps, or the game of ombre: "Great things were now to be achieved at table, / With massy plate for armour, knives and forks / For weapons" (xv.62). The poet explicitly reminds us of the feasts in Homer. But the most relevant literary connection is with the satiric tradition. In both Horace and Juvenal (to say nothing of Petronius) meals are used as symbols of social values. Social ideals and conditions, that is, are dramatized through the communal meal (the *cena*). Byron himself seems to be hinting at this with his mention of the turbot (63; it occurs again at the election dinner, xvi.88). For the turbot (*rhombus*) is an almost indispensable part of the equipment of the satirist who is treating social decay in terms of diet. Pope mentions it twice in his "imitation" of Horace's *Serm.* ii.ii.[10] It is almost as conventional as Pope's and Byron's mechanical references to the appetite of aldermen.

But Byron's dinner party is still more firmly traditional. His stanza 73, comparing the olives and wine of the elaborate feast with those he had eaten, "The grass for my tablecloth, in open air, / On Sunium or Hymettus," corresponds to Horace's and Pope's references to the place of simple olives at the gourmand's table (Horace, 45–6; Pope, 31–6), though the point is rather different. While Horace and his Augustan imitator are speaking "satirically," Byron is at least as interested in developing the *persona* as one who, as he has said of Juan, has "the art of living in all climes with ease" (xv.11). It is the sophistication of the speaker rather than moral indignation at the bill of fare at Norman Abbey that is most at issue here. The point is not a trivial one if the "moral" of *Don Juan* is to be sought in the suave ambivalences of attitude manifested by the speaker.

The episode we are considering is, from this point of view, particularly rich. Consider, for example, the following excerpt from the menu:

> Then there was God knows what "à l'Allemande,"
>   "A l'Espagnole," "timballe," and "salpicon"—
> With things I can't withstand or understand,
>   Though swallowed with much zest upon the whole;
> And "*entremets*" to piddle with at hand,
>   Gently to lull down the subsiding soul;
> While great Lucullus' *Robe triumphal* muffles—
> (*There's fame*)—young partridge fillets, decked with truffles. (xv.66)

The first two lines remind us of the foreign nature of the feast. The dishes are French, and the references to "à l'Allemande" and "A l'Espagnole" heighten the meal's cosmopolitan character. This is not, as we are reminded in 71, "roast beef in our rough John Bull way." And while the speaker is clearly amused, there is hardly any suggestion that he seriously disapproves of such goings-on in the house of an English peer. He enjoys playing with the names just as he would, apparently, enjoy the meal—the dishes described are "things I can't withstand or understand." They are strange and amusing and irresistible to a *bonne vivante* Muse.

The reference to the *entremets* is especially interesting. They are things "to piddle with" in order "gently to lull down the subsiding soul." The tone here is remarkably bland when one considers the source of the allusion (which has apparently escaped the annotators). "Piddle" was one of Pope's words. He uses it, for example, in the same Horatian imitation mentioned above (II.ii.137). Further, and more significantly, the expression "subsiding soul" is clearly derived from this same poem, where "The Soul subsides" is Pope's rendering of the Horatian "animum quoque praegravat" (Horace, 60; Pope, 79). And this, in turn, is the same passage to which Byron refers us in a gloss on his own "very fiery particle" stanza on the death of Keats (*Don Juan* XI.60). This is rather a lofty flight in Horace, and while it is less impressive in Pope's version, Byron is startlingly casual when compared with either of his sources. This is especially striking when one recalls that Byron thought food actually to have a lulling effect on his soul. One must watch the tone carefully. Byron is suggesting that the guests at Norman Abbey were dragging the mind down with the body and fastening a particle of the divine spirit to the earth. But there is little to hint that this is anything worse than amusing. And when we are a little better acquainted with Byron's Prometheanism we may understand how the poet could speak so genially of acquiescing in the power of the "clay."

At any rate, if Byron has any very grim denunciatory purposes in mind he makes very little of his opportunity. He moves on immediately to another theme, exploiting the fact that Lucullus had been a successful general as well as a gourmand. Both in a prose note and in stanza 67 Byron enlarges on the superiority of culinary to military glory. "What are the *fillets* on the Victor's brow / To these?"[11] Perhaps the lines on the great things to be achieved at table were not merely facetious.

We have seen something of how Byron tends to interject allusions to the Fall of Man at strategic points in *Don Juan;* and the dinner party is no exception:

> The mind is lost in mighty contemplation
> Of intellect expanded on two courses;
> And Indigestion's grand multiplication
> Requires arithmetic beyond my forces.

> Who would suppose, from Adam's simple ration,
>   That cookery could have called forth such resources,
>   As form a science and a nomenclature
>   From out the commonest demands of Nature? (xv.69)

The stanza begins with an ironic expression of awe at the vast quantity of intellectual energy expended on devising a meal such as this. There is something magnificent about it. But intellect so employed leads (according to the laws of physiology and assonance) to an indigestion of still greater sublimity. For it is as true of cookery as of poetry that pride "leads the mind to soar too far, / Till our own weakness shows us what we are" (IV.1). And in neither case is the attitude toward the presumption of the artist, poet or cook, quite a simple one. For example, the last four lines of the stanza quoted above contrast the artifice of Norman Abbey with the dietary simplicity of (presumably prelapsarian) Adam. Man's actual needs are few and excess is comic. But Byron does not seem disposed merely to "reason the need." If the "*goût*" leads to the "gout" (72), it is still a refinement of nature. There is art involved, and ingenuity. The poet smiles, but he also appreciates. The versifier of a cookbook is not a man to scorn a tour de force. Luxury, again, is a result of the Fall—but in a way it is one of man's means of dealing with the conditions brought about by the Fall. And again, the emphasis is being placed on the second element, the positive pole of the paradox the poet is engaged in defining.

One can see, then, how essential it is to come to a clear understanding of Byron's attitude towards nature, one that has more in common with Baudelaire than with Rousseau. We think, for example, of his allusion to "ruts, and flints, and lovely Nature's skill" (IX.31), referring to a post road insufficiently refined by art. Or again, at the Battle of Ismail, there seems to be no great moral gain when "the Art of War," however dubious an achievement of civilization, is replaced by "human nature":

> Death is drunk with gore: there's not a street
> Where fights not to the last some desperate heart
>   For those for whom it soon shall cease to beat.
> Here War forgot his own destructive art
>   *In more destroying Nature;* and the heat
> Of Carnage, like the Nile's sun-sodden slime,
> Engendered monstrous shapes of every crime. (VIII.82; my italics)[12]

The real horror of war is the result not of civilization but of the natural fallen heart of man. The human "clay" (a favorite metaphor), when exposed to "the heat / Of Carnage," naturally brings forth "monstrous shapes of every crime." It is as natural for human nature to react to the circumstances of a battlefield with "sub-human" brutality as it is for monsters to be produced from the ooze of the Nile. But the social order is at least largely responsible for the circumstances. This is what Byron is reminding us when he asks, with reference to the Cossacks pursuing the child Leila: "And whom for this at last must we condemn? / Their natures? or their sovereigns, who employ / All arts to teach their subjects to destroy?" (VIII.92). Again, this seems an attitude which it is hardly fair to dismiss as either oversimple or confused.

Of these same Cossacks the poet has observed:

> Matched with *them,*
> The rudest brute that roams Siberia's wild
> Has feelings pure and polished as a gem,—
> The bear is civilised, the wolf is mild. (*ibid.*)

The notion is a familiar one. Man has it in him to be worse than the worst of the beasts if he gives in to his lower instincts. As Juan himself puts it when he refuses to give the crew of the sinking ship access to the grog: "Let us die like men, not sink below / Like brutes" (II.36). For when the ship goes down, carrying with it the appurtenances of civilization, and passengers and crew are set adrift on the sea (whose symbolic suggestions in this connection should be clear enough), man has an admirable opportunity for showing what his nature is (cf. Steffan, p. 192). It is not surprising, therefore, that in this episode the poet should make good use of animal imagery.

We are told, for example, that "like the shark and tiger [man] must have prey" (67). And though Juan had at first declined to join in eating his father's spaniel, he finally gives in when he feels "all the vulture in his jaws" (71). Again, after seven days under a scorching sun on a windless sea, thoughts of cannibalism are to be seen "in their wolfish eyes" (72). Finally, when the men draw lots to decide who is to be eaten, we are told: " 'Twas Nature gnawed them to this resolution" (75). The suggestion seems to be that nature is a beast that seeks to reduce man to its level. This is the same malicious nature we have met only a few stanzas before, where the sea is compared to " . . . a veil, / Which, if withdrawn, would but disclose the frown / Of one whose hate is masked but to assail" (II.49). Nature lures man on with its beauty and its apparent calm, then shows itself in its true savagery. It is this meal (on Pedrillo) and this nature that should be borne in mind as we read of the elaborately "unnatural" banquet at Norman Abbey.

But the shipwreck episode, though less subtle than the banquet scene, is not so simple as is sometimes suggested. The matter-of-fact tone, reminiscent of Swift, may help keep the episode, unsparing as it is, from impressing one as the product of a morbid misanthropy. If it is possible for man to act this way, it is well perhaps to acknowledge the fact. It would be questionable only if the poet were suggesting that the cannibals in the long-boat were an adequate embodiment of what man "really" is. Byron, at least, is not so naive. He is no more suggesting that man is "really" a beast than is Goya in the brutish figures of the *Caprichos*. In both cases the bestial is seen as an aberration from a human norm suggested in the drawings by the prefatory figure of the wide-awake and fully rational artist[13] and in the poem by the complex rationality of the ever-present speaker. Furthermore, the hero himself is carefully preserved from falling completely into animality. He has no part in the cannibalism, and is reluctant even to eat the spaniel's paw. It must be remembered, moreover, that the episode is only one part of a rather long poem; it enjoys no unique authority. Finally, there is in passages such as the following a note of what can almost be called admiration for the sheer toughness of human beings, their ability to hang on to life in the most difficult circumstances:

> 'Tis thus with people in an open boat,
>   They live upon the love of Life, and bear
> More than can be believed, or even thought,
>   And stand like rocks the tempest's wear and tear;
> And hardship still has been the sailor's lot,
> Since Noah's ark went cruising here and there. (II.66)

This feeling for the fineness amidst the meanness of human life is central to Byron's vision in *Don Juan*.

Steffan has recently commented on the contrast between the storm and shipwreck and the Haidée episode. The contrast, he suggests, is the structural basis of Canto II. In the stanzas on the shipwreck nature is seen in its grim, and in the Haidée episode in its cheerful, aspect (cf. Steffan, pp. 193–4). . . . But while it is easy enough to see the point of the usual generalizations about the idyllic life on the isle, it might be well to try to define certain aspects of it a little more closely. One thinks, for example, of the violence out of which Juan comes to the isle in the first place. The only survivor of a savage storm on a treacherous ocean, he is washed up on a shore not conspicuously hospitable (II.104): "The shore looked wild, without a trace of man, / And girt by formidable waves." There are "roaring breakers," "A reef," "boiling surf and bounding spray." Shipwrecks, further, are not uncommon on this coast. Haidée made a fire

>   . . . with such
> Materials as were cast up round the bay,—
>   Some broken planks, and oars, that to the touch
> Were nearly tinder, since, so long they lay,
>   A mast was almost crumbled to a crutch;
> But, by God's grace, here wrecks were in such plenty,
> That there was fuel to have furnished twenty. (II.132)

And while we learn that there is a port "on the other side o' the isle" (III.19), it is the "shoal and bare" coast with its treacherous reefs and currents that is most impressed upon us.[14]

The point is worth mentioning if for no other reason than that, as Byron is careful to point out, it is here, on a coast whose perils have been repeatedly emphasized, that the peculiarly harmonious and ideal love of Juan and Haidée is consummated: "Amidst the barren sand and rocks so rude / She and her wave-worn love had made their bower" (II. 198). Now the violent sea that had wrecked Juan's ship and which beats upon the shore "spills" a "small ripple" on the beach, like "the cream of your champagne" (II. 178). More, these same storms that cost the lives of Juan's shipmates create beauty as they work on the hard rock of the coast. They smooth the pebbles of the beach so that they shine in the moonlight, and they form "hollow halls, with sparry roofs and cells," in one of which Juan and Haidée "turned to rest" (II. 184).

More is involved here than the traditional motif of "beauty in the lap of horror." This is a particularly fine expression of one of the most important qualities of Haidée's isle. It is a place where natural violence is tempered to beauty, but where the violence forms an indispensable basis to the beauty created. There is, for example, the famous "fancy piece" of the "band of children, round a snow-white ram," wreathing "his venerable horns with flowers" (III. 32). Or, more importantly, there is Lambro himself (for it is properly *his* island), the violence of his nature and his life, and the kind of ideal existence made possible by this violence (and which corresponds to another aspect of his nature). For on the simplest level one can hardly ignore the rather dubious economic basis of the island pastoral. Juan and Haidée's idyllic, natural existence, surrounded by slaves, tapestries, fine Persian carpets, and sherbets chilled in porous vessels, is, after all, supported by a career of piracy and murder. This is too simple, of course, since the important point is the use the two lovers make of their opportunities. They dine (and one should bear their by no means austere buffet in mind also when one considers the banquet at Norman Abbey) and dress and move among their luxurious surroundings with a consecrating grace. But this is precisely what I mean. There is no real irony in the vulgar sense. Byron is not so crude as to say, "Yes, Juan and Haidée live beautifully, but look at the evil and violence that supports their existence." It is rather the other way around; he would say, "Yes, Lambro is a man of violence (as nature is violent), but Lambro makes possible the creation of beauty (just as the violence of nature may make beauty)." And this is more than an especially accomplished development of the paradoxes implicit in the relations of art and nature. It looks ahead to the English cantos (cf. the banquet scene already discussed), where this attitude is given definitive expression.

And as violence and disorder lurk behind the most winning manifestations of tranquillity and harmony, the tranquil and harmonious are fated inevitably to dissolve again in the violent and chaotic. This is an apparently immutable law of Byron's world. Haidée was, we are told, "Nature's bride" (II. 202), and the love she shared with Juan is explicitly contrasted in its naturalness with the unnatural situation of woman in society (199–201).

Their union is a kind of act of natural religion: "She loved, and was belovéd—she adored, / And she was worshipped after Nature's fashion" (II. 191).

The completeness of their commitment to and involvement in the processes of nature is dramatized in a rather flashy piece of romantic mingling:

> They looked up to the sky, whose floating glow
>   Spread like a rosy Ocean, vast and bright;
> They gazed upon the glittering sea below,
>   Whence the broad Moon rose circling into sight;
> They heard the waves' splash, and the wind so low,
>   And saw each other's dark eyes darting light
> Into each other. (II. 185)

It is a twilight moment (184) when daylight distinctions are blurred and all nature seems one. [15] The sky as they look at it seems a glowing sea, while the ocean itself is a night sky with the moon rising. The sound of the waves mingles with the sound of the wind. And just as the sky seemed to float like a sea and as the sea bore a moon like the sky, the "dark eyes" of the two lovers darted "light / Into each other." They mingle as sea and sky mingle, natural phenomena among natural phenomena.

But it is precisely because of the completeness of their harmony with nature that they are not exempt from sharing in its less idyllic manifestations. Such involvement in the natural, while it makes possible something so beautiful as the love of the two young "birds," implies also a participation in the vicissitudes inevitable to a fallen nature, particularly in its subjection to mutability:

> The Heart is like the sky, a part of Heaven,
>   But changes night and day, too, like the sky;
> Now o'er it clouds and thunder must be driven,
>   And Darkness and Destruction as on high:
> But when it hath been scorched, and pierced, and riven,
>   Its storms expire in water-drops; the eye
> Pours forth at last the Heart's blood turned to tears,
> Which make the English climate of our years. (II. 214)

While this is primarily an explanation of Juan's unfaithfulness to Julia, it is presented as a general truth applicable to all men. The heart is traditionally that part of us which is most "natural" and which is valued (or distrusted) for that reason. Byron is trying to make clear exactly what is implied in the notion of "natural man." That involvement in the natural which is from one point of view an ideal is from another point of view part of the burden of fallen man, "given up to the law of gravity."

It has been suggested above how much the natural love of Juan and

Haidée owes to Lambro, whose piratical career is presented as a metaphor of the real nature of the activities of great men in the great world (see especially III. 14). But that civilization must at the same time take much of the blame for the idyll's violent dissolution is made quite explicit. [16] Civilization has from one point of view enhanced the idyll, and from another point of view it has contributed to its destruction. As Elizabeth Boyd has observed in this connection: "Evil is inherent in the nature of man; he does not have to learn it from society, though society frequently succeeds in first evoking it." [17] And the hideous effect of this double evil, natural and social, is seen in the death of Haidée.

We have previously seen Haidée's innocent heart heavenly "like the sky." Now we must see it "scorched, and pierced, and riven" by the storms of experience. In the dream that embodies the uneasiness of their last twilight rendezvous (IV. 31–5), Haidée sees herself chained to one of the jagged cliffs of the shore. She has fallen from the paradise of the love idyll to the level of struggling humanity "Chill, and chained to cold earth." The "small ripple spilt upon the beach" (II. 178) has become the "loud roar" of the rough waves rising to drown her (IV. 31). The "shining pebbles" and the "smooth and hardened sand" of the pastoral (II. 184) have become the "sharp shingles" that cut her feet as she pursues the terrifying something in a sheet that has replaced the seemingly secure reality of her love (IV. 32). And the completeness of her (anticipated) union with the forces of nature is dramatized by her tears' joining them in their activity of forming marble icicles in a sea-cave strongly reminiscent of that to which she and Zoe had first borne the half-drowned Juan. [18]

Since it is essential that the implications of what has been suggested thus far be thoroughly grasped before going further, it may be well briefly to reiterate the main points toward which the argument has been moving and the kinds of relation it has been attempting to establish. The underlying principle of Byron's universe seems to be that its elements are in their different ways both means of grace and occasions of sin. [But] the religious image is misleading if one understands it in too moral a sense. The point is not that a thing is good if used properly and bad if used improperly. It simply *is* both good and bad. But it is *good* and *bad*. I make use of theological terminology because Byron does, and he does so because it is expressively necessary for him. The universe, as Byron sees it, is not merely inconveniently arranged, or not arranged at all and so humanly neutral. There is, from man's viewpoint at least, something profoundly wrong about it and about his place in it. But at the same time there is generous provision of means and opportunities of dealing with this wrongness and making it humanly right. But these means and opportunities have a way of being closely allied with the primary causes and manifestations of the wrongness. All this is not what *Don Juan* is about. It is about coming to terms with such a world. But something very like this is what *Don Juan* presupposes.

Examination of the poem makes it clear that the overt contrast between art and nature is in some ways less significant in the world of *Don Juan* than is the contrast between the two aspects of either nature or art taken in themselves. Byron's nature, the authoritative embodiment of his notion of the way things are, is, like the Christian nature, a double one. It is beneficent and normative; and at the same time it is harsh and in need of correction and control. Byron appropriates the traditional paradox, adapting it to the purposes of his own paradoxical vision. Art, the conventional opposite to nature, reflects precisely the same duality. It is good in that it helps make a fallen world bearable; and it is bad in that it conspires to aggravate the condition of fall. Finally, there is love. And we shall find that love, the specific "matter" of *Don Juan,* shares also in this radical duality. . . .[19]

Notes

1. Ernest J. Lovell, Jr., *Byron: The Record of a Quest. Studies in a Poet's Concept and Treatment of Nature* (Austin, Univ. of Texas Press, 1949), p. 250.

2. Helene Richter, *Lord Byron. Persönlichkeit und Werk* (Halle, Niemeyer, 1929), pp. 126–43. William J. Calvert, *Byron. Romantic Paradox* (Chapel Hill, Univ. of North Carolina Press, 1935), passim. Antonio Porta, *Byronismo Italiano* (Milan, Casa Editrice L. F. Cogliati, 1923), pp. 45–62.

3. Cf. Canto VI.94, where we are told that "one Lady's slip . . . [left] a crime on / All generations."

4. Cf. Lovell, esp. pp. 126–7. Lovell's whole discussion of Byron's attitude toward nature should be consulted.

5. *Waiting for God,* tr. Emma Craufurd (New York, Putnam, 1951), p. 128. Could there be an echo of the imagery of the first of the *Holy Sonnets* here? Simone Weil knew the metaphysicals, and the whole section (of "The Love of God and Affliction") is filled with Donnean concepts and images.

6. *Mon Cœur mis à nu,* sec. 59. I am using the translation in Peter Quennel, ed., *The Essence of Laughter* (New York, Meridian, 1956), p. 189. Robert Escarpit, in his ambitious *Lord Byron. Un Tempérament littéraire* (2 vols. Paris, Le Cercle du Livre, 1955), *I*, 153–61, makes a similar point with regard to the position adopted by Byron in his letters attacking William Lisle Bowles. But the Frenchman quotes Chesterton.

7. Exploration as a metaphor for poetic activity occurs more than once. In XIV.101, for example, the poet observes that "The new world would be nothing to the old, / If some Columbus of the moral seas / Would show mankind their souls' antipodes." Or again (XV.27): "We [i.e. "my Muse" and I] surely may find something worth research: / Columbus found a new world in a cutter, etc." The image is basic to *Childe Harold.*

8. Cf. Harold Bloom, *Shelley's Mythmaking* (New Haven, Yale Univ. Press, 1959), pp. 91–2.

9. Steffan, *The Making of a Masterpiece,* vol. 1 of *Don Juan: A Variorum Edition,* ed. Steffan and W. W. Pratt (Austin, Univ. of Texas Press, 1957), 264. See also the admirable essay by Lovell, "Irony and Image in Byron's *Don Juan,*" *The Major English Romantic Poets: A Symposium,* ed. C. D. Thorpe, C. Baker, B. Weaver (Carbondale, Southern Illinois Univ. Press, 1957): 129–48.

10. Pope, ll. 23, 141. See Horace, *Serm.* II.ii.42, 48, 49, 95; VIII.30, or Juvenal, *Sat.* XI.121, and IV passim.

11. Cf. I.128–34. Here, where there is an ambivalence of attitude similar to that found in the stanzas on the dinner, Byron observes that "Vaccination certainly has been / A kind antithesis to Congreve's rockets" (129), and that

> Sir Humphry Davy's lantern, by which coals
> Are safely mined for in the mode he mentions,
>   Tombuctoo travels, voyages to the Poles
> Are ways to benefit mankind, as true,
>   Perhaps, as shooting them at Waterloo. (132)

12. Cf. Selim's comment on the savagery of his band (*Bride of Abydos*, ll. 910–11): "Yet there we follow but the bent assigned/ By *fatal Nature* to man's warring kind" (my italics).

13. Cf. José López-Rey, *Goya's Caprichos* (2 vols. Princeton Univ. Press, 1953), *I*, 75–8.

14. Lovell (p. 206) has called attention to the inhospitable terrain of Haidée's isle, though for a different reason.

15. Byron is fond of this twilight motif, which serves so effectively as a metaphor of the peace, harmony, and wholeness to be found in nature. It is the hour sacred to Juan and Haidée (IV.20), in whom one important aspect of this natural harmony is manifested, and he celebrates it in one of the best-known purple patches in the poem (III.101–9). The poet, who in the previous stanzas (III.94–100) has been attacking Wordsworth for the private nature, the obscurity, and the provinciality of his verse, lovingly endows his own twilight meditation with a wealth of socially accessible allusion. We have two stanzas of sentimental Catholicism (102–3), one of eighteenth-century pantheism (104), references to the literary associations of the Pineta at Ravenna (105–6), and paraphrases of the evening hymns of Sappho and Dante (107 and 108). Byron makes especially effective use of the ambiguities of the image to dramatize the "fall" of Juan and Haidée, reminding us that twilight can not only dramatize oneness, but can also express a close, an ending of something valuable ("the descending sun" of IV.22). It is a useful type of the paradoxical nature of nature in Byron's vision.

16. See IV.28:

> They should have lived together deep in woods,
>   Unseen as sings the nightingale; they were
> Unfit to mix in these thick solitudes
>   Called social, haunts of Hate, and Vice, and Care.

17. Elizabeth French Boyd, *Byron's Don Juan. A Critical Study* (New Brunswick, Rutgers Univ. Press, 1945). p. 62.

18. Cf. the following: "The fire burst forth from her Numidian veins, / Even as the Simoom sweeps the blasted plains" (IV.57). And: "The tears rushed forth from her o'erclouded brain, / Like mountain mists at length dissolved in rain" (IV.66). Coleridge (*Poetry*, 6, 192 n.) calls attention at this point to the cave in *The Island* (IV.121 ff.). A more useful analogue (or even "source") might be the cave in which Shelley's Cythna is imprisoned in *The Revolt of Islam* (VII.12–18).

19. [Ed. note: In the opening paragraph of his next chapter, "The Unforgiven Fire," Ridenour notes that "we should not forget that *Don Juan* is, after all, a poem about a great lover and that it deals largely with love."]

Editor's Bibliographical Note

As indicated in the introduction to this volume, I regard Ridenour's book on *Don Juan*, despite its exclusive focus on Byron's masterpiece, as the one that inaugurated not only the modern era of *Don Juan* criticism but also the modern era of Byron criticism, for it did what all such critical inaugurations should do—precipitate the debates about Byron's poetic achievement that have endured in the history of Byron criticism to this day. This is not to say, of course, that Ridenour addressed all of the issues that still concern the Byron critical cohort, but his fundamental argument for a complex, if shifting and sometimes self-contradictory, artistic coherence in Byron's greatest work has ramified into elaborate and finely detailed subsequent analyses of the wholeness, if not always the comfortable or easily definable coherence, of Byron's total oeuvre.

But Ridenour's achievement in *Don Juan* studies specifically did not emerge from a critical vacuum, for behind his work stand the pioneering books by Elizabeth Boyd, *Byron's "Don Juan"* (New Brunswick: Rutgers University Press, 1945), and by Paul Graham Trueblood, *The Flowering of Byron's Genius: Studies in Byron's "Don Juan"* (Palo Alto: Stanford University Press, 1945). Despite their efforts, however, further early illuminating criticism of *Don Juan* was minimal, what there was being almost totally overshadowed by the persistence of biographical, belletristic, and other less categorizable writers still seduced by the fascinations of Byron's life, personal habits, and drearily repeated minutiae such as how to pronounce "Giaour." Ridenour's dramatic departure from this trend must be seen, however, as in large part enabled by Truman G. Steffan and Willis W. Pratt's monumental four–volume *Byron's "Don Juan": A Variorum Edition* (Austin: University of Texas Press, 1957) with its extraordinary lengthy and detailed critical and scholarly apparatus. Moreover, in the same year Leslie L. Marchand's equally monumental three-volume *Byron: A Biography* (New York: Knopf) also appeared, paradoxically laying to rest by its factual authoritativeness the ghost of "mere" biographical commentary on (or ruminations over) Byron's poetical works.

To all three of these achievements we owe the quite stunning parade of Byron books in the decade of the sixties—all of which continue to deserve attention from serious Byronists and other students of romantic poetry. Since I have commented at some length on this decade in my introduction, I forgo further notice of those books here, noting instead a few additional publications on *Don Juan* not included there: Karl Kroeber, "Byron: The Adventurous Narrative," in his *Romantic Narrative Art* (Madison: University of Wisconsin Press, 1960); Ridenour, "The Mode of Byron's *Don Juan*," *PMLA* 89 (1964): 442–46; Brian Wilkie, "Byron and the Epic of Negation," in his *Romantic Poets and Epic Tradition* (Madison: University of Wisconsin Press, 1965); A. B. England, *Byron's "Don Juan" and Eighteenth-Century Literature* (Lewisburg: Bucknell Univ. Press; London: Associated University Presses, 1974); Peter J. Manning, *Byron and His Fictions* (Detroit: Wayne State University Press, 1978); George de F. Lord, "The Epic of Indeterminacy, *Don Juan*," in his *Trials of the Self: Heroic Ordeals in the Epic Tradition* (Hamden, Conn.: Archon, 1983), 113–56; Bernard Beatty, *Byron's Don Juan* (Kent: Croom Helm, 1985); Jerome J. McGann, "Byron, Mobility and the Poetics of Historical Ventriloquism," *Romanticism Past and Present* 9 (1985): 66–82; Cecil Y. Lang, "Narcissus Jilted: Byron, *Don Juan,* and the Biographical Imperative," in *Historical Studies and Literary Criticism,* ed. Jerome J. McGann (Madison: University of Wisconsin Press, 1985), 143–79; and the essays or chapters of books by McGann (*Beauty of Inflections* excerpt), Beatty, Reiman, Manning, and Wolfson included in this collection.

As several of the above titles suggest, the issue of whether or not *Don Juan* is an epic (and if it is, what relationship this breed of epic has to other more recognizably epic poems) is still very much before us. A particular case in point is the *Studies in Romanticism* symposium publication (Fall 1977) entitled "On Byron" (which I was unable to include in this volume for lack of space). Prompted by the appearance of Jerome J. McGann's *"Don Juan" in Context* but, as the journal editor notes prefatorily, transcending the occasion, Ridenour, McGann, and Reiman spiritedly debate the issue of the "epic" *Don Juan* as well as "Byron's place in the [even more problematic] Romantic movement." On the latter see also the Editor's Bibliographical note to Reiman's essay later in this volume, an essay that includes an expanded version of his contribution to the *SIR* symposium.

For other matters central to the study of *Don Juan* see the bibliographical notes to the essays in this volume by Gleckner, Manning, Wolfson, and McGann ("The Book of Byron" essay). Also useful are Edward E. Bostetter, *Twentieth-Century Interpretations of "Don Juan"* (Englewood Cliffs, N. J.: Prentice Hall, 1969), Harold Bloom, ed., *Lord Byron's Don Juan* (New York: Chelsea House, 1987), Oscar J. Santucho's bibliography of Byron criticism from 1807 to 1974 (*George Gordon, Lord Byron: A Comprehensive Bibliography of Secondary Materials in English, 1807–1974* [Metuchen, N. J.: Scarecrow Press, 1977]), and Charles J. Clancy's *Review of "Don Juan" Criticism 1900–1973* (Salzburg, Austria: University of Salzburg, 1974).

On Reading
Childe Harold's Pilgrimage

Jerome J. McGann

The Poet in the Poem

"I write what's uppermost, without delay," Byron declares in *Don Juan* (XIV, 7) and even adds that his "narrative is not meant for narration" in the proper sense at all. As he says a bit later, "I rattle on exactly as I'd talk / With anybody in a ride or walk" (xiv, 19). His great comic work gives the reader a series of loosely connected tales about Juan's adventures, but even more it gives us a graphic revelation of the mind of the poet who creates these stories. *Don Juan* is a "poem written about itself,"[1] as Hazlitt has noted: throughout we seem to be with Byron while he is actually spinning his rhymes. The key device for creating this illusion of the poet's immediate presence is digression. M. K. Joseph has well said that "the substance of the digression can be related *thematically* to the poem as a whole; but its *dramatic* function in the immediate context is to keep alive our sense of the narrator, interposing him between ourselves and the story."[2]

But "dramatic" is not a term completely appropriate to the presentation of the poet's personality in *Don Juan:* the manifold complications of his psyche are extrapolated in a long series of personal self-exposures, but we are never made to feel that the poem possesses a "dramatic" finality, that the poet acts upon and reacts to a series of experiences which force significant modifications in his character. In a word, *Don Juan* has no plot in which the principal character—the poet himself—can be said to participate. Juan may undergo psychological changes during his picaresque adventures, but the personality of the poet does not develop. We are given, rather, a succession of insights into the rich and complicated quality of his mind and heart. Byron's string of related stories permits him the widest possible range of personal commentary (on history, art, contemporary manners and affairs, philosophy, etc.): the reader thus encounters the poet from so many angles and points of view that he seems not only fully present, but fully presented.

Childe Harold's Pilgrimage, on the other hand, is a poem in which the

From *Fiery Dust: Byron's Poetic Development* (Chicago: University of Chicago Press, 1968), pp. 31–66, © 1968 by The University of Chicago. Reprinted by permission of the publisher and author.

poet is both immediately present to us and involved in a continuity of events in a truly "dramatic" way. He undergoes a succession of psychic changes in the course of the four cantos. At the end of Canto II, for example, he laments that "Time [has] reft whate'er my soul enjoyed" (II, 98), and at the beginning of Canto III he recalls the past in which his "brain became, / In its own eddy boiling and o'erwrought" (III, 7). "Yet am I changed," he adds, and he looks to the future (sts. 4–6) for further and more beneficent changes still. At the end of Canto III he gets a Pisgah sight of Italy (st. 110), and again reviews the past and looks to the future:

> Thus far have I proceeded in a theme
> Renewed with no kind auspices:—to feel
> We are not what we have been, and to deem
> We are not what we should be,—(III, 111)

Canto IV concludes the story ("My task is done," he says in st. 185) of the poet's geographical and psychological peregrinations, and he leaves the reader to benefit by "the Moral of [the] Strain" (186). Through the course of the entire poem the theme unfolds that "to the mind / Which is itself, no changes bring surprise" (IV, 8).

What the substance of the poet's tale of himself is I will discuss more fully later. For now it is important only that we understand the general dramatic nature of the poem, since it is this which will determine how we read it. For example, *The Prelude* is, like *Childe Harold's Pilgrimage,* an autobiographical poem, but its subject is a sequence of events from Wordsworth's past life (i.e., "past" in relation to the "virtual present" of the narrating poet) while the subject of *Childe Harold's Pilgrimage* is a sequence of events that are contemporaneous with the poet's act of narration. *The Prelude* is to *Childe Harold's Pilgrimage* what a reflective autobiographical essay is to a journal or a series of letters. We "get at" Wordsworth's mind through the continuous and developing record of his "present" interpretation of already completed events. *The Prelude* is the externalization of an imaginative dialectic: it is fundamentally a philosophic poem or, better, a cognitive myth whose full implications are gradually unfolded to the reader and the writing poet alike. With the completion of the ascent of Snowdon in Book XIV, Wordsworth has arrived at his most complete definition of the powers of the human imagination. Thus, *The Prelude* amounts to a growing act of imaginative cognition in which the meanings and relationships of the poem's symbols and images are developed into a complete poetic statement of an important human vision (something akin to the vision of Teilhard de Chardin in our own day).

But while we are interested in the mind of the poet in *The Prelude* (as it is symbolized to us in the mythic configuration which is the issue of the poem), in *Childe Harold's Pilgrimage* we are interested in the poet's existential condition. Byron's poem presents a series of actions and reactions in a natural order that we conveniently refer to as "realistic," whereas Wordsworth gives us a series of perceptions and intuitions within an order of experience that we ordinarily call "cognitive." Our relationship to the poet in *Childe Harold's Pilgrimage* is the same as our relationship to Augie March, or to Herzog: all are involved in a play of circumstances, and we are interested in their reactions. The narrating poet of *The Prelude*, however, is the center of an action in the same way that the participating poet is in the *Vita Nuova:* at bottom both poems are not "actions," but acts of revelation. The narrating poet is the "hero" of *Childe Harold's Pilgrimage*, but we could not call the poet the "hero" of *The Prelude* without wrenching the meaning of that specialized term.

Consequently, because no distinction exists in *Childe Harold's Pilgrimage* between the narrator's virtual present and a past series of events about which he writes, and because the poem describes a sequence of "realistic" events in which the narrating poet participates in an immediate way, *Childe Harold's Pilgrimage* places unique demands upon the reader. Aristotle had no experience of a poem like Byron's, but his discussion of narrators, narrative poetry, and drama provides a useful indication of the kind of problem that *Childe Harold's Pilgrimage* presents: ". . . the poet may imitate by narration—in which case he can either take another personality as Homer does, or speak in his own person, unchanged—or he may present all his characters as living and moving before us."[3] In terms of Aristotle's categories, Byron's poem exists somewhere between narrative and drama, for while the poet comes forward in propria persona, he also presents himself as "living and moving before us" in a phenomenal setting. The result is a work whose illusionistic character is pronounced and crucial:

> Is thy face like thy mother's, my fair child!
> Ada! sole daughter of my house and heart?
> When last I saw thy young blue eyes they smiled,
> And then we parted,—not as now we part,
> But with a hope.—
>   Awaking with a start,
> The waters heave around me; and on high
> The winds lift up their voices: I depart,
> Whither I know not; but the hour's gone by,
> When Albion's lessening shores could grieve
>   or glad mine eye (III, 1).

This stanza illustrates narrative illusionism pushed to its extreme limit. The poet's revery in the first four and one-half lines occurs at the same time as his act of narration. Then, with a familiarly Byronic disregard of prose grammar, he suddenly awakens to describe his present situation. In effect, the poet not only records his musings at the time of their actual occurrence, he writes down his sensations immediately upon coming into a condition of exteriorized consciousness. An artist writing in the first person could scarcely objectify his "poetic personality" as a person "living and moving before us" more completely.[4] While the act of poetic illusion here is unmatched in the rest of the poem, it is by no means untypical of the general approach to the material. A little later in the same canto, for example, the poet introduces the Waterloo section in a similarly theatrical way: "Stop!—for thy tread is on an Empire's dust!" (III, 17). In this case not only is the act of narration continuous in time with the experience; the poet addresses us as if we were on the scene with him.

Illusions such as these are staples in the poem, and they exhibit a good deal more daring than any comparable scenes in *The Prelude*. The reasons I have already discussed: Byron's work exists in a realistic continuum while Wordsworth's moves in a world that is not significantly impinged upon by Space, Time, or Circumstance ("that unspiritual God," IV, 125). The past life on which Wordsworth meditates, is, of course, an existential record, but the real meaning of the poem is to be found not in these past events as such, but in the poet's immediate act of recovery. The continuum is mental, timeless, spaceless. But because *Childe Harold's Pilgrimage* is fixed within a realistic environment; and second, because the act of narration and the narrated events occur simultaneously in a virtual present; and finally, because the poem tells the story of the psychological modifications that the narrating poet undergoes during the four cantos, the poem demands that the narrating poet be considered a participant in an action whose future progress he cannot know and whose ultimate issue he is, at all points prior to the climax, only partially aware of.[5] Like a character in a novel or a play, he has neither the author's prevision nor the audience's objectivity, but is immersed in the immediacy of the events he himself recounts. Not only can he not see beyond any particular event; he may be equally unaware of the full significance of an event while it is taking place, or even after it has passed. The audience knows more about Macbeth than the character does himself, at least at the early stages of the play; for that matter, the narrator of *The Aspern Papers* is ignorant of himself and the full meaning of his story from beginning to end. The narrator of *Childe Harold's Pilgrimage* is presented in a similarly dramatic way, and the story of himself that he recounts involves him in a series of important self-discoveries before he is able to offer the reader, at the end of Canto IV, a revelation that is at once his interpretation of the meaning of his own history and his vision of man's fate as well.

CANTO IV: ITS MEANING AND METHOD

Part of the meaning of the poem's great conclusion, which begins at the St. Peter's stanzas in Canto IV, is that the narrating poet has come at last to a complete understanding of what it means to be a pilgrim—for him, what it means to be a man. All along he has been driven by the idea that somewhere, if one searches long enough, a place will be found that will answer to all human aspirations, that will satisfy and complete one's humanity. The poet's first pilgrimage was undertaken out of a disgust of England: "Je haissais ma Patrie," the epigraph from *Le Cosmopolite* states, but after his pilgrimage the poet finds "L'univers est une espèce de livre, dont on n'a lu que la première page quand on n'a vu que son pays. J'en ai feuilleté un assez grand nombre, que j'ai trouvé également mauvaises." In Canto III, the poet's journey to the Swiss Alps is another quest to escape from "the peopled desert" (III, 73) of this world, as well as from his own diseased mind and "degraded form" (III, 74). In stanza 156 of Canto IV he deliberately recalls the conclusion [stanza 109] of Canto III:

> Thou movest—but increasing with the advance,
> Like climbing some great Alp, which still doth rise,
> Deceived by its gigantic elegance—
> Vastness which grows, but grows to harmonize—
> All musical in its immensities;
> Rich marbles, richer paintings—shrines where flame
> The lamps of gold—and haughty dome which vies
> In air with Earth's chief structures, though their frame
> Sits on the firm-set ground—and this the clouds must claim. (IV, 156) . . .

The lines from the third canto echo a number of earlier passages, especially III,62 where the Alps are called "The Palaces of Nature" (hence the appropriateness of the Alp image with respect to St. Peter's, of which the poet asks rhetorically: "what could be / Of earthly structures, in [God's] honour piled / Of a sublimer aspect?" IV, 154).[6] But in the middle of Canto III the Alps only show the poet "How Earth may pierce to Heaven, yet leave vain man below" (III, 62). At the end of the canto he throws off this earlier sense of ineffectualness and declares that he "must pierce" to the "most great and growing region, where / The earth to her embrace compels the powers of air." His search for fulfillment is still not concluded, however, for when he gains the summit of the Alp he is given a prophetic view of Italy, which is presented as a kind of Promised Land ("the throne and grave of empires; still / The fount at which the panting Mind assuages / Her thirst of knowledge . . . the eternal source. . . . ," III, 110). Later, at St. Peter's, the perception of the union of Nature and Supernature, which he sought and partially achieved on the Alp, is finally given him. But now a further understanding comes: that this yearning to possess and exercise godlike powers, to participate in a divine activity, is not capable of fulfillment if human life is to continue. The true end of such a desire is not satisfaction, but creation, and the condition of its being is constant movement, increase, growth.

This theme, which is repeated in the famous Address to Ocean (a mythic vision of an eternal death/life cycle), is a vindication of the act of pilgrimage. In stanzas 157–58[7] the poet tells us not only what pilgrimage means, but also what the method of *Childe Harold's Pilgrimage* has entailed. . . . At St. Peter's the poet gains only an intimation of divine fullness and eternally existing Life; for if he is able, "growing with its growth," to "dilate" his spirit to the size of St. Peter's, still the basilica is only one vast image of the even greater spatial and temporal immensity of Life itself, and his apprehension of the symbolic meaning of the church will pass if he continues simply to live. This is in fact what happens in the poem. Nevertheless, the experience at St. Peter's finally exposes the teleology of the poem and of the life of man as well. The poet is made aware of the necessity of a "piecemeal" apprehension of a life which we never fully comprehend precisely because it involves us in constant passage and possibility. Human life is not something that can be "gained" or "concluded" or "fulfilled," but must simply be "kept" in our experience of consecutive vital particularities. Entering St. Peter's with a highly developed sensitivity to immediate experience, a virtue strengthened by the act of pilgrimage, the poet finds that he is forced to apprehend the basilica moment by moment and item by item. When he does finally gain a sense of the order in the vast disparateness of the church, he is impelled onward to the Vatican Gallery, and eventually, to another mountain prospect from Monte Cavo (sts. 174ff.). The basilica, it turns out, is not a place of fulfillment, but a symbol of a mode of experience and perception: the endless activity of self-discovery and renewed self-development. By such means the soul is forced into a position where it must constantly reconsider its own conception of itself and recreate itself under the influence of fresh experience.

> 'Tis to create, and in creating, live
> A being more intense that we endow
> With form our fancy, gaining as we give
> The life we image, even as I do now—
> What am I? Nothing: but not so art thou,
> Soul of my thought! with whom I traverse earth,
> Invisible but gazing, as I glow
> Mixed with thy spirit, blended with thy birth,
> And feeling still with thee in my crushed feelings' dearth. (III, 6)

We never "gain" definitively the fullness of Life in our imaginatively recreative activities, but are always in the process of gaining anew, of becoming and going somewhere else.

This idea of "piecemeal" apprehension amounts to an analysis of the poetic method in the poem itself. As he contemplates the "immediate objects" at St. Peter's the narrator discovers that his "fond gaze" is "fooled" and "deceived" by his own "gradual" powers, that he has continually to reformulate his understanding of the significance of what he sees. Thus it is in the poem. The poet passes from ignorance to ignorance, but, like the fool who persists in his folly, he eventually comes to see at St. Peter's that comprehension is achieved only in successive, and relatively ignorant, perceptions. To "know oneself" one must submit to immediate and partial acts of perception:

> condense thy soul
> To more immediate objects, and control
> Thy thoughts until thy mind hath got by heart
> Its eloquent proportions . . .
> part by part. . . . (IV, 157)

This present understanding is wisdom for the future since pilgrimage never ends ("Roll on, thou deep and dark blue Ocean—roll!"); but the poet is also thinking of what has already been recorded in the poem, is thinking of his past blindnesses and partial insights. We know this because the stanzas allude to important moments in the poetic record of his past life. Stanza 156 calls up again the principal issue of Canto III, and stanzas 157–58 reinterpret the meaning of the attempt made therein to harmonize his human capabilities with his more than human impulses. The line "Defies at first our Nature's littleness" is surely meant to recall the earlier moments when the poet's sense of human insufficiency weighed heavily upon him:

> Where are the charms and virtues which we dare
> Conceive in boyhood and pursue as men,
> The unreached Paradise of our despair,
> Which o'er-informs the pencil and the pen,
> And overpowers the page where it would bloom again? (IV, 122)[8]

The sense of absolute *vanitas vanitatis* is contravened for good at St. Peter's and the Vatican Gallery. The way in which the narrator comes to a complete understanding of St. Peter's—through cumulative acts of limited perception that eventuate in a general sense of comprehension—is the image of the poet's experience in all four cantos. "We but feel our way to err," he says (IV, 81), as he scours the ruins of Rome for an understanding of the causes of her greatness and her collapse. He identifies himself with Italy—he is "A ruin amidst ruins" (25)—so that his search for a means of her resurrection (55) to her rightful preeminence is a search made in his own behalf as well. Just as he stumbles over the remains of Rome's enigmatic greatness, so he gropes blindly and uncertainly along for a kind of self-knowledge that will eventually set free his "Faculty divine" which "Is chain'd and tortured— cabin'd, cribb'd, confined" (IV, 127). But he is fooled continually with premature expectations and false hopes:

> But Rome is as the desert—where we steer
> Stumbling o'er recollections; now we clap

> Our hands, and cry "Eureka!" "it is clear"—
> When but some false Mirage of ruin rises near. (IV, 81)

Though St. Peter's brings enlightenment, the narrator in the meantime moves along compassed about with darkness, and beset with the constant danger of despair from his own vigorous skepticism.

A Process of Discovery: IV, 128–51

Thus, the narrator does not come before us in the posture of a seer or a prophetic instructor except at certain crucial moments—most notably, at the end of Canto IV. "Mark well my words! they are of your eternal salvation," Blake's poet says at the beginning of *Milton*.[9] Byron's poet does not possess oracular powers like this as part of his being, but seeks after a comparable kind of prophetic insight. Further, because he is dramatically presented to the reader in a succession of virtually present moments, and because he is absolutely divorced from Byron the omniscient artist, his thoughts and actions at particular moments are subject to alteration and revision. The narrator gradually accedes to a prophetic office, but in the meantime he "enlightens" us not as an oracle, but as an exemplum. This fact about the structure of the poem has not been generally recognized, and the failure to do so has led to some misinterpretations of the meanings of certain passages. John Wain, for example, has a fine analysis of the technical merits and demerits of the "Dying Gladiator" passage, but his interpretation of the basic meaning of the lines errs because he does not take into account the sequence of the narrating poet's thoughts as they develop through the whole meditation upon the Coliseum beginning at stanza 128. . . .[10] The central event in the meditation on the Coliseum is the forgiveness-curse sequence (130–37), which grows out of Byron's initial identification of himself and his present fortunes with the wrecked and desolated arena (129–31). After he has cursed his destroyers with his forgiveness, he conjures up yet another image of man's inhumanity to man—the Roman gladiatorial spectacle which took place in the Coliseum. The associative movement of the poet's thought here is rather interesting. He begins with the sight of the ruined arena and then goes on to consider his own ruination. This leads him to think how retribution always pursues such deeds, and he hails "great Nemesis" as his "Avenger."

> And Thou, who never yet of human wrong
> Left the unbalanced scale, great Nemesis!
> Here, where the ancient paid thee homage long—
> Thou, who didst call the Furies from the abyss,
> And round Orestes bade them howl and hiss
> For that unnatural retribution—just,

> Had it but been from hands less near—in this
> Thy former realm, I call thee from the dust!
> Dost thou not hear my heart?—Awake! thou shalt, and must. (132)

After delivering his forgiveness-curse, he considers the destruction of the Gothic gladiator in the Roman circus, and once again he cries out for retributive justice ("Arise! ye Goths, and glut your ire!" 141). In so doing, however, he has altered the significance that the Coliseum originally had for him as an image of his own desolation; it is now the symbol on which Roman brutality is focused.

This associational change in meaning might seem at first to have weakened the poetic structure by breaking the continuity of the poet's thought. Actually, the ambivalent associative value of the Coliseum serves to clarify the whole form of his thoughts on retribution for wrong—ultimately, to clarify the meaning of the forgiveness-curse sequence both for him and for us. The "tit-for-tat moralizing" which seems to be his object in stanzas 140–41 breaks down completely in stanza 142 when he again associates sympathetically with the Coliseum.

> But here, where Murder breathed her bloody stream;—
> And here, where buzzing nations choked the ways,
> And roared or murmured like a mountain stream
> Dashing or winding as its torrent strays;
> Here, where the Roman million's blame or praise
> Was Death or Life—the playthings of a crowd—
> My voice sounds much—and fall the stars' faint rays
> On the arena void—seats crushed—walls bowed—
> And galleries, where my steps seem echoes strangely loud. (142)

His wish for the destruction of the Roman symbol of oppression has been, in fact, tragically fulfilled. As he gazes around he sees the broken vestiges of once great Rome (143–44), and his "voice"—which called out angrily for retribution—now "sounds much" in an "arena void." The hollow echo of his cry is a mournful image of the effects of "tit-for-tat moralizing." "Hath it indeed been plundered, or but cleared? / Alas! developed, opens the decay . . ." (143). Now, "When the stars twinkle through the loops of Time" (144), the poet is able to see the entire picture of the "wretched interchange of wrong for wrong" (III, 69) in the story of Rome's decline and fall. He had criticized this process earlier in Canto III in the history of the French Revolution, and even earlier in Cantos I–II in reference to the Peninsular War. Now he presents this cycle of historical vengeance as the ultimate human horror, the activity that brings about a "Ruin past Redemption's skill" (IV, 145). Elsewhere he calls it the cause of "Man's worst, his second fall" (IV, 97), and in the present context he declares that vengeance of this sort not only brings the oppressor low, but pulls down the whole structure of human values as well (145). The entire world is at present in moral ruins, and the poet uses the Coliseum, destroyed in an act of "just" rage, as the focusing image of man's folly of self-destruction.

This vision of history as an inexorable movement of "tit-for-tat moralizing" is one of the principal themes in all four cantos, just as it is one of the main ideas at the back of Shelley's *Prometheus Unbound*. In *Childe Harold's Pilgrimage* the poet calls it a "base pageant" (IV, 97) of tyranny answering tyranny:

> And thus they plod in sluggish misery,
> Rotting from sire to son, and age to age,
> Proud of their trampled nature, and so die,
> Bequeathing their hereditary rage
> To the new race of inborn slaves, who wage
> War for their chains, and rather than be free,
> Bleed gladiator-like, and still engage
> Within the same Arena where they see
> Their fellows fall before, like leaves of the same tree. (94)

The reference to the bleeding gladiator is clearly an anticipation of the poet's later meditations at the Coliseum, and stands as a subtle portent of the important associational about-face that takes place in stanza 142.

Thus, the Coliseum sequence begins as an attempt to secure eye-for-an-eye justice. Heated by indignation, the poet inclines to disregard his earlier meditations on the theme of vengeance for wrong. But his desire to right "the unbalanced scale" undergoes a series of modifications beginning in stanza 135 when he unexpectedly calls for a *forgiveness*-curse. The modifications are not completed until the scene at the *Caritas Romana*, when the narrator recounts a story that has important thematic parallels both with his forgiveness-curse and with his version of the causes of Rome's destruction. Briefly, the poet tells the story of how a daughter paid back "the debt of blood" (150) to her father by feeding him from her breast while he was in prison. But the poet must be equivocating with the phrase "debt of blood," for its usual meaning—vengeance for suffered wrong (blood for blood)—is obviously not its first meaning here. Rather, the phrase refers to the fact that the daughter owes her very existence to her father. But Byron has a good reason for using the phrase in this unusual way; he wants to keep the idea of vengeance in our minds, to preserve intact the train of associations from the forgiveness-curse sequence to this point. His purpose in doing so becomes clear in stanza 151:

> The starry fable of the Milky Way
> Has not thy story's purity; it is
> A constellation of a sweeter ray,

And sacred Nature triumphs more in this
Reverse of her decree, than in the abyss
Where sparkle distant worlds:—Oh, holiest Nurse!
No drop of that clear stream its way shall miss
To thy Sire's heart, replenishing its source
With life, as our freed souls rejoin the Universe.

Nature pitilessly hews down men and their "worlds" (like Rome), but "this Reverse of her decree"—in which a young girl preserves the life of an old man—is a greater triumph yet. The stanza reaches back to the forgiveness-curse sequence through a complicated but discernible series of associations. The narrator also "reverses" the decree of Nature by forcing Nemesis to balance the scales of Justice not with vengeance but with forgiveness. We are probably also meant to see in the story a loose parallel to Rome in her later years (the aged father) and the emergent Gauls (the younger daughter). Rome is often presented in the last canto as the parent of all subsequent Western civilization (see stanzas 78–79), and history is pictured as a process in which each age bequeaths to the next its "inborn tyranny," its "hereditary rage." The story of the *Caritas Romana* "reverses" this cyclic movement toward death that operated in Nature and history alike, for the daughter seeks to preserve the life of her parent, to pay back the only "debt of blood" that is important for human life. Further, just as the narrating poet's curse is intended to infuse "love" into the "hearts all rocky now" (137), so the girl in the legend replenishes her "Sire's heart" with new "life." By taking the story of the *Caritas Romana* as a principle for living, the "souls" of men are freed from the bondage of a "contentious world" (III, 69) and can "rejoin the Universe"— can attain that "Freedom" which the narrator has been in pursuit of throughout Canto IV (see, for example, stanzas 89–96).

But the *Caritas Romana* not only completes the process of thought between stanzas 128 and 151 (preparing thereby for the triumphant assertion at St. Peter's and the Vatican Gallery which immediately follows), it clarifies and resolves all the poet's stumbling meditations upon bondage and freedom in the last canto. In stanza 96 he blurts out a desperate question:

Can tyrants but by tyrants conquered be,
And Freedom find no champion and no Child
Such as Columbia saw arise . . . ?
. . . .
Has Earth no more
Such seeds within her breast, or Europe no such shore?

He gets intermittent glimpses of such an achievement before the Coliseum sequence, and these partial insights anticipate the idea of a "reversed" decree like the forgiveness-curse and the *Caritas Romana*. The parallel is obvious in the most famous of these stanzas:

> Yet, Freedom! yet thy banner, torn, but flying,
> Streams like the thunder-storm *against* the wind;
> Thy trumpet voice, though broken now and dying,
> The loudest still the Tempest leaves behind;
> Thy tree hath lost its blossoms, and the rind,
> Chopped by the axe, looks rough and little worth,
> But the sap lasts,—and still the seed we find
> Sown deep, even in the bosom of the North;
> So shall a better spring less bitter fruit bring forth. (98)

Here again he senses the need to oppose the tide of bloody events, but this assertion is subsequently overwhelmed by his perception of the constant operation of a death principle to which men deliberately cling. So, later, he contravenes the vision of Egeria ("The nympholepsy of some fond despair," 115):

> Oh, Love! no habitant of earth thou art—
> An unseen Seraph, we believe in thee,—
> A faith whose martyrs are the broken heart,—
> But never yet hath seen, nor e'er shall see
> The naked eye, thy form, as it should be;
> The mind hath made thee, as it peopled Heaven,
> Even with its own desiring phantasy,
> And to a thought such shape and image given,
> As haunts the unquenched soul—parched—
>   wearied—wrung—and riven. (121)

Similarly, he declares against his vision of human creativity which he gained earlier at the Uffizi Gallery (49–52):

> Of its own beauty is the mind diseased,
> And fevers into false creation:—where,
> Where are the forms the sculptor's soul hath seized?
> In him alone. Can Nature show so fair? (122)

As he approaches the crucial events at the Coliseum, his despair at finding a principle of creative and immortalizing love has reached its deepest:

> Few—none—find what they love or could have loved,
> Though accident, blind contact, and the strong
> Necessity of loving, have removed
> Antipathies—but to recur, ere long,
> Envenomed with irrevocable wrong;
> And Circumstance, that unspiritual God
> And Miscreator, makes and helps along
> Our coming evils with a crutch-like rod,
> Whose touch turns Hope to dust,—the dust we all have trod.

> Our life is a false nature—'tis not in
> The harmony of things,—this hard decree,
> This uneradicable taint of Sin.
> This boundless Upas, this all-blasting tree,
> Whose root is Earth. . . . (125–26)

Though his mind thus continually wanders into mazes of uncertainty and hopelessness, he declares in the next stanza that he will continue to "ponder boldly," since the activity of groping thought is, in the end, justified, for his perseverance in meditation finally leads to a clear understanding that Love can and must be made a "habitant of earth."

The *Caritas Romana* modifies the forgiveness-curse sequence by presenting it again to us in a moderated tone. The girl offers her "gentle side" (150) to her father, whereas the poet had earlier "wreaked" the "deep prophetic fulness" of his curse of love (134) upon the heads of his enemies. Readers like Peter Thorslev have often found the forgiveness-curse stanzas offensive— "petty and vindictive," Thorslev calls them.[11] Yet surely this is misplaced Christian sentimentalism (or predisposed moralizing on Byron's biography), for as the stanzas appear in the poem the poet is graphically presented as the sufferer of intolerable wrongs.

> And if my voice break forth, 'tis not that now
> I shrink from what is suffered: let him speak
> Who hath beheld decline upon my brow,
> Or seen my mind's convulsion leave it weak;
> But in this page a record will I seek.
> Not in the air shall these my words disperse,
> Though I be ashes; a far hour shall wreak
> The deep prophetic fulness of this verse,
> And pile on human heads the mountain of my curse!
>
> That curse shall be Forgiveness.—Have I not—
> Hear me, my mother Earth! behold it, Heaven!—
> Have I not had to wrestle with my lot?
> Have I not suffered things to be forgiven?
> Have I not had my brain seared, my heart riven,
> Hopes sapped, name blighted, Life's life lied away?
> And only not to desperation driven,
> Because not altogether of such clay
> As rots into the souls of those whom I survey. (134–35)

The problem with which the poet must deal is a fundamental one, for if the judgment of men upon him is allowed to stand, then "Opinion" becomes an "Omnipotence," and "right / And wrong are accidents" (93) of transient human ethics rather than the absolute points of definition by which an individual must judge his own relation to the Godhead. The poet admits his own guilt: "It is not that I may not have incurred, / For my ancestral faults or mine, the wound / I bleed withal . . ." (133). But if once the principle of "wrong for wrong" is allowed, human integrity becomes impossible ("Man's worst, his second fall"). The evil that he has received at the hands of his detractors must be exposed and cast out, for it lies at the root of the "boundless Upas" which has overspread the earth and kept man in a cycle of self-destruction and moral death. He therefore invokes Nemesis to curse with forgiveness, a gesture which at once turns the destructive power of Nemesis against herself and "reverses" the very idea of cursing. The prophetic style in which the poet's curse is delivered, as well as the ease with which he associates himself with a sublime order of Reality (e.g., "Hear me, my mother Earth! behold it, Heaven!"), makes it impossible to regard his outburst as either "petty" or "vindictive." The prophetic tone is required by the circumstances, for his is not so much a self-defense as a defense of all contingent and erring humanity. It is an assertion of the sacred worth of the individual soul above everything else on earth, including its own sin and weakness and the judgment of other men. The whole scene appears as a terrible last resort for the vindication of the human person against his own and the world's evil, a Jobean cry wrung from a self-confessed sinner asserting that, despite all his weaknesses and perversions, every man must be able to believe that he is "fit for the society of kings" if he is not to die the death, and that if any other man seek to destroy that belief he has committed a fearful wrong that cries to heaven for judgment.

As Mr. Thorslev has noted, however, the narrator's prophetic style does not succeed in obliterating all subjective and personal elements from his curse. Dramatically considered, this fact has two results. First of all, it is a reliable pledge of the truth of the poet's "suffering" that he is unable entirely to forget himself in his role as prophet. But second, because his curse itself borders dangerously upon an act of vendetta, we may tend to forget (with him) that his lips have been touched with a burning coal, and that he has been called upon in extremis to speak a divine, not a human, truth. The cases of Job, Jeremiah, and especially Jonah indicate how often these two results tend to correlate with each other. It is the function of stanzas 138–51 to take the curse out of the poet's tone of voice: that is, the element of prophetic anathema must stand (the tone of a divine utterance), but when the afflatus leaves him, no trace of cursing must remain in his more intimate tone and more personal attitudes. This process begins at the end of stanza 137 when he looks to a future reconciliation in love, and it is completed in the poet's meditation upon the *Caritas Romana* where pity and gentleness are the predominant motifs.

Stanzas 128–51 present Byron's accession to a more perfect understanding of the good and evil in himself and his world. In addition, they repeat the method of the whole canto, in which the poet rummages about the museum of Italy for a solution to the problem of human evil. He alternates between periods of hopefulness and expectancy (for example, stanza 47) and spells of terrible despair; but even after the climax has been passed—in the last thirty-three stanzas of the poem—he finds that the truth he has discovered is not The Truth, but the way to Truth. Once again we are given a statement of the necessity of constant development and painful growth. In the Coliseum sequence, as elsewhere, the narrator is the prototype of groping, stumbling humanity who is, nevertheless, called to a high and splendid destiny; in the end, by "pondering boldly" and by preserving always a responsiveness to new sensations and attitudes, he is enlightened not to a goal, but to the glory of what he is even now engaged in seeking. Gide's famous remark—"Je ne suis jamais, je deviens"—could not be more appositely applied than to the last canto of *Childe Harold's Pilgrimage*.

DRAMATIC ACTION IN CANTOS I–II

But the first two cantos also dramatize the narrating poet in a process of "becoming," only in this case he portrays himself advancing to a condition of mental anguish and futility. I suspect that most readers who regard Cantos I–II as a versified travel book do so because the narrator is so "impressionable" in them. Unlike the exuberant poet of Cantos III and IV, the narrator of 1812 never influences events himself, but is always acted upon. Even his satirical set pieces and declamatory sequences are not hurled forth from a position of strength; they are responses to an earlier disagreeable impression or stimulus, purely reflex movements. But it is just because this is true that Cantos I–II are primarily personal, not objectively descriptive documents, or satirical, or didactic. John Wilson says they reveal "a mind . . . enslaved to itself,"[12] and in fact we find Byron's self-consciousness and sensitivity are themselves the predominant causes of his perplexities, for they subject him to ambiguous, even contradictory, attitudes in quick succession. Everything is equivocal to him: in Portugal are both natural beauty and abject weakness and corruption; in Albania, vigor and bravery as well as vendetta and blood-lust; in Greece, beauty and a heritage of the world's most noble values, but also complete spiritual enervation. As he passes through these countries and observes their manners he gives us not so much a picture of them as a moving picture of his reactions to them; and it is upon the sequence of the narrator's reactions as they are presented in the poem that the structure of the first two cantos, like the last, is built. . . .

. . . as we [can see] from the stanzas on Spain, his personality in the early cantos is as unstable as his forms of thought are equivocal. We cannot take anything he says as a conclusive statement on any subject because his mind is constantly veering off toward different points of view. But if his thoughts are not engaging as precepts, the movement of his mind is exceedingly interesting and instructive as a psychological exemplum. Without a fixed center of established values and modes of reasoning in which he is willing to put his trust, the poet is moved along by circumstances, his own skepticism, and the habit of associational responsiveness, until by the end of Canto II he has passed through various stages of disenchantment with his environment to an attitude of total alienation. His opinions, as ideas, are strictly of secondary poetic importance; what matters is that they are his, and that in them we can read the temper of his mind. . . .

In the early cantos, then, we see that the mind of the poet is objectified to us in much the same way that it is in the later cantos: we observe him thinking and acting, and frequently perceive significance where he remains without self-knowledge. This is true because a similar process is repeated in all four cantos: the poet tells us his story, but because the telling and the living seem to have occurred simultaneously, the poet in the poem can know nothing about himself beyond the stanza he is immediately writing (the moment he is immediately living). He is thus a prejudiced participant in the action which he himself narrates. This is a matter of art, not chance, for it proceeds from the method in which Byron has chosen to cast his poem. Though the poet *in* the poem is presented to us as the artist *of* the poem, he in fact shows no signs of artistic objectivity. He has to acquire consciousness and self-knowledge in the course of the poem; only Byron the artist, who is refined out of poetic existence, possesses such objectivity, and his consciousness is built into the poem's structure, not into the narrator's character. This really basic fact about the form of the whole poem (why it is "dramatic" in character) can be forgotten only at the risk of fundamental misreading.

Those long-suffering stanzas at the beginning of Canto I (2–13), for example, have often been rather harshly treated by contemporary critics for just this reason. As it is, they have weaknesses enough in basic matters of execution; but we ought not to find fault indiscriminately. The lapses in these early stanzas are the same kind that we encounter throughout the first two cantos: thoughtless rhythm, overly generalized metaphors, functionless verbosity, neglect of diction for the sake of rhyme.

> For he through Sin's long labyrinth had run,
> Nor made atonement when he did amiss,
> Had sighed to many though he loved but one,
> And that loved one, alas! could ne'er be his.
> Ah, happy she! to 'scape from him whose kiss
> Had been pollution unto aught so chaste;
> Who soon had left her charms for vulgar bliss,
> And spoiled her goodly lands to gild his waste,
> Nor calm domestic peace had ever deigned to taste. (5)

Critics like to attack the opening stanzas for their Spenserian diction, yet this stanza—which is probably the worst in the early group—is entirely free of it, while stanza 2, which is full of such diction, develops a raffish charm by exploiting the antique language for some important comic effects. Not only are the faults of the opening stanzas not a function of their Spenserian diction, the general meaning of the lines is specifically related to the way the narrating poet uses it. The antique language helps to reveal the poet's attitudes to the reader. [13]

I will return to the second stanza again in a moment, for we can appreciate it more easily once we have elucidated the purpose of the whole introductory passage. We make our first assessment of the narrator's character in stanzas 1–13, and the contrast between this initial picture and those presented at various other significant moments later in the poem is an important index to the overall psychological movement. The poet begins by invoking the blessing of the Muse:

> Oh, thou! in Hellas deemed of heavenly birth,
> Muse! formed or fabled at the Minstrel's will!
> Since shamed full oft by later lyres on earth,
> Mine dares not call thee from thy sacred Hill:
> Yet there I've wandered by thy vaunted rill;
> Yes! sighed o'er Delphi's long deserted shrine,
> Where, save that feeble fountain, all is still;
> Nor mote my shell awake the weary Nine
> To grace so plain a tale—this lowly lay of mine. (1)

He has already told us in the Preface that most of the poem was written "amidst the scenes which it attempts to describe." The first stanza, however, manifestly belongs to a period subsequent to his visit to Greece (ll. 5–6), which is to say—in terms of the poem's own time sequence—after the conclusion to Canto II. He addresses us first in the approximate present, then, and we find that his melancholy feelings occasioned by the passing of greatness (ll. 6–7) as well as the sense of his own ineffectuality (ll. 4, 8–9) parallel the state of his mind as we see it at the end of Canto II (see especially stanzas 92 and 98). Moreover, the contempt he expresses for the host of "louder Minstrels in these later days" (II, 94) is foreshadowed here in the disdain he feels for the "later lyres on earth" who now shame the Muse's ancient glory. Finally, the poet's gloom is also a function of the general social corruption which is suggested by the symbolism of the stanza: waste and infertility surround Parnassus, the mountain sacred to Apollo and the Muses, and the symbolic apex of literature, art, and culture. At the end of Canto II he also finds himself alone and desolate in a corrupted world (97), left "deserted" by the deaths of all those close to him who gave meaning to his existence (96). The relationship between Greece and the lonely poet is explicitly drawn in II, 92.

> The parted bosom clings to wonted home,
> If aught that's kindred cheer the welcome hearth;
> He that is lonely—hither let him roam,
> And gaze complacent on congenial earth.
> Greece is no lightsome land of social mirth:
> But he whom Sadness sootheth may abide,
> And scarce regret the region of his birth,
> When wandering slow by Delphi's sacred side,
> Or gazing o'er the plains where Greek and Persian died.

The allusion to the motto from *Le Cosmopolite* fixes the stanzas as an important statement of what the narrator has learned so far on his pilgrimage with Harold.

When the narrative proper begins in stanza 2, however, there is an abrupt change in the tone of the poet's voice. No reader can miss this *fact,* but generally the reason for it is overlooked. Northrop Frye, for example, finds the poet's "semi-facetious" manner in stanzas 2–13 merely "pointless."[14] I do not think this is accurate. The point is that the poet at the end of the first pilgrimage is "A sadder and a wiser man" than he was at the beginning.[15] The epigraph from *Le Cosmopolite* states this clearly. The theme of Cantos I–II is "Consciousness awaking to her woes" (I, 92), the painful education of the poet into a more sensitive and reliable subjective moral awareness, one that he did not possess at the start. The tonal contrast between stanzas 1 and 2 is the poem's initial forecast of the direction in which the first two cantos will ultimately move (that is, toward the tone of st. 1).

Stanzas 2–13 are about equally divided between sardonic mockery and earnest satire or reflection. One of the many editors of the poem, Andrew J. George, discusses the vein of cynical irresponsibility in this way: "These . . . stanzas have doubtless deterred many from reading the poem. There is in them something of the *Don Juan,* that spirit of melodrama and affectation which is distinctly Byronic. . . . There is here something of a motiveless malignity which would shock those mortals afflicted with the disease which Dean Hole called piosity."[16] Yet why should we censure the poetic mockery in a passage like stanza 2? We learn a great deal about the narrator in a very short space, certainly much more than we do about Harold. A few general facts are detailed about Harold's life, but the specific thrust of this stanza is its ironic attack upon the sensibilities of the conventionally moral, as Mr. George has noted. The attack is not "motiveless," however, for "piosity" is a disease (as Byron frequently tells us in *Hours of Idleness*), and the poet suggests here that it is quite as symptomatic of social and moral degeneracy as is "riot most uncouth." But the poet seems disinclined to take the objects of his ridicule very seriously, at least here, so that his tone remains cavalier and almost bantering. His mocking use of syntax and diction robs everything in the stanza of moral significance except his own jocose cynicism. "Virtue's ways," "Concubines and carnal companie," "riot most uncouth," even the "shameless wight" himself are all reduced to a dead level of absurdity. This tendency to complete moral nihilism is characteristic of all the early stanzas. When he alludes to the history of Harold's "vast and venerable" (7) hall he resorts again to his irresponsible humor.

> Monastic dome! condemned to uses vile!
> Where superstition once had made her den
> Now Paphian girls were known to sing and smile;
> And monks might deem their time was come agen,
> If ancient tales say true, nor wrong these holy men.

Stanzas 2–13 display this kind of urbane mockery quite often, and it is a significant characteristic of the narrator's early state of mind. He likes to set himself up as a gadfly to all conventional moral systems and attitudes, attacking or hooting at them for their hypocrisy, or selfishness, or self-righteousness. Thus he gets his joke at the expense of the hypocritical monks of those "ancient tales," and in stanza 2 he mocks the propriety-bound attitudes of conventional British morality. Yet this cynicism into which he retreats is only the reverse of the more serious attitudes toward his society which also appear in these early stanzas. In fact, the opening stanzas display a fairly constant alternation between seriousness and persiflage, and it is this kind of indecisiveness that comes across as the most apparent trait of the narrator's character at this point. Thus, if he is contemptuous of self-righteous piosity, he is equally opposed to the gentlemanly pursuit of dissolute pleasures that is especially characteristic of the upper class (compare *Hours of Idleness,* "Granta, A Medley," st. 13–16). He attacks them as "The heartless parasites of present cheer" (9), and in this case the line betrays no tone of levity whatever. The glimpse we get into the narrator's mind here recalls several remarks in the first stanza of the canto, just as it foreshadows the loneliness described in the conclusion to Canto II, as well as the declamation in II, 26 on society's "Minions of splendour, shrinking from distress."

Insofar as Harold is the product of a sentimental eighteenth-century education he too is mocked by the narrator. "Sickly sensibility" is a persistent object of satire in *Hours of Idleness.* But as in that early volume Byron's own feelings about "the man of feeling" are frequently equivocal, so here:

> And now Childe Harold was sore sick at heart,
> And from his fellow Bacchanals would flee;
> 'Tis said, at times the sullen tear would start,
> But Pride congealed the drop within his ee:
> Apart he stalked in joyless reverie,
> And from his native land resolved to go,

And visit scorching climes beyond the sea;
With pleasure drugged, he almost longed for woe,
And e'en for change of scene would seek the shades below. (6)

The archaisms in the first four lines tend to deflate Harold's conventionally melancholic pose, but the tone of the stanza undergoes a gradual metamorphosis in the second half. The "semi-facetious" antique style at the beginning is the sign of the narrator's skeptical smile, just as it is in the earlier line "Ah me! in sooth he was a shameless wight." The tone grows more complicated, however, for it is difficult to know just how seriously lines 5–9 are to be taken. A line like the eighth is particularly problematical, for it has no Spenserianisms to mitigate its rather grim signification.

A similar effect is produced in stanza 4:

Childe Harold basked him in the Noontide sun,
Disporting there like any other fly;
Nor deemed before his little day was done
One blast might chill him into misery.
But long ere scarce a third of his passed by,
Worse than Adversity the Childe befell;
He felt the fulness of Satiety:
Then loathed he in his native land to dwell,
Which seemed to him more lone than Eremite's sad cell.

The first line of the stanza echoes a line in a famous speech by Jaques in *As You Like It* (II, vii, 12–34), in which the theme of evil Fortune and the ravages of Time is paramount. . . .[17] Jaques, Hamlet, Sterne, and the Byron of *Don Juan* are all famous for their ability to hold mockery and melancholy in a delicate—and significant—equipoise. The allusion here is thus most apposite, for it not only supports the tone of comic reduction on which the stanza opens, but prepares us for the darker moods that flit through the later parts of the passage. After the third line, the tone becomes equivocal, as it did in the middle of stanza 6. The straightforward meaning of the seventh line, for example, conflicts with the ironic tone maintained at the stylistic level. This kind of effect happens frequently in the early stanzas ("something of the *Don Juan*," as A. J. George said), and it serves to convince us that the narrator's character is a complicated mixture of cynical humor and melancholy seriousness. He can laugh at Harold's "Paphian girls," but at the same time he is seriously opposed to Harold's dissolute "flatterers" and repelled by the effects of irresponsible pleasure-seeking; he finds Harold a bit ridiculous and without the capacity for effective self-examination (Harold does not begin to learn the art of "Meditation" until I, 27, and even then he flees it), but the narrator is likewise sensible of the Childe's pained and gloomy condition (8). He can, for example, smile ironically at Harold's "vast and venerable pile" which was

"So old, it seemed only not to fall" (7), and in the very next line cut across his own humor with a serious qualification: "Yet strength was pillared in each massy aisle." That the poetry in this case is completely undistinguished does not affect its evident intention. He is also an adept at self-mockery; we frequently find him deflating his sympathetic responses with a sudden ironic thrust, as in stanza 9:

> And none did love him! though to hall and bower
> He gathered revellers from far and near,
> He knew them flatterers of the festal hour,
> The heartless Parasites of present cheer,
> Yea! none did love him—not his lemans dear—
> But pomp and power alone are Woman's care,
> And where these are light Eros finds a feere;
> Maidens, like moths, are ever caught by glare,
> And Mammon wins his way where Seraphs might despair.

Byron had much trouble with the composition of this stanza, which originally was completely somber in tone;

> And few could love him, for in hall and bower,
> An evil smile, just bordering on a sneer,
> Curled on his lip een in the festal hour
> As if he deemed no mortal might him cheer—
> To gentle dames still less could he be dear—
> But pomp and power alone are woman's care,
> And where these are let no possessor fear,
> The Sex are slaves to ⎫
> Love shrinks outshone by ⎬ Mammon's dazzling glare
> That Daimon wins his way, where Angels might despair.[18]

Revising the stanza, Byron takes away Harold's "evil smile" in order to make him appear just sympathetically melancholy. The evil is transferred to the "flatterers of the festal hour, / The heartless Parasites of present cheer" with whom the Childe consorts. But the "gentle dames" in the first form of the stanza are not at all attractive creatures, so Byron decides to tone the narrator's description down. They become "moths" caught (unwittingly) by Mammon's "glare" rather than the willing and even deliberate "slaves" to his enticements. The phrase "light Eros finds a feere," a very late addition,[19] supports the narrator's new tone of indulgent mockery toward the ladies. The new fifth line ("Yea! none did love him—not his lemans dear—") was clearly a decisive addition, for in it we observe the narrator making an abrupt effort to sound less concerned, to appear more sardonically disinterested. The original seriousness of the stanza still hovers around the playful satire in the last five lines, and the reader is left uncertain as to just how much bite the narrator's irony has in it. This equivocalness seems to me perfectly functional, however, since it reflects again that basic emotional duality in the narrator's character which we find exemplified throughout the opening stanzas.

Perhaps no commentary on the early stanzas of Canto I reveals so well the precise tone of the poet's voice there as does the following passage in a letter from Byron to Francis Hodgson. The letter is especially interesting because it was written just after Byron had finished the first draft of Cantos I–II. He seems to have had the opening stanzas specifically in his thoughts when he wrote to Hodgson, for not only is the substance of the following passage very close to that in the poem, the tonal quality duplicates stanzas 2–13 nearly perfectly.

> I hope you will find me an altered personage,—I do not mean in body but in manner, for I begin to find out that nothing but virtue will do in this damned world. I am tolerably sick of vice, which I have tried in its agreeable varieties, and mean, on my return, to cut all my dissolute acquaintance, leave off wine and carnal company, and betake myself to politics and decorum. I am very serious and cynical, and a good deal disposed to moralise; but fortunately for you the coming homily is cut off by default of pen and defection of paper. (Letter of 5 May 1810)

William Borst found it "hard to say"[20] just how serious Byron's declarations in this letter were, and his equivocal reaction is a sensitive reflection of Byron's own attitude. There is a certain wicked perversity in the trick of the final sentence (which closes the letter) where Byron dexterously tiptoes away from taking any responsibility for what he has just said; for he himself does not know his own mind at this point, and he refuses to become too deeply involved in his volitional impulses and emotional responses. At the same time, it is perfectly clear that he has experienced some sort of psychic reaction against "vice," even if he as yet has no idea what might or even ought to be done about it. So he substitutes irony for commitment.

CONCLUSION

The way we naturally read passages like these from Byron's dramatic and self-revelatory prose can help us keep our responses true to the self-dramatizing nature of *Childe Harold's Pilgrimage*. The narrator's style in the poem—the way he expresses himself, the momentary attitudes that he reveals—are as much a part of the poem's meaning in Cantos I–II as they are in III and IV. The Preface of 1812 announces the tonal fluctuations that we do in fact find throughout the early cantos, and I think it would be a mistake to assume that Byron did not see how such a technique would contribute to the realization of the narrator's character in the poem. For his part, Andrew Rutherford acknowledges that the poet "does succeed in presenting different aspects of his personality" in the poem, but he goes on to say that Byron "fails to unite them into a coherent artistic whole—a failure which must be attributed in part to careless workmanship and lack of planning, but also to his inability at this stage to resolve the conflicts in his nature, to develop a consistent attitude toward life . . ." (p.33). We shall see that his argument about lack of planning cannot be maintained in the face of the existing MSS. If Byron failed to present a "coherent artistic whole" it is not because he did not try very hard to do so; this he said himself in his Preface.

In this chapter I have tried to show how *Childe Harold's Pilgrimage* gives us the poet's history (Arnold's "real Lord Byron") in the form of the protagonist's own immediate record of his life; and, further, that this kind of poetic method ("dramatic") places special demands upon the way we must read the poem. I have also tried to make some preliminary suggestions about what sort of person the narrating poet is at different points in the poem, and how his story tends to develop from the earlier to the later cantos. On the basis of these initial observations, I must dissent from Rutherford's statement that Cantos I–II do not arrange themselves into a "coherent artistic whole." This fairly widespread opinion exerts a strong claim to validity in Rutherford's presentation because (*a*) a good deal of the verse in the early cantos is either mediocre or worse, and (*b*) Rutherford's other point—that the two cantos do not "develop a consistent attitude toward life"—is clearly an accurate description of the specifically ethical development of the cantos. The narrator's sensibility is dislocated, and this condition only becomes more aggravated as the cantos proceed. Yet *Hamlet* is the story of a similar type of mind, nor do the eighteenth and nineteenth centuries show any lack of novels and poems which take such men for their heroes; the literature of our own day abounds in "alienated" personalities. The fact that the poet in the poem does not attain a consistent attitude toward life has nothing whatever to do with the question of the aesthetic "consistency" of these early cantos. The logical conclusion of this view is that which Ernest J. Lovell, Jr. arrived at some time ago: that Byron's poetry is, as a whole, hopelessly crippled by its inability to offer us a "consistent attitude toward life" like Wordsworth's.[21] A critical argument, like this, from moral precept is always hazardous, for it may turn out that the poetry in question espouses a different ethical position altogether. Such is the present case, for Byron, like his beloved Montaigne, deliberately sought to avoid the kind of ethical consistency that Wordsworth sought. In the end, his poetry embraces alienation, skepticism, constant change, as it were by necessity, and attempts to show how man achieves a Godlike sovereignty (or a childlike innocence) even in a "waste and icy clime" (*Don Juan* VII, 2).

Byron did not think ideology of paramount importance for such an achievement. Certain positive concepts remain crucial for him (e.g., love, personal integrity, strength of will), but he almost never treats these programmatically. Works like *Sardanapalus* and *The Island* show a marked commitment to the idea of an earthly paradise, but even in them ideology is sidestepped for dramatic and symbolic presentation. Goethe was right: Byron could not write philosophic poetry, and he rarely tried (his satires, for example, are not interesting because they are arguments but because they are passionate self-dramatizations). We can abstract certain predominant Byronic ideas and themes from his works, but—as readers have always discovered—we must not expect that they will submit to the convenience of programmatic definition. Byron's "coherence," as a whole, becomes realized in the definition of his various, metahistorical character; the coherence of his individual works, on the other hand, depends upon *poiesis,* the symbolic organization of immediate and dramatic materials. A work like *Childe Harold's Pilgrimage* illustrates both of these facts about Byron's poetry, for on the one hand it contains the story (or at least *a* story) of his metahistory, and on the other it presents that metahistory in a dramatic and symbolic form. Byron-the-narrator tells his own story and in the process not only discovers what his life means, but finds that its meaning proliferates and develops as the story continues. The poem is a journal that eventuates in an autobiography, for the overall coherence that the latter form pretends to and that the former (at least by intention) does not, becomes realized in the total work within the narrator's own act of self-discovery. *Our* experience of the work involves the perception of this self-dramatization and self-discovery in the narrating poet, whose purpose in writing is "to create" himself—"and in creating live / A being more intense."

Notes

1. William Hazlitt, *The Spirit of the Age,* in *The Complete Works of William Hazlitt,* ed. P.P. Howe, 11 (London, 1930–34): 75.
2. *Byron the Poet* (London, 1964), p.199.
3. *Aristotle's Poetics,* ed. and trans, S.H. Butcher, in *Aristotle's Theory of Poetry and Fine Art* (London, 1907), p.13.
4. Susanne K. Langer's remarks on Illusionism in the literary arts, and the difference between the illusions of "drama" and "literature," suggest how *Childe Harold's Pilgrimage* tends to fall somewhere between the two categories. "Drama is not, in the strict sense, 'literature.' Yet it is a poetic art, because it creates the primary illusion of all poetry—virtual history. . . . It is a fabric of illusory experiences, and that is the essential product of poesis. . . . Literature projects the image of life in the mode of virtual memory; language is its essential material; the sound and meaning of words, the familiar or unusual use and order, even their presentation on the printed page, create the illusion of life as a realm of events—completed, lived, as words formulate them—events that compose a Past. But Drama presents the poetic illusion in a different light: not finished realities, or 'events,' but immediate, visible responses of human beings, make its semblance of life." *Feeling and Form* (New York, 1953), p.306. Though *Childe Harold's Pilgrimage* cannot but exist in the medium of "virtual memory" which is the printed

word, its mode of presentation seeks to persuade us that we are reading the "immediate, visible responses" of a human being: not emotion recollected in tranquillity and filtered through an artistic consciousness, but an unmediated expression of self.

5. The distinction here is between the poet's artistic consciousness of his work and his human consciousness of himself as a man in an environment. The poet who appears as the narrator of *Childe Harold's Pilgrimage* does not possess an artistic consciousness with respect to the work he relates. In this he differs from the "poets" of *Don Juan* and *The Prelude* alike, both of whom make their artistic consciousness part of the substance of their works. Both are, in other words, poems written about themselves, about the act of writing poetry. An interesting discussion of this problem can be found in Robert M. Durling's *The Figure of the Poet in the Renaissance Epic* (Cambridge, Mass., 1965), pp. 2–6. He departs somewhat from Wayne C. Booth's pioneering work on this and related matters in his well-known *Rhetoric of Fiction* (Chicago, 1961).

6. The mountain image is the focus of the whole third canto. See, for example, stanzas 14, 40, 67, 72, 91, 96, and 109.

7. I have benefited in general from reading George Ridenour's unpublished doctoral thesis "Byron and the Romantic Pilgrimage" (New Haven, 1955). My interpretation of these stanzas in particular is simply an extrapolation of Ridenour's view.

8. See also III, 62, where the gigantic Alps make the poet painfully aware of his littleness; and IV, 17, where the poet speaks of Venice (the "fairy city of the heart") as one of the "charms" conceived in innocent "boyhood."

9. *Poetry and Prose of William Blake,* ed. Geoffrey Keynes (London, 1961), p. 376.

10. "The Search for Identity," in *Byron: A Collection of Essays,* ed. Paul West (Englewood Cliffs, 1963), pp. 163–64.

11. *The Byronic Hero* (Minneapolis, 1962), p. 140.

12. Review of Lord Byron, "The Fourth Canto of Childe Harold," *Blackwood's Magazine 3* (May, 1818): 217.

13. Andrew Rutherford states the prevailing objection against the Spenserian diction very well: "Byron cannot justify his archaisms as Beattie does his occasional use of 'old words' in *The Minstrel,* by saying they are appropriate to his subject, for Childe Harold, though referred to as a pilgrim, is a contemporary figure, and there is no point in using pseudo-medieval jargon to describe his actions" (*Byron: A Critical Study* [Palo Alto, 1961], pp. 26–27). One does not have to defend every instance of Byron's use of archaic language to see that it is often most appropriate to the subject of the poem—to the revelation of the narrator's personality, that is. As I shall try to show in the discussion below, the highly derivative character of this language makes it a focus of the narrator's self-consciousness: a tension is set up in the early stanzas of the poem between the narrator's use of his artificial Spenserian diction and his more normal declamatory-meditative-conversational language.

14. "Lord Byron," in *Fables of Identity* (New York, 1963), p. 182.

15. Coleridge's *Rime of the Ancient Mariner* was a favorite of Byron's, and may have influenced the form of *Childe Harold's Pilgrimage.* The wanderer motif needs no emphasis, but one might recall that Coleridge's poem also begins with a picture of the principal character after the fact, and that both the mariner and Byron's narrator start their journeys in a certain careless atmosphere. Byron alludes specifically to Coleridge's poem in Harold's "Good Night" lyric, stanza 9, lines 1–2.

16. *Childe Harold's Pilgrimage,* ed. Andrew J. George (New York, 1907), p. 184.

17. In fact, the entire passage in which the line occurs is pertinent to Byron's point: see II, vii, 12–34.

18. This is transcribed from the original MS of the canto in the Murray collection.

19. It does not appear in the Murray MS, but it does appear in the Dallas transcript made in late July or early August, 1811.

20. *Lord Byron's First Pilgrimage* (New Haven, 1948), p. 114.

21. Ernest J. Lovell, *Byron: The Record of a Quest* (Austin, Texas, 1949), p.41, for example.

Editor's Bibliographical Note

While critical commentary on *Childe Harold's Pilgrimage* is virtually legion, before and after McGann's book, and while McGann himself has since progressively modified (abjured, *I* think, is too strong a word) what in retrospect he characterizes as an inadequate critical approach to Byron in this his first book, I continue to maintain (along with others) that it remains one of the best introductions we have to how to read Byron's first great poem. Since all other major Byron critics have written extensively on *Childe Harold* in one book or another (especially those whose names most frequently appear in these bibliographical notes), I shall not list them again here—although I do want to note particularly my own extensive and detailed analyses of the entire poem in *Byron and the Ruins of Paradise* (Baltimore: Johns Hopkins University Press, 1967), 39–90, 225–50, 267–97, and Peter J. Manning's less extensive but critically illuminating and different approach to all four cantos in *Byron and His Fictions* (Detroit: Wayne State University Press, 1978), 21–35, 62–71, 90–99. In addition I offer what I regard to be among the best journal essays published from the sixties to the present—with a prefatory reminder about George Ridenour's Yale doctoral dissertation on *Childe Harold,* to which McGann refers in one of his notes above, and about Harold Bloom's essay on Byron in *The Visionary Company* (New York: Doubleday, 1961), 232–74. Those essays (and an occasional book chapter) are Ward Pafford, "Byron and the Mind of Man: *Childe Harold* III and IV, and *Manfred*," *Studies in Romanticism* 2 (1962): 105–27; Kenneth A. Bruffee, "The Synthetic Hero and the Narrative Structure of *Childe Harold* III," *Studies in English Literature* 6 (1966): 669–88; R. W. Harris, "*Childe Harold* and *Don Juan*," in his *Romanticism and the Social Order, 1780–1830* (London: Blandford Press, 1969), 328–66; Carl Woodring, "Nature, Art, Reason, and Imagination in *Childe Harold*," in *Romantic and Victorian,* ed. W. P. Elledge and R. L. Hoffman (Cranbury: Fairleigh Dickinson University Press, 1971), 147–57; Francis Berry, "The Poet of *Childe Harold*," in *Byron: A Symposium,* ed. John D. Jump (London: Macmillan, 1975), 35–51; Paul H. Fry, "The Absent Dead: Wordsworth, Byron, and the Epitaph," *Studies in Romanticism* 17 (1978): 413–33; John A. Hodgson, "The Structures of *Childe Harold* III," *Studies in Romanticism* 18 (1979): 363–82; Sheila Emerson, "Byron's 'one word': The Language of Self-Expression in *Childe Harold* III," *Studies in Romanticism* 20 (1981): 363–82; Bernard A. Hirsch, "The Erosion of the Narrator's World View in *Childe Harold's Pilgrimage,* I–II," *Modern Language Quarterly* 42 (1981): 347–68; Michael Vicario, "The Implications of Form in *Childe Harold's Pilgrimage*," *Keats-Shelley Journal* 33 (1984): 103–29; Cecil Y. Lang, "Narcissus Jilted: Byron, *Don Juan,* and the Biographical Imperative," in *Historical Studies and Literary Criticism,* ed. Jerome J. McGann (Madison: University of Wisconsin Press, 1985), 143–79; Vincent Newey, "Authoring the Self: *Childe Harold* III and IV," in *Byron and the Limits of Fiction,* ed. Bernard Beatty and Newey (Liverpool: Liverpool University Press, 1988), 148–90.

Byron and the
World of Fact

MICHAEL G. COOKE

The world is a perpetual caricature of itself; at every moment it is the mockery
and the contradiction of what it is pretending to be.

—George Santayana

Hours of Idleness, Byron's early portmanteau of assorted experimental poems,
offers in the lines "To Romance" a remarkable preview of his teetering
between irreconcilable positions which can be characterized as idealism and
actuality, knowledge (or perhaps intellect acting upon empirical knowledge)
and faith. Byron renounces romance, but he does so with ill-concealed regret:
"'t is hard to quit the dreams / Which haunt the unsuspicious soul." Similarly, his equating of romance with "childish joys" loses some of its authority
when we see that his new attitude grows out of disillusionment, not maturity. Even as he offers his strictures on romance, which is now "but a name," a
purely fabricated world of "deceit" and "Affectation" and "sickly Sensibility,"
he is forced to be correspondingly hard on himself as erstwhile believer
("Fond fool"). Evidently he as well as his world must be changed.

The terms of the change, however, seem neither consistent nor feasible.
Does Byron "leave [the] realm" of romance (st. 1) or do they "perish" in
"oblivion's blackening lake" (st. 8)? In other words, does he create or only
passively witness change? To compound the problem, the poem is rather
imprecise in representing the "Truth" supposed to take the place of the
"realms of air." It is so overwhelmingly given over to describing and decrying
romance that the protestation, "[I] leave thy realms for those of Truth,"
suggests a fairly vague inclination toward an object, rather than an assured
destination. If the past world is certainly dead for the poet, the new one—
truth not being a product of mere volition—seems almost as certainly power-
less to be born. [1]

The clue to this failure on both fronts lies in the fact that Byron is
unwittingly "flying" from discovered Truth no less than from exposed Romance. One presupposes the other, and differs from it only in direction of

From *The Blind Man Traces the Circle: On the Patterns and Philosophy of Byron's Poetry.* © 1969 by Princeton
University Press. Reprinted by permission.

focus. But Byron, ready for neither literary realism nor practical cynicism, somehow keeps at arm's length the poem's only tangible truth, that romantic courtesy is a hypochondriacal hypocrisy. It is all too clear that he is "leaving," or rather yearning "for [realms] of Truth" which genuinely will embody spirituality, friendship, and fidelity; he is in a special way raising the desirable over the actual, the ideal over the known. Though formality of tone and of diction, and a tight structural regularity give the poem the air of an embryonic ode to rationality, Byron perhaps betrays its latent bias by entitling it "To Romance."

Elsewhere in *Hours of Idleness* he designates his muse as "the simple truth" ("Answer to Some Elegant Verses"). But this can amount to no more than an argumentative challenge offered at once to contemporary literature and to himself. A reliable mark of his resolved position presents itself in the complications and mutations of his "truth."[2] Beyond the evidence already brought up, we find Byron in effect defying his muse: "Truth!—wherefore did thy hated beam / Awake me to a world like this?" ("I Would I Were a Careless Child"). In this cry he makes explicit the aversion to crude material truth which gives rise to subconscious tension in "To Romance." A higher and more comprehensive truth appears momentarily as the object of Childe Harold's aspirations (II.xxvii.6–9), but disappointment here proves correspondingly keener and more definitive, as the hero cannot even become acquainted with that truth—it is as inaccessible as swarming facts are insistent. And Byron conveys the impression that an innate incapacity causes the Childe's frustration, for "as he gazed on truth his aching eyes grew dim" (l. 9). Whether the eyes ache from straining to see or from inability to accommodate the sight, the result is the bleak negation implied in the phrase "grew dim."

On that sort of negation, as a matter of fact, Byron has no monopoly in the romantic period. We may recall John Wilson's troubled acknowledgement of the "subjects of darkness and mystery which afford, at some period or other in his life, so much disquiet . . . so much agony to the mind of every reflecting modern."[3] And it is clear that a certain negation takes a central place in the "Ode to a Nightingale," in the "Ode: Intimations of Immortality," and in "Dejection: An Ode," besides being at least thematically important in such poems as the "Hymn to Intellectual Beauty" and "Europe: A Prophecy." A potentially disabling apprehension of mortality and finitude is not easily separated from the imaginative transcendency of romanticism. Byron claims special attention, in the last analysis, in that he tries such a miscellany of nostrums against mortality: the inexhaustible will, for example, tradition (artistic *or* historical), nature as direct metaphysical healer *or* as propitious symbol, the mystical spirit of youth, personal love, "the right of thought". . . ; and in that he so candidly details its protean recrudescence.

His aggravated difficulty in reaching a state of belief . . . , we may suppose, [was] because he expected an "age of imagination" to cope with a disorderly "repertory of facts" (*DJ* XIV.xiii), and because he saw no escape from "the inadequacy of [our] state to [our] conceptions." According to Blake, the desire of man being infinite, the possession is infinite. With his less categorical habits of mind, Byron could not have so serenely abolished the other possibility in logic, that his destitution might be so. This is not to suggest that Byron's position looks desperate or defeatist. He is kept from that in the first place by the very inconclusiveness of the analytical process, and even more important by his own unquenchable desire for the sort of dream ("To Edward Noel Long, Esq.") or truth (*Childe Harold*) which is self-sufficient, stable, beautiful, and withal potent against the confusions of the empirical order. Surely an almost puritanical desire plays a large part in his refusal of seductive substitutes for truth.

His concern for facts nevertheless engenders a problem of evaluation. Keats cried Byron down for representing what he had seen, rather than what he imagined (he himself found the matter of imagination to be like Adam's dream, not like the Redcrosse Knight's); but Ruskin praised Byron on those very grounds, saying that he "spoke only of what he had seen, and known; and spoke without exaggeration, without mystery, without enmity, and without mercy" (*Works*, XXXV, 149). The issue between Keats and Ruskin, it will be found, is essentially superficial; the expression of praise or blame tends to obscure the way both writers conceive of Byron's work as strong in receptivity, not in creativity, as attaining to reproductive credibility but wanting in imaginative or conceptual authority. Indeed Byron vaunted himself on his fidelity to fact. Though we need not be credulous of his claims—*Sardanapalus* has only the most exiguous foundation in history, and the liberties Byron takes with his source material for *Marino Faliero* indicate a very elastic obedience to facts—the proposition that he is a poet of the seen gets undeniable support from the want of an imposing, or imposed philosophical unity in his work, and even more from the material use of himself as a subject. Yet there is a compatibility, even a sort of continuity among the elements, insofar as they make up a spectrum of obligatory responses to an experimental, or at best obscurely regulated, order. The apparent self-display of Byron's work may have the stamp and the value of a positively human independence-cum-humility: he deals with himself, like Thoreau perhaps, as the subject on which he is best qualified to speak, making himself a legitimate point of departure for more inclusive discussion. It is important to note, moreover, that he deals with himself, and with his "facts," in terms having the insistence of experience or evidence, rather than of dogma. The fluid character of his work may likewise convey not a wanton stirring up but a precise vision of the encountered world.

Byron's lifelong habit of making self-conscious—if not self-explanatory—references to his style gives prima facie support to the contention that his most "licentious" work has not a random form, but an unconventional, rationally chosen form, and would also tend to reveal the mere proposition that he sees, his "repertory of facts," as no more than a prelude to recognition of the way he sees, of the conceptual implications of subject matter and form. One is wary of dictating a convenient pattern into the copiousness and variety of, say, *Don Juan;* but it is to be remembered that Byron's handling of his material, though often emotionally descriptive or dramatic in immediacy and involvement, as a rule takes direction from a reflective, even abstractive frame of mind.

On the strength of the remarks Byron made in situations free from polemics, it is easy to conclude that the "cosmos" of his poetry is *"feeling* not intellect" (Clement Tyson Goode, *Byron as Critic,* Weimar, 1923, p. 86). Byron associates poetry with compelling, unWordsworthian emotion and inarticulate, obscure visions of "new" man.

> What is Poesy but to create
> From overfeeling Good and Ill; and aim
> At an external life beyond our fate,
> And be the new Prometheus of new men . . . ?
> ("The Prophecy of Dante," IV, 11–14)

"What is Poetry?—the feeling of a Former world and a Future" (*LJ,* V, 189); "Are not the *passions* the food and fuel of poesy?" (*LJ* V, 55); "Poetry is the expression of an *excited passion*" (*LJ,* V, 318). And the emotion identified with poetry has about it something pathological: the impulse to poetry reveals, the production of poetry relieves a virulence in the creator. "Poetry is the lava of the imagination whose eruption prevents an earthquake" (*LJ,* III, 405; see also *Childe Harold* III.iv).

> And the unquiet feelings which first woke
> Song in the world, will seek what then they sought;
> As on the beach the waves at last are broke,
> Thus to the extreme verge the passions brought
> Dash into poetry, which is but passion. . . . (*Don Juan* IV.cvi)

As poetry for Byron precludes self-possession, it readily turns into a sort of possession: "As for poesy, mine is the *dream* of my sleeping Passions; when they are awake, I cannot speak their language, only in their Somnambulism" (*LJ,* IV, 43). The emphasis on incontinent passion in all the foregoing statements culminates in a dictum which could as well be an indictment of much of Augustan poetry, and in particular of the *Essay on Man:* "Poetry is in itself passion, and does not systematize. It assails, but does not argue; it may be wrong, but it does not assume pretensions to Optimism" (*LJ,* V, 582). Still the passion Byron claims for poetry is not uncensored, not unalloyed by measures of knowledge and logic. Perhaps it would be most accurate to say that passion, in Byron's case, governs the inception of poetry more com-pletely than its process or content. He shows reflection and passion com-bined, though not reconciled.

We might note that despite the common assumption that Byron is characteristically given to "admiration of heroic activity,"[4] remarkably few of his heroes rank among men of prowess. They are heroes who bear the primary stamp of consciousness—of elected indomitability, of careful aloofness and gloom, of contemptuous intelligence and passion. They are little given to action; at one extreme they even, like Don Juan, largely give up practical choice. But they all either exercise the "right of thought" to a critical degree (e.g., Sardanapalus or Mazeppa), or they are met in a context critically colored by its exercise (e.g., Don Juan or Napoleon).

It will hardly seem surprising then that the question of knowledge should occupy a central position in Byron's work. The protean elusiveness of certitude—facts being relentless but not necessarily clear—furnishes a high-light for his adopted ottava rima stanza equally with his most sustained philosophical disquisition. He may set himself up as the celebrant of the world of fact, but he is also partly its victim, one who comes into it with an initial bias toward hope and love, and as a seeker after truth. It is as such that he develops the negative reflex of characterizing it as a wilderness of fact, and more aggressively, of maintaining with volleys of logic and laughter the unbalancing relation of seeker and universe. To study the apparent confusions of imagery and structure in his work, and the apparent rootlessness of his attitudes toward characters, actions, and ideas is to see them as strategies, as means to a comprehensive end which, paradoxically perhaps, exchanges the hieratic finality of "I affirm" for the profane unpredictability of "I would affirm." Hence what one may call the imagery of contradiction in *Don Juan,* "Mazeppa," and *Childe Harold* III–IV.[5]

With the ambivalent proposal, already seen, that Napoleon's page in French history is the "brightest or blackest," Byron graphically indicates how the tortuous ways of experience baffle and betray the aim of judgment. Of course, each of the alternatives may be preferred to the other, but neither can be denied; each conclusion is valid without invalidating its antithesis. This kind of rhetorical impasse occurs often enough to be of moment in Byron's work, and is unusual enough to warrant special attention. Byron clearly poses a problem different from what we meet in the *Epistle to Dr. Arbuthnot* where Pope writes: "All Bedlam or Parnassus is let out." No real choice is invited, or possible, between Bedlam and Parnassus. The "Bedlamites" have ludi-crously usurped the name of Parnassus, but since they must remain what they are, their "Parnassus" equals Bedlam—the two terms become convertible, one: as Boileau would have it: "C'est en vain qu'au Parnasse le téméraire auteur / Pense de l'art des vers atteindre la hauteur." Far from thus signaliz-ing sameness by the appearance of opposition, Byron offers a real but indis-soluble opposition, where no one seems to know more or better than his adversary, where not just a particular standard of judgment, but the very operation of judgment is called into question. . . .

Pope's approach, holding up in principle at least a general standard of judgment, prevails in poetry right through the romantic period.[6] It is almost to be expected, then, that the new tack Byron takes maintains itself on more than an ambivalent particle.[7] Ambivalence, or readiness to face up to duality—Byron might call it reality—occurs in a variety of forms in his work, and perhaps nowhere more notably than in his use of imagery and allusion. One finds images that are applied to a single person or situation seemingly at odds with one another; the same image applied to dissimilar persons or situations; and allusions to a single source so manipulated as to throw credit and blame on one character or situation, or else either credit or blame on antagonistic characters or situations.[8] The effect is the gradual establishment of an almost schematic displacement that can offer an unusual, if not a comfortable perspective on the familiar world.

A combination of images occurring in two separate stanzas of *Childe Harold* illustrates the indifference Byron may be said to show to our habitual experience and expectation. The first stanza, from Canto III, deprecates man's aspirations by means of the images of mountain-top and tempest.

> He who ascends to mountain-tops, shall find
> The loftiest peaks most wrapt in clouds and snow;
> He who surpasses or subdues mankind,
> Must look down on the hate of those below.
> Though high *above* the sun of glory glow,
> And far *beneath* the earth and ocean spread,
> *Round* him are icy rocks, and loudly blow
> Contending tempests on his naked head,
> And thus reward the toils which to
>   those summits led. (xlv)

The second stanza, from Canto IV, celebrates man's triumph over adversity in terms of the same images:

> But from their nature will the tannen grow
> Loftiest on loftiest and least sheltered rocks,
> Rooted in barrenness, where nought below
> Of soil supports them 'gainst the Alpine shocks
> Of eddying storms; yet springs the trunk, and mocks
> The howling tempest, till its height and frame
> Are worthy of the mountains from whose blocks
> Of bleak, gray granite into life it came,
> And grew a giant tree;—the mind may grow the same. (xx)

This self-contrasted imagery met within one poem and one year is articulated with key parallels that rule out the possibility of haphazard composition; both passages weight the meaning of mountain and tempest by bringing in a variable relation of what is above to what is below, and by rating man according to the security of his purchase in his environment. The absence of actual effort to go higher, and indeed the absence of a higher point to go toward in the second excerpt can be acknowledged as material without qualification of the basic point that Byron has skillfully reused and reformed a single complex of terms. The reformation is easy enough to analyze, if not to assimilate. In III.xlv Byron summarizes the state of things as done and known (shall, must); in IV.xx he enunciates a possibility, an appealing prospect (may). How, though, are the two related? How, and where, will the world of fact and the world of promise meet? The uncanny repetition of the images of one world in the other poses a problem virtually epistemological, and that problem cannot well be attempted until we see how Byron exploits the protean versatility of his images not simply at the point of presentation but also in reminiscent or associated passages.

The two passages in question prima facie bespeak man's vain ambition, and contrariwise his inborn power; but associated stanzas in both cantos quietly upset such impressions and further complicate the process of definition. The man who appears in a dramatic moment of failure in III.xlv is not ultimately derided; something like a compassionate regard for him supervenes by virtue of the forty-seventh stanza, where the man who aspires survives, indeed withstands the failure of his aspiration:

> And there they [castles] stand, as stands a lofty mind,
> Worn, but unstooping to the baser crowd,
> All tenantless, save to the crannying wind,
> Or holding dark communion with the cloud.

For in these lines "unstooping to the baser crowd" and "holding dark communion with the cloud" make positive, in terms of spiritual character and quality, two adverse outward circumstances of the earlier stanza: peaks capped with clouds and the hate of the earthbound. We have in effect gone past accidents and variables which exalt or degrade a man (xlv) and come to a bare but far from inconsiderable minimum (xlvii).

A comparable revision is in evidence between IV.xx and IV.xxi. The active, irresistible self-achievement of the mind shifts toward a passive state of elementary stoicism, in which one does not wonderfully "spring" and "grow" but "bear."

> Existence may be borne, and the deep root
> Of life and sufferance make its firm abode
> In bare and desolated bosoms: mute
> The camel labours with the heaviest load,
> And the wolf dies in silence,—not bestow'd

> In vain should such example be; if they,
> Things of ignoble or of savage mood,
> Endure and shrink not, we of nobler clay
> May temper it to bear,—it is but for a day.

This compounded qualification of point of view, with images revising themselves and continually undergoing further adjustment in context, is a legitimate procedure for any writer and, for Byron, works basically as a refinement of a total picture, or perhaps rather an adventure in inclusiveness. The first two cantos reveal Byron explicitly concerned with the confusions of experience—the words "mingle," "mix," and "blend," as often as not appear without overtones of harmony, solution, or integration. Again and again they show indiscriminacy, and shattering identities (see, for example, I.xxix, xxxiv, xli, lxxi; II.xxiii, xliv, lvii–lix). It may be plausible, then, especially in view of the purposely reflective temper of the final two cantos, to see the imagery of contradiction therein as part of the subsequent process of reassessment and recognition. It challenges our confidence in our reactions, laying bare the simplifications and prematurities which make experience regular at the expense of ignoring an ever-present fluidity or ambivalence. Byron accuses us, and Keats would have borne him a clear second, of binding ourselves and calling "some mode the best one" (*DJ* XIV.ii), even when "System" boils down to a perversion of the unnatural: it "doth reverse the Titan's breakfast" (*ibid*). In this light it would be appropriate to turn to the poem not for the massive stability that absorbs the bombardment of details, but the undazzled and unwearied reorientation that takes them as they come.

Mazeppa is as much given to action as Childe Harold to rumination; his aphorism (1. 524) and his philosophizing (ll. 718ff.) are barely removed from practical experience of what suffering does to the "bold" or of how the prospect of death affects various classes of men, and so belong to a different order from Childe Harold's considerations of time, knowledge, heroism, nature, etc. Where the peculiarities of imagery in *Childe Harold* might conceivably be suspected of artificiality, those same peculiarities in "Mazeppa" can only come of naturalism, expressing a personal impulse to describe and relate, with relatively little of the abstract purpose to analyze and define. The forms of experience in "Mazeppa" justify the formulations of the intellect in *Childe Harold*.

A pattern of unpredictability, summarized in the question "What mortal his own doom may guess?," is prominent in "Mazeppa," notwithstanding its quasi-allegorical use of space. "Will" and "guide"—internal and external promoters of our purposes—work incongruously, if they work. Between Charles and Casimir, contrasting kings, neither fortune nor reason seems to secure a choice, so that the fate of kingdoms as well as of persons appears somehow impenetrable. Mazeppa's experience proves wholly congruous with such a framework. The concealed social anomaly of the love between page and countess[9] foreshadows—I do not think it precipitates—a world in which even perception has no guarantee. From the moment the cuckolded Count calls for "the horse" as if it were a fixed instrument of torture like the rack, the canons of expectation prove idle, and there is an increasing resort to imagery to handle the demands of actuality. The animal is likened to a torrent (l. 374), and to a meteor (l. 426), to a mountain-roe (l. 511),[10] to snow (l. 512), to a frustrated child (ll. 518–519), and to a wilful woman (ll. 519–520). All these images clearly share a common object of conveying driving energy and motion, though the last two seem concerned more with its emotional source than with its physical form; it is equally clear that no two chime together perfectly even in terms of energy and motion, so that we seem to witness the conflict of collaborating objects. Oppositions among the first four images are perhaps most numerous, but their ultimate value seems to depend on the child-woman images, which with their almost mathematical arrangement have been set up for special consideration: "Untired, untamed, and worse than wild— / All furious as a favoured child / Balked of its wish; or—fiercer still— / A woman piqued—who has her will!" Not only do these lines come at the end of a section, but they serve at once to re-open and to culminate the aforementioned series of images. More important yet, they show Byron purposefully revising his metaphor ("or fiercer still") without eliminating an antithesis, and offering something beyond, and not instead of, what has been given before. The affluence of images presents a series of perspectives as a sort of cubist unity to the eye, but for the mind. The limitations of the eye, in fact, lead to a strange effect, as the final images tend to make the response to the horse human as well as logical. The child in a tantrum and the woman with the upper hand all but defy visualization in terms of the horse; the reader is tempted to think he is learning what certain people as well as a certain horse may be like. But this counts less than the penetration into Mazeppa's mind through witnessing his continual effort to portray his horse and his ride. It is a mind grappling with the actuality of the senses with a competence hardly superior to that of the fastened body: Mazeppa in the one experience finds the inorganic, the organic, and the human, summer and winter, fire and water, the earthly and the celestial, the horizontal and the vertical, flowing and piling. Implicitly he has found a paradoxical definition of the possibilities of experience, in what could stand as the Byronic version of Wordsworth's mysteries of the known.

In the end Mazeppa's images for the borderland between self-possession and exhausted insensibility, having the same mixed character as those for his ride (ll. 544–560), may seem to intimate that he has been deranged all along. But any such impression is dispelled with the observation that he fetches the analogy for delirium from plain everyday experience of waves which "at the same time upheave and whelm." He even takes it for granted that the reader ("thee") is acquainted with the phenomenon, and can thereby gain access to the extraordinary world.[11] The vocabulary of the tale, moreover, bears pervasive witness to the difficult points of identity between distinct beings and states. A herd of horses in the forest is called a "troop" and a "squadron," with surprising associations with military regimentation, and then startlingly termed "the wild" and the "free." The word "wild" is used differently here than in numerous instances concerning the original horse of vengeance, and we further find both words, "wild" and "free," used of the eyes of the Cossack maid whom Mazeppa first sees upon his recovery of consciousness in human habitation and care. Other information is forthcoming, for example, about the maiden's eyes, but that too can cause a start—the wild and free eyes look "bright" and "gentle"! In short, not only is "wild" in itself a complex term, but it is used of complex subjects. The horses band together in an orderly way, even having "a patriarch of their breed," though they are not subject to any rational discipline; the girl is compassionate and generous, though not motivated by custom or prescription; the burdened horse heeds nothing but its own desires and impulses, which have been exacerbated with fury and fright into the further wildness that makes a "faint and low" voice "a sudden trumpet's clang" (ll. 456–459).

Mazeppa obviously feels a certain respect or affection for each of these "wild" things, but his very use of the word tends to stamp him as an observer of the forms—he is certainly punctilious as an old warrior in the care of his horse, and he seems to have been amazed, in the midst of his youthful ordeal, at the natural sight of "a thousand horse—and none to ride!" The unconventional peculiarities of his imagery thus seem not just impressive, but ineluctable. And if we consider the implications of his struggle with imagery as well as the obvious facts that he is reliving, and not just relating the events of his past, we may infer a psychological pressure, a sort of narrative compulsion as a major feature of his performance. The tale will be told, once begun; and if there is humor in its being told in part to a sleeping audience, this humor is not without a strong tinge of poignancy. The episode of his ride becomes in a way analogous to the voyage of the Ancient Mariner, though Mazeppa's story is triggered from without, not from within, as only befits one who has turned into a grizzled soldier instead of a weird prophetic figure.

The narrator of *Don Juan* is too self-conscious and analytical for naturalism, and too much of an empiricist for orthodoxy, but finds use for the same sort of polyform imagery as Mazeppa. This has the initial advantage of seeming most apt to his easy-going, onward, excursive manner of speech. It goes deeper, and means more than that. No easy consistency, no protected schematization of imagery or otherwise goes by him unscanned or unscathed; his garrulity and levity, insistent enough in themselves, are mounted with barbs of agnostic opinion occasionally honed into aphorism. He is never dogmatic, but he is somehow portentous. His agnosticism ("such things are, which I can not explain," III.xlvii) has deep roots in his character and every encouragement not only from everyday events: "the Fates / Change horses [with the moon], / Leaving at last not much besides chronology" (XIV.ciii), but also from the experimental world of science: "What opposite discoveries we have seen" (I.cxxix). It is hardly fortuitous that changes and oppositions in imagery fairly abound in the expanse of *Don Juan*. If they do not dominate the poem's fabric, they are stitched into it with remarkable deftness, overlapping with each other and even picking up threads of allusion for special effects.

We find Juan and Haidee both likened to birds (II.clxviii and cxc), but for quite distinct and even conflicting relations of protector to pet and mate to mate. And such rapid adaptation of the guise under which a particular image operates confronts the reader often enough to suggest that generalizations concerning a given image or category of imagery must yield place to continual discriminations within categories as a critical response to Byron's method and design. The bird imagery of the Haidee episode, in fact, is less striking in its frequency than in the variety of its uses. In IV.xiv, though the idea of mates does occur, Byron presents the bird to embody not a kind of practical domestic relationship between two people, but a mystical oneness based on intuition, and foregoing it would seem both language and sense experience. Shortly again, in IV.xix, an analogy with the loves of nightingales and doves suggests naturalistic spontaneity and simplicity. If, however, these can all be seen as favorable, appealing uses of the "bird imagery," giving Juan and Haidee a positive stature and luster, they do not long go unqualified. In the end Byron virtually recants, with a twist of the bird imagery, what that imagery has seemed to say. Falling into a subjunctive mood, he makes use of the conception of a bird to tell us what Juan and Haidee are not, and so cannot do: "They should have lived together deep in woods, / Unseen as sings the nightingale . . ."(IV.xxviii).

The image of the lily, also used of both Juan and Haidee, appears less troublesome, since the two of them come before us in similar extremities (II.cx and IV.lix), and since the image varies in accordance with who is looking (II.xc and clxxvi) or what is being looked at (III.lxxvi and IV.lxx). But a series of Biblical allusions enters and perplexes the case of the lily and the bird alike. The "lily" Juan has been "providentially" washed up on the island shore (II.cvii) and Haidee has "cheered him both / With food and raiment" (cxxiii), deeming herself bound " 'to take him in, / A stranger' " (cxxix). We are made mindful of a benevolent order of nature, and within that of a specifically Christian charity.

And he said unto his disciples, Therefore I say unto you, Be not anxious for *your* life, what ye shall eat; nor yet for your body, what ye shall put on. For the life is more than the food, and the body than the raiment. Consider the ravens, that they sow not, neither reap; which have no store-chambers nor barn; and God feedeth them: of how much more value are ye than the birds! . . . Consider the lilies, how they grow: they toil not, neither do they spin; yet I say unto you, Even Solomon in all his glory was not arrayed like one of these.

(Luke 12. 22–27; American Standard Version)[12]

But this order proves at best idle when Haidee is the "lily." Unlike the barely breathing Juan, with his largely bodily needs, she is in a situation transcending questions of material self-preservation: "Food she refused, and raiment" (IV.lxviii). And Byron, pointedly telling us she "wither'd" (lxix, lxx) forces us to behold the violation of the order of happiness: "In vain the dews of Heaven descend above / The bleeding flower and blasted fruit of love" (lxx).

It seems unlikely that Byron is impugning the Christian scheme here; Haidee incarnates it even though her total experience does not fall neatly in its scope. The Christian scheme is portrayed as best, but not commonest. [13] His concern with the empirical order of circumstance, "that unspiritual god / And miscreator" (*CH* IV.cxxv) requires Byron to include what is inimical to the order of perfection, and also to admit its presence within that very order. Thus Haidee, if she is "lily" and "bird," is also something antipathetic to them, "snake," in the special way of one "who pours his length, / And hurls at once his venom and his strength" (II.cxvii)—within perfection resides the quality of self-destruction, or as Blackstone cryptically puts it, "innocence is its own deepest guilt." [14] In addition there are those who on whatever grounds oppose perfection, such as Lambro, the "snake" that destroys not itself but others (III.xlviii, IV.xlviii). Here again, however, the clear distinction in imagery is overlaid and largely overborne by the implied fact that Haidee defends Juan in part as a mother (II.cliii, clviii), while Lambro attacks him (and to that extent Haidee herself!) with the parental instincts of the "cubless tigress" (II.lviii). [15] And finally the text hums with the continual reminder that time opposes perfection; it is riddled with forebodings (e.g. II.clxii, clxxiii, clxxxviii, cxcii; III.l, lxv; IV.viii–ix, xv, xxii–xxiv, xxx–xxxv). No wonder that the narrator calls himself Cassandra (IV.lii).

Ultimately time and circumstances seem more to blame than Lambro, for whom Byron evidently has ambivalent feelings. Allusions to *The Odyssey* make this quite plain. We could think Juan is like Odysseus when he is washed ashore, but it would have to be conceded that Byron hardly highlights this possibility (II.cvii–cx). [16] It is certain, however, that he is thinking of Odysseus when Lambro makes his appearance (III.xxii–xxiii, li, lii); we are obliged to think of Lambro as a man and paterfamilias flagrantly wronged. "The notable lack of hostility toward Lambro" is ultimately explained by an ineradicable sense of this experience of wrong, and not just "by the fact that Byron is simply assuming that of course he *would* act as he does" (Ridenour, p. 83). Byron accounts clearly for any such assumption by the powerful allusion to Odysseus. That this comparison in the final analysis fails wholly to vindicate his conduct and damns Haidee's as little as it does depends on the way Byron shifts the focus in mid-allusion, making Lambro "the Cyclops" (lvii), and making Haidee, in the midst of impious artificiality and luxury, as "pure as Psyche ere she grew a wife" (lxxiv). It would be hard to show everyone in the right, or in the wrong, on the strength of Byron's kaleidoscope of images and allusions. Indeed, Haidee seems as unimaginable without Lambro as he is inhuman without her. What the images and allusions imply is an oddly prolific world engendering more than it can reconcile or maintain. Its undeniable moments of splendor—Juan in shipwreck, Haidee in love, and later, the Tartar Khan in battle—have no patent, but it is well to remember that we see them intimately before the telescope wheels us to the more inclusive view, and that the turns of the rhetoric are at once the narrator's practice and his obligation. He knows he is going to surprise, knows he is going to laugh before we do, but he too knows the poignancy of the mutable: "And if I laugh at any mortal thing, / 'T is that I may not weep . . ." (IV.iv).

As of the writing of *Childe Harold* IV (1817–18) it is possible to recognize as a hallmark of Byron's poetry a certain "meditative" or "contemplative" response to the content of experience and to the weight of mutability and mortality therein (cf. IV.xix, xxv, lxxvi, cxxviii, clvii–viii). The way he presents dreams of destruction furnishes a fair idea of the change. An obsessive nightmare of all-annihilating death batters into the reader's consciousness in "Darkness" (1816), but the poem suffers from the great disability of a nightmare, that it is a dissociated phenomenon which, if momentarily compelling, will soon be found wanting in substance. Certainly the "Darkness" that is "the Universe" in Byron's piece bears no comparison with Pope's "Universal Darkness," and largely because it has something merely arbitrary and external about it as corresponding to one man's isolated depression and not to an artistically, philosophically established state of things. [17] Two later nightmares of time show a clear gain in comprehensiveness, and in real power. Haidee's nightmare of the future in *Don Juan* IV.xcix (1819) and the hero's nightmare of the past in *Sardanapalus* IV.i (1821) have all the immediacy with none of the insularity of "Darkness," being designed as salient foci in a conceptual, and dramatic, and psychological frame of obvious complexity.

Both these nightmares strengthen characterization and thematic aims in the respective works. We know Haidee's nature, in the peculiar terms of the poem, much better than we know her thoughts. But her strongest assertion of her nature, that defiant challenge levelled at Lambro: "I knew / Your nature's firmness—know your daughter's too," emphatically reminds us that her parsimony with words coexists with a full apprehension of what she is and in what circumstances. Her life of bright harmonious instinct rests on clear deliberate principle—she *knew*. And her nightmarish sleep tells us more completely than anything else the gist of what she knew, namely, how harsh and hurtful a version of the Juan episode resided in the normal play of the conditions of her life. There is more wistful hope than conviction in her claim that Lambro "will forgive" her and Juan (IV.xxxviii). What at last can she mean in stating that she knew her father's nature? Is it inquisiturient to wonder whether Lambro has *always* held her in the shelter, in the chains of a paternal puritanism? Has Haidee as well as Juan stumbled into an interlude of love and grace? Certainly there may be doubt whether Lambro has, or could have left "the violence of his nature and his life" whenever his foot touched shore, whether "a kind of ideal life" has ever been "made possible by this violence" (Ridenour, p. 45). Her nightmare, revealing enough in itself, reacts intriguingly with other facets of the text.

The nightmare of Sardanapalus does not, like Haidee's, break through a cover of silence, but a cover of speech. Easy and articulate, Sardanapalus succeeds in keeping from himself no less than from us an inner sense of discomfort and danger under the downward burden of time, until its grotesque manifestation in his dream. The dynamism of the dream, significantly, carries the king, who will in reality compromise with his pacifist and hedonistic views, within range of reconciliation with his ancestors. The reconciliation fails, but the manner of failure still leaves Sardanapalus more closely bound to his past than before: he wishes in vain to maintain contact with the "hero" Nimrod, and wishes, again in vain, to break contact with the "crone" Semiramis. The nightmare, then, lays bare not just the unsuspected dimension, inside Sardanapalus, of his struggle against the set rhythms of society and history, but also an unsuspected ambivalence in that struggle. The implied failure of all the available options, to continue in his adopted course, to adhere to Nimrod, and to repudiate Semiramis may further remind us that Byron usually appears more pessimistic about the individual in history than about institutions. In *Sardanapalus* Byron most graphically shows his sense of "that dark compulsion that binds the race to its habitual conflicts."[18]

The enriched reverberations of the later nightmares in *Don Juan* and *Sardanapalus* as against that of "Darkness" fairly reflect an overall gain in power for Byron, and in particular show a capacity for condensed psychological dramatization that handsomely balances his more discursive vein. Yet it is not unlikely that the discursive vein provided the life-blood of such dramatic moments; the dramas are weakest not in conflict or dialogue, but in thematic comprehension and exactness. Great emphasis must be laid on the fact that apparent confusion in his work results from an extraordinary accuracy in rendering the simultaneity of plural states. Critics have seen this more readily in local passages than in Byron's writing at large, and have taken it as a random occurrence when it is a keynote of Byron's style. With the reservation that the stanza is typical, not "curious," I would like to quote Ridenour's impeccable analysis of this technique in *Don Juan* VII.xliii, for convenience first giving the lines:

> They fell as thick as harvests beneath hail,
> Grass before scythes, or corn below the sickle,
> Proving that trite old truth, that life's as frail
> As any other boon for which men stickle.
> The Turkish batteries thrash'd them like a flail,
> Or a good boxer, into a sad pickle
> Putting the very bravest, who were knock'd
> Upon the head, before their guns were cock'd.

Now Ridenour:

> The first line by itself could easily be taken "straight." There is nothing overtly humorous about it. But the two variants in the introductory simile provided by the second line make us feel less secure. There is suddenly something unnerving about this cold-blooded toying with images of violent death. We cannot react as we would, say, to a developed Homeric simile using the same tenor and vehicle. This feeling is only increased by the offhand cynicism of lines 3–4 and the flippant versions of the simile in 5–6. . . . But at the same time we are aware of something else, of pity for them simply as men taking a beating, a pity controlled but not negated by the passages of superficial cynicism. (*Style,* pp. 72–73)

It is in the light of Byron's ever more frequent production of such chords of effortlessly controlled atonality that it becomes fitting to dwell on the analytical strength and range of *Childe Harold* IV. In place of the feverish and futile race for "transcendence rather than . . . analysis of the Self" which Marshall sees in *Childe Harold* III,[19] Byron in the concluding canto is by and large reconciled to his own person (that would make an important, if inconspicuous reason for his abandoning the tortuous, faint line between Harold and himself)—and hence *less insistent on it.* He speaks in his own person, but he speaks less self-consciously and more humanely. Not that self-centered remarks altogether disappear. One of Byron's most strident vauntings occupies a place in this canto (cxxxi ff.). But there is a curious duality in his outburst, which is in part meant for a profession of forgiveness and love, of full human harmony in the self; and besides, the stanzas on the singular speaker are clearly shown as eccentric (xxv, cxxxiv). One senses here a desperate reactive rush to fill the vacuum created by the removal of hostility. But the act of compensation entails its own turbulence, and as Marshall astutely indicates in the case of "The Prophecy of Dante," does not lend itself to the simplicity of a sudden affirmation: "The recognition of his vindictiveness is for the speaker the real beginning of his purge of . . . hatred and of his *ascent toward* positive affirmation. Psychologically, however, the loss of such an emotional force as the hatred itself, albeit negative, leaves him for the moment extremely close to despair" (*The Structure,* p. 129; italics added). Perhaps, though, "despair" does not quite fit the case. Like Byron in *Childe Harold* IV, Dante goes on to express an overweening expectation of his status before posterity, betraying withal some residue of antagonism in forecasting God's corrective rod on those who have trespassed against him. In like manner, in the "curse" of forgiveness, as Rutherford penetratingly says, we perceive not "genuine emotional or spiritual change, but rather . . . continued self-approval" (*Byron: A Critical Study,* Edinburgh, 1961, pp. 94–95). The only likely extenuation is offered by G. Wilson Knight, to wit, that Byron "is cursing, as it were, through tears" (*Byron and Shakespeare,* London and New York, 1966, p. 202).

The "meditative" method of *Childe Harold* IV, locally spotlighted in the key recognition of the "developing" nature of things (xxxiii, cxliii, clxi), and of the corresponding fact that "Our outward sense is but of gradual grasp" (see sts. clvii–clviii), projects itself at once in the arrangement of the opening stanzas. The dramatic first lines focus on the narrator less for himself than for his presence at a geographical and temporal vantage point from which to come to terms with the complex length of human history, whether cultural, political, or biographical; the latter category of course includes his own life. Significantly he begins by proposing to himself certain basic structural norms, in a sequence which could be supposed to follow a typical life-pattern. The first is imagination, or "beings of the mind" (v). The second, "strong reality" (vi), is virtually the converse of the first, and is made up of the special class of things which penetrate the mind from without, filling it with *their* existence instead of its own notions. Neither of these appealing possibilities wins final approval, though Byron brings them back for elaboration in terms of Art, and of Empire and Nature respectively, thus incidentally making Art and Nature important foci but not, as sometimes claimed, the final concerns of the canto. What he puts before both arbitrary predominance of the mind and its waxen docility is a new life designated as "waking Reason" (vii). This is unrelated to classical Reason, with its assumption and promotion of a strict universe of clear rule, order, and harmony; like the Wordsworthian Imagination, it is progressively cognitive and conceptual, but it precludes the *teleology* of Wordsworth's gift, relying on that discriminating totality of awareness which exacts poise rather than producing ecstasy in the possessor.

The mood associated with "waking Reason" is one of nearly stoical resignation (x, xxi), a spiritual condition which requires positive achievement and thus must be distinguished from earlier Childe-ish jadedness or apathy. The poem confronts the radical problem of reconciling the ubiquitous evidence of degeneration and death with the periodic manifestations of things whose perpetuation we would desire. In its first major phase, up to the middle of stanza lxi, Byron considers Empire and Art, and sees, in spite of the obvious losses to time, outstanding possibilities of survival—here "dust . . . is / Even itself an immortality" (liv). The section on Nature which follows (lxi.5–lxxvii) cites certain consolations, such as the fact that nature yields a "suspension of disgust" (lxviii), but it stresses human ineffectualness, the sure death of "fragile . . . clay."

There is a chiasmic reversal of these attitudes in the succeeding stanzas (lxix–cxxx), which deal with Empire, Art and Nature all together, as elements of a more basic consideration of the possibilities of knowledge. Thus at first general fragility and incertitude are projected, most graphically perhaps in the passage on Metella: "Thus much alone we know—Metella died, / The wealthiest Roman's wife. Behold his love or pride!" Pessimism is made explicit in the poem's initial summary of the meaning of history:

> There is the moral of all human tales:
> 'T is but the same rehearsal of the past
> First Freedom and then Glory—when that fails,
> Wealth, vice, corruption,—barbarism at last.
> And History, with all her volumes vast,
> Hath but *one* page. . . . (cviii)

Such pessimism reaches its intensest force in the concluding stanza of the section, "Our life is a false nature . . ." (cxxvi). This is the nadir, the exaggeration of despair which "waking Reason" will not countenance, though it cannot utterly controvert it. The next brief phase (cxxvii–cxxx) qualifies despair by suggesting the possibility of a resolution, the possiblility of light, making uncanny use of the Coliseum as a fused emblem of art, empire, and nature in deathless realization, and offering a more balanced conception of Time as "beautifier," "corrector," and "avenger." But of course it must be noted that the Coliseum passage redeems despair by qualification, instead of true affirmation. However ruefully, Byron is prepared to own that "the colossal fabric's form . . . will not bear the brightness of the day" (cxliii). It turns out, too, that some of his claims in the propitious moonlight really reflect the logic of his expectations ("for divine / Should be the light which streams here"), and tend to disregard what may be more important, his abiding conviction and his experience; and the way he frames the strange and moving scene where daughter nourishes father, with examples of impiety (Cain) and impropriety (Hadrian's "Mole"), sets off the excellence of her action at the cost of proposing a negative value for the generality of things that are given birth.

The chiasmic structure of the canto to this point[20] contains and stabilizes the very variation of mood which tends to produce weltering in *Childe Harold* III. This equilibrium, alike the product and the vindication of waking Reason, is more than formal of course. It reflects the narrator's accommodation with human experience, historically taken, just as the accommodation must underlie his proposal of reconciliation with living humankind (cxxxi–cxxxvii). The remainder of the canto apparently assumes that the new entente is unblemished and complete ("The seal is set.—Now welcome, thou dread power!", cxxxviii), but it repeats the difficulty Byron has with the immediate world, making his "curse" of "Forgiveness" seem a coercive conversion of terms.[21] Unlike that of the dying Gladiator or of Laocoön, his own suffering ultimately lacks the benefit of the critical perspective supplied by time or art. The mind that comes to terms with the fates of, say, Dante and Petrarch is too involved in the fresh fate of Princess Charlotte to handle it serenely. The magnificent human confidence of its identification with St. Peter's collapses, with the disappointment of the messianic hope in the Princess' expected child, into a gloom closely akin to the earlier state of despair; the image of the ill-omened "meteor" firmly links the two (clxx, cxxiv).

The conception of the single life as a bubble floating on, or sinking into the ocean, in youth and at death respectively (clxxxiv, clxxix), may seem the final dispassionate statement of the casual, and insubstantial quality of life; it is a picture of nature thinly tolerating then annihilating man and whatever is generated by him. But Byron's "prying into the abyss" has yielded him an undeniable, if not an unqualified composition of spirit. To add the character of Time and destroyer is not to recant all faith in the beautifier, the corrector. . . . One might seem, through what he himself calls the "loops of time," to discern the means of escaping his indictment. The very griefs which mar his trembling resignation arise from no dishonorable weaknesses. He is capable, to the end, of at least a Lawrentian hope in nature (clxxvi–clxxvii), and also of recreating, as an inalienable intuition, that former contact with eternity when, with terrifyingly cautionless, charmed innocence, he rested his hand on the "mane" of the "dread, fathomless" ocean. And he is in posssession of that intelligence with respect to the past which can declare mankind rid of an immemorial onus: "And if it be Prometheus stole from Heaven / The fire which we endure, it was repaid. . . ." In the final analysis, perhaps, the achievement of waking Reason is a chiaroscuro one, tempering and yet heightening pain, leading to praise and pride and then again to belittlement and dismay, settling our account with an archaic mythology but coming up short of a new frame of reference: the old benefit of fire cannot be dispensed with, and now is something "we endure." If, as Byron asserts, "we can recall . . . visions" of "brightest," godly moments, we end up only with "things" that "look like gods below." No special emphasis need be put on "below" to bring out an undertone of compromise and making-do in this resemblance to the divine.

Still it is hard to resolve whether the degree of failure offsets or sets off the partial success. *Childe Harold* IV announces and embodies a major new attitude, not a manifesto. Its "meditative" orientation does not demand solutions, but holds it necessary, proper, and cardinal to "ponder boldly" (cxxvii), so that the recognition of true problems becomes a substantial value, as does the accurate gauging of how, and how far a comprehensive conceptual scheme can be defended. Even at this point it would seem necessary to challenge the rather compromising summary of Byron's work and mind offered by Carlyle upon receiving the news of the poet's death: "Poor Byron! And but a young man; still struggling amid the perplexities, and sorrows, and aberrations, of a mind not arrived at maturity or settled in its proper place in life." Aside from the reflection that one man's maturity is another man's arrogance, Byron conjures up an empirical definition of one's proper place as where it is possible, all things considered, to be. Strictly speaking he is *grappling* with perplexities, not in a situation to be settled by any arbitrary number of falls, but as a root condition of existence. And *Childe Harold* IV thus takes on pivotal significance with its unflinching presentation of a mind that sacrifices tidiness to inclusiveness, a mind whose virtue it is to work *ex necessitate rei,* rather than ex cathedra.[22]

For all its lack of resolution, that mind attains a viable state in being at once personal and analytical, idealistic and undemanding, humble and uncompromising. In *Don Juan,* its position is duly expanded into a philosophy, and complemented with a full-fledged personality.

Notes

[Ed. Note: The parenthetical abbreviations *DJ, LJ,* and *CH* used in this essay refer to, respectively, Byron's *Don Juan,* the E.H. Coleridge and Rowland Prothero edition of *The Works of Lord Byron* (London: John Murray, 1898–1904), six volumes of which contain Byron's *Letters and Journals (LJ),* and *Childe Harold's Pilgrimage (CH).*]

1. Ridenour reads the poem essentially as a "Popean" opposition of truth to romance (*The Style of "Don Juan,"* New Haven, 1960, pp. 92–93); this is somewhat oversimplified, and entails an unfortunate distortion of the temper of Byron's work.

2. Ruskin in *Praeterita* praises Byron for his "measured and living *truth*" (*Works,* ed. E.T. Cook and A. Wedderburn, London, 1908, xxxv, 148), but this can only be truth as a summary abstraction and distillation from the Byron corpus, the perception that made Ruskin call Byron "the truest . . . Seer of the Nineteenth Century" (XXXIV, 397). It is not any of the truths which attracted and exercised Byron.

3. "Childe Harold's Pilgrimage: Canto the Fourth," *Edinburgh Review,* xxx (1818), 96.

4. M.K. Joseph, *Byron the Poet,* London 1964, 126.

5. For other discussions of Byron's imagery, with different emphases from mine, see Ernest J. Lovell, Jr., "Irony and Image in *Don Juan,*" in *English Romantic Poets: Modern Essays in Criticism,* ed. M. H. Abrams, New York, 1960, pp. 228ff.; Joseph, *Byron the Poet,* pp. 212ff.; and John William Harrison, "The Imagery of Byron's Romantic Narratives and Dramas," Univ. of Colorado Ph.D., 1958, L.C. Card no. Mic 59-829.

6. The poet who most strikingly anticipates Byron, so far as I have found, is Andrew Marvell, in "The Character of Holland" and preeminently in "An Horatian Ode," with its pervasive and unfaltering dualism. In fact Byron's treatment of Cromwell (*CH* IV.lxxxv) has much in common with Marvell's . . .

7. Other examples may be given a quick survey. In Fez, "all is Eden, or a wilderness" (*DJ* IV.liv); hell-fire is said to be prepared for people who give "Pleasure or pain to one another" (*DJ* II.cxcii); Gulbeyaz has the beauty to make "A Kingdom or confusion anywhere" (*DJ* v.cxxix); Byron declares in *Childe Harold* that "Man with his God must strive: / Or, it may be, with demons" (IV.xxxiv), and again he interprets Napoleon's response to "the turning tide" as "wisdom, coldness, or deep pride" (III.xxxix). The stanzas following the description of the Fez and those leading up to the comment on Napoleon also abound in oscillations of viewpoint which, though not always dependent on the ambiguous "or," help to show how intimately it is bound up with Byron's way of seeing. One final example will all but explicitly sum up the operation of the particle: "Juan [was] flatter'd by her [Catherine's] love, or lust;— / I cannot stop to alter words once written, / And the two are so mix'd up with human dust, / That he who *names one,* both perchance may hit on" (*DJ* IX.lxxvii); and Byron repeats the indistinguishable alternative, "love or lust," in XII.iv.

8. The phenomenon described here may recall the romantic "contraries," which Blake and Coleridge and Wordsworth severally recognize and exploit. But Byron is not aiming at that dialectical synthesis or reconciliation of "opposite and discordant qualities" which was, according to Charles J. Smith, "almost a compulsion" for Wordsworth ("The Contrarieties:

Wordsworth's Dualistic Imagery," *PMLA*, LXIX [1954], 1193). This in part because he is more interested than Wordsworth in the distinctive logic of events, and in part because, if he "strains" after a "cosmic philosophy" and a "monistic faith" (G. Wilson Knight, *The Burning Oracle*, Oxford, 1939, p. 280), he does so by probing experience for unforeseen possibilities of analysis of its Gordian knot, not by striking it through.

9. Byron energetically attracts our attention to the anomaly with an oxymoron: "The happy *page*, who was the *lord* / Of one soft heart" (italics added).

10. There are some intriguing reminiscences between the present narrative time and the remembered vital time of the tale. This comparison of wild horse and roe has been anticipated in that of steed and fawn in ll. 76–77. Byron's control of context proves more than adroit enough to keep a basic distinction clear—the metaphor indicates docility in one case, and wild tirelessness in the other; the imagery of contradiction is compounded here.

11. If the shipwreck seems a somewhat infrequent and hence contrived occasion for the comparison, we may recall Byron's demonstration of the self-contradictions of anyone's experience, involving cases of simultaneous "scorching and drenching": "Did he never spill a dish of tea over himself . . . ? Did he never swim in the sea at Noonday with the sun in his eyes and on his head, which all the foam of Ocean could not cool? Did he never draw his foot out of a tub of too hot water . . . ? Was he ever [becoming rhetorical and mischievous] in a cauldron of boiling oil?" (*LJ*, IV, 341–342).

12. An extensive list of Biblical allusions in the Byron corpus is to be found in Arthur Pönitz, *Byron und die Bibel*, Leipzig, 1906. [See also the more recent and far more inclusive *Byron and the Bible: A Compendium of Biblical Usage* by Travis Looper, Metuchen, N.J. and London, 1978. Editor's note.]

13. Byron's dispraise of the distortions and petrifactions of Christian ideals and practice is eloquently treated by C. N. Stavrou in his article on "Religion in Byron's *Don Juan*" SEL, III (1963), 567–594.

14. Bernard Blackstone, *The Lost Travellers: A Romantic Theme with Variations*, London, 1962, 203.

15. Byron reaffirms the instinctive, incontrovertible force of mother love in the harem episode (V.cxxxii–cxxxiii); the strength of these statements puts the conduct of the calculating, formal mother, Donna Inez, in an even more unfavorable light.

16. Brian Wilkie, in his study of *Romantic Poets and Epic Tradition*, points out allusions to Homer's and to Dante's Ulysses at earlier stages of the shipwreck episode (Madison and Milwaukee, 1965, pp. 204–205); and Karl Kroeber and Bernard Blackstone, who both undiscriminatingly accept the Edenic overtones of Haidée's island life, observe that Byron compares Lambro to Ulysses on his return home (respectively, *Romantic Narrative Art*, Madison, Wisconsin, 1960, p. 157, and *The Lost Travellers*, p. 207). [For a more recent, penetrating study of Byron's use of *The Odyssey* see Hermione DeAlmeida, *Byron and Joyce Through Homer: "Don Juan" and "Ulysses,"* N.Y., 1981. Editor's note.]

17. A more favorable view of Byron's poem as a "visionary lyric" is presented by Karl Kroeber in his study of *Romantic Narrative Art*, and in more general terms of poetic power by Blackstone in *The Lost Travellers*.

18. G. Wilson Knight, *The Starlit Dome*, London, 1941, p. 91.

19. *The Structure of Byron's Major Poems*, Philadelphia, 1962, p. 74.

20. For a more detailed picture of the organization of *Childe Harold* IV according to the sequence of single topics and subjects, the reader should consult Joseph's *Byron the Poet*, pp. 83ff.

21. Gleckner calls the idea of forgiveness "new and somewhat startling," and aptly points out that "in the original skeletal manuscript . . . the curse remained but a curse" (*Byron and the Ruins of Paradise*, Baltimore, 1967, p. 290). Byron has not so much revised or repudiated the curse as reinforced it with singularity.

22. Rutherford suggestively argues that in *Childe Harold* IV Byron's style is being modulated toward harmony with the *Don Juan* style (*Byron: A Critical Study*, pp. 100–101).

Editor's Bibliographical Note

With this wide-ranging essay on Byron's "world of fact" should be compared the Gleckner and Reiman pieces in this collection as well as Jerome J. McGann's *Fiery Dust: Byron's Poetic Development* (Chicago and London: University of Chicago Press, 1968) and the slim but pertinent *Byron and the Mythology of Fact* by Anne Barton (Nottingham: University of Nottingham, 1968). For a quite different view of "fact" in Byron, approached via German idealism, see Mark Kipperman, *Beyond Enchantment: German Idealism and English Romantic Poetry* (Philadelphia: University of Pennsylvania Press, 1986). On Byron's alleged skepticism see the bibliographical note to Reiman's essay in this collection and Truman Guy Steffan's elaborate edition and discussion of *Lord Byron's "Cain": Twelve Essays and a Text with Variants and Annotations* (Austin: University of Texas Press, 1968). Although most of the book-length studies in the last 25 to 30 years that purport to comment on the entire Byron corpus have at least a word or two to say of "Mazeppa," it is still a relatively neglected poem. The most useful critical commentaries are in McGann's *Fiery Dust*, William H. Marshall's *The Structure of Byron's Major Poems* (Philadelphia: University of Pennsylvania Press, 1962), and especially Peter J. Manning, *Byron and His Fictions* (Detroit: Wayne State University Press, 1978); but see also Hubert F. Babinski, *The Mazeppa Legend in European Romanticism* (New York: Columbia University Press, 1974). For other studies of *Childe Harold* see the Editor's earlier Bibliographical Note to McGann's essay, and for those on *Don Juan* see the earlier Editor's Bibiographical note to Ridenour's essay.

From Selfish Spleen to Equanimity:
Byron's Satires

ROBERT F. GLECKNER

Although there has been much ado, of late especially, about whether *Don Juan* is an epic—and that is, despite McGann's recent demurrer,[1] a legitimate issue for critical discussion—extraordinarily enough, amid the staggering bulk of Byron criticism and scholarship, from outrageous and even tasteless trivia to the magisterial biographical and editorial work of Marchand and the critical renaissance of the last fifteen years or so, Claude Fuess's *Byron as a Satirist in Verse,* written in 1912, remains the only full-length study of Byron's satires. To be sure, we continue our efforts to analyze and define (or at worst to codify and categorize) the mode of the early satires, as well as *Beppo, The Vision of Judgment,* and *Don Juan,* to locate them in this, that, or the other context, and from most of these efforts we have learned much. But aside from these and isolated insights elsewhere into the shorter poems we have but nibbled at the larger issue. Robert Hume, capitalizing on F. R. Leavis' early assumption of "Byron's incapacity for Augustan satire," writes negatively of the early satires while telling us little about what they are;[2] Mary Clearman solidly establishes Juvenal's first satire as the "blueprint" for *English Bards and Scotch Reviewers;*[3] T. S. Eliot, Frye, and others mention in passing that Byron's satire is more like Burns's than Pope's, Dryden's, or Swift's;[4] and most recently Bernard Blackstone startlingly pronounces *The Curse of Minerva* a masterpiece of "barbed intelligence," but reserves his analytical and critical powers for a provocative reading of *The Waltz.*[5]

On the other hand there are those who, like Frye, R. C. Elliott, Ronald Knox, Paulson, Rosenheim, Worcester, Kernan, and Highet,[6] have surveyed the whole tradition of comedy and satire, "placing" Byron somewhere in it. Yet the fact remains that we do not yet know precisely how Byron's satiric and comic verse fits into or emerges out of his own canonical context. A number of us in recent years have been at some pains to discern a fundamental coherence in Byron's total poetical endeavor—and despite the fact that all of us did not arrive at the same conclusions, these essays toward a holistic view seem to me salutary. Yet even in these studies there is a kind of critical

Studies in Romanticism 18 (1979): 173–205. Courtesy of Trustees of Boston University.

awkwardness attendant upon integrating the satiric and "Romantic" poetry, a tentativeness that belies our general critical growth beyond W. F. Calvert's *Romantic Paradox*.[7] Part of the problem is Byron's remarkable range, even if we define that range solely in terms of satiric works from the youthful crudities of "To a Knot of Ungenerous Critics," "Soliloquy of a Bard in the Country," "On a Change of Masters at a Great Public School," and "Granta— A Medley" (among other early poems now generally included under the title *Hours of Idleness*) to the unduly neglected epigrams, to the sudden outpouring of *English Bards, Hints from Horace*, and *The Curse of Minerva*, to Cantos I and II of *Childe Harold* (which McGann rightly reminds us were largely satiric in first draft),[8] and on to *The Waltz, The Blues, The Vision of Judgment, Beppo, The Morgante, The Age of Bronze*, and of course *Don Juan*.

I apologize for this dry rehearsal of titles, but it may serve to remind us that his "satires" span not only Byron's entire career but interfoliate with everything else he wrote in such a way that the amalgam that is the total canon argues dramatically against any bifurcated labeling. While I am not prepared to argue here that the Turkish Tales and plays are satiric or even that when Byron is least satiric or comic the impulse behind his verse participates in that spirit, less promising approaches have been taken toward these still troublesome works. What I should like to do is take a fresh look at a few of Byron's poems, mostly early, as the basis for a theory of satiric-comic-Romantic coherence or development—focusing on Byron's own changing responses to his work, both matter and manner, tenor and vehicle—culminating in the multi-facetedness of *Don Juan*. If the roots of that almost unclassifiable poem are variously traceable not only in the great tradition of all satire but in the novel and Restoration comedy as well, they are also, even more helpfully I think, discernible in Byron's own early work.

Most recently Jerome McGann has done something of this sort (though the coherence he finds is quite different from my own view) by arguing that Byron's early attraction to Juvenal modulated into an allegiance to Horace, to "the *sermo merus* style" and the kind of self-effacement which McGann associates with Byron's having gained, as he himself says in *Don Juan*, "a deal of judgment" (1.215).[9] I do not intend to argue that issue here, but rather to take another tack, suggestively begun by Michael Cooke in *The Blind Man Traces the Circle*.[10] What is satiric or comic (and, finally, poetic) in Byron hinges, perhaps not surprisingly, on what he means by truth; and we could do worse in our overview of his total poetic performance than to study the evolution of that idea. In *Hours of Idleness* Byron's idea of truth is predictably naive and simplistic, as Ridenour and others have noted, yet it is nevertheless suggestive by virtue of its frequent coupling with other thematic nodes. For example, in one of the keynote poems of *Hours of Idleness*, "I Would I Were a Careless Child," truth is crudely opposed to dreams:

> Once I beheld a splendid dream,
>   A visionary scene of bliss:
> Truth!—wherefore did thy hated beam
>   Awake me to a world like this?

We need only a hand-wringing "Alas!" to complete the familiar rhetorical posturing: what *was* "real" or "true" is now no more. But the triteness should not put us off entirely, for Byron is also saying that what he announces as real (his careless childhood) was not real after all, not even when he was a part of it. It was only a "splendid dream" (note the tense: "Once I *beheld* a splendid dream"), a "visionary scene of bliss." The Wordsworthian past is as fictional as the most sentimental "soft primitivism" (to use Lovejoy's apt term):

> I would I were a careless child,
>   Still dwelling in my Highland cave,
> Or roaming through the dusky wild,
>   Or bounding o'er the dark blue wave.

While the child of *Tintern Abbey* bounding "o'er the mountains" "like a roe" attains to an imaginative reality, the force of Byron's lines does the reverse for his. The poetic fiction obtrudes: there was, and Byron knows it, no "Highland cave," no "dusky wild"—no real "scenes my youth hath known before." *That* past was as much wish-fulfillment as the concluding lines of the poem:

> O! that to me the wings were given
>   Which bear the turtle to her nest!
> Then would I cleave the vault of heaven,
>   To flee away, and be at rest.

To return now to "the rocks I love, / Which sound to Ocean's wildest roar"— even though he cannot quite become a careless child again—would be just as disillusioning and painful an experience as awaking now "to a world like this."

The "parent" of these dreams is Romance which, in his poem "To Romance," Byron defines as:

> Auspicious queen of childish joys,
> Who lead'st along, in airy dance,
>   Thy votive train of girls and boys;
> At length, in spells no longer bound,
>   I break the fetters of my youth;
> No more I tread thy mystic round,
>   But leave thy realms for those of Truth.[11]

The confusion inherent in the collocation of "spells" and "fetters," and of the self-consciously literary "votive train," "mystic round," and "airy dance" with the hackneyed prosiness of "childish joys"[12] emerges even more clearly in the poem's later assertion that Romance is "but a name," its realm a place where "every nymph a goddess [only] seems." The truth is that Romance is deceitful, filled with affectation and "sickly Sensibility." It is with "shame," then, that the speaker acknowledges its sway: "Repentent, now thy reign is o'er; / No more thy precepts I obey, / No more on fancied pinions soar"—not even, presumably, the pinions that will enable him to "cleave the vault of heaven, / To flee away, and be at rest"—only seemingly contradicting his earlier wish to be placed "among the rocks I love." What the speaker—and Byron—seem not to recognize is that the descendental truth of the present is no different from the transcendental truth of the past and future. In the companion poem, "Farewell to the Muse," transcendental reality or truth is associated firmly with poetry, with those same "fancied pinions" of the Muse whom he will now abjure. Yet in this poem, interestingly, it is not the Muse which is fledged but rather "Apathy" and "Visions"—the first wafting away "feelings of childhood," the second fleeing never to return. And this time Byron *does* write "Alas!" His final hope in the poem is the preposterous wish "that the present at least will be sweet"—so complete an evasion of the claims of any sort of truth that one must sympathize with Goethe's charge.

But there is yet another side to the coin. In "The First Kiss of Love" the speaker (some version of Byron's psyche obviously) lashes out at the "fictions of flimsy romance, / Those tissues of falsehood which folly has wove!"—in favor of the heady touch of real lips in the first kiss of love. He will have no "pastoral passions" like those of "rhymers, whose bosoms with phantasy glow." Yet the real thing, which we expect to be advanced in contrast to fictional Arcadias and the dictates of the muse, is clad in the most egregious poetic diction—"mild beam of the soul-breathing glance," "rapture," "the effusions that spring from the heart"—all rushing pantingly toward the extraordinary association of the sensuous kiss with the revival of Eden. Truth, then, lies not in the "cold compositions of art" but it does reside in the dream of paradise regained. To quote yet another early lyric, his heart is his lyre but his muse "the simple truth" ("Answer to Some Elegant Verses," l. 24).

Even given the excesses of these puerile attempts at profundity, the fact remains that amid all the confusion and melodrama "truth" has already settled in Byron's mind as, more often than not, anti-Romantic, anti-past, anti-dream, anti-fancy, anti-poetic. Needless to say, despite his farewell to the muse in 1807–09 he did not stop writing what he called Romance; but it is far from coincidental that his first *major* effort was *English Bards and Scotch Reviewers*. Byron was 21 and even before the *Edinburgh Review*'s caustic attack on *Hours of Idleness* he had relegated his own poems to the same illusionary past of which they spoke. Brougham's review, then, was but the catalyst that transformed his original draft of *British Bards* into the more disjointed and unsteady *English Bards and Scotch Reviewers*. Truth was beckoning to him, but his uneasy and ill-conceived flirtations with its power and full meaning led him merely to personal abuse, what in *Hints from Horace* (uncritically lumping together Dryden, Pope, and Swift) he advanced as the essence of satire, "selfish spleen" (ll. 115–16). Thus in *English Bards* he presents himself as ". . . now, so callous grown, so changed since youth, / I've learn'd to think and sternly speak the truth" (ll. 1057–58). The implicit contrast here is obvious: poetry is feeling, the same feeling that produced his own earlier "schoolboy freak," a "scrawl" and "flood of rhyme" with "nothing in't" (ll. 47–52). Thinking produces something else, like Jeffrey's prose; and so he will make his "own review" and grandly be not a poet but "self-constituted judge of poesy" (l. 62). It is this simple dichotomizing that leads to the generally unnoticed confusion at the beginning of *English Bards*. "Fools are my theme, let satire be my song" (l. 6), the Juvenalian speaker announces— only to withdraw from that stance 30 lines later: "but not belong / To me the arrows of satiric song."[13] Similarly, his own "grey goose-quill" turns out to be not only the "Slave of [his] thoughts, obedient to [his] will" but also "That mighty instrument of little men / . . . foredoom'd to aid the mental throes" of poetasters (ll. 7–12). And if, like Pope, he will "descend to Truth," he will also "soar to-day"—not to the vault of heaven this time but, in a revealing mixed metaphor, along the "path" which, though plain, is "full of thorns" (ll. 23–25).

The passage at once moves descendentally toward "thinking" as the proper, even the only path to truth, yet ascends on the wings of poesy derived from the feathers of his own "especial pen." Byron will thus be, as if in spite of himself, the poet of satiric song and with the very instrument of poetry, attack poetry. Perhaps with an innate sense of his own compulsion to rhyme, which is hinted at in the beginning of the poem and echoed at the end, and with his already developing awareness that the classical and neo-classical satiric mode was not so congenial a vehicle as he had thought, toward the end of *English Bards* he offers to step down from the critical pulpit as quickly as he had mounted it:

> Truth! rouse some *genuine* bard, and guide his hand
> To drive this pestilence from out the land.
> E'en I—least thinking of a thoughtless throng,
> Just skill'd to know the right and choose the wrong,
> ....
> E'en I must raise my voice, e'en I must feel
> Such scenes, such men, destroy the common weal.
> (ll. 687–96; my italics)

Finally Byron muddies the waters even more by referring to his own forthcoming grand tour, bidding us a curious adieu (apropos nothing—but perhaps with the satiric muse in mind, and at least a second thought about his own splenetic performance). Should he return, he says, from the exotic beauties of the east, "no tempting press / Shall drag my journal from the

desk's recess" (ll. 1023–24). Only coxcombs print. Such a commercial prosti-
tution of one's self is neither dream nor truth: ". . . quite content, [he] no
more shall interpose / To stun the public ear—at least with prose" (ll. 1035–
36). That final promise, however seemingly facetious, betrays not merely a
gnawing literary ambition (despite all his protestations to the contrary), but a
deep-seated confusion about how he should write and what he should write if
he is to be something other than a coxcomb or a "poet."

All in all, then, as everyone has noticed, *English Bards* not only waffles
in its aim but is filled with confusion about the nature of poetry and art and,
above all, about Byron's own vocation. He will embrace truth, yet as the last
phrase above indicates, he will not give up the kind of poetry which in his
mind is associated with illusion and dream. He will even forsake feeling since
he is now "so callous grown," and yet he is aware that compulsively he will
continue to feel—more and more strongly—about his world. He will take
up the same pen that produced *Hours of Idleness* and transform it into a
weapon which somehow soars despite stooping to truth. No "distempered
dream" will be his inspiration, his Muse, no "eastern vision" (a marvellous
adumbration of his yet-to-be-written tales); he will, rather, "err with Pope"
(ll. 24, 102). But, finally, what he isolates to praise in Pope is not his
"thought" but rather "Pope's pure strain" which "Sought the rapt soul to
charm" much as Otway's scenes "melt" us (ll. 109–10, 115). Similarly
Rogers, Campbell, Burns, Gifford, Sotheby, and MacNeil (who?) are the
"genuine sons" of Apollo, those "Who, least affecting, still affect the most: /
Feel as they write, and write but as they feel" (ll. 815–18). Byron's fumbling
and self-contradictory efforts to isolate the truth (both its source and the
artistic means of embodying it) could not be more obvious. The truth of the
thinking mind seemed to demand but the facts; the truth of the heart and
feelings required vision and genuineness. If the "selfish spleen" of *English
Bards* seemed right at the time, in the long run (*pace* Pope, Dryden, and "the
muses' violated laws") the ideal poet emerging out of *English Bards and Scotch
Reviewers* is clearly the author of *Childe Harold:*

> Blest is the man who dares approach the bower
> Where dwelt the muses at their natal hour;
> Whose steps have press'd, whose eye has mark'd afar,
> The clime that nursed the sons of song and war,
> The scenes which glory still must hover o'er,
> Her place of birth, her own Achaian shore.
> But doubly blest is he whose heart expands
> With hallow'd feelings for those classic lands;
> Who rends the veil of ages long gone by,
> And views their remnants with a poet's eye! (ll. 867–76)

Even with this remarkable foreshadowing of *Childe Harold's Pilgrimage* we
must note here parenthetically that a few months after Byron put the finish-

ing touches to the proofsheets of *English Bards,* a different genuineness emerged unobtrusively to remain unpublished until after his death—the delightfully rollicking "Huzza! Hodgson, We Are Going," with its own kind of truth:

> Still to laugh by far the best is,
>   Then laugh on—as I do now,
>   Laugh at all things,
>   Great and small things,
>   Sick or well, at sea or shore;
>   While we're quaffing,
>   Let's have laughing—
> Who the devil cares for more?

It is difficult to believe that Byron did not recall this when the idea of *Don Juan* struck him: "Do you suppose that I could have any intention but to giggle and make giggle?—a playful satire with as little poetry as could be helped—was what I meant" (letter to Murray, 12 August 1819).

In 1809, though, the "truth" was *Childe Harold's Pilgrimage,* Byron's first major essay on the relationship between the essentially bifurcated and ultimately confusing truths of *English Bards.* It will be "poetic" in the sense of Spenserian Romance, however bastardized, and yet it will be the truth in that, as the original manuscript shows, its prevailing mode will be satiric. The main formal device that Byron chose to try to manage this paradox is the essentially dual point of view (if we ignore that of Harold himself for the moment)—that of the Hobhouse-like no-nonsense narrator of facts, and that of the poet. As I have indicated elsewhere,[14] however, despite all of Byron's considerable efforts simultaneously to divide and unite these diverse strands of dramatic truth, the first two cantos, as everyone agrees, betray a notable lack of coherence. His poetic capacities were not yet up to the steadying of what was, basically, a conceptual wobble.

But there are moments of sureness, harbingers, however unlikely, of the confident fusion of modes and truths in *Don Juan.* One such moment occurs at the outset of Canto II. The invocation to the muse, "that blue-eyed maid of heaven," is conventional—yet unconventional in that she is Athena, who, "alas, / Didst never yet one mortal song inspire— / Goddess of Wisdom" (II.1). Despite this avowed allegiance, however, the initial imaginative tack is that of the "doubly blest" poet portrayed at the end of *English Bards,* whose

>   heart expands
> With hallow'd feelings for those classic lands:
> [And] rends the veil of ages long gone by,
> And views their remnants with a poet's eye!

The operative muse, then, is less Athena than her ruined temple, the prey of "men who never felt the sacred glow" (II.1). Such men, of course, are those attacked willy-nilly in *English Bards and Scotch Reviewers*—as well as here the Moslem passer-by whom Byron summons from his lethargy in stanza 3 and the "light Greek" who indifferently "carols by" in stanza 10.

With remarkable sureness Byron picks up the questions of stanza 2 ("Where are thy men of might? thy grand in soul?") and extends his emergent image pattern of ruins to the burial urn, which is metonymically "a nation's sepulchre" (stanza 3) as well as the empty grave of the "vanish'd Hero" of stanza 5, and thence to the skull:

> Ambition's airy hall,
> The dome of Thought, the palace of the Soul.
> ....
> The gay recess of Wisdom and of Wit
> And Passion's host—

all subsumed in the introductory phrase "a temple where a God may dwell" (stanzas 5–6). In this context the dreams earlier associated with the flimsiness of illusionary Romance become momentarily an imaginative truth like that of the boy in Forster's "The Celestial Omnibus":

> . . . if, as holiest men have deem'd, there be
> A land of souls beyond the sable shore,
> ....
> How sweet it were in concert to adore
> With those who made our mortal labours light!
> To hear each voice we fear'd to hear no more!
> Behold each mighty shade reveal'd to sight. (st. 8)

Only in such a fusion of past and future, the truth of feeling, can the speaker, in the shrewd late addition of stanza 9, "dream that we may meet again" and thus "woo the vision to [his] vacant breast." The recollection of Athena's vanished power, of Greece's men of might and grand in soul, of the exiled hero, of the wisdom and passion of the now hollow skull, and of his own lover is as true as it is illusory and false—for finally the world dictates that "all saint, sage, or sophist ever writ" cannot "people this lonely tower, this tenement refit," this past revive (st. 6).

And so, as he will consistently in *Don Juan,* the speaker must turn to what is here, the "unshaken base" of the ruined temple of Jupiter which "ev'n . . . Fancy's eye"—the eye of the poet-dreamer-romantic—cannot restore to its original grandeur. If it is Time that "hath labour'd to deface" it, mercifully Time also left at least a "latent grandeur" (st. 10). Only man, personified by Lord Elgin, takes the giant step beyond defacement to destruction.

Byron had already attacked Elgin in *English Bards* for wasting "useless thousands on [his] Phidian freaks, / Misshapen monuments and maim'd

antiques" and for making "grand saloons a general mart / For all the mutilated blocks of art" (ll. 1029–32)—the emphasis clearly on the commercial-
ization of British archeology and travelogue-mongers rather than the impact
of their enterprise on Greece: "Of Dardan tours let dilettanti tell, / I leave
topography to rapid Gell" (ll. 1033–34). Nor is there much sense here that
such activities are a violation of truths sacred to the mind and heart. They are
merely trivializations, like the poetic and dramatic works lampooned in the
rest of the poem. Byron later accurately described his effort in *English Bards*
as insensitive and surly, "a fit / Of wrath and rhyme" which he ejaculated to
show his wit "when juvenile and curly" (*Don Juan*, x.19). The conclusion of
English Bards, then, as I have noted, is predictably ambiguous: the speaker
won't contribute to this trivialization, this touristy money-grubbing, but the
door is left more than ajar for some poetic enterprise—with little or no
indication that it will aim at any sort of "truth."

But in Canto II of *Childe Harold* the imaginative truths inherent in the
image patterns of the opening stanzas provide a poetic context for the satiric
personification of the same truth that awoke the speaker of "I Would I Were a
Careless Child" to "a world like this." The attack on that personification,
Lord Elgin, then, is quite different from its original version—toned down
apparently at Dallas' insistence but, more importantly, refocussed by Byron
to avoid at once the spleen of *English Bards* and the obtrusive personal details
of Elgin's life and character, both of which militated against the passage's
harmonious absorption in the poetic framework he had established so well.[15]
The result of such artistic control, though not unequivocally successful, is
still a remarkably effective blend of the truth of the past (Grecian glory) and
the present (Grecian ruins and their perpetrators) in the mindlessness and
heartlessness of Elgin's depredations.

Byron's own awareness of the growing shape of these opening stanzas is
reflected in his belated insertion of a coda, stanza 15, which, despite the
jumble of memorable and clumsy poetic execution and the out-of-key concluding lines on England, fuses the earlier conflicting claims of truth as well
as the historical and personal past and the historical and personal present:
"Cold is the heart, fair Greece, that looks on thee / Nor feels as lovers o'er the
dust they loved."[16]

While he was still revising *Childe Harold*, having learned much from
that critical retrospection, Byron again took up the Elgin business in *The
Curse of Minerva*. Although I cannot agree with Blackstone's estimate of it as a
great poem (p. 57), it deserves better than we have given it, especially since
it is Byron's first attempt to give *dramatic* form to his developing sense of the
interrelatedness of several modes of truth. Taking his cue from a cancelled
line in stanza 13 of *Childe Harold* ("Oh that Minerva's voice lent its keen aid
to mine"), Byron imagines Minerva's appearance in her own devastated temple (his first portrait, we might note, of the "ruin amidst ruins" figure) to
personally curse Lord Elgin. But were the poem merely a diatribe, albeit by

an alter-ego, it would warrant little attention here.[17] Instead Byron rather deftly constructs a dramatic setting to contrast with the vision of ruin and decay that opens Canto II—the lovely, lyrical hymm to the sunset over "fair Greece"—evoking not only peace and beauty but also what Carl Woodring has aptly called "worth"[18]—all surprisingly cast in the heroic couplets Byron seemed to associate only with satire. This "magic shore," for the speaker, lives only "in poets' lore"; in poetry alone the past returns and the "present seem'd to cease" (ll. 57–61). Although no poet, as we shall see, the speaker is clearly a poet-manqué, moved deeply by the scene. Into this past (made imaginatively present) steps the real present, "Minerva's self; but, ah! how changed":

> Her idle aegis bore no Gorgon now;
> Her helm was dinted, and the broken lance
> Seem'd weak and shaftless e'en to mortal glance;
> The olive branch, which still she deign'd to clasp,
> Shrunk from her touch and wither'd in her grasp;
> And, ah! though still the brightest of the sky,
> Celestial tears bedimm'd her large blue eye;
> Round the rent casque her owlet circled slow,
> And mourn'd his mistress with a shriek of woe! (ll. 75, 80–88)

Through *her* eyes the speaker's poetic vision narrows in line 99 to the dark reality of "vacant, violated fane" (reminiscent of the skull image in *Childe Harold*), which in a sense becomes the speaker of the curse as well as an oracle of the future.

Instead of Elgin, the initial target is the speaker for being a Briton, "once a noble name," whose country sent the spoiler worse than Turk or Goth (ll. 90–97). The speaker protests; as a "true-born Briton" he disclaims responsibility: "England owns him not: / Athena, no! thy plunderer was a Scot" (ll. 126–28). It is, he insists, that "bastard land" of "meanness, sophistry, and mist," that has dispatched "her scheming children far and wide" (ll. 131–44). This jingoistic protestation of his own and his country's innocence, sufficient in itself to cement Byron's efforts to divorce himself from the speaker, is halted abruptly by the curse itself—first on "the head of him who did this deed" and next on "the state receiver of his pilfer'd prey" (ll. 163–174): "Hers were the deeds that taught her lawless son / To do what oft Britannia's self had done" (ll. 211–212). "Your city saddens," Minerva continues, warming to her role:

> loud though Revel howls,
> Here Famine faints and yonder Rapine prowls.
> See all alike of more or less bereft;
> No misers tremble when there's nothing left. (ll. 241–44)

Elgin has receded far into the background as Minerva's voice assumes oracular power. In a sense he has been diminished to merely witting tool, the operative occasion for the prophetic attack on the future of the speaker and upon his land. The tawdry vulgarization of the Grecian marbles into a "stone shop" around which coxcombs creep and lascivious females leer (ll. 182 ff.) Minerva magnifies and transforms into a vision of England's self-destruction. The furies, war, ignominious death, havoc, rape, and a final apocalyptic conflagration shall engulf her. Amid all, in a devastating parody of her own ruination, she decrees a statue of Elgin, turned to stone by her Gorgon shield, standing unscathed on into eternity (ll. 207 ff.).

Unlike the juvenile brashness of *English Bards* and beyond the carefully reconstructed and modulated elegy opening Canto II of *Childe Harold,* in *The Curse of Minerva* Byron allows the truth to speak out in its several voices, lyric and satiric, descriptive and prophetic,[19] through dramatically realized characters that reflect his own growing sense of the interrelatedness of multiple truths as well as his own ability to hold these in suspension with a kind of grace despite the pressures on him to chase, endlessly and futilely, what Cooke calls that "truth . . . which is self-sufficient, stable, beautiful, and withal potent against the confusions of the empirical order" (*Blind Man Traces the Circle,* p. 96).

But the poem is not quite so neat as I have made it out to be. Despite its achievement, despite Byron's shrewd distancing of himself from the speaker—and from the curse—the whole lacks, finally, equanimity. He is not yet able to disclaim responsibility as it were, and thus to extricate himself from the self-lacerating despair of his Cassandra role or from the role of self-righteous judge and jury. In short he has not yet learned how to make use of his comic sense.

It may seem an unfortunate un-Byronic digression to turn here from satire and the idea of a comic sense to the tales, but I should like to argue that in them can be found, however curiously, adumbrations of equanimity and poise of spirit, both of which undergird Byron's comedy. *The Giaour* has recently come to be recognized as an unusually interesting and revealing document in Byron's struggle for a form, vehicle, or structure suitable to the needs of which he was only gradually becoming aware. It is also, as a direct result of that struggle, a foundation-stone of the carefully constructed psychic posture that will emerge full-blown only in the precarious sanity of *Don Juan*—no matter how the melodramatic and all-too assiduously cultivated melancholy and gloom of this "Fragment of a Turkish Tale" tend to benumb our sensibilities.

Unlike *The Curse of Minerva,* which precedes it by less than two years (during which Byron was otherwise occupied by refurbishing and reshaping Cantos I and II of *Childe Harold*), *The Giaour* is obviously not satiric. Yet Byron's effort in *The Curse* to objectify points of view in realized (or near-realized) characters, and thus to vacate the judgment seat so to speak, is in *The Giaour* elaborately and self-consciously expanded. If the poem is accretively structured, as it certainly is, we miss the essential point of its accretiveness if we ignore the fact that virtually all of Byron's revisions add new points of view or strengthen and clarify existing ones. Our sense of the poem's wholeness depends directly on the poet's ability to "maneuver us into the position of seeing all the points of view represented at once."[20] Moreover, such maneuvering effects a disengagement of the poet from responsibility for the actions and opinions of his characters—to the point (fully developed only in *Don Juan*) of suggesting the poem as writing itself, as in a sense self-created. This fundamental, though paradoxical, self-effacement amid apparently blatant self-advertisement and exploitation seems to me a neglected clue to the dynamics of Byron's poetry, and perhaps especially to the "style" (in Ridenour's inclusive sense) of *Don Juan*. The striking effort in *The Giaour* at once to embody both the narrative and the attitudes toward the narrative in multiple and variously perceptive articulators, and to absorb all of these points of view (as Byron was simultaneously trying to do in the first two cantos of *Childe Harold*) into the voice of the poet seems to me finally unsuccessful, for Byron's own emotional engagement in the history and psychology of the Giaour himself precluded finally the kind of "escape" that only his maturer sense of the world's "comedy" would permit him. Such a failure, however, should not obscure Byron's notable attempt for the first time in his poetry to avoid taking sides in the network of character conflicts (and allegiances) and even to refuse flatly to tell us exactly what the full story was. We have what I described as "the public guesses" (Gleckner, p. 113) as to what happened (retailed by the fisherman from a variety of sources including mere rumor) and the fragmented accounts of Hassan's lone remaining soldier, the Monk, and of course the Giaour himself. Taken together, their "broken tale was all we knew / Of her he loved, or him he slew" (ll. 1333–34). Otherwise "of his name or race" we have neither "token" nor "trace" except what the Monk, who heard the Giaour's confession, may know but cannot reveal (ll. 1329–31). Similarly, if the "common crowd" can see in the Giaour only waywardness and a "fitting doom" (ll. 866–867), Byron draws no such conclusion. The end of the poem, then, is not the mere trumpery of perpetuated mysteriousness for its own sake that is often charged against Byron's tales, but rather a shrewd displacement of acknowledged authority on the part of the poet in the settled calm of simple fact: "He pass'd" (l. 1329). Yet if the poem "cheers no heroes, advances no cause (private or public), asserts no values" (Gleckner, p. 106), its tonal resonances are distinctly and militantly negative, and the acknowledged hopelessness of even the noblest of man's endeavors severely qualifies that apparent calm or objective aplomb of the concluding lines.

Successive tales register Byron's persistent experiments in the manipulation of point of view which reflect at once an equally persistent probing for the avenues to truth and a less than settled awareness of what his own attitude ought to be toward that truth once found. Not that he did not know his own mind and heart; those burned steadily with a most un-Pateresque gem-like flame. But whether to allow that flame to appear nakedly in public or to mask it or even to try to snuff it out—that was the question he was beginning to recognize as lurking at the core of his art. Of these subsequent tales none is more important with respect to that question than *Parisina*. Like *The Giaour* neither comic nor satiric, it nevertheless succeeds in establishing for the first time in Byron's work his own conviction of the impossibility of certain judgment—or, if one is unwilling to go quite that far—the shocked recognition that the act of judgment, moral or otherwise, is a tragically mistaken effort on man's past to play a role for which he is manifestly unqualified and unsuited. The truth lies, serenely or jarringly, in what is. "It is just there," as Ortega y Gasset puts it in a relevant context, "confronting us, affirming its mute, terrible materiality in the face of all phantoms." "Terribly self-sufficient" it "rejects whatever 'meanings' we may give it,"[21] implacably belies what man conceives it to be, and frustrates his usurped power to decide why it is what it is or what it ought to be. Such usurpation, I hasten to add, has little to do in Byron's mind (though it may in Azo's) with playing God. For if, as he once remarked, "a *Creator* is a more natural imagination than a fortuitous concourse of atoms,"[22] all of human experience and intellectual enterprise urge upon man the truth that the world is, as he says in a revealing self-quotation, "a sad jar of atoms."[23]

In *Parisina* Byron has his narrator deliberately tempt us into seeing a grimly judgmental and vengeful God (not merely a conveniently imagined creator) at work. As Hugo is about to be beheaded on Azo's orders for what all agree is his "sin," "the crowd in a speechless circle gather / To see the Son fall by the doom of the Father!" (ll. 405–06). But while deliberately tempting us into mythic identifications, Byron is careful to show us that Hugo is no Christ-figure anymore than Azo is a Jehovah, much less a loving God. Both are mere mortals, both innocent, both guilty. The fluctuating judgments on the actions of the several characters made by Byron's narrator throughout the poem merely underscore the dramatically enacted futility of assigning blame or responsibility. If it is "right" that Hugo die, Azo *is* God; but if it is "wrong" Azo is Pilate. What is known is that Hugo is executed, Parisina goes mad and disappears like Browning's last duchess, Azo lives on like a lightning-shattered tree trunk, and law and order and peace reign in his kingdom—the facts of the story as the poet, not the narrator, presents them. What we don't know is what the poet confesses is unknown and unknowable:

> . . . Parisina's fate lies hid
> Like dust beneath the coffin lid:
> Whether in convent she abode,
> And won to heaven her dreary road
> By blighted and remorseful years
> Of scourge, and fast, and sleepless tears;

Of if she fell by bowl or steel,
For that dark love she dared to feel;
Or if, upon the moment smote,
She died by tortures less remote,—
Like him she saw upon the block,
With heart that shared the headsman's shock,
In quicken'd brokenness that came
In pity o'er her shatter'd frame,—
None knew—and none can ever know.
But whatsoe'er its end below,
Her life began and closed in woe! (ll. 513–29)

But the self-protectiveness inherent in Byron's superimposition of a narrator between himself and his tale, and in the endlessly oscillating pendulum-movement between praise and blame, cause and effect, is finally cold comfort for the poet; for the overall impact of *Parisina,* on Byron as well as the reader, is of Coleridge's nightmare world of death-in-life couched almost satirically in the accouterments of a deliberately anti-comic all's well that ends well within the established canons of law and order, right and wrong. Though Byron pens no epitaph for the dead, the concluding lines on Azo's tortured life break through the narrator-mask to expose Byron's own deeply felt compassion (and anger) at eternally erring man. The siege of Ismail in *Don Juan* will be no different, though manifestly more bloody. But, more important, after the epitaph-like conclusion of the "Tartar Khan" episode (*Don Juan* VIII. 104–19), the poet's final word is his outrageous emulation of, without the self-aggrandizement inherent in, Suwarrow's "witty" rhyming, "like Nero o'er a burning city"—

All very accurate, you must allow
And *epic,* if plain truth should prove no bar;
For I have drawn much less with a long bow
Than my forerunners. Carelessly I sing. (VIII. 138)

We have perennially taken that last adverb to be the key to Byron's colloquial mode in *Don Juan.* Perhaps it is. But it is also a skillfully submerged projection of an attitude toward *what* is in his poem: not the quiet facetiousness which he tells us early on will be his prevailing note, that sort of attitude implicit in the modern locution, "I could care less," but rather the hard-won repression of felt concern in favor of the solidity of mere plain truth-telling. In *Parisina* there is no such carelessness.

One might fruitfully pursue Byron's further attempts at dissociating himself (i.e. his "feeling" self) from his poetry in the series of plays—but suffice it to say here that if they develop a kind of objectivity unavailable in other poetic forms (execpt perhaps the dramatic monologue, which, we should remind ourselves, Byron experimented with between his work on the tales and his foray into drama), they taught him little about the unplumbed capacities of his comic sense. (It is no accident, I suppose, that the closest Byron comes to dramatic comedy is in the dialogue form embedded in *The Vision of Judgment,* achieved well after *Don Juan* was in full swing.)

And so we must now turn to that final masterpiece. From the preceding I hope it is clear that I think *Don Juan* an impossible dream without the experiments in *Childe Harold, The Curse of Minerva, The Giaour,* and *Parisina, et al.* This is not to denigrate the idea that in *Beppo* he found a form and style congenial to his "mobility" and pen, but it is to say that the manner of *Beppo,* and Byron's stance vis-à-vis that manner and its content, would have been far less likely without his earlier essays into the nature of truth—and especially his growing awareness of his own relationship to that truth. Rutherford, it seems to me, is quite wrong in saying that in *Beppo* Byron finally found "a form and a convention which would enable him to express adequately his own complex nature."[24] On the contrary, *Beppo* represents a daring attempt to transform a Turkish Tale into a comedy. M. K. Joseph's description of it— "like one of the Turkish Tales turned inside-out"[25]—while unusually perceptive amid the plethora of more conventional views, is neither precisely right nor sensitive to the unacknowledged critical sense and considerable courage involved in this enterprise. For we need to ask ourselves, as no one has to my knowledge, why Byron would want to turn a Turkish Tale upside down or inside out. If the time was fortuitous for some happy versifying, as J. D. Jump suggests, that fortuitousness was hardly inspiration for Byron merely to "express his delight in his Italian existence."[26] Laughter is *Beppo's* mode to be sure, but what is laughed at? The same ruinousness that informed *Childe Harold* and the tales—hypocrisy, lost youth and beauty and innocence, the Fall, self-exile, the corruptions of society and politics, the grimness of man's fate, *"The World"* and its inexorable ways—but all now supremely trivialized. The invention of the "broken Dandy" narrator (the comic version of *The Giaour's* fisherman or the narrator of *Parisina*), the insistent digressiveness, the flexible play of the *ottava rima,* and the diminution of the "Byronic hero" to a Restoration comedy cuckold all bespeak Byron's insulation of himself against the responsibility for and the heart-wounding consequences of his clear perception that Venice *circa* 1780 was no less the world than that of the Giaour, Azo, Mazeppa, or the prisoner of Chillon. He allows the facts of his story as Piero Segati told them at dinner in August 1817 to control his poem just as the stanza form determines the poem's progress or "lingering." As a result, rather than allowing Byron "to express adequately his own complete nature" the mode of *Beppo* disguises or represses that true nature and submerges it in the laughter so effectively that most readers tend to agree with Jump that it is "one of the most cheerful poems in the English language" (*Byron,* p. 95). In one sense I suppose it is (though I have argued against that view),[27] but in that very cheerfulness Byron has so completely absented himself that the truth he saw clearly enough—and perhaps was even moved and angered by—is obscured in its very trivialization. As Lockhart wrote about "the Italian weavers of merry rima ottava: their merriment is nothing, because they have nothing but their merriment."[28] Almost as if in response to his own recognition of this fact, a few months later Byron penned the "Ode on Venice" in his old self-torturing manner—the same Venice as Beppo's but now an "empty Oyster Shell" (letter to Hoppner, 28 Oct. 1819) where "Mirth is madness, and but smiles to slay," where "Hope is nothing but a false delay," and where freedom is "the mere numbness of [the] chain" (ll. 35–44). *There* is the world, the untrivializable truth in all its rawness, "The everlasting *to be* which *hath been*" (l. 59). And it is that truth which *Don Juan* will essay. It will be as funny as *Beppo* but far less fun.

In Canto IX of *Don Juan* Byron apparently has his final say about Pyrrho, to whose brand of skepticism he has often been accused of subscribing. The entire passage is worth pausing upon, for its associative sequence speaks directly to the issues I have been discussing. Byron opens the canto with an attack, not unlike those in *English Bards* and *The Curse of Minerva*, on Wellington, that "best of cut-throats" (IX.4), moves on to Napoleon who "abused" his great opportunity to free "fallen Europe from the unity / Of tyrants" and thus be "blest from shore to shore" (IX.9), and thence to all war-mongers who cause Death himself to laugh and scorn at all they are and do:

> And thus Death laughs,—it is sad merriment,
>   But still it *is* so; and with such example
> Why should not Life be equally content
>   With his superior, in a smile to trample
> Upon the nothings which are daily spent
>   Like bubbles on an ocean much less ample
> Than the eternal deluge. . . . (IX.13)

The italicization in the second line is crucial, for it signals us to see that though the macabre death's-head is "sad" it still articulates a kind of "merriment" that Life may properly emulate whether or not we are tempted thereby to trample "Upon the nothings" of this world. The recall of the fourth stanza of Canto IV ("And if I laugh at any mortal thing; / 'T is that I may not weep") is deliberate, though the modulation of laughter to the "melancholy merriment" occasioned by our "checker'd . . . human lot" (VIII.89) is even more important. Since we "cannot always bring" ourselves "to apathy" in the face of "what we least wish to behold," since Lethe's fabled spring is, however seductive and desirable, nonreachable, and since the laughter of Death is not, finally, laughter at all, for without its "fleshy bar" it can no longer flex its face from "*ear* to *ear*"—what is left is but a smile, the smile of recognition and suppressed self-involvement, the sober merriment of what I have called equanimity. The skull of Byron's only half-facetious early carpe diem poem,

"Lines Inscribed upon a Cup Formed from a Skull," and those of *Childe Harold* II and *The Curse of Minerva* have now reached their ultimate avatar.[29]

From the precariousness of this balance between Graveyard School gothic and a joke in poor taste the opening stanzaic sequence of Canto IX moves on with a certain kind of logic to the question of existence itself. " 'To be, or not to be? that is the question,' " Byron quotes, only to be sidetracked momentarily into a brief discussion of fame and the deflationary assertion that it's better to "have a sound digestion" (IX.14). Then back to the question, now considerably trivialized by the application of digestive juices: " 'To be, or not to be?' Ere I decide, / I should be glad to know that which *is being?*" (IX.16). And since speculation on *that* question is vain, Byron will enlist on no side until all sides agree—that is, never. But he does enlist on a side, of course, namely that which avers that it doesn't make a damned bit of difference. He will eschew all philosophizing and all determinations of what reality is (or, we might add, what ultimate "truth" is). That position in turn seems to throw him into Montaigne's camp:

> 'Que scais-je?' was the motto of Montaigne,
>   As also of the first academicians:
> That all is dubious which man may attain,
>   Was one of their most favourite positions.
> There's no such thing as certainty, that's plain
>   As any of Mortality's conditions;
> So little do we know what we're about in
> This world, I doubt if doubt itself be doubting. (IX.17)

McGann accepts this as the final word on "Byron's skepticism. . . . Byron doubts all things, scrupulously, but in the full event of this skepticism he wonders if 'doubt itself be doubting.' . . . The wonder is justified."[30] But this ignores the following stanza and its reduction of Pyrrhonism to a kind of absurdity:

> It is a pleasant voyage perhaps to float,
>   Like Pyrrho, on a sea of speculation;
> But what if carrying sail capsize the boat?
>   Your wise men don't know much of navigation;
> And swimming along in the abyss of thought
>   Is apt to tire.

Whatever "reality" or "truth" is, it is as "plain / As any of Mortality's conditions," which anyone who knows much about navigation knows. *Don Juan* then is no such "pleasant voyage," though its "merriment" serves both as ballast and rudder to keep the craft afloat and on course, to maintain the even keel unavilable to the "wise" who, ignorant of navigation, habitually end up shipwrecks battling the waves in the abyss of their own thought.[31] Byron returns to this passage again in Canto XIV to make the same point:

> If from great nature's or our own abyss
>   Of thought we could but snatch a certainty,
> Perhaps mankind might find the path they miss—
>   But then 't would spoil much good philosophy.
> One system eats another up. . . . (XIV. 1)

Wisdom, and hence truth, emerges not from plunging into the abyss of one's psyche and thrashing around vainly for the shore but rather in clear-sightedly (sicklied o'er with no pale cast of thought) receiving what is without analysis beyond what the "story," which "must / Tell for itself" (IX.77), provides in unvarnished fashion. The only sanity in the face of the truths that story tells is in a kind of poised and sober playfulness, a tolerant if precarious spectatorship that topples compulsively into self-involvement but always with a Huck-Finn-like "I been there before" manages to regain its equilibrium. If "poesy" is a kind of Baconian "straw, borne on by human breath, / . . . according as the mind glows" (XIV.8), or, more solemnly, "A paper kite which flies 'twixt life and death, / A shadow which the onward soul behind throws" (XIV.8), Byron's metaphoric choice is neither of these. His poesy's a "bubble, not blown up for praise" and least of all for instruction, but rather "just to play with, as an infant plays" (XIV.8). His muse, in the oft-quoted lines, merely "gathers a repertory of facts" (XIV. 13) without judgment or arrangement or assignment of cause and effect:

> 'T is sad to hack into the roots of things,
>   They are so much intertwisted with the earth;
> So that the branch a goodly verdure flings,
>   I reck not if an acorn gave it birth. (XIV.59)

And there is, of course, plenty of verdure in *Don Juan*.

It is in this total context of lilliputianizing Pyrrho that the familiar lines of XIV.3 must be read: "For me, I know nought; nothing I deny, / Admit, reject, contemn. . . ." "What's this to the purpose? you will say," he asks. As much to the purpose as anything else in the poem is Byron's inevitable (and only possible) answer, for his "sole excuse is—'t is my way" (XIV.7). And that way is, to retrieve an earlier nautical metaphor, to sail not "before the wind" (IX.26) but rather "In the wind's eye" (X.4): only "Frail mariners afloat without a chart" do otherwise (XIV.74). And if the achievement of his "poesy" is something less than that of the discoverer of stars, in taking up his "paltry sheet of paper" his "internal spirit" nevertheless cuts "a caper" at his own discovery of the truth (X.3).

Here, then, seems to me the key to the equanimity gained, after the long apprenticeship I have been sketching, in *Don Juan*. As McGann has recently pointed out, *Don Juan* started out as "an amusing and gossipy tale after the *Beppo* manner [and] ended in a complex mixture of comedy and tragic pathos."[32] One needn't, I think, accept McGann's interpretation of the precise nature of that "mixture" to recognize that it emerges, as it were, out of the writing of the poem itself. While there is the familiar foolery in Byron's oft-repeated claim that he doesn't know what comes next—neither fact nor word—there is a fundamental seriousness about the confession. For the true nature of *Don Juan* is discovered only gradually by Byron as it emerged from his mind and pen—and more importantly from the facts as they uncovered themselves to him. As a consequence he also had to learn how to respond to his own poem without merely yielding to, or even indulging, those responses in such fashion that the resultant poem would become, in a large sense, a form of self-torture, an artistic magnification of the psychic consequences of his vision of the way things are. One possibility he feared was the spleen that characterized his early satires. Aside from the aesthetic dead-end that he quickly realized such an attitude to represent, he later came to see that "'t is in vain such sallies to permit" (*Don Juan* x.19), the vanity being inherent both in the self-righteous presumption involved and in the impossibility of certainty or reform. A second possibility was the dramatic self-effacement developed in the early tales and perfected particularly in *Parisina, The Prisoner of Chillon,* and the plays. But there, despite the "objectivity" of the form and the self-protection, even self-exculpation, inherent in that form, the thought, as Byron said in another but related context, burned "through, through . . . yes, yes, through,"[33] and his self-lacerating vision of mankind's inevitable doom led to the compulsively repeated act of creation, which paradoxically merely exacerbated his sense of the human tragedy. The third possibility was the insouciance of *Beppo* and the early manner of *Don Juan* itself. That is to giggle and make giggle, to be a little quietly facetious about everything, in a sense to abandon the quest for truth and court the kind of indifference calculated to the easier maintenance of his own sanity which was so sorely battered by his self-assumed prophetic role. However tempting that escape route must have seemed, it is no small measure of his greatness as a poet that he rejected it almost as suddenly as he found it.

How to continue to play the role of vates without being vatic, that is without Cain's "rage and fury against the inadequacy of his state to his conceptions," and without suffering (at least openly) the passionate consequences of his own perceptions became one of his central tasks in *Don Juan,* once he had decided the poem was going to be something other than another *Beppo.* More simply, how does one "play" seriously with the eternal verities and complexities? We know from Canto II that his will not be "a weeping muse" no matter what the cause (II.16), whether the immediate context is Juan's tearful departure from Spain, or the captive Jews' lament "by Babel's waters," or Byron's own all-too-vividly and readily recalled self-exile. "Such light griefs are not a thing to die on," he concludes un-Manfredlike, for there is neither comprehensible explanation nor help for them. The studied self-control inherent in the phrase "such light griefs" should not, I think, be confused with a hardened cynicism. Although obviously some steeling of the heart in the manner of his earlier heroes was surely going on in Byron's psyche, his capacity to feel deeply and to remember vulnerably never lessened. As he wrote once to Moore, "I have been all my life trying to harden my heart, and have not yet quite succeeded."[34] But out of his own experience with this oscillation (reflected in the "wobbling" I spoke of earlier) and, more important, his own persistent artistic attempts to shape and thus control it artistically, comes a hard-won psychic stance, neither merely defensive nor resignedly acceptive or accommodative, that manifests itself in a variety of ways in *Don Juan*. I have already looked at some of these ways above, and others have been charted by other commentators. But they all have a kind of gestural signature that has not been sufficiently noted.

That signature is the shoulder shrug, accompanied by the kind of "merriment" symbolized by the death's-head smile of Canto IX. No giggles now, no quiet facetiousness, no tears (despite their consistent presence in the very act of repressing or submerging them), no futile rage, but that poise of spirit[35] and firm consciousness of his own unassailable sanity[36] indissociable from what I have called simply a "comic sense." To be or not to be is no longer a question of interest—or if it is, an unperturbed recognition of its unanswerableness constitutes the wisdom so perturbably sought in its asking. Neither is Montaigne's "Que scais-je" the question, or if *it* is, *Don Juan*, eternally writing itself and infinitely revelatory of the facts, is the eloquent answer. And if "there's no such thing as certainty," there is nevertheless the "plainness" of "Mortality's conditions," knowledge of whose chameleon-like fluctuations and even contradictions is the bedrock of authorial psychic health[37] and a sound digestion in a mad, mad, mad, mad world.

The shoulder-shrug, then, is ubiquitous in *Don Juan* just as it is in that extraordinarily Juanesque film *It's a Mad, Mad, Mad, Mad World*. Even as early as Canto I we find:

> Revenge in person's certainly no virtue,
> But then 't is not *my* fault, if *others* hurt you.

> And if your quarrels should rip up old stories,
>   And help them with a lie or two additional,
> *I*'m not to blame, as you well know. . . . (I.30–31)

As to love, if people go beyond the proper bounds (whatever they may be construed to be), "'t is quite a crime, / But not my fault" (I.80). Again, in Canto III we are told that

> Haidée and Juan were not married, but
>   The fault was theirs, not mine; it is not fair,
> Chaste reader, then, in any way to put
>   The blame on me. . . . (III.12)

Similarly "Gulbeyaz was extremely wrong," but though Byron privately may "own it, . . . deplore it, . . . condemn it" he detests the illusions of fiction "even in song, / And so must tell the truth, howe'er you blame it" (VI.8). In Canto VII he is indignant that

> They accuse me—*Me*—the present writer of
> The present poem—of—I know not what—
> A tendency to under-rate and scoff
> At human power and virtue, and all that;
> ....
> Good God! I wonder what they would be at!

For he has said only what everyone else has said before him, "Who knew this life was not worth a potato. / 'T is not their fault, nor mine, if this be so" (VII.3–4). In matters of aesthetic taste with respect to what should or should not be included in his poem, the narrator simply asserts the fact for it is his job to record what life speaks. Thus in the bizarre scene following the siege of Ismail, a Russian officer striding over the heaps of slain "felt his heel / Seized fast" by a not-yet-dead Turk. The regimental surgeon cuts off the Turk's head but still the teeth "stuck faster than a skewer" (VIII.83–85). Conscious of the unbelievable grotesquerie of the incident Byron shrugs and comments, "But then the fact's a fact" (86). And so on. Such passages, in various permutations, are legion, a chorus of verbal shoulder hunches, a seam of perspicuity and professed innocence that hems the whole crazy quilt together. The truth is not *his*—although he makes abundant attempts to explore its complexity and even contradiction. To explore, not solve, for the former, as Cooke reminds us, is "an act of spirit" (*Blind Man Traces the Circle*, p. 210), the latter of philosophy. The world may even be, he says, "a glorious blunder," the result of sheer happenstance; or it may be "according / To the old text" (XI.3–4). If so, so much the better: it may indeed "turn out so."

> . . . our days are too brief for affording
> Space to dispute what *no one* ever could
> Decide, and *every body one day* will
> Know very clearly—or at least lie still.
>
> And therefore will I leave off metaphysical
> Discussion, which is neither here nor there:

and make instead a bargain with the reader: "If I agree that what is, is; then this I call / Being quite perspicuous and extremely fair" (XI.4–5; Byron's italics). The deliberate alteration of Pope's "Whatever is, is right" is a crucial indicator of Byron's stance throughout the poem. Rightness has as little to do with the truth as morality. Fairness with the reader is all, but a fairness born of the mutually acknowledged futility of explanation, argument, and judgment. In *Jerusalem* Blake's Eternals, contemplating with horror the death that is, to them (and to Blake), mere physical life, say:

> What seems to Be: Is: To those to whom
> It seems to Be, & is productive of the most dreadful
> Consequences to those to whom it seems to Be: even of
> Torments, Despair, Eternal Death. . . .[38]

In a sense the early Byron suffered such consequences, for "What seems to Be" indeed was to him what is, purged of self-cultivated or externally imposed illusion. And out of both his perceptiveness and his responses he made his poems. If for Blake "the Divine Mercy / Steps beyond and Redeems Man in the Body of Jesus" (*Jerusalem* 32:54–55), for Byron there is neither mercy nor divinity, and redemption is Manfred-like to refuse to succumb to the power of that reality and thus to die—if not to live—on one's own terms. Indeed if one could imaginatively conjure up a comic *Manfred,* he would have some insight into the nature of Byron's poise of spirit in *Don Juan*—neither merely equilibristic (whether or not as a function of tolerance and forgiveness, as McGann suggests), for that smacks of a Urizenic and hence deadly reconciliation, nor "counter-heroic" in its blend of "humanism and stoicism" as Cooke suggests,[39] but rather grandly heroic in its unflinching honesty, neither mawkish nor self-cripplingly, because self-consciously, confessional.

When the sea of Time and Space "poured in amain upon the Giants of Albion"—that is, the four Zoas and hence all mankind—"many of the Eternal Ones laughed after their manner" (*Jerusalem* 32:40–43). Byron's laughter is not much different, his perspective essentially the same, his realized helplessness in the face of man's glory as well as his folly and cruelty emerging now in the unflappable voice of the anti-satirist whose "spirit of genial sanity," as F. M. Cornford defined the temper of comedy,[40] precludes his falling back (at least for long) into the alluring arms of Romance and "poetry" as much as it rescues him from the self-satisfying rancor of conventional satire. If earlier Byron believed with Blake's Isaiah "that the voice of honest indignation is the voice of God,"[41] his new-found prophetic voice, though punctuated with indignation here and there, has modulated from God's to man's. He is no longer interested in removing mountains, however capable he is of a "firm perswasion," but only in sketching the "world exactly as it goes" (VIII.89).

And that brings me to my final point. It *is* the world that goes; the poet doesn't make it go, nor does he profess to understand why it goes like it does. The poem, then, formally embodies this going, Byron the "sketcher" merely observing (as well as being a part of) its going through uncolored glasses and creating a form which in its formlessness is an image of that going. As several other Byron scholars have pointed out, the poem thus is not only autonomously self-creating but also self-perpetuating. "I cannot stop to alter words once written," Byron confesses (*Don Juan* IX.77), seemingly adding to the sum of evidence for careless composition and verbal impetuosity (the famous tiger's leap). Yet the comment has less to do with the revision of language or image or meter than it does with the revision of Truth (capital "T") once it has spoken.

> I ne'er decide what I shall say, and this I call
>   Much too poetical: men should know why
> They write, and for what end; but, note or text,
> I never know the word which will come next. (IX.41)

The poem is not his fault—and in a sense not even his responsibility except as a kind of amanuensis.[42] If never deciding what one will say in his poem is "too poetical," deciding what to say and for what purpose must be the mode of prose, undifferentiable as always in Byron from satire. Unlike the simplistic dichotomy of truth and illusion, satire and Romance we saw in the early poems, this poem, at once "poetic" and anti-satiric, is now the truth self-revealed, kaleidoscopic and encyclopedic, Romantic and satiric, lyric and prophetic, epic and comic, serious and burlesque, all genres subsumed in no genre, sui generis. And Truth's "story" which "must / Tell for itself" (IX.77), "*will* be read" (X.28; Byron's italics) by the poet who in some sense is also the reader of his poem. Each canto and stanza and line and word become for him the as yet "unread events of time" (XI.90): "I tell the tale as it is told, nor dare / To venture a solution: 'Davus sum!' "—not Oedipus the unriddler (XIII.12–13). Once again, as so often in his poetry, Byron's self-quotation is marvellously revealing. In *Childish Recollections* Byron's name for his friend John Tattersall is Davus,

> For ever foremost in the ranks of fun,
> The laughing herald of the harmless pun;
> ....
> Candid and liberal, with a heart of steel
> In danger's path, though not untaught to feel. (ll. 265–72)

This extraordinary linking of Terence's dispassionate story-teller and the harmless laughing herald—modified by the paradoxical merriment of the death's-head—is as clear a definition of his own mode and mood in *Don Juan* as Byron ever gave us. The satirist in him, however, now submerged (or sublimated), continued to gnaw at his innards:

> If I sneer sometimes,
> It is because I cannot well do less,
>   And now and then it also suits my rhymes.
> I should be very willing to redress
>   Men's wrongs, and rather check than punish crimes; (XIII.8)

but, as Cervantes had demonstrated, "all such efforts fail." His muse now will be not a gadfly but a butterfly, which "hath but her wings, / Not strings, and flits through ether without aim" (XIII.89). And if he therefore "cannot fly," he can "yet flutter" (XV.27).

The butterfly image is a useful one, its erratic flight, momentariness of touchdowns, and airiness of its apparent unconcern match perfectly the kind of play that Byron means his poem to be: ". . . in my slight way I may proceed / To play upon the surface of humanity. / I write the world . . ." (XV.60)—or, better, the world writes itself through him. In that play is what Mark Schorer called, in a totally different context, a "moving splendor"[43] in the face of all truths, petty and apocalyptic. If he is not Oedipus nor was meant to be, there is a considerable heroism in such a triumphant yet precarious equanimity, pulsingly aware as it was of the steady, never fully repressible claims of a thinking mind and feeling heart. Their descendental and transcendental forays into the self-revelatory world of the poem are both under-cut by comic shiftings of focus from the matter to the medium of expression[44] whose anti-poetic outrages paradoxically preserve the truth from the self-righteousness of the satirist as well as from the self-indulgence of the poet of Romance.

In a celebrated passage in Canto IV Byron wrote: "And if I laugh at any mortal thing, / 'T is that I may not weep." But we too often forget that the passage continues: ". . . and if I weep, / 'T is that our nature cannot always bring / Itself to apathy." Needless to say, *Don Juan* is not an apathetic poem. Yet neither is it satiric, however much it may be epic in the various senses it has been defined as such from Paul Elmer More's day to ours. Even laughter is finally not its mode, nor Byron's aim. Though "the older that one grows / Inclines us more to laugh than scold" (*Beppo,* lxxix), laughter "leaves us so doubly serious shortly after." In its own way it smacks of the spleen he left behind so long ago—or stoops to mere burlesque.[45] Frank McConnell has recently tried to define the Byronic stance or mode of *Don Juan* as one of miser-like collection, assimilation, and "vacation" (somewhat in the sense of Paul West's idea of elimination and Byron's own well-known lava and earth-quake metaphor).[46] James Thompson, citing Byron's "lack of faith in the therapeutic nature of satire," defines the poem as "serious comic explora-tion."[47] These and other recent attempts to move us away from some satiric mold or formula into which we may comfortably pour *Don Juan* seem to me, whatever their intrinsic merit or persuasiveness, salutary developments. Eliot said that "to satirize humanity in general requires either a more genial talent than Byron's, such as that of Rabelais, or else a more profoundly tortured one, such as Swift's."[48] What I am arguing in a sense is that Byron has struggled his way toward that very geniality—not of Rabelais, perhaps, but surely at least like Sterne's. Perhaps genial is wrong, though it is close. Sincere maybe—the way Byron himself uses that word to describe Juan who, now in England, had learned "the art of living in all climes with ease":

> Sincere he was—at least you could not doubt it,
> In listening merely to his voice's tone.
> ....
> By nature soft, his whole address held off
> Suspicion: though not timid, his regard
> Was such as rather seem'd to keep aloof,
> To shield himself than put you on your guard:
> Perhaps 't was hardly quite assured enough,
> But modesty 's at times its own reward,
> Like virtue; and the absence of pretension
> Will go much farther than there's need to mention.
>
> Serene, accomplish'd, cheerful but not loud;
> Insinuating without insinuation;
> Observant of the foibles of the crowd
> ....
> . . . without a struggle for priority,
> He neither brook'd nor claim'd superiority. (xv. 11–15)

Having "felt and seen / That which humanity may bear, or bear not" (XIV. 49), Juan (and Byron) can with supreme self-control transmit to all of us "that true nature which sublimes / Whate'er it shows with truth" (XIV. 16). Cooke concludes that *Don Juan* does not result in a "final, all-encompassing serenity" (*Blind Man Traces the Circle,* p. 141). I think it does, if we understand that serenity to be a Blakean marriage of heaven and hell rather than a Wordsworthian coming to terms. If there is laughter in *Don Juan* it is ours, not Byron's, just as our tears or anger rise at the story-telling itself, not at any directed verdict by its transcriber. Byron aptly sees himself as "a moderate Presbyterian," not a pulpit thumper nor an atheist; his smiles "sincere or not at all" (xv. 91, 96).

His muse then was not Minerva after all, however much he may have wanted her to be; nor was his muse the upside-down "Muse etcetera" that he hails—but rather his own unique muse of serious play, poised precariously yet somehow sure-footedly on Truth's tightrope. Only such a muse could afford him the grand and moving compassion for the sad truths of the present that *Don Juan* in toto reveals to us as well as its uncorruptible and indestructible belief in the bright truths of the past—and at least perhaps the future. If the future's "full contents I do not give ye," Byron says, "it is because I do not know them yet" (XIV. 68). But he has, for man (for the future), "a modest hope" (xv. 22). The truth of the satirist and the truth of the poet of Romance have finally made their peace.

Notes

1. Jerome J. McGann, *"Don Juan" in Context* (Chicago and London: U. of Chicago Press, 1976), p. xii.

2. "The Non-Augustan Nature of Byron's Early 'Satires,' " *Revue des Langues Vivantes,* 34 (1968), 495–503. Leavis' view is in "Byron's Satire," *Revaluation* (New York: W. W. Norton, 1936), pp. 148–153.

3. "A Blueprint for *English Bards and Scotch Reviewers: The First Satire of Juvenal*," *Keats-Shelley Journal,* 19 (1970), 87–99.

4. See particularly Frye's introduction to the Byron selections in *Major British Writers,* rev. ed., ed. G. B. Harrison (New York: Harcourt Brace, 1959) and Eliot's essay on Byron in *On Poetry and Poets* (1943: rpt. New York: Noonday Press, 1961).

5. *Byron: A Survey* (London: Longman, 1975), p. 7.

6. See, e.g., Frye's *Anatomy of Criticism* (Princeton: Princeton U. Press, 1957); Robert Elliott's *The Power of Satire: Magic, Ritual, Art* (Princeton: Princeton U. Press, 1960); Ronald Knox's *Essays in Satire* (London: Sheed and Ward, 1928); Ronald Paulson's "A Theory of Satire" in his edited *Satire: Modern Essays in Criticism* (Englewood Cliffs, N.J.: Prentice Hall, 1971); Edward Rosenheim's "The Satiric Spectrum" in *ibid.;* David Worcester's *The Art of Satire* (Cambridge, Mass.: Harvard U. Press, 1940); Alvin Kernan's *The Plot of Satire* (New Haven: Yale U. Press, 1965); and Gilbert Highet's *The Anatomy of Satire* (Princeton: Princeton U. Press, 1962). See also the essay by W. Ruddick, "Don Juan in Search of Freedom: Byron's Emergence as a Satirist," in *Byron: A Symposium,* ed. J. Jump (London: The Macmillan Press, 1975), pp. 113–37. It is at least interesting to note, however, that in their anthology, *Satire* (Cleveland and New York: World Publishing Co., 1967), John Russell and Ashley Brown do not include any Byron.

7. (Chapel Hill: U. of North Carolina Press, 1925).

8. Jerome J. McGann, *Fiery Dust: Byron's Poetic Development* (Chicago: U. of Chicago Press, 1968), p. 75.

9. *"Don Juan" in Context.* The particular points referred to here are on pp. 15–17. See also what seems to me the more persuasive argument for Byron's assimilation and transformation of his classical satiric forebears in *Don Juan* in Frederick L. Beaty's "Byron's Imitations of Juvenal and Persius," *SiR,* 15 (1976), 333–55. All references to *Childe Harold's Pilgrimage* and *Don Juan* will be, as here, by canto and stanza numbers. The text used is *The Poetical Works of Byron,* rev. ed., intro. by Robert F. Gleckner, text by Paul E. More (Boston: Houghton Mifflin, 1975).

10. (Princeton: Princeton U. Press, 1969). See esp. Ch. IV.

11. Cf. George M. Ridenour's different interpretation of this poem in *The Style of "Don Juan"* (New Haven: Yale U. Press, 1960), pp. 92–93, as well as Cooke's in *The Blind Man Traces the Circle* (Princeton: Princeton University Press, 1969), pp. 91–92.

12. A measure of this triteness may be seen if we compare Byron's phrase to the rejuvenation accorded the same idea in Blake's "The Ecchoing Green."

13. Lines 37–38. He had made the same withdrawal earlier in "Childish Recollections": though "truth indignant" swell his bosom,

> Away with themes like this! . . .
> ....
> Let keener bards delight in satire's sting,
> My fancy soars not on Detraction's wing. (ll. 77–80)

14. *Byron and the Ruins of Paradise* (Baltimore: The Johns Hopkins U. Press, 1967), esp. Chs. 2–3.

15. Perhaps inspired by Moore's and Dallas' criticisms, Byron in a later appended note to stanza 12 of Canto II tried very hard to convince his reader of his "objectivity": "On this occasion I speak impartially. I am not a collector or admirer of collections, consequently no rival; but I have some early prepossession in favour of Greece, and do not think the honour of England advanced by plunder, whether of India or Attica." But though in a third note Byron even apologizes for a small error in an earlier note, his notes generally to this section of Canto II

are as unrelievedly scathing as the omitted or revised original stanzas 11–13 and the two unnumbered stanzas indicated in manuscript to follow stanza 13.

16. Cf. II.93, with its splendid opening lines: "Let such approach this consecrated land, / And pass in peace along the magic waste." The reference back to Elgin and his "despicable agents" is obvious.

17. One might recall here that Dryden's major premise in "A Discourse Concerning the Original and Progress of Satire" is that "satire originated in some sort of rude curse which manifests no more than the ill will of the speaker." Byron's effort in *The Curse* to lift himself beyond such rudeness is notable in itself.

18. "Nature, Art, Reason, and Imagination in *Childe Harold*," in *Romantic and Victorian*, ed. W. P. Elledge and R. L. Hoffman (Rutherford, N.J.: Fairleigh Dickinson U. Press, 1971), p. 157.

19. Cf. Blackstone's description of the poem as an amalgam of satire, description, polemic, apology, prophecy, and vision (*Byron: A Survey* [London: Longman, 1975], p. 59), though he seems unaware of the dramatically conceived structure Byron invents to try to achieve an harmonious amalgam.

20. Gleckner, *Byron and the Ruins of Paradise*, p. 116. For a fuller presentation and demonstration of the point I've summarized here, as well as Byron's care in the building of his multi-perspectived poem, see pp. 96–117.

21. *Meditations on Quixote* (New York: W. W. Norton, 1961), pp. 144–45. In fact Ortega's entire discussion of the ambiguity of "realism," the relationship of myth to fact and epic to comedy is pertinent to my point.

22. 1821 Journal (*Letters and Journals*, ed. R. E. Prothero [London: John Murray, 1901], v, 459).

23. Ibid., v, 457.

24. Andrew Rutherford, *Byron: A Critical Study* (Palo Alto: Stanford U. Press, 1961), p. 102.

25. *Byron the Poet* (London: Gollancz, 1964), p. 135.

26. *Byron* (London: Routledge & Kegan Paul, 1972), 91–92.

27. *Byron and the Ruins of Paradise*, pp. 301–07.

28. John Bull, *Letter to the Right Honorable Lord Byron* (London: William Wright, 1821).

29. For another echo of the skull image see *Childe Harold* IV.79. The death's-head "merriment" in a very real sense subsumes stanza 109 of Canto IV of *Childe Harold*: "Admire, exult—despise—laugh, weep,—for here / There is such matter for all feeling:—Man! / Thou pendulum betwixt a smile and tear." His substantial progress toward the equanimity I have been talking about can be measured by the fact that Byron's original version of the second line above was "Oh, ho, ho, ho—thou creature of a Man!"—perhaps a "slip" of his *Beppo* and *Don Juan* pen which was busily at work at the same time Canto IV of *Childe Harold* evolved.

30. "*Don Juan*" in Context, p. 123.

31. Cf. Cooke's comment on this stanza and his sense of Byron's diversion from Pyrrho (as well as Socrates, Hume, and Montaigne) in *The Blind Traces the Circle*, Ch. VI. One might also recall Byron's final "demotion" of Pyrrho to one of the supernumeraries who, to paraphrase Eliot in *Prufrock*, Byron uses to swell a progress, start a scene or two at the Amundevilles' gathering: "There was Lord Pyrrho, too, the great freethinker, / And Sir John Pottledeep, the mighty drinker" (XIII.84).

32. "*Don Juan*" in Context, p. 124.

33. Journal of November 1813, in Leslie A. Marchand, ed., *Byron's Letters and Journals* (Cambridge: Harvard U. Press, 1974), III, 209.

34. Marchand, *Letters and Journals*, IV, 125.

35. Willis Pratt uses this phrase in a different context in "Byron and Some Current Patterns of Thought," *The Major English Romantic Poets*, ed. C. D. Thorpe *et al.* (Carbondale: Southern Illinois U. Press, 1957), p. 151. Perhaps this is what Frye misses in the poem when

he speaks of the absence of any "sense of engagement or participation" or "moral involvement" on Byron's part (*Fables of Identity* [New York: Harcourt Brace, 1963], pp. 184, 187). On the other hand what he says elsewhere of *Tristram Shandy* as an "anatomy" seems to me pertinent to *Don Juan* ("Specific Continuous Forms" [from *The Anatomy of Criticism*] in *Perspectives on Fiction*, ed. J. L. Calderwood and H. E. Toliver [New York: Oxford U. Press, 1968], pp. 97–98).

36. Cf. McGann, *Fiery Dust*, p. 284.

37. The phrase is Michael Cooke's (*The Blind Man Traces the Circle*, p. 212) but his definition of it (as applied to Byron's *The Island*) seems to me to lean awkwardly on Lamb's essay "On the Artificial Comedy of the Last Century," in which such health is associated with an escape from "serious" drama's intense confirmation of our experience of reality and from "our coxcombical moral sense."

38. Plate 32[36], lines 51–54. Subsequent references to Blake will be thus, by plate and line number, as found in David V. Erdman's *The Poetry and Prose of William Blake* (Garden City: Doubleday & Co., 1965).

39. McGann, *Fiery Dust*, p. 296; Cooke, *The Blind Man Traces the Circle*, p. 181. Cf. Rutherford, *Byron: A Critical Study*, pp. 100–101.

40. *The Origins of Attic Comedy* (Garden City: Doubleday & Co., 1961), p. 184. Cooke at one point goes so far as to identify *Don Juan* as "satire manqué" (*The Blind Man Traces the Circle*, p. 145), but if that means as it seems to, that Byron is thus a satirist manqué, I cannot agree. His position is stronger and more "positive" than that. Perhaps mock-satiric? Indeed, Byron's own sense of at least the nonsatiric nature of *Don Juan* tends to be confirmed by several letters from Ravenna in the early 1820s in which he threatens to work up a new *English Bards and Scotch Reviewers* to attack the "fools" whose "nonsense" Murray insists on sending him. See, e.g., his letter to Murray of 24 September 1821 and, even better, the one of 9 October 1821 about his new *Vision of Judgment:* "I just piddle a little with these trifles to keep my hand in for the new *English Bards*, etc., which I perceive some of your people are in want of, and which I only wait for a short visit to your country . . . to commence. I have not *sought* it; but if I *do* begin, it shall go hard." The best that came out of his "early *English Bards* style" (letter to Hunt, 10 January 1823), though, was the lame and wooden *Age of Bronze*.

41. *The Marriage of Heaven and Hell*, Plate 12.

42. My point is certainly similar to, though obviously not identical with, Ricardo Quintana's definition of *Gulliver's Travels* as "situational satire": "Once the situation has been suggested, once its tone, its flavour have been given, it promptly takes command of itself and proceeds to grow and organize by virtue of its own inherent principles. . . . It is to be observed that the satirist is himself not involved: he is as much an observer, as much outside all the fuss and nonsense, as we are. . . . For the incidents which come to pass no one can be held responsible, any more than for the ideas and emotions which appear" ("Situation as Satirical Method," in Jonathan Swift, *Gulliver's Travels*, ed. Robert A. Greenberg [New York: W. W. Norton, 1961], p. 346—orig. pub. in *University of Toronto Quarterly*, 1948). It goes without saying that Byron is no Swift, nor wanted to be.

43. "Technique as Discovery," in *Perspectives on Fiction*, p. 216 (orig. pub. in *Hudson Review*, 1948).

44. This nice idea is Harriet MacKenzie's in *Byron's Laughter: In Life and Poetry* (Los Angeles: Lyman House, 1939), p. 147, though she seriously errs in applying it not to *Don Juan* but to *English Bards and Scotch Reviewers*.

45. A. B. England seems to me, finally, quite wrong in placing *Don Juan* in the tradition of Hudibrastic burlesque (*Byron's "Don Juan" and Eighteenth-Century Literature* [Lewisburg, Penn.: Bucknell U. Press, 1975]).

46. "Byron as Antipoet," in *Byron's Poetry*, ed. McConnell (New York: W. W. Norton, 1978), p. 423, orig. pub. as "Byron's Reductions: 'Much Too Poetical,' " *ELH*, 1970. Cf. West's *Byron and the Spoiler's Art* (London: Chatto & Windus, 1960).

47. "Byron's Plays and *Don Juan*," in McConnell, *Byron's Poetry*, p. 415 (orig. pub. in

Bucknell Review, 1967). I might also mention Cooke's casting about for a "definition" in "Byron's *Don Juan:* The Obsession and Self-Discipline of Spontaneity," *SiR,* 14 (1975), where *Don Juan* is "an epical elegy tinged with mythical and translunary vision" (p. 294), "a generic hybrid confession and satire, in epic guise" (p. 295), "a compound of plangent skepticism and sardonic merriment and undying dreams of human magnificence" and hence a poem that "falls somewhere between the picaresque and the *Bildungsroman*" (p. 302).

    48. *On Poetry and Poets,* p. 237.

Editor's Bibliographical Note

The critical literature on *Don Juan* is, of course, enormous and I need not recapitulate what is presented elsewhere in this volume, in the introduction and bibliographical notes (especially but not exclusively those to Ridenour's essay). I shall content myself here, then, with pointing the reader back to the footnotes in my essay as well as pointing to those other contributions to the study of *Don Juan* that, in my judgment, advance our understanding of its particular and, as I suggest in my essay, sui generis brand of satire. Works already cited in my essay's notes will be included by author's last name and date here to indicate critical continuities.

    Certainly the first major works of this kind, still useful though critically conventional, are Elizabeth Boyd, *Byron's "Don Juan"* (New Brunswick: Rutgers University Press, 1945), and Paul S. Trueblood, *The Flowering of Byron's Genius* (Palo Alto: Stanford University Press, 1945), neither of which was succeeded valuably until Ridenour's seminal *The Style of "Don Juan"* and its host of successors in the great decade of the sixties. The most useful of those for the study of *Don Juan* as satire are, in chronological order, the books by Rutherford (1961), William H. Marshall (*The Structure of Byron's Major Poems* [Philadelphia: University of Pennsylvania Press, 1962]), E.E. Bostetter (*The Romantic Ventriloquists* [Seattle: University of Washington Press, 1963]), Joseph (1964), Kernan (1965), McGann (1968; even more important his 1976 *"Don Juan" in Context*), and Cooke (*Blind Man,* 1969). While there have been other critical books and articles in the last 20 years, none, it seems to me, fully measure up to these except for Beatty's *Byron's Don Juan* and Frederick Garber's *Self, Text, and Romantic Irony* (Princeton: Princeton University Press, 1988). Also recent is Frederick L. Beaty's, *Byron the Satirist* (DeKalb: Northern Illinois University Press, 1985), which supercedes in all ways Fuess's early book, *Byron as a Satirist in Verse* (New York: Columbia University Press, 1912).

    In addition to Beaty's treatment of *The Vision of Judgment,* however, the following should also be consulted: John D. Jump, "Byron's *Vision of Judgment,*" *Bulletin of the John Rylands Library* 51 (1968): 122–36; William Walling, "Tradition and Revolution: Byron's *Vision of Judgment,*" *The Wordsworth Circle* 3 (1972): 223–31; Stuart Peterfreund, "The Politics of 'Neutral Space' in Byron's *Vision of Judgment,*" *Modern Language Quarterly* 40 (1979): 275–91; Peter T. Murphy, "Vision of Success: Byron and Southey," *Studies in Romanticism* 24 (1985): 355–73; and Edward T. Duffy, "Byron Representing Himself against Southey," in *History and Myth,* ed. S. C. Behrendt (Detroit: Wayne State University Press, 1990), 188–201. See also Jerome Christensen's "*Marino Faliero* and the Fault of Byron's Satire," *Studies in Romanticism* 24 (1985): 313–33.

    With my somewhat narrower view of Byron's career in this essay, compare the more capacious analyses by the Byron critics of the sixties, especially Marshall, Joseph, McGann, and Cooke—and, more recently, Manning, McGann (*Beauty of Inflections* [Oxford: Clarendon Press, 1985]), Reiman, and Garber (all of whose works appear in excerpts in this volume). And see also Christensen's essay reprinted later in this book.

Don Juan and Byron's Imperceptiveness
to the English Word

Peter J. Manning

In a famous essay which mixes praise and contempt in characteristic fashion, T. S. Eliot observed in 1937: "Of Byron one can say, as of no other English poet of his eminence, that he added nothing to the language, that he discovered nothing in the sounds, and developed nothing in the meaning, of individual words. I cannot think of any poet of his distinction who might so easily have been an accomplished foreigner writing English."[1] From this stigma of "imperceptiveness . . . to the English word" Byron and Byron criticism have yet wholly to recover.[2] The condemnation is best challenged by examining the assumptions on which it rests.

Eliot's privileging of the word is true to his symbolist heritage. Implicit in the negative verdict on Byron is the recommendation of an evocative poetry, one that gathers itself into a dense concentration of almost magically suggestive power, a poetry marked by moments at which meaning seems to overflow mere connotation, by nodal points at which meanings accumulated throughout an entire work converge and are released. The sense of an investment of meaning beyond the capacity of words creates a brief illusion of intensity and inclusiveness. A standard that invokes the word thus tends to acquire the hieratic associations of the Word, the authoritative utterance in which not only meaning but also being seem actually to reside. For Coleridge, the most reflective theorist of this mode among the English Romantics, symbolism was, as J. Robert Barth has recently reiterated, intimately bound up with a sacramental view of the world.[3] At its extreme, however, Eliot's position values the single pregnant phrase, the resonant, gnomic aphorism. Keats's Grecian Urn, animated by the inquiries of its beholder, itself speaks only teasingly or remains silent. Unheard melodies can be judged sweeter than real ones because with them the gap between signifier and signified is widest, and the power of suggestion verges therefore on the infinite.

Other premises for poetry are possible, and attitudes other than awed contemplation are appropriate ends. One could sketch a poetics based not on the word but on words: that is, not on the charge granted the individual

Studies in Romanticism 18 (Summer 1979): 207–33. Courtesy of the Trustees of Boston University.

word (whether through special diction, as the focus of an imagistic or narrative pattern, or by an aura of numinous presence), but on the relationship between words in themselves unremarkable. In contrast to Eliot's bias toward the symbolic, hence the static, one might urge the disjunctive and the dynamic; in place of Eliot's favoring of "full" speech, one might posit a discourse based on absence, one that never offers the consolations of climax or comprehensiveness, never holds forth the promise of an order suddenly made manifest. *Don Juan* exemplifies these procedures, and its richness refutes Eliot's judgment of "this imperceptiveness of Byron's to the English word" by revealing the narrowness of Eliot's criteria. I shall argue that it is precisely in proportion to his refusal to exalt the individual word that Byron is able to display the multiple functions of language itself.

I

The language of *Don Juan* can be approached through the role of language as it is conceptualized *in* the poem. The most satisfying starting-point is paradoxically a scene in which language is unnecessary, Byron's depiction of the embrace of Juan and Haidée. "They had not spoken; but they felt allured, / As if their souls and lips each other beckon'd," the narrator observes (II. 187):

> They fear'd no eyes nor ears on that lone beach,
> They felt no terrors from the night, they were
> All in all to each other: though their speech
> Was broken words, they *thought* a language there,—
> And all the burning tongues the passions teach
> Found in one sigh the best interpreter
> Of nature's oracle—first love,—that all
> Which Eve has left her daughters since her fall. (II. 189)

Byron develops the theme of Juan's and Haidée's ability to communicate without the mediation of words from the moment that Juan arrives on the island. Haidée, infatuated with her handsome shipwrecked guest, imagines that Juan calls to her, though he is asleep: "she thought . . . He had pronounced her name—but she forgot / That at this moment Juan knew it not" (II. 135). Conversation remains impossible even when Juan revives because Juan and Haidée have no common language, but that barrier proves crossable. "Her eyes were eloquent," comments the narrator on Juan's bewilderment by Haidée's Romaic, even if "her words would pose" (II. 150):

> Now Juan could not understand a word,
> Being no Grecian; but he had an ear,
> And her voice was the warble of a bird,
> So soft, so sweet, so delicately clear,

> That finer, simpler music ne'er was heard;
> The sort of sound we echo with a tear,
> Without knowing why—an overpowering tone,
> Whence Melody descends as from a throne. (II. 151)

This characterization of Haidée's voice presents a familiar Romantic figure, at once pathetic and sublime. Voice is here an absolute presence, capable of doing without the agency of words and directly inspiring a response from its hearers. The less Haidée and Juan can talk, the more intensely they share:

> And then fair Haidée tried her tongue at speaking,
> But not a word could Juan comprehend,
> Although he listen'd so that the young Greek in
> Her earnestness would ne'er have made an end. (II. 161)

Freedom from language becomes the very mark of intimacy:

> And then she had recourse to nods, and signs,
> And smiles, and sparkles of the speaking eye,
> And read (the only book she could) the lines
> Of his fair face, and found, by sympathy,
> The answer eloquent, where the soul shines
> And darts in one quick glance a long reply;
> And thus in every look she saw exprest
> A world of words, and things at which she guess'd.
>
> And now, by dint of fingers and of eyes,
> And words repeated after her, he took
> A lesson in her tongue; but by surmise,
> No doubt, less of her language than her look:
> As he who studies fervently the skies
> Turns oftener to the stars than to his book,
> Thus Juan learn'd his alpha beta better
> From Haidée's glance than any graven letter. (II. 162–63)

Just before the return of Lambro brings it to an end Byron presents again the preternatural harmony between Juan and Haidée:

> The gentle pressure, and the thrilling touch,
> The least glance better understood than words,
> Which still said all, and ne'er could say too much;
> A language, too, but like to that of birds,
> Known but to them, at least appearing such
> As but to lovers a true sense affords;
> Sweet playful phrases, which would seem absurd
> To those who have ceased to hear such, or ne'er heard. . . . (IV. 14)

The poem puts forward two analogies to the communion that ordinary language is too clumsy to express. The first is mythical and honorific: "They were alone once more; for them to be / Thus was another Eden" (iv. 10). Byron delineates the privacy of Juan and Haidée as a mutual transparency, a vision of complete reciprocal love seemingly prior to the fall into selfhood. This formulation is co-ordinate with another of differing tenor; the poem continues: "All these were theirs, for they were children still, / And children still they should have been" (iv. 15). The second analogy introduces an infantile coloring into the paradisal scene.

Haidée and Juan both appear as children to the narrator, enmeshed in a bewildering adult world, but within the story their roles are clearly distinguished: Haidée functions as the mother of the infantile Juan. Famished and half-drowned, Juan is reborn from the sea and nursed back to health in Haidée's warm, well-provisioned, and womb-like cave. As the weakened Juan sleeps, Haidée "bent o'er him, and he lay beneath, / Hush'd as the babe upon its mother's breast" (ii. 148); when he revives, Haidée, "who watch'd him like a mother, would have fed / Him past all bounds" (ii. 158).

These similes and the narrative configuration in which they occur place the ideal wordlessness of Haidée and Juan in parallel to the symbiotic union of mother and infant, at that early stage of human development before the infant comes to see himself as separate from the mother. Language at this level is a secret and subtle bond, a process of ceaseless and delicate adjustment, of needs understood and gratified before they are expressed. The figurative identification of the erotic sublime, as it were, with the dyad of mother and infant has important consequences for the conceptualization of language in *Don Juan*.

Juan participates briefly in a state anterior to the formation of an independent identity, but this fantasy of boundary-less bliss conflicts with the continued integrity of the adult who imagines it. To aspire toward the condition of Haidée and Juan carries the threat of self-abolition: to an autonomous being the idealized fusion is equivalent to a dangerous dissolution.[4] Inevitably, the beloved Haidée is therefore also a figure of death. As many critics have remarked, ominous overtones surround her from the moment of her introduction:

> Her hair, I said, was auburn; but her eyes
> Were black as death, their lashes the same hue,
> Of downcast length, in whose silk shadow lies
> Deepest attraction, for when to the view
> Forth from its raven fringe the full glance flies,
> Ne'er with such force the swiftest arrow flew;
> 'Tis as the snake late coil'd, who pours his length,
> And hurls at once his venom and his strength. (ii. 117)

Even Haidée's most maternally protective gestures bear, in exact relation to their nurturing power, vampiric suggestions:

> And then she stopp'd, and stood as if in awe,
> (For sleep is awful) and on tiptoe crept
> And wrapt him closer, lest the air, too raw,
> Should reach his blood, then o'er him still as death
> Bent, with hush'd lips, that drank his scarce-drawn breath. (II. 143)

These sinister aspects are reinforced by the two other instances of wordlessness in *Don Juan* with which the episode of Haidée and Juan is thematically connected. The first concerns the grotesque "misshapen pigmies, deaf and dumb" (v.88), who guard Gulbeyaz's door:

> Their duty was—for they were strong, and though
> They looked so little, did strong things at times—
> To ope this door, which they could really do,
> The hinges being as smooth as Rogers' rhymes;
> And now and then with tough strings of the bow,
> As is the custom of those eastern climes,
> To give some rebel Pacha a cravat;
> For mutes are generally used for that.
>
> They spoke by signs—that is, not spoke at all; (v.89–90)

Through the seemingly capricious comparison with the verse of Samuel Rogers, Byron links "smooth" writing to muteness and death, while the slant rhyme of "do" with "though" and "bow" makes clear that he himself rates lithe movement above euphony.[5] The conversation between Juan and General Lascy during the battle of Ismail displays a second, but different, linking of speechlessness and death; this exchange, like that between Juan and Haidée, is marked by linguistic incompatibility.

> Juan, to whom he spoke in German, knew
> As much of German as of Sanscrit, and
> In answer made an inclination to
> The General who held him in command;
> ....
> Short speeches pass between two men who speak
> No common language; and besides, in time
> Of war and taking towns, when many a shriek
> Rings o'er the dialogue, and many a crime
> Is perpetrated ere a word can break
> Upon the ear, and sounds of horror chime

In like church bells, with sigh, howl, groan, yell, prayer,
There cannot be much conversation there. (VIII.57–58)

Byron's description of Juan's enthusiasm for battle recalls several features of the episode of Juan and Haidée and so brings the two episodes into
relationship:

> —I say not *the* first
> But of the first, our little friend Don Juan
> Walked o'er the walls of Ismail, as if nurst
> Amidst such scenes—though this was quite a new one
> To him, and I should hope to *most.* The thirst
> Of glory, which so pierces through and through one,
> Pervaded him—although a generous creature,
> As warm in heart as feminine in feature.
>
> And here he was—*who upon Woman's breast,*
> *Even from a child, felt like a child;* howe'er
> The man in all the rest might be confest,
> To him it was Elysium to be there;
> And he could even withstand that awkward test
> Which Rousseau points out to the dubious fair,
> "Observe your lover when he *leaves* your arms";
> But Juan never left them, while they had charms,
>
> Unless compelled by fate, or wave, or wind,
> Or near relations, who are much the same.
> (VIII.52–54; italics added in 53)

The end of this sequence reminds the reader of Juan's enforced departure from
Julia as well as from Haidée, and the incongruity of echoing Juan's amorous
exploits in the midst of carnage is Byron's means of reinforcing the fundamental kinship of the opposites. Juan is "nursed" in battle as he is nursed by
Haidée; for Juan to be alone with Haidée "was another Eden" (IV. 10), and for
him to be fighting "was Elysium" (VIII.53). Byron announces "fierce loves
and faithless wars" (VII.8) as his subject, and the reversal of Spenser is
possible because at one level love and war function identically. The link
between the two actions is passion, etymologically the root of passivity.
Juan's much-remarked passivity might be considered as the annulment of
psychological distance, the consequence of an overwhelming presence. The
thirst for glory "pervades" Juan, or, to cite the *O.E.D.* definitions, it diffuses
and spreads through or into every part of him, it permeates and saturates
him. Common to the intensity of war and love is an obliteration of detachment, and, as the introduction of the configuration both here and in the

Haidée episode insinuates, the prototype of this experience, erasing the outlines of the self, is the fusion of infant and mother.

The fantasy of fusion is situated at two poles: it is a fantasy of origins, of mother and infant, and it returns as a fantasy of prospective conclusions in sexual union, or in war and death. These become prominent in Byron's portrayal of the lustful Empress Catherine whose troops destroy Ismail. Catherine's infatuation with Juan establishes the equivalence of the "oh!" of sexual joy and the "ah!" of misery:

> Oh Catherine! (for of all interjections
> To thee both *oh!* and *ah!* belong of right
> In love and war) how odd are the connections
> Of human thoughts, which jostle in their flight!
> Just now *your's* were cut out in different sections:
> *First* Ismail's capture caught your fancy quite;
> *Next* of new knights, the fresh and glorious hatch;
> And thirdly, he who brought you the dispatch! (IX.65)

Byron began the description of Catherine by expanding upon Horace's ascription of war to sexual passion: "nam fuit ante Helenam cunnus taeterrima belli / causa" (Satire I.3.107–08). The *double entendres* of that passage are not more remarkable than its insistence that the gate of life and death is one:

> Oh, thou "teterrima Causa" of all "belli"—
> Thou gate of Life and Death—thou nondescript!
> Whence is our exit and our entrance,—well I
> May pause in pondering how all Souls are dipt
> In thy perennial fountain:—how man fell, I
> Know not, since Knowledge saw her branches stript
> Of her first fruit; but how he falls and rises
> *Since, Thou* hast settled beyond all surmises.
>
> Some call thee "the worst Cause of war," but I
> Maintain thou art the *best:* for after all
> From thee we come, to thee we go,·and why
> To get at thee not batter down a wall,
> Or waste a world? Since no one can deny
> Thou dost replenish worlds both great and small:
> With, or without thee, all things at a stand
> Are, or would be, thou Sea of Life's dry Land!
>
> Catherine, who was the grand Epitome
> Of that great Cause of war, or peace, or what
> You please (it causes all things which be,
> So you may take your choice of this or that)—(IX.55–57)

Catherine, at once aggression and sexual passion, birth and death, source and end, is an image of woman as the terrifying and engulfing force who must be resisted. The light she retrospectively casts alters the impression made by Juan and Haidée. Their intimacy offers the sole example of complete communication in *Don Juan,* and Byron's treatment of it, in itself and as part of the series culminating in Catherine, suggests how the fantasy union presses toward a lethal silence. Catherine's Russian is as foreign to Juan as Haidée's Romaic, nor does Catherine speak directly in the poem. If Haidée and Juan transcend the usual barriers of the self, the poem also delineates the limitations inherent in their ecstasy. Insofar as their love is perfect it is finished, incapable of development: "for they were children still, / And children still they should have been" (IV. 15). Haidée and Juan reach a state of atemporal happiness, but from the human perspective such freedom from time is stasis and death. The narrator observes as Haidée and Juan join their lives on the beach that she

> had nought to fear,
> Hope, care, nor love beyond, her heart beat *here.*
>
> And oh! that quickening of the heart, that beat!
> How much it costs us! (II.202–03)

What the illusion of the all-encompassing *here* costs is the past and still more the future, the change of the self in time. The totality of Juan's and Haidée's passion is a fearful exclusion, but the countervailing claims of the life they sublimely reject are kept before the reader by the interventions of the narrator. He enables us to perceive that the fantasy of full speech and full understanding, with its attendant values of wholeness, presence, and atemporality, is not an isolated ideal: the thematic networks within which it exists in *Don Juan* expose its connection with silence and the death silence figures. Juan's passion annihilates him on the breast of Haidée, and an ultimate value of silence brings to an end the role of the poet. The narrator and Juan, the poet and the character, are equally endangered: the Latin root of "infant" means "he who does not speak." The episode of Haidée and Juan is Byron's version of the *Ode on a Grecian Urn:* in Byron's meditation on his lovers, as in Keats's, the values of an encompassing, symbolic, finally static imagination are set against the humbler commitments and narrative imaginings of the speaker himself. Both poets at last withdraw from the potent ideal they have imagined—the figures on the urn, Juan and Haidée—to face the imperfections of "breathing human passion." But whereas Keats throughout his career remains uncertain what language to put in place of the ennobling fictions of epic and romance that he repeatedly elaborated only to reject, Byron deploys a language which acknowledges and enacts the inescapable facts of absence and loss while affirming human vitality. "You have so many 'divine' poems,"

Byron vexedly exclaimed to his publisher, "is it nothing to have written a *Human* one?"[6] The style of *Don Juan* is co-ordinate with the role of speech in the poem: it is best studied through the plot it represents.

II

Somewhat later in his essay on Byron, Eliot turns to "a long passage of self-portraiture from *Lara*" already singled out by Charles Du Bos in *Byron et la besoin de la fatalité* and declares: "Du Bos deserves full credit for recognizing its importance; and Byron deserves all the credit that Du Bos gives him for having written it. This passage strikes me also as a masterpiece of self-analysis, but of a self that is largely a deliberate fabrication—a fabrication that is only completed in the actual writing of the lines. The reason why Byron understood this self so well, is that it is largely his own invention; and it is only the self that he invented that he understood perfectly." Eliot here brilliantly specifies the self-creation Byron wrought in the Byronic hero, but the creation was not wholly uncontingent. If the Byronic hero was no simple transcription of Byron but a fabrication, it was nonetheless a fiction responsive to the fears and desires of its author. The role required of the Byronic hero is displayed in the relationship in *Don Juan* between Juan and Lara's descendant, Haidée's father Lambro.

At first glance Lambro functions merely as a *senex* who intrudes upon the lovers and puts an end to their happiness. Insofar as Haidée's love imperils Juan, however, Lambro is also a savior who rescues Juan from an absorption he is too weak to withstand. Byron's two heroes are the opposing faces of a single figure (biographically, Juan embodies parts of Byron's childhood and Lambro, returning to his shattered home, expresses aspects of Byron's response to his broken marriage—see, e.g., III.51–52). *Don Juan* presents in the temporal sequence of drama the continuum of a psychological strategy: the stern warrior is the protagonist Byron generates to preserve the passive child from collapsing back into his mother. Alfonso's interruption of Juan's affair with Julia in Canto I operates as a similarly providential occurrence, because Juan risks being crushed by the older women for whom he has become the pawn; his mother, Inez, who contrived at the affair for her own reasons, and Julia, suddenly transformed at the end of the canto from a sympathetically self-deceiving lover into a skillfully deceitful intriguer.[7]

As the defense Julia makes on the night the lovers are discovered (I.145–47) reaches its climax, Byron's rhetoric rises toward the sublime: ". . . pale / She lay, her dark eyes flashing through their tears, / Like skies that rain and lighten" (I.158). While the tide of Julia's apology breaks over Alfonso and his posse Juan lies inert, hidden in the bed between Julia and her maid, "half-smother'd" (I.165), in danger of "suffocation by that pretty pair"

(I. 166). Here as elsewhere in *Don Juan,* the powerful speech of others is a menace to the hero.

The erotic triangle in both these episodes bears unmistakable Oedipal overtones, and in both the function of the father-figure as a principle of difference is apparent. By forcibly separating Juan from the mother whose love overwhelms him, Lambro, like Alfonso before him, makes possible Juan's independence. Moreover, even as the child models his identity on the father whom he cannot supplant, so Juan asserts himself in responding to this older rival. Attacked by Alfonso, Juan is driven to act: "His blood was up: though young, he was a Tartar, / And not at all disposed to prove a martyr" (I. 184). So too, after his weakness and silence in Canto II and his position in Canto III as Haidée's consort, dependent on her for wealth and status, Juan achieves a brief autonomy in his defiance of Lambro: " 'Young man, your sword'; so Lambro once more said: / Juan replied, 'Not while this arm is free' " (IV. 40). This confrontation is virtually the first time that Byron presents Juan in direct discourse, and his speech is the proof of his temporary self-sufficiency.[8]

When Lambro overcomes Juan and casts him forth he sets in renewed motion the oscillating and ambiguous journey whose curves shape *Don Juan.* In his passivity Juan falls into a repetitive series at each stage of which he is almost absorbed by a dominating woman—Julia, Haidée, the "imperious" Gulbeyaz, the devouring Catherine, the "full-blown" Fitz-Fulke, and Adeline, "the fair most fatal Juan ever met" (XIII. 12); circumstances free him from her, but only to propel him toward the subsequent lapse. The journey is ambiguous because this potentially deadly woman, mother and lover, is a figure of desire and because Juan's freedom consists only of this endless chain of disruptions and losses.

Two alternatives to this dilemma would seem to exist in *Don Juan.* One is typified by Lambro, whose isolated marauding life and coolly powerful manner show him as the avatar of the hero who fills Byron's earlier works. The absolute masculine will with which Lambro crushes Juan and re-establishes his priority, however, *Don Juan* exposes as no solution at all. His contest is depicted by the narrative as more with Haidée herself than with her love-object. Haidée's resistance to Lambro (IV. 44–45) is uncolored by the irony with which Byron tinges Juan's and the extended pathetic description of her death (IV. 54–71) completes the eclipse of Juan's moment of bravery. In exerting his authority over Haidée, Lambro destroys the peace of his home: the desolate fate he brings on his island and himself (IV. 72) reveals that he too cannot exist apart from the mother-figure. The second solution is embodied in the narrator, who is not so much in the story as above it, but whose words are shaped by the same exigencies as those his story witnesses.

Don Juan locates the origin of language in the Edenic harmony of mother and child: Haidée teaches Juan his "alpha beta" (II. 163). The narrator develops the myth from his own experience:

> 'Tis pleasing to be school'd in a strange tongue
> By female lips and eyes—that is, I mean,
> When both the teacher and the taught are young,
> As was the case, at least, where I have been;
> They smile so when one's right, and when one's wrong
> They smile still more, and then there intervene
> Pressure of hands, perhaps even a chaste kiss;—
> I learn'd the little that I know by this: (II.164)

Language here figures as innately sexualized: talk is desire. Byron underscores the connection in writing of Italy in *Beppo:*

> I love the language, that soft bastard Latin,
> Which melts like kisses from a female mouth,
> And sounds as if it should be writ on satin,
> With syllables which breathe of the sweet South,
> And gentle liquids gliding all so pat in,
> That not a single accent seems uncouth,
> Like our own harsh, northern whistling, grunting guttural,
> Which we're obliged to hiss, and spit, and sputter all.
>
> I like the women too. . . . (44–45)

Yet the consummation of the desire for women must be resisted, deferred, because it would annihilate the poet's voice. As the puns on death and dying in Elizabethan poetry reveal, orgasm is "the little death." It is also, as a rejected stanza of *Don Juan* suggests, a phenomenon literally beyond language:

> But Oh! that I were dead—for while alive—
> Would that I ne'er had loved—Oh Woman—Woman—
> All that I write or wrote can ne'er revive
> To paint a sole sensation—though quite common—
> Of those in which the Body seemed to drive
> My soul from out me at thy single summon
> Expiring in the hope of sensation. . . . (XVII.13)

Juan's career and the narrator's reflections thus place language between two equally dangerous termini, both of which are approached with desire yet self-protectively put off. At one extreme looms the power of erotic bliss to annul self and voice, at the other the similar threat of the fusion of infant with mother.

In this schema language exists as the unresolved middle between the states that would abrogate it. Moreover, this middle is a middle of repetitions, for the story *Don Juan* tells is of the loss of the desired object in the necessary separation from her, the yearning for her, and the fresh flight from her. Human existence, as the poem sees it, perpetually re-enacts the primary liberating catastrophe of separation. A repetition is also a re-petition, a re-asking: the repetitions of the poem set forth again and again the mournful questions "How did I become separate?" "Who am I?" Women as much as men exemplify the pattern: once begun, they too must re-enact their initiating gesture:

> In her first passion woman loves her lover,
> In all the others all she loves is love,
> Which grows a habit she can ne'er get over,
> And fits her loosely—like an easy glove,
> As you may find, whene'er you like to prove her:
> One man alone at first her heart can move;
> She then prefers him in the plural number,
> Not finding that the additions much encumber.
>
> I know not if the fault be men's or theirs;
> But one thing's pretty sure; a woman planted—
> (Unless at once she plunge for life in prayers)—
> After a decent time must be gallanted;
> Although, no doubt, her first of love affairs
> Is that to which her heart is wholly granted;
> Yet there are some, they say, who have had *none*,
> But those who have ne'er end with only *one*. (III.3–4)

The last stanza illustrates the every-varying inter-penetrations of the story level and the narrative commentary in *Don Juan,* the two aspects Robert Escarpit has distinguished as "le temps fictif" and "le temps psychologique."[9] This inter-penetration breaks down any simple distinction between the story and its telling: there is only the modulation of language. The narrator's seemingly unmotivated generalization recalls Julia, banished to a convent a canto earlier, and her imposed constancy is the fate his fluid mode avoids. Juan vows eternal fidelity:

> "And oh! if e'er I should forget, I swear—
> But that's impossible, and cannot be—
> Sooner shall this blue ocean melt itself to air,
> Sooner shall earth resolve itself to sea,
> Than I resign thine image, Oh! my fair!
> Or think of anything excepting thee; (II.19)

This protestation is notoriously interrupted by retching, and happily, for Juan's romantic dedication to a single image is the willed counterpart to Julia's unwilling stasis. Juan can go forward because he forgets, and because he is prevented from ever looking back. Similarly, Byron's refusal to linger over the episode of Juan and Haidée is a refusal of fixation, a refusal of the seductions of completion and finality. He writes their story not as a self-contained heroico-pathetic romance like his own earlier tales, but as part of an ongoing narrative whose rhythms undo the authority both of its dreams of bliss and of its conclusion. Byron repudiates his own temptation by the totalizing fantasy of Juan and Haidée (IV.52–53, 74), passionate union or faithful death, to affirm the vital multiplicity of his own independent existence: not for him the diminishing pledge not to "think of anything else, excepting thee." In so doing he restores the intermediate space in which language (and hence his poem) can continue to exist. The space is empty, and marked by absence and lack, but it is an emptiness that invites filling by the imagination of the poet.

III

At the end of the first canto of *Don Juan* Byron threatens to promulgate a definitive set of "poetical commandments": "I'll call the work 'Longinus o'er a Bottle, / Or, Every Poet his *own* Aristotle'" (I.204). In no respect does Byron differ more greatly from the rules than in his departure from the Aristotelean precept that a work of literature should have a beginning, a middle, and an end: *Don Juan* is all middle. The epic conventionally begins *in medias res,* but at the actual middle point of epic is a stabilizing device, a place about which the story can be organized: Odysseus narrating his adventures, Aeneas describing the fall of Troy to Dido, Raphael recounting the war in Heaven to Adam and Eve as an instructive example. In *Don Juan,* however, the condition of unfinishedness is not merely an aspect of the story, a temporary fiction exposed when the whole is complete, but one that attaches to the poet himself and influences the ongoing creation of his text.

 The lines of *Don Juan* which the notion of indeterminacy perhaps first brings to mind are the melodramatic ones at the end of Canto XV:

> Between two worlds life hovers like a star,
> 'Twixt night and morn, upon the horizon's verge:
> How little do we know that which we are!
> How less what we may be! (XV.99)

This fundamental unsettledness speaks in other tones as well:

> Of all the barbarous Middle Ages, that
> Which is the most barbarous is the middle age
> Of man; it is—I really scarce know what;
> But when we hover between fool and sage,
> And don't know justly what we would be at,—
> A period something like a printed page,

> Black letter upon foolscap, while our hair
> Grows grizzled, and we are not what we were,—
>
> Too old for youth,—too young, at thirty-five,
> To herd with boys, or hoard with good threescore,—
> I wonder people should be left alive;
> But since they are, that epoch is a bore: (XII. 1–2)

This reflection has been prepared for by the allusions to Dante in the previous cantos (e.g., X.27), but Byron transforms the tradition that thirty-five, as the midpoint of man's allotted span of years, is a moment of decision; the era which in *The Divine Comedy* marks a crisis becomes in *Don Juan* a particularly anomalous stage in which meaningful choice seems impossible. The stanzas connect the uncertainties of middle life directly to the paradoxes of a text— "A period something like a printed page, / Black letter upon white foolscap"—and this odd conjunction recurs at the opening of the fifteenth canto, where Byron opposes the fertile indeterminacy of his text to the brevity of life and the blankness of boredom:

> Ah! What should follow slips from my reflection:
> Whatever follows ne'ertheless may be
> As àpropos of hope or retrospection,
> As though the lurking thought had follow'd free.
> All present life is but an Interjection,
> An "Oh!" or "Ah!" of joy or misery,
> Or a "Ha! ha!" or "Bah!" a yawn, or "pooh!"
> Of which perhaps the latter is most true.
>
> But, more or less, the whole's a syncope
> Or a singultus—emblems of Emotion,
> The grand Antithesis to great Ennui, (XV. 1–2)

Here is another form of the paradox already noted. The contradiction recurs, for the "syncope" of emotion which combats boredom itself abolishes consciousness: a syncope is also the loss of syllables and sounds in the middle of a word, hence also the emblem of the cutting-short of the poet's voice. The sexual overtones of the "Oh!" of "Joy" and their equivalence to the "Ah!" of "Misery" recall the dangerous themes previously developed in the portrait of Catherine (see IX.65 quoted above).

The intermediate position *Don Juan* occupies thus appears as a positive *modus vivendi*. The repeated suspension of the story functions on two levels. Juan is caught between infantile unconsciousness and sexual self-annihilation, and the poem's interruption of all his affairs corresponds to a refusal to allow passion its obliterating force. The narrator, yearning for both states, is also caught between his lost youth ("No more—no more—Oh! never more on me / The freshness of the heart can fall like dew" [I.214]), and a future which must ultimately be death. His refusal to treat life according to the familiar pattern of crisis-autobiography is a dissent from the notion of a fixed identity, of a life stiffening into shape once and for all, just as his refusal to precipitate a single final meaning is a mode of ensuring the inexhaustible vitality of his text. On both levels he is committed to filling the empty present, to staving off closure at any cost: "the past tense, / The dreary 'Fuimus' of all things human," which "must be declined" (XIII.40), must be resisted as long as possible. The pun on "decline" again links life and language by operating brilliantly in both contexts. The poem's insistence on its own indeterminacy and arbitrariness is its style of freedom: by rejecting the points of fullness, origin and end, Byron devotes himself to a discourse of absences, fragments, and losses which can yet keep the moment open.

The characteristic mode of this discourse is excursive, associative, metonymic, in contrast to the kind of metaphoric, symbolic concentration lauded by Eliot. As we have seen, Byron's resistance to such nodes of convergence is a matter both of substance and of technique: he denies the fatal power of certain meanings by continuing past them, and refuses permanence to identifications and identity. *Don Juan* is thus an anti-sublime poem, a poem which no sooner reaches a point of intensity than it undoes its own effects: the poem advances by negating the obsessions to which it returns, and then moving on, again and again. [10] Insofar as Juan represents aspects of Byron's own life, for example, they are admitted only by negation: Juan's crises are Juan's, never acknowledged as the narrator's. Byron, in contrast to Coleridge and Wordsworth, deliberately stays on the surface (as much as he can), and that is why, despite the extravagantly artificial manner of *Don Juan*, he appears as a realist. [11]

The narrative of *Don Juan* seems to be set free of the constraints of purposefulness:

> I ne'er decide what I shall say, and this I call
> Much too poetical. Men should know why
> They write, and for what end; but, note or text,
> I never know the word which will come next. (IX.41)

Don Juan abounds in this sort of confession, each a protest against a vision of complete authorial control. Byron renounces the goal of a fictitious (and factitious) unity, of a designed poem whose meaning would be thoroughly determinate, thoroughly subservient to an end. In so doing he reinstates the power of language to initiate an endless play of meanings, a range of possibilities unrestricted by the demands of an author obviously shaping, or invested in, his work: compare, for example, the increasing pressure Wordsworth places on his narrative in the later books of *The Prelude* as he strives to make his lived experience accord with a scheme in which "All [is] gratulant, if rightly understood" (1805, XIII.385).[12] Byron's structureless habit of proceeding enables him to combat his anxieties by playing them out; it allows him to take on as his own some of the characteristics of the women whom he has placed as the potent other, desired and feared. His characterization of his poem is suggestively similar to that which he gives of women's letters:

> The earth has nothing like a She epistle,
> And hardly heaven—because it never ends.
> I love the mystery of a female missal,
> Which, like a creed, ne'er says all it intends,
> But full of cunning as Ulysses' whistle,
> When he allured poor Dolon. . . . (XIII.105)

The digressive manner of *Don Juan* bespeaks a relaxation of will which permits ominous material to surface: instead of repression, whose indefinite force heightens the sublime, the associative chains of *Don Juan* work toward expression and neutralization.[13] Symbolic and metaphoric poetry achieves its richness through compression and ambiguity: *Don Juan,* which, like women's letters, also "ne'er says all it intends," creates its vitality by extended meanings—inexhaustible sequences rather than pregnant points.

Eliot remarks that "if Byron had distilled his verse, there would have been nothing whatever left," but he is uninterested in the positive implications of his witticism. Byron's manner liberates his unconscious: it enables him to write a poem that can continually surprise its author. The long poem for which the Romantics strove, only to find their aspirations turn into an onerous task or poignant failure, is for Byron a spontaneous, ceaselessly proliferating process. Novelty, rather than inevitability, marks the growth of *Don Juan.* The result is a poetry of surprising conjunctions and momentary delights. Consider, for example, the last quoted stanza. "The earth has nothing like a She epistle" sounds, apart from the oddity and false literariness of "She epistle," like a cliché, but the weakly descriptive phrase acquires force when a buried comparison is released in the second line: "And hardly heaven." This in turn becomes the starting point of a brief but consistent series of religious terms: "mystery," "missal," and "creed." If, as the revisions printed in the variorum suggest, Byron was trapped into "whistle" by the need to rhyme with "epistle" and "missal," he resourcefully overcame the awkwardness with the allusion to Dolon and Ulysses. The unexpected change of context, from Christian to classical, is found elsewhere, notably in the clash between epic and Christian values which Byron insists that the reader confront with Siege of Ismail. The poem repeatedly draws on epic tradition: Ismail is the modern counterpart of Troy, and Juan's wanderings are a skewed version of Odysseus', as the echoes of the *Odyssey* in the Haidée episode make explicit.[14] The linking of female letters to epic craftiness insinuates again the replacement in *Don Juan* of physical adventure by the greater psychological perilousness of "cruizing o'er the ocean woman" (XIII.40). Moreover, the juxtaposition of religious terms and deception—"you had better / Take care what you reply to such a letter" ends the stanza—connects the seemingly chance allusion to the theme of hypocritical piety running throughout the poem: think of Donna Inez keeping the erotically ornamented "family Missal" for herself (I.46). It also recalls the elaborate love-letter written by the convent-bound Julia in Canto I. Byron drops the allusions at the close of the stanza, but not before they have provoked trains of association that send the reader over the whole poem. To read *Don Juan* is to encounter a succession of such tantalizing occasions, a succession which is not determined by an obvious logic, which is inconsecutive but not therefore inconsequential. The sequences begin with license but as they develop become meaningful: they are justified by what they unfold, and so rise above irrelevance. *Don Juan* is not so much "fortuitous," as Jerome McGann describes it, as it is "overdetermined": it is because the "fortuitous" happenings can be situated in many overlapping configurations that they possess meaning.[15] The reader may explore each occasion or not, as he chooses, before the flow of the narrator's talk carries him on to the next. The poem, then, is not precisely the "grand poetic riddle" (VIII.139) the narrator once calls it. Riddling is part of its appeal, but—to use a word which in its various forms occurs twenty-three times in the poem—it is rather a multiplicity of "puzzles." *Don Juan* asks less for comprehensive interpretation than for participation.

This range of meaning is possible only when the radically private language of mother and child represented in the relationship of Juan and Haidée is broken by the separation of the child from the mother. The taboos of the Oedipus complex send the son forth on his metonymic career, seeking satisfaction not in his mother but in a surrogate for her, not striving to usurp his father in actuality but to become like him in another setting. The Oedipus complex is thus, as Freud insisted, the foundation of culture, because it is through the Oedipus complex that the child passes from the family to his broader culture. To do so is to pass from the private language of mother and child to the pre-existent terms of the culture, to dream nostalgically of that lost transparency of communication but to feel oneself doomed to speak in the always slightly misfitting words the culture provides; at this level the ever-present allusions of *Don Juan* are the emblem of the pre-emption of the narrator's own voice by the babble of all who have preceded him. "Doomed" but also "enabled": in *Don Juan* Byron exploits this dilemma instead of concealing it by a myth of symbolic plenitude.

To illustrate the strengths of Byron's manner it may be useful to turn once more to Coleridge. Arguing in the *Biographia Literaria* against Wordsworth's assertion that the *Lyrical Ballads* were written in "the real language of men," Coleridge examines the fallacy on which the statement rests:

Every man's language varies, according to the extent of his knowledge, the activity of his faculties, and the depth or quickness of his feelings. Every man's language has, first, its *individualities;* secondly, the common properties of the *class* to which he belongs; and thirdly, words and phrases of universal use. The language of Hooker, Bacon, Bishop Taylor, and Burke differs from the common language of the learned class only by the superior number and novelty of the thoughts and relations which they had to convey. The language of Algernon Sidney differs not at all from that which every well-educated gentleman would wish to write, and (with due allowances for the undeliberateness, and less connected train, of thinking proper and natural to conversation) such as he would wish to talk. Neither one or the other differ half so much from the general language of cultivated society, as the language of Mr. Wordsworth's homeliest composition differs from that of a common peasant. For "real" therefore we must substitute *ordinary,* or *lingua communis.* And this, we have proved, is no more to be found in the phraseology of low and rustic life than in that of any other class. . . . Anterior to cultivation the lingua communis of every country, as Dante has well observed, exists every where in parts and nowhere as a whole.[16]

In the Preface to the *Lyrical Ballads* Wordsworth had espoused a view of language as deriving directly from objects; Coleridge exposes the mistake of this "natural" view by maintaining that "the best part of human language . . . is derived from reflection on the acts of the mind itself," and is "formed by a voluntary appropriation of fixed symbols to internal acts" (II.39–40). He thus restores language to the distinctively human matrix in which it comes into being, and his formulation permits a recasting of Eliot's critique. To say that Byron "added nothing to the language" is, in Coleridge's more discriminating framework, to indicate the lack of any strongly idiosyncratic "individualities" in his style, but also to throw the emphasis on its "common properties" and "words and phrases of *universal* use."

Byron cherishes the membership of *Don Juan* in the linguistic community to which it ineluctably belongs. The words he speaks have a history of their own, meanings they carry with them from their innumerable uses outside and prior to the poem. They are his only for an instant, loaned to him only briefly for his own purposes, before they return to their larger ongoing life. "If, fallen in evil days on evil tongues," Byron writes in the Dedication to *Don Juan,* "Milton appeal'd to the Avenger, Time," and continues: ". . . Time, the Avenger, execrates his wrongs, / And makes the word 'Miltonic' mean *'sublime'* " (l. 10). Of more interest than Byron's enlistment of Milton to lambaste Southey is his highlighting of the historical process by which words acquire meaning. The allusion to *Paradise Lost* is typical of *Don Juan,* a veritable echo-chamber reverberating with phrases, imitations, parodies, and halfheard fragments from Homer, Virgil, Dante, Shakespeare, Milton, Pope, and scores or lesser figures. These shadowy presences augment Byron's voice by locating him within his tradition: even were it true, as Eliot charges, that Byron added nothing to the language, one might yet reply that through him a whole tradition is summoned and renovated. His contempt for the "insolent . . . wish," as he saw it, of Southey, Coleridge, and Wordsworth "to supersede all warblers here below" (Dedication, 3) is the corollary of his refusal to give superordinate value to the concept of originality which, given his consciousness of, and commitment to, the public continuities of language, could only seem to him an impoverishing mystification.

Allusion is only a special case of the way in which *Don Juan* continually unmasks the illusion of its own autonomy in order to reap the benefits of acknowledging all that lies outside it. To choose words already invested with significance by their recognizability as literature—allusions—is in one respect to beg the central issue, because one of the fundamental questions raised by *Don Juan* concerns the conventional distinctions between the literary and the non-literary. Macassar oil, Congreve's rockets, the brand names of ships' pumps, and all the other odd objects that find their way from daily life into *Don Juan,* on the one hand, and the highwaymen's slang, parodied jargons, and the mention of pox and like taboo subjects, on the other, constitute a challenge, less socially radical than Wordsworth's but kindred and no less far-reaching, to the notion of a specialized poetic diction. *Don Juan,* building on the comic precedents of the previous century,[17] demonstrates more thoroughly than does Wordsworth's own work the contention of the Preface to the *Lyrical Ballads* "that there neither is, nor can be, any essential difference between the language of prose and metrical composition." The conversation poem which "affects not to be poetry," that undertaking about whose implications Coleridge remained uneasy, reaches a triumphant apogee in *Don Juan.*[18]

Yet to speak, as in the title of Ronald Bottrall's essay, of "Byron and the Colloquial Tradition in English Poetry," is still somewhat to underestimate the ramifications of *Don Juan,* because the poem places itself in relation not only to a tradition *within* literary history but also to what would seem to stand outside it.[19] *Don Juan* could scarcely exist without the conventions Byron manipulates to make his meaning. If his "narration [of her genealogy] / May have suggested" (1.59) that Julia will be the culmination, that is only because of the expectations of a pattern held by readers and writers within a given culture, their common literary competence. But Byron does not privilege these patterns or, to put it more accurately, he privileges them by calling attention to their artificiality. To read *Don Juan* is to be made aware of the arbitrary agreements on which the making and maintaining of meaning rest. The relationship between flamboyant literariness and ostentatious anti-, or non-, literariness is a differential one: each throws the other into relief, and both together direct our attention to the functioning of language, to the conventions by which it works and the domains into which historically it has divided itself. By unveiling the artificiality of his own procedures Byron displays the fictiveness of language generally and the delicate and complex consensus through which it is preserved. The myriad slippages and maladjustments of that social network create the gaps in which his irony and satire operate.

Don Juan, to return to the quotation from Coleridge, can imitate "the indeliberateness, and less connected train, of thinking proper and natural to conversation" because it sees conversation as an exemplary act performed in language, hence different in degree only, not kind, from literature. Byron repeatedly announces a freedom guided only by his own intelligent curiosity: "So on I ramble, now and then narrating, / Now pondering" (IX.42). By refusing to mark itself off absolutely from everyday life, by denying that it constitutes any sort of special experience, *Don Juan* gains the power to include its opposite within itself. "This narrative is not meant for narration," the narrator comments, "But a mere airy and fantastic basis, / To build up common things with common places" (XIV.7). Byron had chosen as the motto for the first cantos of *Don Juan* "Difficile est propria communia dicere," a phrase he had translated in *Hints from Horace* as "Whate'er the critic says or poet sings / Tis no slight task to write on common things." He thereby directly connects the difficulty of his art to the prosaic nature of his medium: because his words claim no magic in themselves and because he regularly turns us outward from his words to their uses elsewhere, Byron demonstrates with remarkable clarity the basis of poetry not in "individual words," as Eliot implies, but in the relationship they mutually establish. Though seeing that Byron must be quoted at length to make his effect, Eliot does not recognize the alternate conception of language his practice successfully illustrates: individually colorless counters are transformed into a compelling series by the unexpected but self-validating connections Byron fabricates between them. The aggregative and associative mode of the poem is a virtual paradigm of Coleridge's definitions of the Fancy, but the loss of the intensity Coleridge ascribed to the Imagination only is more than offset by the revelation of the power of language itself, both within and without this particular poem. Despite Byron's evident pride in his achievement, *Don Juan* is almost less concerned with its own status as a unique *parole,* to use a Saussurean distinction, than it is with the overall function of *langue. Don Juan* advances its claim to our interest not so much by conveying *a* meaning as by making its readers aware of the prior conventions on which any sharable meanings whatever depend.[20] Or, to remain with Coleridge, to read *Don Juan* is to be made aware of the characteristics of that "lingua communis [which] . . . exists everywhere in parts and nowhere as a whole."

Despite such declarations as that of Wordsworth in the Prospectus to *The Recluse* that he would employ "words / Which speak of nothing more than what we are," the poetics of Romanticism habitually resorts to a language of intimation. If the period is one of Natural Supernaturalism, as its most magisterial recent description would have it, that terminology itself betrays the very binary opposition the poetry seeks to mediate. In the Preface to the

Lyrical Ballads Wordsworth sets forth his aims in a fashion which similarly maintains a distinction: he proposed, he says, "to choose incidents and situations from common life" and "to throw over them a certain coloring of imagination, whereby ordinary things should be presented to the mind in an unusual way." To see merely the object is the sign of Peter Bell's imaginative poverty: "A primrose by a river's brim / A yellow primrose was to him, / And it was nothing more" (ll. 58–60). Though he insists on the "real," Wordsworth takes the object as instrumental to the transforming imagination. For Coleridge likewise the symbol is defined by its embodiment of a realm beyond itself: it "is characterized by a translucence of the Special in the Individual, or of the General in the Especial or of the Universal in the General. Above all by the translucence of the Eternal in and through the Temporal."[21] But in poetry there can be only words, and this illusion of depth and timelessness is a linguistic conjuring trick, a sleight of hand performed in language and inseparable from it. Byron's satiric and anti-sublime deconstructions strip away this illusion, insisting that we recognize that it is through our own language that we create the images that enchant us. He stresses not the "mystery" putatively residing in the object but the "doubt" caused by our own fallible mental activities. Paradoxically, it is by thus affirming the priority of our constructions that Byron returns us to the object world, but not as an empirical, objective given. To stretch Oscar Wilde, he too knows that it is only shallow people who do not judge by appearances: *Don Juan* shows that "the real" is the totality of our conventions, the agreed-upon social vision of reality. Here too Coleridge provides a useful gloss. In a footnote to Chapter IV of the *Biographia Literaria* he discusses the evolutionary process by which synonyms initially "used promiscuously" gradually distinguish themselves from each other: "When this distinction has been so naturalized and of such general currency that the language itself does as it were *think* for us (like the sliding rule which is the mechanic's safe substitute for arithmetical knowledge) we then say, that it is evident to *common sense*" (i.63). *Don Juan* continually lays bare the dangers of this "common sense" by correcting delusion, attacking cant, brutally reiterating the brutal "facts" of war and death, but simultaneously calling to our attention the sway of language and the social bonds on which it in turn rests. "I write the world" (xv.60), Byron can declare, because in writing he fully enters the transpersonal medium in which "the world" represents (and misrepresents) itself to itself.

Language in *Don Juan* thus points not to a supralinguistic reality (and hence is spared the agonizing doubt of language characteristic of a Shelley) but to a community of speakers and readers in the world their language builds up. In his influential *Romantic Image* (1957; rpt. New York: Random House-Vintage, 1964) Frank Kermode showed how "inextricably associated" in the Romantic-Symbolist tradition are the beliefs "in the image as a radiant truth out of space and time, and in the necessary isolation or estrangement of men who can perceive it" (p. 2). These views may be found throughout *Childe Harold* and occasionally in *Don Juan,* but the nature of the latter poem qualifies the statements made within it. Even as he reduced the magical image Byron restored the poet to his fellow-men. Their common habitation in language binds together the two central figures of *Don Juan,* the narrator and the reader his fiction projects: the isolation Byron-as-Juan suffers is recuperated in the affiliation of Byron-as-narrator to his audience.

Though the web of words which is *Don Juan* reveals "the class to which [Byron] belongs," and the aristocratic Whig liberalism of his principles, the poem is remarkably unprescriptive of its reader. Assent, or the maneuvering of the reader into a point of view congruent with that of the author, is only one of the many and successive aims of the poem: the implicitly dramatized responses range from shock and anger to laughter at the author's image of himself, the narrator. The most generous aspect of *Don Juan* is the depth and variety of the experiences it acknowledges: the poem solicits the reader to bring with him all the works of literature he has read, all the political controversies in which he is enmeshed, all the mundane objects through which he moves, all his conflicting passions as child, parent, and lover. The poem functions not so much centripetally, directing attention to its uniqueness (though it does so gleefully), as much as centrifugally, returning each reader to the complex of private and public experienes which make up his particular life.[22] The comprehensiveness of *Don Juan* and the much debated question of its status as epic are subjects that can be reformulated in terms of the inclusiveness of the response it figures but does not restrict. There is no single perfect reading of *Don Juan:* the text enfranchises all that infinite series of readings, neither idiosyncratic nor stock, which the common cultural context of author and reader empowers. It earns this richness because it is shaped not by the concept of uniqueness but of difference. The narrator demonstrates that identity exists only through the roles furnished by his culture, and hence is something both his and not his. To avert a threatening alienation, an imprisonment in a role, he must continually repudiate the stances he adopts, defining himself not by fixed points but by the shifting pattern of his movement between them. At one level *Don Juan* is a prolonged elegy for the loss of the union of mother and child represented by Haidée and Juan, but the poem also deploys a tenacious and resilient resistance to the temptations of that fantasy. The attempt to master the conflict perpetuates it: the repetitions of *Don Juan* reiterate the dilemma, revealing Byron's continued subjection to, as well as his conquest of, his desires and fears. The place of language in *Don Juan* is inevitably ambiguous: the situations in which it might be superseded by transparency of communication Byron rejects as self-destructive, and so he remains trapped, his reliance on language the sign of all that he has lost. Language for Byron can never be what it briefly is for Haidée and Juan, private and innocent: every fresh employment of it further implicates him in the continuum of history and society. Caught in words, however, Byron makes the exposure and exploitation of their treacherous wealth serve his ends. By displaying the unavoidable inauthenticity of language he liberates its fictiveness and sets in motion the self created only through it. He unmasks the illusion of full meaning dear to Eliot and the symbolists, asking us to recognize that poetry can be made not only by saturating the individual word, but also by ceaselessly uncovering the paradoxes hid in the use of ordinary words. The contra-dictions at the center of an existence defined by a language that is creative but inevitably conventional, his but not his, a means of connection but a story of separation, a mode of recovery but an admission of loss, a fantasy of wholeness that is desired but resisted, Byron accepts and makes generate the elaborate play which enlarges the narrator and animates the words of *Don Juan*.

Notes

1. "Byron," *On Poetry and Poets* (1943: rpt. New York: Noonday, 1964), pp. 232–33.

2. I mean only to indicate that this accusation has not been rebutted, not to underrate the excellent studies of Byron's style. In addition to the works cited below I would single out George M. Ridenour, *The Style of DON JUAN* (New Haven: Yale U. Press, 1960), M. K. Joseph, *Byron The Poet* (London: Gollancz, 1964), and W. W. Robson, "Byron as Poet," rpt. in his *Critical Essays* (London: Routledge, 1966), pp. 148–88. Two recent essays of relevance are Bernard Beatty's "Lord Byron: poetry and precedent," in *Literature of the Romantic Period 1750–1850,* ed. R. T. Davies and B. G. Beatty (New York: Barnes and Noble, 1976), pp. 114–34, and Francis Berry's "The Poet of *Childe Harold,*" in *Byron: A Symposium,* ed. John D. Jump (New York: Barnes and Noble, 1975), pp. 35–51, which also takes up Eliot's critique.

3. *The Symbolic Imagination: Coleridge and the Romantic Tradition* (Princeton: Princeton U. Press, 1977).

4. See on this subject Jean Laplanche, *Life and Death in Psychoanalysis,* tr. Jeffrey Mehlman (Baltimore: Johns Hopkins U. Press, 1976).

5. A variant for line 4 shows the original contrast to have been between the quiet of the doors and the vitality of Byron's own speaking voice: "The hinges being much smoother than these rhymes."

6. Letter of April 6, 1819, *Byron's Letters and Journals,* ed. Leslie A. Marchand, VI (Cambridge, Mass.: Harvard, U. Press, 1976), 105.

7. To the degree that Inez connives at the affair she and Julia converge. Juan's affair with Julia thereby seems a displacement of maternal incest: Alfonso's intervention is thus punishment for the forbidden act and rescue from a dangerous absorption.

8. Juan first speaks in the poem during the second canto, when his farewell is quickly cut short by seasickness (II.18–20), and when he bars the panicky crew from the grog (II.36), where Byron takes his speech directly from a scene in his sources. He is unheard during the subsequent 180 stanzas of Canto II and throughout Canto III.

9. *Lord Byron: Un Tempérament Littéraire,* 2 vols. (Paris: Cercle du Livre, 1957), II, 58.

10. It could not, of course, repeatedly undo the sublime if it did not repeatedly strive for it. This movement is akin to that described as "desublimating" by Thomas Weiskel, *The Romantic Sublime* (Baltimore: Johns Hopkins U. Press, 1976). I have not used the term because the relation between "the sublime" and "sublimation" within Weiskel's otherwise stimulating argument remains problematic.

11. Roman Jakobson proposed the relationships of metaphor to symbolism and meton-

ymy to realism in section 5, "The Metaphoric and Metonymic Poles," of his essay, "Two Aspects of Language and Two Types of Aphasic Disturbances," Roman Jakobson and Morris Halle, *Fundamentals of Language,* 2nd rev. ed. (The Hague: Mouton, 1971), pp. 69–96.

12. The notion of free play is taken from Jacques Derrida; see, for example, "Structure, Sign, and Play in the Discourse of the Human Sciences," *The Structuralist Controversy,* ed. Richard Macksey and Eugenio Donato (Baltimore: Johns Hopkins U. Press, 1972), pp. 247–65.

13. The relationship of repression and the sublime is a theme of the recent criticism of Harold Bloom; see *A Map of Misreading* (New York: Oxford U. Press, 1975).

14. E.g., III.23, on Lambro's arrival: "An honest gentleman at his return / May not have the good fortune of Ulysses." The allusions are studied in my *Byron and his Fictions* (Detroit: Wayne State U. Press, 1978).

15. "Fortuitous" is a word McGann often uses to describe the growth of the poem in *DON JUAN In Context* (Chicago: U. of Chicago Press, 1976). The accretive chains, however, are often generated by the anxieties aroused by certain recurrent subjects, such as women. The motives for the resulting digressions and evasions are partly concealed from Byron himself. These gaps and switches suggest that the meaning of *Don Juan,* to use a Lacanian phrase, is not simply one that Byron speaks but one that speaks him. It is precisely such "arbitrary" links as the rhyme forces between epic craft and female cunning which show the connection and inscription of personal and cultural themes in the unconscious. *Don Juan* seems to me a little less rationally experimental, less scientifically instructive and more anarchic (as well as obsessive) than it appears in McGann's presentation. *DON JUAN In Context* is nonetheless the most penetrating discussion yet of the mode of the poem; that, starting from such different premises, my conclusions should often coincide with McGann's I wishfully interpret as corroboration of their general rightness.

16. John Shawcross, ed., *Biographia Literaria,* 2 vols. (Oxford: Clarendon Press, 1907), II, 41–42. Subsequent page references are incorporated in the text.

17. A. B. England has explored Byron's affinities with Butler and Swift as well as the more commonly cited Pope and Fielding in *Byron's DON JUAN and Eighteenth-Century Literature* (Lewisburg, Penn.: Bucknell U. Press, 1975).

18. See Max F. Schulz, *The Poetic Voices of Coleridge* (Detroit: Wayne State U. Press, 1964), pp. 81, 179.

19. *Criterion,* 18 (1939), 204–24, and rpt. in M. H. Abrams, ed., *English Romantic Poets: Modern Essays in Criticism* (New York: Oxford U. Press, 1960), pp. 210–27. Bottrall answers Eliot by arguing that Byron's "interest was rather in the fundamental rhythmic movement of speech than in the word."

20. In an essay of that title Roland Barthes locates "the structuralist activity" in the reconstruction of an object in order to show its rules of functioning (tr. Richard Howard, *Partisan Review,* 34 [1967], 82–88). The structuralist critic Barthes describes focuses not on the content of meanings but on the act of producing them: he "recreates the course taken by meaning, he need not designate it." A criticism based on these principles reveals virtues in Byron ignored by the still-prevailing organicist or apocalyptic camps.

21. "The Statesman's Manual," *Lay Sermons,* ed. R. J. White, *Collected Works of Samuel Taylor Coleridge,* VI (London: Routledge, 1972), 30.

22. Ruskin commented long ago on a conjunction between the prose-like directness in Byron and the suggestive freedom he grants the reader. Observing that "He is the best poet who can by the fewest words touch the greatest number of secret chords of thought in the reader's own mind, and set *them* to work in their own way," Ruskin chooses as specific example a couplet from *The Siege of Corinth:* " 'Tis midnight: on the mountains brown—The Pale round moon shines deeply down.' Now the first eleven words are not poetry, except by their measure and preparation for rhyme; they are simple information, which might just as well have been given in prose—it *is* prose, in fact: It is twelve o'clock—the moon is pale—it is round—it is

shining on brown mountains. Any fool, who had seen it, could tell us that. At last comes the poetry, in the single epithet, 'deeply.' Had he said 'softly' or 'brightly' it would still have been simple information. But of all the readers of that couplet, probably not two received exactly the same impression from the 'deeply,' and yet received more from that than from all the rest together. Some will refer the expression to the fall of the steep beams, and plunge down with them from rock to rock into the woody darkness of the cloven ravines, down to the undermost pool of eddying black water, whose echo is lost among their leafage; others will think of the deep *feeling* of the pure light, of the thousand memories and emotions that rise out of their rest, and are seen white and cold in its rays. This is the reason of the power of the single epithet, and this is its *mystery*." Quoted in *Byron: The Critical Heritage,* ed. Andrew Rutherford (New York: Barnes and Noble, 1970), pp. 426–27.

Editor's Bibliographical Note

Although Byron's language had received some attention before Manning's essay, as he indicates no one had yet taken up Eliot's pontifical denigration of it. But there were defenses of a sort of Byron's linguistic practice, albeit notably silent with respect to Eliot. The most useful of these are Ronald Bottrall, "Byron and the Colloquial Tradition in English Poetry," *Criterion* 18 (January 1939): 204–24; Marius Bewley, "The Colloquial Mode of Byron," *Scrutiny* 16 (March 1949): 8–23; and especially George M. Ridenour's chapter in *The Style of "Don Juan"* (New Haven: Yale University Press, 1960) entitled "Carelessly I Sing." Also worthy of note are Roland Bartel, "Byron's Respect for Language," *Papers on English Language and Literature* 1 (1965): 373–78; Frank D. McConnell, "Byron's Reductions: 'Much Too Poetical,' " *ELH* 37 (1970): 415–32; Peter Porter, "Byron and the Moral North: The Englishness of *Don Juan,*" *Encounter* 43 (August 1974): 65–72; Lindsay Waters, "The 'Desultory Rhyme' of *Don Juan:* Byron, Pulci, and the Improvisatory Style," *ELH* 45 (1978): 429–42; and L. E. Marshall, " *'Words* Are *Things'*: Byron and the Prophetic Efficacy of Language," *Studies in English Literature* 25 (1985): 801–22. Less directly pertinent but lively nevertheless is Sheila Emerson, 'Byron's 'one word': The Language of Self-Expression in *Childe Harold* III," *Studies in Romanticism* 20 (1981): 363–82. See also Frederick Garber's chapter in *Self, Text, and Romantic Irony* entitled "Self and the Language of Satire," a shorter version of which appeared in *Thalia* 5 (1983): 35–44. Although less directly relevant to these studies of Byron's language, three recent essays, all appearing in the Winter 1988 special Byron issue of *Studies in Romanticism,* provocatively blend language, prosody, poetic form, and politics: Susan Wolfson, "Couplets, Self, and *The Corsair*" (491–513); Kurt Heinzelman, "Politics, Memory, and the Lyric: Collaboration as Style in Byron's *Hebrew Melodies*" (515–27); and William Keach, "Political Inflections in Byron's *Ottava Rima*" (551–62).

Byron's Poetry of Politics:
The Economic Basis
of the "Poetical Character"

KURT HEINZELMAN

How many have I seen, how many have we all of us known, young, with promising poetic insides, who produce one book and die of it? For in our time, at least, the little public that does read new poetry is not twice bored by the same aspirant, and if a man's first book has not in it some sign of a serious struggle with the bases of the art he has small likelihood of meeting them in the second. But the man who has some standard reasonably high—consider, says Longinus, in what mood Diogenes or Sophocles would have listened to your effusion—does, while he is striving to bring his work within reach of his own conception of it, get rid of the first froth of verse, which is in nearly every case quite like the first verse-froth of everyone else. He emerges decently clean after some reasonable purgation, not nearly a master, but licensed, an initiate, with some chance of conserving his will to speak and of seeing it mature and strengthen with the ripening and strengthening of the mind itself until, by the favour of the gods, he come upon some lasting excellence.

So, on the subject of first books, wrote Ezra Pound[1]—who published his at his own expense in Italy, a good place (if one is an English poet) to exorcize one's first verse-froth. In Pound's own poetic apprenticeship, the proprietary rights of authorship exacted many pragmatic compromises. In the first place, to be properly credited as an author (to be credible in such utterances as the one quoted above), one needed the collateral of a first book, however acquired. "Striving to bring his work within reach of his own conception of it," Pound discovered that any "serious struggle with the bases of the art" must be fought on several fronts—economic as well as psychic. Only through such psychoeconomic struggle would the young poet gain the "character," in the fullest sense of the word, of an author.

Years after publishing his first book, Pound was still writing music reviews in London, trying to earn a livelihood; he was also working at his true vocation, "a long poem." An immediate model for these cantos was *Don Juan*,[2] in which Byron anticipated Pound's concern with the economic bases

Reprinted from *Texas Studies in Language and Literature* 23 (Fall 1981): 361–88 by permission of the author and publisher.

that underlie the psychic struggle for a poetical self—that is, for a sense of one's identity as an author. Carl Woodring also points out that "Byron is rare among [Romantic poets], and among English poets generally, in using political activities metaphorically as the vehicle to make more pungent the tenor of his thought."[3] Woodring's first generalization is, I believe, mistaken— Byron was not so rare in this regard; but the gist of the second part cannot be overemphasized, although Woodring's own pungent way of putting it here is potentially misleading. To say that Byron (or any other poet) applied his metaphors to enhance his thought implies that metaphorical vehicles are like spray paint: their gloss highlights and brightens the surface without permeating the substance beneath. But Byron's metaphors penetrate more deeply. In this essay I will argue that they derive more directly than Byron scholars usually believe from the same kind of psychoeconomic struggle for an authorial "character" to which Pound bears witness.

The author of *Don Juan,* as a beginning poet in the years 1806 to 1808, had acquired his sense of "conception," of *poietikis,* through his Augustan education at Harrow, an education which produced a more skeptical attitude toward the hieratic function of poetry than Pound's. Where Byron specifically differed from Pound was in the way he understood the "character" of the author. For Byron, one's socioeconomic (i.e., class) status would affect not merely the kind of poetry one wrote but, more important, the kind of attitude one took toward it. To labor at poetry in the Grub Street sense was vulgar, and Byron never failed to satirize the socioeconomic rewards sought by artisan-artists, even when, in his later career, he willingly accepted royalties for his own work. To harbor a hieratic sense of the poet's vocation was equally vulgar because sentimental and naive. Southey, the poet laureate, was frequently assailed for fostering a "romantic" sense of vocation which led to writing bad poetry. Both of Byron's attitudes are conventional, but merely to identify them as such does not resolve the agony of the poetical character—a conflict, as Pound describes it, between youthful excess of will and properly licensed authority. In fact, the more conventional Byron's attitudes were in his youthful work, the more this tension resisted resolution. As license for his authority (as an author), the young Byron appealed both to his "promising poetic insides" and to his social status as a lord. Such a socioeconomic appeal, however, only heightened the irony that, as a lord, he had an unseemly train of economic encumbrances and fiscal liabilities and that, as a poet, he was highly derivative. Some reviewers castigated him for the baldness of his special pleading; Byron eventually castigated himself for the ironic bankruptcy of it. Reversing Pound's dictum, the young Byron found himself striving to bring his conception of his own worth as an author within reach of the work.

The first paragraph of Byron's Preface to his first published book, *Hours of Idleness* (1807), reveals how ambivalent Byron was: "In submitting to the public eye the following collection, I have not only to combat the difficulties that writers of verse generally encounter, but may incur the charge of presumption for obtruding myself on the world when, without doubt, I might be, at my age, more usefully employed." For Pound, the *agon* of character building occurs in respect to two audiences: (1) the "little public" that reads poetry at all and (2) the audience of Diogenes and Sophocles, the great dead. From the former the neophyte will find little if any economic reward, only a kind of impatient curiosity; from the latter he will learn if his poetic name is a true one. But Byron attempts to sever the question of mastering artistic discipline from the question of "poetical character." While acknowledging the "difficulties" of the first, he belittles the seriousness and utility of the second. His aristocratic disdain for "the public eye" derives from his "situation" as a lord, and this disdain is exacerbated by just such a (public) declaration of his "reputation and feelings." Byron concludes: "It is highly improbable, from my situation and pursuits hereafter, that I should ever obtrude myself a second time on the public" (Preface, 1807). This gesture declares a Poundian apprenticeship supererogatory, for Byron is saying that he will produce one book and *gladly* die of it. And yet, quoting "the opinion of Dr. Johnson on the Poems of a noble relation of mine, 'That when a man of rank appeared in the character of an author, he deserved to have his merit handsomely allowed' " (Preface, 1807), Byron reveals that he wants public approbation, too, and that he wants it for *this* work.

For Dr. Johnson, the lives of the poets may or may not determine the life of their poetry, but in his criticism, poets' lives do precede discussion of their work. Such biographical precedence (still a prominent concern in Byron scholarship) both reassured and distressed Byron himself. In his youthful work especially, he appealed alternatively to his biographical character as "a man of rank" and to his aesthetic character as a poet, depending upon which kind of emotional support he needed.[4] According to Jerome J. McGann, the "conflicted aspects" of Byron's characterization of himself did not contradict his persistent "concern for public recognition as a validating condition of achievement."[5] But how would this validation occur? Byron's Preface belittles his own poetical character for having no character—for being useless, idle, and trifling, for having no significant "rank." At the same time, as "a man of rank" he sees his authorial self as an indiscreet problem. Byron's conventional deprecation of his own public authority leads here to a dilemma of aesthetic valorization: How can he both earn public approbation for the labor of his poetry and at the same time devalue the public personage that created the poems? Denying his own "character" as an author, can he still claim authority for his work?

Byron's "first" volume of poems actually comprises four separate editions issued over two years. Some aesthetic permutations occurred in that time, but the most important change is the mode of self-advertisement. The first of the four volumes, *Fugitive Pieces* (1806), was a lark; "never intended to meet the public eye," it was privately produced for the "amusement or approbation" of friends (dedication page). In that stock phrase, the "or" has the rhetorical force of "and therefore," as if approbation and amusement were interchangeable modes of credit. When one of those friends objected to a poem as being "rather too warmly drawn," the poem was suppressed and the volume withdrawn.[6] But early in the next year (1807), a slightly altered version of the same volume [including the dedication] appeared under the title *Poems on Various Occasions*. The next version, *Hours of Idleness,* appeared later that year and continued to draw upon the earlier volumes for its content and even for its formal layout ("Fugitive Pieces" was one of the section subheads). *Hours of Idleness* was, however, a more august and "finished" product. It sported a "literary" title, supplied by the publisher, John Ridge of Newark; it came in full public dress, parading a subtitle, mottos, epigraphs, and the soon-to-be infamous preface, all supplied by the poet himself, who for the first time identified himself by name, rank, and age ("A Minor") on the title page. For Byron, this public act of self-identification was also susceptible of more private irony. To his friends (such as Edward Noel Long), he merely said: "you will behold an 'Old friend with a new face.' "[7]

This trying on of faces, which became a trying out of selves as well as a testing of one's audience, is precisely the luxury that such seriatim production made possible.[8] If, in the beginning, his audience was his friends, then in *Hours of Idleness* the elaborately naive "character" of the poet-as-minor was needed to avoid being held publicly accountable for that original intention. But in his fourth version of this same first volume, Byron's pose will be less evident, as we shall see. In his private correspondence, Byron will express a more overtly professional curiosity about the production of *Poems Original and Translated* (1808). While still maintaining a putative disinterest in the commercial aspects of publishing a "second edition," Byron will also evidence a greater self-understanding of the *quality* of that disinterestedness.

Through this process of nominating one authorial self, finding it unacceptable, and then discarding it for another, Byron evolved a kind of aesthetic stratagem which he explored more fully *as* a stratagem in *Don Juan.* It is a stratagem based on the idea of speculation in the economic sense, a risking of an immediate investment on future prospects in hopes of a disproportionately large return. Psychologically, this velleity is a form of play that banks the psychic resources of the present on an imaginary projection of what the future might hold. Economically, we must remember, Byron was doing something similar during the period leading up to his majority in 1808. As is well documented, the Byron estate at this time was in financial disarray, and Byron's mother needed to concoct elaborate loans to get her and her son through. Partly because of his prodigious expenses at Cambridge and partly because of his largesse to friends as economically strapped as himself, Byron increased his loans, sometimes resorting to the complicated fiscal maneuvering described by Doris L. Moore:

> The consequence [of Byron's profligacy as a minor] was that he could not produce the interest on the loans his mother had raised for him, and he was borrowing afresh. To run up debts while still a minor was a costly and intricate operation. One of Byron's ways of doing it was to undertake to pay annuities, when he came of age, to persons whose capital was secured by an insurance on his life effected by some other part at his expense. The premiums fell due relentlessly at moments of greatest inconvenience.[9]

While a minor, therefore, Byron was not living in debt so much as he was living on credit, the collateral for which was literally himself and his future prospects, and his creditors were often the very "friends" who nominally comprised the original audience for his poetry. To image himself as a public author would be tantamount to attaining a more mature and unencumbered sense of economic identity for himself. He never put it this crudely. By the time he was prepared to put it directly at all, his directness had the rich burden of self-irony. That irony has, as Byron may have wished, distracted his readers, even scholarly ones, from considering seriously the economic basis of his "poetical character."[10]

The issue of self-authorization is manifested in the early poems as a concern with nominating the self to an authentic "name." In a poem of 1803, originally untitled when it appeared in the privately printed and anonymous volume *Fugitive Pieces* (1806), Byron asserts:

> My *epitaph* shall be my name alone:
> If *that* with honour fail to crown my clay,
> Oh! may no other fame my deeds repay!
> *That*, only *that*, shall single out the spot;
> By that remember'd, or with that forgot.

In the poem's first publication, the thrice-repeated "that" lacks the very antecedent—a specific name—which its repetitions affirm. Only when reprinted as "A Fragment" in *Hours of Idleness* is Byron's name given. But even so, the "other fame," which in the poem probably means "ill repute," is, according to the Preface to *Hours of Idleness*, poetic fame itself. The author's "deeds" *as a poet* remain not merely unnamed but analogically related to ignominy.

In "Elegy on Newstead Abbey," a poem that recounts the political history of Byron's ancestral home, the speaker identifies himself as "The last and youngest of a noble line" who "holds thy mouldering turrets in his sway." Here Byron nominates himself as a nobleman, albeit a lord of ruins, but the poem curiously refuses to name a poetic self at the same time. It is curious because the passage quoted above could easily accommodate such a nomination. In this poem Byron himself is writing in (and using the clichés of) "a noble line" of country-house poetry, and the double meaning of "line" could be used to reconcile empirical self and poetic vocation. In fact, the next line reads: "Deserted now, he scans thy gray worn towers"—where again "scans" could have become a weighted word. Instead, the peculiar grammar that makes the "he" rather than the "towers" sound "deserted now" merely shows us Byron's own self-desertion of the poetical character.

Naming becomes a most perilous act when the nominating vehicle, poetry itself, is divested of any intrinsic authority. The ironies in the last stanza of "The Tear," one of only two poems that Byron signed with his name in the otherwise anonymous *Fugitive Pieces* (and one of seventeen poems from that volume that he reprinted as late as 1808), exhaust Byron's capacity to harmonize them:

> May no marble bestow
> The splendour of woe,
> Which the children of Vanity rear;
> No fiction of fame
> Shall blazon my name
> All I ask, all I wish, is a *Tear*.
> (Byron, 26 October 1806)

The "fiction" he rejects here—literally an epitaph—is linked to what he calls earlier in the poem "a fanciful wreath / In Glory's romantic career"—that is, military fame. But it is linked also to the fiction-making career of poetry, and so, both ways to fame—that of romantic public action and that of equally romantic poetic fancy—are rejected in favor of the "Truth" (l. 3) of the heart's affection, symbolized by a tear. When friendship's tears have such authority, then the whole idea of an honorable name is stripped of any public consequence. And yet the inscriptive force of this very stanza belies its own renunciations. The last line of this lugubriously affirmative stanza, which is stamped with Byron's name and the date like an epitaph, does not reject *fame* as a fiction; indeed, it specifies just what kind of temporal approbation is required and from whom.

At the end of the 1807 Preface, Byron claims that he does not want to "triumph in honours granted solely to a title"—that is, merely to a name. At the same time, he agrees with Dr. Johnson in admiring Carlisle, whose "works have long received the meed of public applause to which, by their intrinsic worth, they are well entitled." To what intrinsic worth does Byron's (titled) name entitle *him?*—that question provides the subtext of "The Tear." The Preface seeks to discriminate between the "intrinsic worth" of Byron's poems and the intrinsic worthlessness of their author's "character," a discrimination that makes the act of naming oneself either pathetic or self-aggrandizing. "The Tear" tries to hold a middle ground, countering pathos with a putative disdain for fame. Rejecting all aggrandizing fictions, however, the speaker's name becomes blazoned here with its own act of self-effacement, a brilliant sentimentalizing of that private "Vanity" which is publicly being deprecated.

The poems in *Hours of Idleness* and the Preface to them are not working at cross-purposes, then. They speak to the same burden of identifying the author's "character" as an author but without appearing to understand how and why this becomes a dilemma. The root of the dilemma is that Byron's rather conventional descriptions of (and special pleadings for) himself as author did not satisfactorily reflect the enthusiasms expressed in his verse nor did they authentically represent the ("vulgar") pride he took in making his verse accomplished. So, on the one hand, he invokes the modesty topos to his Cambridge acquaintance, William Bankes: "in fact I never looked beyond the Moment of Composition, & published merely at the Request of my Friends.—Notwithstanding so much has been said concerning the 'Genus irritabile Vatum' we shall never quarrel on the Subject, poetic fame is by no means the '*acme*' of my Wishes" (6 March 1807). One sees that this modesty is both sincere *and* a topos when one recognizes how Byron's language echoes what Thomas Moore said as "editor" of *The Poetical Works of the Late Thomas Little, Esq.*—indeed, how Byron quotes Moore almost verbatim.[11] In a follow-up letter to Bankes, this topos has acquired the name of action: "Contrary to my former Intention, I am now preparing a volume for the Public at large, . . . This is a hazardous experiment, but want of better employment, the encouragement I have met with, & my own Vanity, induce me to stand the Test" (*Letters*, p. 112). A mock heroism colors the tone of certain phrases here, but when Byron speaks of hazard, he is also serious. The recipient of this letter was not one of those who gave Byron unqualified encouragement.

In 1807 Byron had no clear sense of how to hold the mirror up to his own social status, and the economic tropes in the following May 14 letter (to E. N. Long) show the consequent strain of representing himself as a poet: "I am tired of versifying, & am irrevocably determined to rhyme no more, an employment I merely adopted '*pour passer le Temps*' when this work [*Hours of Idleness*] is accomplished, I shall have obtained all the *Eclat* I desire at present, when it shall be said that I published before I was 20; the merit of the contents is of little Consequence, provided they are not absolutely execrable, the novelty of the *Deed* (which though not unprecedented, is at least uncommon, particularly amongst *Patricians*) will secure some share of Credit" (14 May 1807). This ingeniously ingenuous passage says not only that he will rhyme no more but also that he will avoid writing more rhymes like Moore. As a patrician, his poetic employment was a labor to pass the time; but whatever his doubts about the merit of the volume, he is not content to drop the economic metaphor. His work becomes a deed, a proprietary contract, signifying not only the prodigality of its author (who is not even old enough to hold deeds) but also the incremental value of that prodigality (it secures some share of credit). Byron borrows the social connotations of this common economic metaphor to show that his work is "uncommon" (i.e., more than common, baronial) even among patricians. By means of wit, he is claiming proprietary rights of authorship *in spite of* the actual poems he produced, and he is grounding that claim in an elaborate economic trope: his "employment" is more prodigious, of *greater* "Consequence" perhaps, precisely because his work is accomplished with the nonutilitarian genius of youth.

The wit is undeniable and, by itself, not immature, but what put Byron at hazard in the "hazardous experiment" of publication was the logical fragility of this psychoeconomic investment of himself, as Brougham in the *Edinburgh Review* unkindly pointed out: "He is at best, he says, but an intruder into the groves of Parnassus; he never lived in a garret, like thorough-bred poets; and 'though he once roved a careless mountaineer in the Highlands of Scotland,' has not of late enjoyed the advantage. Moreover, he expects no profit from his publication. . . . Therefore, let us take what we get and be thankful."[12] Brougham's references to "thorough-bred," to "advantage," and to what *we* get are devastating. Reading Byron's Preface with immunity to its wit, Brougham refused to let Byron's poetic economics pass as *only* a witty trope; he insisted that Byron acknowledge both the *hauteur* and the exploitative potential in his economic metaphors. Byron, who read the review while preparing for a second edition of *Hours of Idleness,* was, "As an author, cut to atoms" (*Letters,* pp. 158–59). Someone took his jeu d'esprit seriously, although Byron, it might be argued, was never as callous about either his metaphors or his economics as Brougham intimates. In any case, he made Brougham's economic critique his own when he spoke thereafter in his private correspondence about how "Literary abuse" and "pecuniary embarrassment" (29 February 1808) had helped to work "a complete Bankruptcy of Constitution" (14 March 1808).

But Byron was already exercising his economic fictions in a less breezy way as he prepared the second edition of *Hours of Idleness.* When Ridge suggested this second edition less than six months after the original publication, Byron first cautioned against it, until "the first at least is entirely sold." He also acknowledged that "the work is your property, & you may dispose of it as you please" (*Letters,* p. 137). Explicitly relinquishing proprietary rights (in the strictest sense), Byron seems to speak as an (economically) concerned outsider. And yet in this same letter he also encloses well-conceived plans for the second edition, which would include changing the title "simply to 'poems' by Ld. Byron," cutting the preface, and adding a dedication. Even before the Brougham review, therefore, Byron began to remove the self-consciousness of both the earlier publisher-supplied title and the author-supplied disclaimer-preface. By the end of this letter, Byron is mentioning poems he would like to add and those he would alter: "These I will send when we have decided, *when, where,* & *how,* we are to publish, a new Edition." The key word is "we." Whoever owns the property, there *will* be a second edition then—one over which the author has begun to exercise authority in a newly authoritative, although polite, way. While he is more conscious of himself *as* producer, he is also less boyishly self-conscious about that self-consciousness.

His next letter to Ridge (20 November 1807) attends in greater detail to preparations for the new edition—from the kind of paper and design to the nature of the illustrations and the way in which the errata will be updated; he assumes that the edition is well under way, repeats the note of economic caution, and concludes, "Do you think, the others will be sold before the next are ready, what says Crosby? remember I have advised you not to risk it a second time, & it is not too late to retract.—However you must abide by your own discretion." At last Byron has established a more workable relationship between himself and his publisher. He chooses to act here as a kind of economic adviser to the publication of the book while also overseeing the economics of its publication in a new way—to his credit, having it both ways at once. The aesthetic dilemma he felt over *Hours of Idleness* is now sublimated into economic concern for the well-being of his publishing agents. Byron can courteously relinquish proprietary claims and yet act as a proprietor in an almost economically innocent sense of caretaker or guide. In this "contractual" way, he is, I believe, seeing himself here for the first time as an author—seeing himself, that is, in the abstract, as the figure of a poet.

To find out "what says Crosby," Byron took it upon himself to write Crosby *in propria persona* on 1 December 1807 (or one month before Byron left Cambridge for good and about seven weeks before his twentieth birthday).[13] The letter further documents Byron's newly integrated role (and it is in the letters, I am arguing, where this role is initially contracted). He reiterates his surprise at Ridge's proposal and asks Crosby point-blank for "a satisfactory reason for his proceeding" and for an economic judgment of Ridge's "premature undertaking" of a second edition—thus significantly forgetting at this moment that *Hours of Idleness* was itself, according to the author's preface, the premature undertaking. More significantly, Byron refers to an article in *The Eclectic Review* that "quits the work, to criticise the author, and expresses a doubt whether I am not a Musselman, or a Pagan," an attack on the *person* of the author that interestingly prefigures not only the personal blast to come in the *Edinburgh Review* but also the Turkish personae of his early majority. Here it discomforts Byron enough to conclude: "I am tired of my state of authorship, & was in hopes, I & my work might repose together in a happy state of oblivion, when Mr. Ridge's Intimation discomposed me not a little."

Byron's reference to his "state of authorship" is again an ironic (and modest) allusion to the nominal condition of authorship that had persisted from the moment the first edition appeared, but here the irony results in a kind of existential fatigue, caused not so much by reviewers as by the fragility or preciosity (Byron himself refers to his book in this letter as "my *precious* publication") of his labors. His wish for "a happy state of oblivion" (even though he was working on several long poems at precisely this time) perfectly balances his reference to "my state of authorship" and perhaps dramatizes the end of the line for the "species of composition" that these "first" books had utilized. One cannot be in a state of authorship and also wish for oblivion, as Byron's subliminal and probably unintended pun on "discomposed" bears witness. "Mr. Ridge's Intimation discomposed me," Byron says, "not a little." The fact is that it discomposed his juvenile, his more tenuous and tendentious, vision of himself as a composer. The new edition of 1808 would terminate his self-professed "Lease of Infancy" (*Letters,* p. 113). Whatever the contractual zeal needed to recast *Hours of Idleness* as *Poems, Original and Translated,* it would now have to be more "professional," or at least to bespeak a more authentic disinterestedness.

We can infer from Byron's follow-up letter to Crosby of 22 December 1807 (*Letters,* pp. 140–41) that Crosby replied satisfactorily to Byron's doubts about the economic wisdom of a second edition, for Byron adds in a postscript, "I am rejoiced that Ridge has not lost by the Undertaking." But this letter, while mentioning in passing yet another favorable review of the former volume (this from the *Monthly Review*), is almost wholly concerned with making arrangements for a *new* volume of poetry to be published by Crosby—its form, a "satire"; its subject, "the poetry of the present Day." (This is *British Bards,* eventually published in 1809 as *English Bards and Scotch Reviewers,* Byron's first public departure from the mode of *Fugitive Pieces* and *Hours of Idleness.*) This new poem is, in effect, a resolution of the "discomposing" he had expressed on the first of December, for here the young poet turns from his own "state of authorship" to consider, in his twenty-first year, the state of British authorship as such. Patently satirical—and, as he informs Crosby, necessarily anonymous this time—the voice will aspire to an overt "political" status that the earlier poems did not have. The anonymity is not merely a defensive reaction to the personal attack by Brougham, for Byron had decided on that strategy months before the review appeared; rather, Byron's public anonymity this time would be just that—an authorial stratagem.

However socially conscious all of Byron's footwork may now seem in retrospect, he was also thinking at this time, and for the first time, of *poetic* consciousness, which relies on different conventions and posits a different sense of utility. Rather than bank on his private identity for either special pleading or ingratiating humility, he here subsumes that "self" into the oratorical objectives of his satire. This time, the private "I" is not merely a subject; it becomes the voice of a "character" who becomes, in turn, the principal questioner of the aesthetic premises and the public morality of poetry itself. So, in *English Bards,* the author's own premises, his juridical claim to authority, would need to be proven by the poem itself. Here his poetry alone would have to prove its author credible.

Brougham, the Whig reviewer in a "Scotch" journal, would not let "politics and poetry" remain "different things," Byron complained (*Letters,* p. 159). But Byron came, reluctantly, to agree: the economics of the poet's character could not be separated from the economics of his imagination as a poet. In addressing, now, the poetic economics of Byron's subsequent authorial character, I am not referring to politics in poetry (i.e., to the appropriation in verse of political "content") nor to poetry in politics (i.e., to the utilitarian ways poetry may affect political action), the two rubrics under which Woodring categorizes "using political activities metaphorically" (p. 7). The former rubric implies a more radical separation of form and content than is, I believe, true of Romantic literature; the latter—which Woodring also rejects—may lead to the kind of Southeyan political cheerleading that Byron excoriated. My own perspective derives from a well-known passage in one of Byron's later letters where he refers enthusiastically to "the *very* poetry of politics."[14] In context he seems to mean by "poetry" the idea of nationalistic self-determination (of Italy, in this case). For Byron, "poetry," in its most incisive usage, always has this political sense of self-identification. By the same token, "politics" in Byron's time had not suffered its modern division into the discrete disciplines of "political economy" and "political science" (or "government"). It still meant not only economics but also the whole intellectual concern designated "moral philosophy." To focus on the poetry *of* (not in or for) politics is to imagine the two neither as form and content nor as cause and effect; it is, rather, to see them as modeling one another, as involved in a dynamic metaphorical exchange. Such a focus on "the economics of the imagination," as I have called it elsewhere,[15] allows one to address empirical economic and political "facts" as if they were integral to the question of self-determination—of individual identity. "As if" is the key phrase, for in speaking of metaphor in this (Romantic) way we are also speaking of the public, political status (and value) of the private imagination itself.

Neither Byron nor his fellow Romantics invented this way of thinking about metaphor. Such thinking was already evident in the language of what Blake called the "Fiends of Commerce," what Wordsworth called "statists," and what Shelley called "legislators"—that is, in the language of Adam Smith, Malthus, Ricardo, Bentham, and the Coleridge of the "method," all of whom were equally concerned with the question of metaphorical modeling. Their problem was, first, how to posit political economy and moral philosophy so that the two subjects had at least a prima facie claim to being contiguous, and then, how to support and to codify that modeling. Their initial efforts were rhetorical; they attempted to redistribute questions of economic price versus natural value and of public goods versus private necessities into a new taxonomy, into a "science" which privileged economic knowledge and the *homo economicus* who possessed it. The burden of the Romantic poets (and of their successors) was not how to unmask or to refute this "science": that was simple—they merely called it "dismal." The burden was how to redeem it or, failing that, how to find a place in it for the poet's labor and for the value of *his* vocation. In this attempt they discovered that the economic modeling of our very language is by no means the least significant effect wrought by Western economic thought—an effect which, paradoxically, their own artistic productions helped both to sustain and to complicate. In Byron's later poetry this paradoxical effect is disclosed in all its irony.

We must look then to Byron's poetry for this disclosure and not to what Byron, in the manner of most of the Romantics, eventually wrote *about* economic matters. At issue here is not the poet's polemics against commerce but the aesthetic and cultural pressure produced when the question of poetry's authority is specifically identified with the political consciousness of the author. In Byron's early career, this identification became a problem when the poet tried to imagine a poetical character to match his private status as a lord. In the years of his majority, the "poetry of politics" became an overt concern, although no work from that period seems to me to engage the economic basis of the poetical character as directly as *Don Juan*. *The Curse of Minerva* and *Waltz* discuss paper money economics, for example; and the political plays, as John P. Farrell has recently shown, address the moral dilemma—the tragedy—of political action as such. When political exigencies demand that one abandon a privileged (in all senses of the word) privacy and accept "a public and iconographic self," as Farrell argues in reference to Sardanapalus, that act of ideological engagement becomes (for Byron) morally compromising—a predicament that is apposite to the dilemma of self-identification that we have been studying in respect to the poetical character of Byron's early work.[16]

For various reasons, however, it is often difficult to distinguish the values held by the Byronic heroes of these works (ca. 1810–18) from the social value that Byron himself wished to affirm in poetry as such: this heuristic difficulty is identified in *Don Juan*. There he confronted the theoretical problem of how a poet represents his economic consciousness as an authentic "fact" of his artistic identity and of how poetry serves as both the mimetic vehicle and the "proof" that such mimesis has value. In *Don Juan* we find the kind of troping of economics that Byron was unable (or unwilling) to risk in his early work (though he troped it freely in his letters). At the same time, this troping generates a more ambitious understanding and ordering of political "facts" within the context of the artist's private needs and public aspirations. Significantly, *Don Juan* itself is also a more overtly economic commodity than, say, Byron's plays. And unlike the Turkish tales which gained him so much popularity, his "epic" poem is also overtly—even self-aggrandizingly—conscious of its own status as a commodity. The antichrematistics of his youthful work, his refusal to accept royalties (or even to participate enthusiastically as a public poet), had been subsumed by the "fact" of writing itself. The Byron of the *Don Juan* period not only accepts income from his work but is acutely aware that "Byron" is both a political and a salable "thing." On the one hand, *Don Juan* uses the ironies of this self-conscious commercialism to preempt the kind of criticism of the author which Byron himself had launched against Wordsworth, Southey, and the artisan poets—those who work for a salary. On the other hand, Byron's satire of the practical economics of his day is embedded, in *Don Juan*, in the poetic strategies of the poem itself. It is one matter to write about the deflationary trends that followed the institution of paper money, but in *Don Juan* Byron derives from that "fact" a poetic correlative, as Carl Woodring has intimated: " 'I want a hero,' he begins—an odd pursuit when gazettes have brought the price of heroes down to tuppence a peck and exposure to battle has so reduced their value that he can pack them six to a line— 'Joubert, Hoche, Marceau, Lannes, Dessaix, Moreau' " (p. 201). Desire is mediated by the price of heroes, and prosody reflects the deflation of pop-culture publishing. But Byron as author is not morally indisposed to trading on any of this.

In Cantos III and XII of *Don Juan*, Byron directs his satire against "the character of an author" in the two economic contexts that perplexed his own authorial identity as a young man. In Canto III the mercantilist-pirate Lambro's "time-serving poet,"[17] who works for wages, is like the kind of vulgar author whom the 1807 Preface was at pains to prevent Byron from becoming: a turncoat, a common laborer. In Canto XII, the poet is a miser, one who hoards his money, "that most pure imagination" (XII, ii). He is the 1807 Preface's "man of rank" par excellence. A figure of prodigious genius (like the poet as titled minor), the miser becomes "the intellectual Lord of *all*" (XII, xi). In *Don Juan* this figure of the worldly lord is so conceived as to be above moral praise or blame (or care). Through this nomination he is made vulnerable to precisely the kind of irony that Byron in 1807 could not clearly see in his own position.

I do not mean to suggest that in *Don Juan* these two fictive characters are necessarily posited by the narrator as complementary (the cantos in which they appear were published several years apart) nor that they are *Don Juan*'s only depictions of the poet. The minstrel and the poet-miser merely represent the same crisis of poetic identity that we have witnessed in Byron's early work. As satirized in *Don Juan*, this crisis is mediated by Byron's own implicated presence in his poem. Both cantos explicitly compare Byron's own youthful exertions as a poet to the careers of these fictive characters (see III, lxxxiii and XII, xvii), a Byronic technique that Michael Cooke has aptly called "the material use of himself as a subject" (p. 96). For our purposes the key word is "material." *Don Juan*'s representation of the character of the author in explicitly economic situations allows Byron to play out, by means of such representation, the psychomachia witnessed in his early work. The underlying action of this psychomachia is not the quasi-Christian redemptive pattern spoken of by Pound, in which the poet undergoes a purgation and emerges from his early work reasonably cleansed and strengthened. Rather, the action of *Don Juan*'s psychomachia is the more typically Byronic patterning of psychological, socio-economic, and cultural "facts" so as to disclose the disparities between them. In ethics the name for such disparity is hypocrisy, but Byron is equally concerned with the epistemological implications of this disparity: how our attempts to order the world of "facts" fail to coincide with the ideas of order by which we *say* we live. And the two symbolizations, the two ideas of order, explicitly at issue in these cantos are economics and poetry.

Lambro's minstrel makes poetic capital of any occasion—"His Muse made increment of anything" (III, lxxxv)—but he can make nothing actually happen in the world of facts. On the other hand, the miser *could* make anything happen, thanks to his capital reserve, his stock of imagination in the form of money, but his principle of action is to hoard, to make nothing occur. Although he possesses the means to act, this potential remains most potent only as long as he does not expend it. As a poet of time, the minstrel can only sing of loss; all his songs are implicitly elegiac. Also a poet of time, the miser can only "sing" of a speculative future, which might be improved by his investments, but which remains merely imaginary. So he troubles no one; is neither a bore nor a nuisance. But his lack of troubles is morally deafening. Cutting across these polar expressions of the temporally compromised economist-poet is the author of *Don Juan* himself, for whom neither fictive persona is a wholly acceptable "character of an author," yet who finds himself needing to define his own labor, the writing of *Don Juan,* in context with and in answer to them.

Following the panoramic narration of Lambro's approach to home in Canto III, the focus narrows to a "suite" of characters who make Juan and Haidee's "new establishment complete." Among these entertainers—dwarfs, dancing girls, and black eunuchs—the most important is the poet, another kind of freak, "He being paid to satirise or flatter" (III, lxxviii). Both satire and flattery color Byron's ensuing description of him. As Lambro's house poet in this pseudoodyssey, the minstrel resembles the orator Demodokos in *The Odyssey.* But this singer, "a sad trimmer" (III, lxxxii) who adjusts the tenor of his lyre to suit the generosity of those who commission it, also gives the traditional practice of *imitatio* the lie: "He praised the present, and abused the past, / Reversing the good custom of old days." Haidee and the others may be flattered that their present life is thus praised, but, in disabusing the past of any nostalgic golden age, the minstrel is also showing Haidee just how ironic and precarious her Edenic island solitude really is. Even as he sings of the present, her father is getting nearer.

The minstrel does not need the illusory promises of a golden age to work a profit for his songs. Singing of time, he renders time as a self-investment by trading upon the poetic conventions of whatever nation he happens to be visiting. In France he writes chansons, in Spain romance ballads, and so on. On Lambro's Greek isle, his anacreontic song, "The Isles of Greece" (between sts. lxxxvi and lxxxvii), initially pays tribute to the heroism and to the lyric accomplishment of Greece "when Greece was young" (III, lxxxvii). It ends, however, not only by satirizing these but also by satirizing itself.

Consider, for example, the refrain of the lyric, "Fill high the bowl with

Samian wine." As Willis Pratt has shown, this is not mere nostalgia for good wine; the Samians, it is also implied, betrayed the classical Greek *arete* just as nineteenth-century Greeks were betraying their democratic legacy by accepting Turkish domination.[18] At the same time, the wine is explicitly said to have "made Anacreon's song divine" (st. 11)—a poet who served Polycrates, a tyrant famous for his piracy,[19] which is also the traditional practice of the Mycenaean kings in *The Iliad* and of Lambro in *Don Juan.* Anacreon, then, turns out to be an ironic exemplar of the glory that was Greek poetry. But there is a further irony. In his own poetry Anacreon admits to being a failed "orator" or epic poet: he is merely a lyric poet. Byron, who included translations of Anacreon in his early volumes, was, as a neophyte poet, like Anacreon in following the lyric impulse, the poetics of feeling, and in not looking beyond "the moment of composition." Now, as the "epic" poet of *Don Juan,* he inserts this lyric into the text in order to ask: "For what is left the poet here?" (st. 6). For, along with the degeneration of the Greek *arete* has come a degeneration of lyric poetry: "And must thy Lyre, so long divine, / Degenerate into hands like mine?" (st. 5). "The Isles of Greece" is, then, a self-implicating, self-satirizing song, and the impotence of those hands is precisely the issue.

At the end of the lyric, Byron's hands are also seen to be in the till. The narrative that resumes following the lyric tells us that we have not heard what Lambro's minstrel "sung" but only what he "would, or could, or should have sung" (III, lxxxvii). At this one moment of composition, therefore, the identity of the fictive poet and the identity of the Byronic narrator are conflated, thus allowing Byron to turn a poetic profit by voicing his own sympathies for a prophetic idea of Greece that is also, ironically, a kind of elegy for his own "warm youth" (III, lxxxiii). So, while the wage-earning poet of Canto III is initially contrasted to the wage-scorning youthful Byron, he is also compared to the author of *Don Juan* in the lyric where their identities fuse. Borrowing from tradition and past literary conventions in order to work his own profit, the degenerate lyricist, who has no passions of his own, no authorial "self," accrues to himself whatever feelings are convenient for his mercantilist purposes—his capitalism thus parodying both genuine *imitatio* and genuine "feeling":

> His strain displayed some feeling—right or wrong;
> And feeling, in a poet, is the source
> Of others' feeling; but they are such liars,
> And take all colours—like the hands of dyers. (III, lxxxvii)

Poets' lyres make them liars, and Byron is also asking if such lyrics have degenerated into (capitalistic) hands like *his.*

In the next stanza (III, lxxxviii), Byron launches into a meditation upon the power of the dyer's hand both to glorify and to demythologize history.

Because "words are things" (III, lxxxviii), that which is written enters into the same "repertory of facts" (XIV, xiii) as events and actions.[20] Poetry *is* economics, or at least a poet's words can have the same effect on the "facts." The writer's power to reshape historical time in his own image through the supererogatory power of the Imagination alone leads Byron to "digress" about his contemporaries and the inflated value of "Romantic" diction as a currency of exchange (III, xciii–xcv). Wordsworth stands out for his "drowsy, frowzy" (III, xciv), nontraditional use of common language: " 'Pedlars,' and 'Boats,' and 'Waggons!' Oh, ye shades / Of Pope and Dryden, are we come to this?" (III, c). This lament, however, reads like an unwitting fulfillment of Pope's own prophecy that what Chaucer's language is, Dryden's will be. Moreover, while criticizing Wordsworth's "Waggon," Byron manages to spin his own incremental rhymes with "dragon" and "nag on"—the last being more ostentatiously vulgar than anything Wordsworth penned. As usual in *Don Juan*, Wordsworth is ridiculed not for his democratized aesthetics but for failing to follow it through, now that he has become, like Lambro's poet, a hired writer, paid off by the Excise Office.[21] But it is Byron himself who, ironically, is also "degenerating."

In stanza ci the feast ends and the poet's song is done, but the incremental poetics set in motion by Lambro's minstrel continue for the rest of the canto to infect the author's own narrative. Three acts of *imitatio* bring the canto to a close. The "Ave Maria," sung at vespers on the island while Juan and Haidee admire the sunset, irrupts as stanzas cii and ciii of Byron's own poem, to be followed by an expansive translation of a Sappho fragment in stanza cvii and by an equally free imitation of Dante's *Purgatorio* in stanza cviii. The narrator, now left with what he calls "the transactions of my hero" (III, cx), finds his own poem already engaged in a transaction with the same poetic past that the minstrel exploited. The insight that ends the canto is that to write on anything at all is to engage in a "transaction," an economic exchange not only with one's predecessors or even with one's contemporaries in the art but with the "business" (as Byron calls it in XII, xxiii) of one's own narrative.

The canto ends with an act of abrupt economy. "I must cut down / (In copying) this long canto into two" (III, cxi), he concludes, citing Aristotle as an authority that epic poems are long. So the double meaning of "copying" locates precisely the whole irony of Canto III. In copying over his manuscript to make a fair copy, Byron copies or imitates the classical dictum about epic length. But such imitation mangles the message—or at least translates it into another kind of transaction. For Byron's canto is too long, "*too* epic" (III, cxi). And yet in cutting down the one long canto, he does not economize but incrementally lengthens the poem with another installment, Canto IV, thus turning Aristotle to a profit and showing that his *own* muse can make an increment of anything. Whereas the minstrel traded on time for his livelihood, Byron defers to the past, to Aristotle's *poietikis* (III, cxi), in order to lengthen time, to expand the time in which, narratively, he works his own poetic transactions.

Canto III ends, therefore, by expressing the poet's potential for creating time, an ironic variation on the practice of Lambro's poet. Byron alleviates the "tediousness" (III, cxi) of a long canto by minting a new one, thus simultaneously shortening and lengthening time. By apportioning narrative time according to this poetic economy, the narrator moves to substantiate his nomination of himself to the title of epic poet. The final irony, though, is that he finds himself capitalizing on his own willful imagination in the same way as Lambro's poet—or as Wordsworth—with only the consoling difference that *he* at least knows the cost of such self-(de)-generation.

Byron's comic capitulation to his own irony in Canto III acquires an unexpected sublimity in Canto XII, where the themes discussed above are rethreaded and projected in the figure of the poet-miser:

> He is your only poet;—Passion, pure
>   And sparkling on from heap to heap, displays,
> *Possessed,* the ore, of which *mere hopes* allure
>   Nations athwart the deep. (XII, viii)

By possessing the object of his passion, an object that other men and nations can only hope for, the miser might be said to "own" his passion in a way that Lambro's poet, with his dyer's hand, does not. In this stanza Byron makes it clear that what the miser possesses are precious gems, later equated with "ready money" (XII, xii) and "cash" (XII, xiv). And so, a secondary irony turns on the disparity between such "real" substances and the paper money being used in Byron's time:

> O Gold! I still prefer thee unto paper,
> Which makes bank credit like a bank of *vapour.* (XII, iv)
>
> ....
> How beauteous are rouleaus! how charming chests
>   Containing ingots, bags of dollars, coins,
> (Not of old victors, all whose heads and crests
>   Weigh not the thin ore where their visage shines,
> But) of fine unclipped gold, where dully rests
>   Some likeness, which the glittering cirque confines,
> Of modern, reigning, sterling, stupid stamp!—
> Yes! ready money *is* Aladdin's lamp. (XII, xii)

In distinguishing between "things" of substance, such as ingots and coins, and mere verbal promises on paper, Byron discloses a tertiary irony. He identifies *himself* as a speculator on paper: "I'm serious—so are all men upon paper; / And why should I not form my speculation, / And hold up to the Sun my little taper?" (XII, xxi). By characterizing himself as a paper speculator, Byron opens an ironic distance between the miser who is "your only poet" and Byron's own poetic project. To understand how this irony works, we must see Byron's poetic speculations in their larger contexts.

The miser's claim to being a poet rests upon "your" (i.e., society's, the reader's) willingness to regard his economically valuable possessions as capable of generating "pure" (because completely useful and functional) speculations. Byron's (poetic) speculations, which run counter to these, have merely the diminutive value of a taper held to the sun. This ironic juxtaposing of a poet's "means" with the means of exchange is a tactic used by many poets of the period. Byron's earliest poetic guide and lifelong friend, Thomas Moore, wrote an ode on cash; Thomas Love Peacock did a whole volume of what he called *Paper Money Lyrics;* and Keats pointedly named his goddess "Moneta" in the *Fall of Hyperion.*[22] Byron's acquaintance, Samuel Rogers, the so-called banker-poet, seemed to embody in his dual vocation both concerns. Byron's own money passage in Canto XII is perhaps most directly connected, however, to Shelley's assertion in his *Defence of Poetry* that money is the "visible incarnation" of the "principle of the self" and thus the direct antithesis of "Poetry." As the empirical embodiment of one's self-interest (following the pun on "principal"), money for Shelley betokens the failure of the self to experience that sympathetic going out of the self in interest toward others that he calls "love." Byron, however, grounds his discussion of money's metaphysical consequence in a more patently empirical context than Shelley's.

Behind the miser's love of "substantial" moneys (things like precious metals and gems that come from mines) is Byron's Rochdale estate and the complex ironies of what "mining" and personal possession mean. Until shortly before Byron's death, the Rochdale estate provided income from mining, not from rents. Hence, the income was subject to parish rates and tithes, for it was the source of the income that determined whether it was taxable (in this case, by the Church). "In a sense," Woodring says, "this is exactly the protest against commercialism that Coleridge was making" (p. 208)—which means, of course, that Byron's is not a protest against commercialism as such but against the hypocrisy of a capitalistic Church. The social and public advantage of taxation is not the issue: the ecclesiastical mining of one's private income is. The moral rationale for parish rates is the Golden Rule, the idea of unselfish Christian charity, but the taking of tithes by the Church is neither a selfless action nor a politically disinterested one. It is a way, in fact, of avoiding political accountability by appealing to a higher (Christian) economics.

The miser's wisdom is calibrated to just such a "superior" economy:

> Perhaps he hath great projects in his mind,
>   To build a college, or to found a race,
> A hospital, a church,—and leave behind

> Some dome surmounted by his meagre face;
> Perhaps he fain would liberate Mankind
>   Even with the very ore which makes them base;
> Perhaps he would be wealthiest of his nation,
>   Or revel in the joys of calculation.
>
> But whether all, or each, or none of these
>   May be the hoarder's principle of action,
> The fool will call such mania a disease:—
>   What is his *own?* Go—look at each transaction,
> Wars, revels, loves—do these bring men more ease
>   Than the mere plodding through each "vulgar fraction"?
> Or do they benefit Mankind? Lean Miser!
> Let spendthrifts' heirs inquire of yours—who's wiser? (XII, x–xi)

The repetition of "perhaps" is the source of the miser's "joy," for his "great" principle of action is to remain innocent of any single principle of action, any ideological identification of *his* responsibilities. Perhaps the miser's "lean" and hungry look betrays a realization that he would do better to "liberate Mankind" *from* as well as *with* "the very ore which makes them base." But Byron's strategy here is not to ask what specific actions would benefit mankind but to wonder if *any* of man's "transactions" is free of "disease." Underlying the seemingly beneficial utility of money, its veritable dance of imaginative options, is a radical equivocation of terms which Byron underscores by quoting two lines from Scott's *Lay of the Last Minstrel* (the title of which may ironically recall Lambro's capitalist minstrel in Canto III): "Love rules the Camp, the Court, the Grove,—for Love / Is Heaven, and Heaven is Love" (XII, xii). Byron then dissects these capitalized abstractions to show that what constitutes their disease is the way they capitalize on the base term that defines them—Cash:

> But if Love don't, *Cash* does, and Cash alone:
>   Cash rules the Grove, and fells it too besides;
> Without cash, camps were thin, and courts were none;
>   Without cash, Malthus tells you—"take no brides,"
> So Cash rules Love the ruler, on his own
>   High ground, as virgin Cynthia sways the tides:
> And as for "Heaven being Love," why not say honey
> Is way? Heaven is not Love, 't is Matrimony. (XII, xiv)

The key phrase is "why not say"; for what you say, in Byron's richest epistemology, determines what "things" are. Each act of naming nominates language to the status of "fact," and each verbal act is such a nomination. Here his magnificently sophistical argument for why Cash rules (as in the quasi-etymological puns that couple married love with mother-money) further discloses a poet who is manipulating language as thoroughly as a miser manipulates his capital. The poem seems to imagine the empirical value and utilitarian status of the miser's "poetry" as originating in a moral vacuum; at the same time, the narrator rushes in to fill that vacuum with a principle of verbal action: irony.

For Byron, one characteristic of an author is that he must use his poem not only to speculate upon the utility of things but to speculate with those things which are words—and the latter speculations prove just as morally elusive, just as ironic, as the miser's:

> I perch upon an humbler promontory,
>   Amidst Life's infinite variety:
> With no great care for what is nicknamed Glory,
>   But speculating as I cast mine eye
> On what may suit or may not suit my story,
>   And never straining hard to versify,
> I rattle on exactly as I'd talk
> With anybody in a ride or walk. (XV, xix)

McGann cites this stanza as an example of Byron's speculative craft in the fullest sense of "speculate."[23] But it is the economic sense of the word, which McGann does not enumerate in his list of the word's "entire significance," that expresses Byron's most radical insight into the poet's compromised "character." When a poet speculates on paper, he necessarily speculates with the utility of language. But this poetic form of speculation reveals only that irony is deflationary and that poems on paper are not likely to be worth any more than deflated paper money. The exploitative potential of economic language becomes the ironic result of economic speculation and thought.

How does poetry avoid imitating the very disease that it would expose (and, by satirizing, cure)? Or, in terms of the economic tropes that Byron develops in *Don Juan,* how does a poet avoid being implicated by the same economics upon which his poem is capitalizing? The answer may reside in the character of that imaginary interlocutor of Canto XV, xix, who is Byron's fictive representation of the reader. Each attempt to nominate the poet to an office of public utility and poetry to a position of value meets a similar predicament: the figure of the reader. Since poetry's utility cannot be willed by the poet but must depend upon the willingness of the reader to profit from it, it must become, lacking such response, merely a form of self-serving private capitalism, like the miser's. But even *with* such a response, the poet risks selling out to such approbation—he risks becoming a mere entertainer, like Lambro's minstrel.

We began this essay by considering the young Byron's attempts to define himself as "usefully employed." At that time he divided the question of utility so as to distinguish between his character *as* an author and his larger political potential as a Whig lord. In *Don Juan* the question is reconstituted so that Byron *must* ask, and by means of his art, how publicly useful the work of imagination is. One kind of reply that he makes is self-deflating and comic: "And though these lines should only line portmanteaus, / Trade will be all the better for these Cantos" (XIV, xiv). This comedy should not distract us from Byron's serious hope that his cantos will have a functional significance, that their fictive orderings may engender social exchanges for "the better." Here, imagining that his poem may become a "thing" to "line portmanteaus," he perceives not merely a disparity between his authorial intent and the uses to which his labor is actually put by the "Gent. reader" (XIV, vii); but he also witnesses the commoditization of his labor into the system of production and exchange that the poem attempted to represent. The vulnerability of the author's "character" to the characterizations of his work made by the public is not the critical point. The deeper irony is that, through his representations of the minstrel and the miser, Byron has shown himself able to understand the amassing irony of such vulnerability but without being able to do anything about it.

In speculating upon the factual world in which we live and upon that which might make it "better," *Don Juan* thus speculates upon its own psychoeconomic integrity. Increasingly, in *Don Juan,* these speculations are brought together in the same moment of composition.

Don Juan might be read as a sublimation of the young Byron's fear that his character as an author and as a man of rank would bankrupt one another, that the "fact" of composing would dispossess him of his reputation and feelings. Quoting Pope, Byron asks in Canto XIV the same question that he put to himself in 1807:

> But "why then publish?"—There are no rewards
>   Of fame or profit when the World grows weary.
> I ask in turn,—Why do you play at cards?
>   Why drink? Why read?—To make some hour less dreary.
> It occupies me to turn back regards
>   On what I've seen or pondered, sad or cheery;
> And what I write I cast upon the stream,
> To swim or sink—I have had at least my dream. (XIV, xi)

The value affirmed here is still "the moment of composition," which Byron calls his "dream." This "moment" is a kind of spot of time, caught between the precompositionary act of turning one's regard back to the past and the postcompositionary act of casting one's pages on the stream of an uncertain futurity. Such a transaction with time curiously combines the temporal poetics of Lambro's poet and the daydream poetics of the poet-miser into the ongoing, self-sustaining, but never sufficient act of writing, which has no certain utility beyond its own exercise. That moment of composition stands for the self's complicity with time and for the self's power to transact with *it*. But the self is as much degenerated by this labor as triumphant over it. When Byron says in Canto XII, turning from his palinode about money and misers to his own narrative story, "And now to business" (XII, xxiii), he is identifying by means of this commercial trope his inability to stop the process of composition from becoming reified, from acquiring a commodity status. Answering the question "why publish" with the question "why read," *Don Juan* confronts its own imaginative economics head-on, yielding a kind of fictive coinage that deflates at the moment of issue its own self-inflationary tendencies. What the poet possesses, then, is not his own. The poem, cast upon the platitudinous stream of time, invites us to recall here its opening line: "I want a hero." In time, however, this desire has become, like the poem itself, the property of its readers, if they want it. Even more perversely, the lack of that hero is precisely what continues to authorize desire and to authenticate this whole poetic/proprietary exchange.

Ironically, in the seventeen years or so between his "first" book(s) and the "last" cantos of the unfinished *Don Juan*, Byron's idea of poetry as "fugitive pieces" takes a literalizing turn. It is also ironic that the "idleness" of the 1807 title should be so literally redefined as a necessarily dissatisfied and incomplete labor and that fame should so much resemble dispossession of the self. Byron's precarious socioeconomic situation in 1807 as an indebted, titled minor emerges in *Don Juan* as the psychoeconomic predicament of poetry itself (or at least of such poetry as *Don Juan*). What we have traced as the empirical, biographical dilemma in 1807 of the man of rank trying to realize his character as an author is finally reassessed as a contradiction inherent in any imaginative act that tries to account for its own inherent value: "But what's this to the purpose? you will say. / Gent. reader, nothing; a mere speculation, / For which my sole excuse is—'t is my way" (XIV, vii).

Notes

1. *Selected Prose, 1909–1965*, ed. William Cookson (New York: New Directions, 1975), pp. 34–35.
2. See *The Letters of Ezra Pound, 1907–1941*, ed. D. D. Paige (New York: Harcourt, Brace and World, 1950), p. 58.
3. *Politics in English Romantic Poetry* (Cambridge: Harvard Univ. Press, 1970), p. 10.
4. Stendahl, writing in 1830, remembered Byron in 1817: "He cherished in his bosom two contradictory inclinations. He wished to be received as a man of rank, and admired as a brilliant poet" (*His Very Self and Voice: Collected Conversations of Lord Byron*, ed. Ernest J. Lovell, Jr. [New York: Macmillan, 1954], p. 203). The roots of this contradiction are the subject of Jerome J. McGann's *Fiery Dust: Byron's Poetic Development* (Chicago: Univ. of Chicago Press, 1968); see esp. pp. 3–28.
5. McGann, *Fiery Dust*, pp. 20–21.

6. See Leslie A. Marchand, *Byron: A Portrait* (New York: Alfred A. Knopf, 1970), p. 42.

7. *"In My Hot Youth"*: *Byron's Letters and Journals, Volume I, 1798–1810*, ed. Leslie A. Marchand (London: John Murray, 1973), p. 115; hereafter referred to as *Letters*).

8. Byron's physiological metaphor above, like his economic metaphors to be studied below, is quite accurate, for he literally did engage in changing (by trimming down) his portly physique during the period that *Hours of Idleness* was in press, his notation of weight loss often coming in his letters immediately after mention of his upcoming literary production, as if he were acquiring a new self all around (see *Letters*, pp. 115, 117).

9. *Lord Byron: Accounts Rendered* (New York: Harper & Row, 1974), pp. 90–91. See pages 82–96 for a full account of Byron's economic transactions as a minor.

10. Jerome J. McGann notes that Byron continued throughout his life to disavow his poetic "vocation" and to renounce poetry as that which "should only occupy the idle"; he concludes, I think justly, that "Byron had to transform in his mind his sense of a literary life." (*Don Juan in Context* [Chicago: Univ. of Chicago Press, 1976], pp. 6–7). I am arguing here that the transformational process began almost immediately, from the first moment that Byron was nominally an "author."

11. Thomas Moore writes in the preface to *The Poetical Works of the Late Thomas Little, Esq.*, 3rd ed. (London, 1803) that the "author, as unambitious as indolent, scarce ever looked beyond the moment of composition" (p. v).

12. Henry P. Brougham, unsigned review, *Edinburgh Review*, XI (Feb. 1808), 285–89; rpt. in *Byron: The Critical Heritage*, ed. Andrew Rutherford (New York: Barnes & Noble, 1970), p. 32.

13. Unpublished letter, Humanities Research Center, University of Texas at Austin. Copyright by John Murray.

14. *The Works of Lord Byron: Letters and Journals*, ed. Rowland E. Prothero (London: John Murray, 1898–1901), V, 205.

15. *The Economics of the Imagination* (Amherst: Univ. of Massachusetts Press, 1980).

16. John P. Farrell, *Revolution as Tragedy: The Dilemma of the Moderate from Scott to Arnold* (Ithaca: Cornell Univ. Press, 1980), p. 167.

17. The phrase is Michael G. Cooke's in *The Blind Man Traces the Circle: On the Patterns and Philosophy of Byron's Poetry* (Princeton: Princeton Univ. Press, 1969), p. 167.

18. *Byron's Don Juan: Notes on the Variorum Edition, Volume IV* (Austin: Univ. of Texas Press, 1957), p. 95.

19. For Polycrates' economic practices, both legal and piratical, see A. R. Burn, *The Lyric Age of Greece* (1960; rpt. New York: Minerva Press, 1968), pp. 314–17.

20. Byron elsewhere identifies the phrase "words are things" as the coinage of a capitalist, the economist and statesman Mirabeau (see Pratt, p. 97).

21. See *Don Juan*, Dedication, stanza vi for Byron's most overt reference to Wordsworth's (economic) sell-out.

22. For Moneta's economic significance, see K. K. Ruthven, "Keats and *Dea Moneta*," in *Studies in Romanticism*, 15 (1975), 445–59; for the use of such poetic economics in other Romantic writers, see Heinzelman, pp. 11–33, 196–233.

23. McGann, *Don Juan in Context*, p. 143: "Byron calls his method in *Don Juan* a 'speculating' one (XV, 19), but the word has been, in his usage, returned to its entire significance. Byron's 'speculations' are visions (intuitions, insights), views (opinions), speculations (experimental operations), and acts of seeing (physical engagements)."

Editor's Bibliographical Note

There is little in Byron studies that is quite comparable to Heinzelman's stimulating essay, except for the Christensen piece on Byron's "career" included in this volume; but on the almost symbiotic relationship in Byron's mind between the economic and political, see Peter J. Manning's fine essay, "Tales and Politics: *The Corsair, Lara,* and *The White Doe of Rylstone,"* in *Byron: Poetry and Politics,* ed. E. A. Stürzl and J. Hogg (Univ. of Salzburg, 1981). Nevertheless, Jerome J. McGann's evolving argument about Byron's development of a "poetic character" forms an important contrapuntal as well as reinforcing view. That argument is first conceived in *Fiery Dust: Byron's Poetic Development* (Chicago and London: University of Chicago Press, 1968), modified and redirected in *"Don Juan" in Context* (Chicago: University of Chicago Press, 1976), and most fully developed in the excerpt from *The Beauty of Inflections* (Oxford: Oxford University Press, 1985) included in this volume. I single out McGann's work here because in many ways it has been the most influential body of Byron criticism in recent years; but it needs to be remembered that at the core of much of that criticism, especially in the last two decades or so, is the difficult issue of Byron's acute sense of the necessity for fashioning a poetic self. I select here but a few of what I regard to be the most interesting publications in very recent years: Peter J. Manning, *Byron and His Fictions* (Detroit: Wayne State University Press, 1978), a carefully modulated and revealing Freudian approach; Malcolm Kelsall, *Byron's Politics* (Sussex and Totowa: Harvester Press and Barnes & Noble, 1987), the best book to date on Byron's political self; Frederick W. Shilstone, *Byron and the Myth of Tradition* (Lincoln: University of Nebraska Press, 1988), a "biography" of the poet's "consciousness" struggling to define itself in conflict with tradition. Disappointing but worth consulting is Philip Martin, *Byron: A Poet Before His Public* (Cambridge: Cambridge University Press, 1982).

There is also little to compare to Heinzelman's detailed analysis of the series of Byron's first poetic volumes culminating in what we now refer to as *Hours of Idleness.* In fact, those early poems are still relatively unstudied, except for isolated comments in essays dealing with Byron's lyrics. The most extensive discussion of the early poems are in Robert F. Gleckner, *Byron and the Ruins of Paradise* (Baltimore: Johns Hopkins University Press, 1967); McGann, *Fiery Dust;* Cooke, *The Blind Man Traces the Circle: On the Patterns and Philosophy of Byron's Poetry* (Princeton: Princeton University Press, 1969); and Shilstone, *Byron and the Myth of Tradition.* For the biographical background of *Hours of Idleness* see Willis W. Pratt, *Byron at Southwell: The Making of a Poet* (Austin: University of Texas Press, 1948), and, most recently, the excellent notes to these youthful poems in the first volume of McGann's superb *Lord Byron: The Complete Poetical Works* (Oxford: Oxford University Press, 1980).

Byron's Career:
The Speculative Stage

JEROME CHRISTENSEN

I

On the problem that Byron presents to literary historians Macaulay was acute:

> It is always difficult to separate the literary character of a man who lives in our own time from his personal character. It is peculiarly difficult to make this separation in the case of Lord Byron. For it is scarcely too much to say, that Lord Byron never wrote without some reference, direct or indirect, to himself. The interest excited by the events of his life mingles itself in our minds, and probably in the minds of almost all our readers, with the interest which properly belongs to his works. A generation must pass away before it will be possible to form a fair judgment of his books, considered merely as books. At present they are not only books, but relics.[1]

Macaulay was a good diagnostician but a faulty prognosticator. More than one generation has passed away; we have had discriminations of romanticisms that pigeonhole Byron, antithetical structures that satanize him, theoretical paradigms that abstract him, and comprehensive surveys that ignore him— we still lack a fair, historically informed judgment of Byron's books, "considered merely as books." But the projections continue. When, in 1976, M. H. Abrams was called to account for the exclusion of Byron from his authoritative history of high romanticism, *Natural Supernaturalism,* he offered a prediction not unlike Macaulay's. Abrams forecasted a history that would "focus on . . . the ironic perspective in general and the theory and practice of 'Romantic irony' in particular. . . . In this plot, the hero among the English Romantics will be Byron, a poet I . . . deliberately left out because . . . as I said, 'in his greatest work [he] speaks with an ironic counter-voice and deliberately opens a satirical perspective on the vatic stance of his Romantic contemporaries.' "[2]

More fortunate than Macaulay, Abrams did not have to wait even for

ELH 52 (1985): 59–84. Reprinted by permission of the Johns Hopkins University Press.

one generation to see his projection realized. In the last few years his call has been answered by four studies of romantic irony: Michael G. Cooke's *Acts of Inclusion,* Anne K. Mellor's *English Romantic Irony,* Tilottama Rajan's *Dark Interpreter,* and David Simpson's *Irony and Authority in Romantic Poetry*—the first two of which grant Byron the eminence Abrams indicated he deserves, the last two referring to him only in passing. Yet amidst this chorus of respondents not a single voice professes to situate Byronic irony within a historical plot.[3] It could not be any other way. Despite the ostensible catholicity of his pluralism, in calling for the history of the ironic counter-voice Abrams has projected what is in fact an impossible history; for, according to the idealist metaphysics that informs Abrams's pluralism at all points, the counter-voice, like the echo, cannot have a genuine history of its own.

There is no future in trying to counter Abrams by inventing a history more true than his. But it may be possible to do something different: to follow the script of circumstance and write a romantic history impossible to voice. Such a history could begin with nothing better than this Byron whom history has already designated as a misfit in the plot of providence, a poet whom Macaulay has aptly described as a "relic." Macaulay's characterization would have seemed apposite but a shade parochial to the writer who, in the journal entitled "Detached Thoughts," conjectured that "man may be the relic of some higher material being wrecked in a former world."[4] Byron imagines his residual status as synecdoche for the condition of man in general. That man is not, however, conceived as the visible symbol of some ultimately intelligible whole, but as an enigmatic remnant of a historically contingent catastrophe. The generic ill-fittedness of man, left over in this place where he finds himself thinking detached thoughts, is not and never can be proof of his secret affiliations with a transcendent spirit, but it is circumstantial evidence of the wreck of a material being, about which we can never expect to receive direct testimony. Although the evidence of circumstance may never cohere to tell the full story, it remains, for Byron and Byronist, the only evidence at hand; and its telling inadequacy at least prevents a definitive falsification of man's estate. We may suspect that a history of leftover man, man the relic, may ultimately be impossible, but we can be confident that it will be circumstantial.

The historical catastrophe to which Byron hearkens could, and properly should, be characterized in various ways, each of which in the typical Byronic mix confounds the personal with the epochal: socially, as the sense that the aristocratic status to which he had risen suddenly failed to count as the sort of privilege it once did; poetically, as the disappearance of the kind of civically virtuous, authoritative poetic practice he associated with the name Pope; politically, in the decisive and, as we shall see, instructive failure of Napoleon Bonaparte to translate the Alexandrian dream of world empire into actuality; philosophically, by the success of skeptical empiricism in stripping man of his pretensions to sure knowledge and native power. But whichever version of the catastrophe is emphasized, to write a history about Byron, the writer who remains, is to write a history of his career.

The poetic career, in the sense in which I want to use it and in the way Byron opted to practice it, should be sharply distinguished from the poetic vocation in either its classical, primarily Virgilian, or its romantic, finally puritan, format.[5] The classical, as Edward Said has described it, "required taking certain memorial steps and imitating a ritual progress. . . ." Pope is the pattern here. Both his attentiveness to Virgilian precedent and his complete confidence in the propriety and authority of his imitation allowed Pope to accommodate himself to the exigencies of the marketplace without fear of corruption, with no anxiety that he could be mistaken for one of the hacks he abused. The romantic rejection of that model did not entail a break with the vocational norm. Abrams's work has definitively established that vocation has a "high" romantic sense, which entails an ethos of revolution rather than recapitulation and which adheres to the Augustinian, radically Protestant conception of the spirit's progress. The neoclassical vocation was undertaken as the appropriate return on a bookish education, was retricted to a privileged class, and imitated antique models. The romantic vocation, on the contrary, conformed to no such decorum; it responded to a *call* and obeyed a transcendental economy which rendered historical progress as a fall away from that original voice—a deficit redeemable only by a return to the original calling. If Pope's *Dunciad* is the exemplary poem of the Augustan vocation, Wordsworth's *Prelude,* as Abrams has shown in *Natural Supernaturalism,* is preeminent among the romantic kind.[7] Byron's poetry, unrepentantly renegade, neither imitates a progress nor heeds any call. He has no poetic vocation. Among those early nineteenth-century poems that have entered the canon, Byron's relics alone direct us toward a history of the course of the writer's material existence, the disposition of his texts in a career.

A history of Byron's poetic career requires replacing the ideal standards of propriety and originality with an empirical criterion, "the true touchstone of desert—success."[8] Byron's success can be gauged by diverse indices, some almost strictly quantitative. One can determine the number of his books printed and circulated, count the reviews of and testimonials to his work, weigh the deference paid by booksellers and printers, enumerate the imitators and plagiarists, measure the proliferation of anecdotes and memoirs. So much would attest to Byron's poetic success as a fact of commerce. But because success is also a social, cultural, and political fact, its evidences are also, if not "subjective," surely intersubjective, transactive in complicated ways. For example, as a social fact, the successful career is recognized as such by influential contemporaries of the writer; indeed, it was the case with Byron's career that those contemporaries were usually associates of one kind or another who had developed an interest in the career—whether that interest was acknowledged explicitly, as it was by John Murray, Byron's publisher, or implicitly, as with the *Blackwood's* reviewer of *Don Juan,* who unwittingly adopted Byron's imagery to excoriate Byron's work.[9] Moreover, a successful career reproduces itself in the careers of others. Samuel Smiles's rosy recollection of John Murray, *A Publisher and His Friends,*[10] would not have been possible were it not for the successful careers of Gifford, Scott, Byron, and others. A pure success story, Murray's "life" is an epiphenomenon of commerce. The book moves in triumphal procession from letter to letter as though conducting an advertising campaign (N.B.: Smiles's *Memoir* was issued by the publishing house that Murray built). Smiles does not doubt the propriety of sacrificing temporal continuity to the end of displaying the transcendental unity of the copyrighted properties held by Murray, the shapeliness of those well-wrought careers that made Murray's life not only coherent but possible. Correspondingly, if we read the critics Francis Jeffrey and John Gibson Lockhart, it is because of Byron's successful career. Jeffrey, in particular, rose to the occasion of Byron and became an important critic as a consequence of his vigorous attempt to engage poetry which, though it violated his standards of excellence, imposed itself on him as an empirically unignorable force—a force which he tapped in his attempt to retain and augment his own power to impose a certain standard of taste on his readers.[11] Contrarily, if we ignore Jeffrey, it is because of his dismissal of Wordsworth and because of our cultivated disregard for the relevance of successs to Wordsworth's greatness. For the Wordsworthian it seems sufficient to quote the notorious judgment on *The Excursion,* "This will never do," and close the book on the Edinburgh reviewer. Yet Wordsworth's triumph over his detractors is less an example of surpassing virtue properly rewarded than an effect of Coleridge's rhetorical forcefulness in dramatizing (see book 4 of the *Biographia Literaria*) the imposition of Wordsworth on *him,* in purifying that act of all taint of policy, and, in a move taken explicitly against Jeffrey, in rendering that primal scene as the mythic premise for a new theory of poetry and for the institution of modern criticism.

A social practice, the successful career can be planned but not fully controlled. The statement, "If I do this, then such and such will occur," may inaugurate a career, but it does not ordain success. A comparison will be illustrative. The teleology of the vocation is the promise, if not of worldly success, then of spiritual fulfillment. A function of the prophetic voice and vision, the vocation has nothing to do with prediction, with what Blake named "futurity," because it denies the inevitability of time's advance. Absorbed by its call, the vocation imagines its consummation as a contemplative presence, what Angus Fletcher has called "the prophetic moment."[12] If the mysteries of a vocation are due to its prophetic mode, the mysteries of a career—at least for the novice—are due to its profit mode, for the attainment of success, a goal that warrants an arsenal of strategems, remains chancy just so far as it remains a mystery how the surplus value of success is generated out of mere succession. There is what Byron calls "a mystery in the craft" of publishing that makes all "literary products . . . so fluctuating and uncertain" that a writer "can make no near calculation" (*BLJ*, 10:58, 42). The poet may make texts, but there is also a strong and occasionally countervailing "sense in which text and writer both are 'made' by the contexts within which they are produced and read" (Miller, 197). For the nineteenth-century maker, laboring under the hegemony of industrial capital rather than royal court, the rub lay not so much in being made by a context, mysterious at its center, but in being unable clearly to identify the context, mysteriously without center, which makes him. In the absence of any certainty that either context or power is centered, the choice between acquiescing in or resisting what is being made of one's work seems meaningless. Shelley's Prometheus emblematizes the irony of resistance. But the course of collaboration runs no smoother. The difficulty that the moral philosopher has in deriving virtue from the springs of self-love is shared by even the most single-minded careerist who, in a world where, as Byron says, "there is nothing but time" (*BLJ*, 9:171), tries to turn time into money, and who, the trick turned, tries to make the power of money his own.

Unlike the vocation, which announces itself with the fanfare of creation or fall, Byron's career does not presume a transcendence of or divorce from everyday life so much as a strategic separation, involving a complicated succession of adjustments, negotiations, and compensations. Here are the parting words of Lady Byron to her husband, words which mark, if not announce, a separation, words which adumbrate, if not inaugurate, Byron's career:

Dearest B.

The child is quite well and the best of travellers. I hope you are *good* and remember my medical prayers and injunctions. Don't give yourself up to the abominable trade of versifying—nor to brandy—nor to anything that is not *lawful* and *right*.

Though *I* disobey in writing to you, let me hear of *your* obedience at Kirkby.

Ada's love to you with mine.

Pip[13]

This letter was not notably efficacious. Byron did not become "*good.*" Indeed, under the circumstances (the expressions of affection, it transpired, disguised Lady Byron's unyielding determination never to see nor allow their daughter to see Byron again) it should not have been surprising if Lady Byron's injunctions came to act as provocations. About brandy no comment is necessary; Byron was not so limited in his imagination of possible intoxicants as his wife. But it was part of the relentless elaboration of the separation that Byron did give himself up to the "abominable trade of versifying," a calculated self-abandonment that involved him with people who, however impeccably lawful they might have been, were, as tradesmen, not quite "right" in Lady Byron's fastidious usage.

Chief among those associates was John Murray, the publisher of almost all of Byron's poetry for almost all of the poet's career. Byron's relations with Murray can be roughly divided into four phases of self-abandonment: *first,* the highly mediated period of aristocratic amusement in 1811 and 1812 when Byron's dealings with Murray were left with conspicuous negligence to the management of Charles Dallas, who obtained as a gift the copyright to *Childe Harold's Pilgrimage; second,* a period in 1813–16 of direct if desultory correspondence between Byron and Murray that followed the astonishing success of *Childe Harold* and the early oriental romances—a period during which Byron vacillated in his response to Murray's offers of substantial sums of money for such poems as *The Giaour* and *The Corsair; third,* the earnest and businesslike negotiations with Murray over payment for Byron's poetry, beginning with *Childe Harold III* in 1816; *fourth;* the break with Murray and the formation in 1822 of an alternative publishing connection with John Hunt, editor of *The Liberal*—a commitment qualified only by Byron's decision, made soon before his death, to publish the continuation of *Don Juan* himself. More generally, those phases could be grouped thematically according to three distinct and successive modes: the first two, when Byron was a self-conscious amateur, under the mode of observation; the third, when he combined with Murray, under the mode of speculation; the last two, under the mode of coincidence. Those distinctions are rough and ready versions of the higher-toned three-part structures (unity, multiplicity, unity) embraced by idealizing historians of romanticism. I hope that mine will not withstand much scrutiny. From the perspective of speculation, for example, the supposedly earlier stage of observation looks like a mystified version of the speculation it will knowingly become; from the perspective of coincidence the notions of "earlier," "later," and "stage" have neither cognitive value nor rhetorical force—they look like futile attempts to contain a contingency that mocks all aspirations to mastery. The justification for the particular terms lies in their relatively frequent and evidently charged appearance in the discourse of Byron and his contemporaries. For example, George Ellis in *The Quarterly Review* explicitly identifies two distinct Byrons—the earlier, sensational observer, whom he likes, and another impious investigator into hidden metaphysical causes, who makes him uneasy—and, with what I can only call prophetic intuition, finds evidence of the speculative mode infecting *The Corsair* and *Lara,* well before the dramatic supersession of monocular observation by dialectical ingenuity in *Childe Harold III.*[14]

My three-step movement has some parallels with the taxonomy of Renaissance poets proposed by Richard Helgerson in his instructive essay "The Elizabethan Laureate: Self-Presentation and the Literary System."[15] Helgerson characterizes the three career models available in the late sixteenth century as the amateur, the professional, and the laureate. Now the models of the amateur and professional roughly correspond to my phases of observation and speculation, but there is no analogy for the laureate in "coincidence." Indeed, Byron's stance, though clearly antiprofessional, is specifically adopted in scornful opposition to the degradation of official poetic virtue that Robert Southey's laureateship represents. It is the impossibility of either a public spirit or a private voice that drives and shapes Byron's poetic career. Moreover, it is a mark of Byron's own historicism (the poet of Popean couplets as well as Spenserian stanzas) that the very index that identifies a Renaissance commitment to a rational and responsible poetic course (laureateship) within a synchronic literary system is supplanted in the Byronic career by a phase of irreducible contingency. So much might plausibly and parenthetically be argued for the theoretical status of my stages. But the real justification of my fragile taxonomy is its tactical usefulness, which can be proven only in its application.

II

The pivotal phase is that of speculation, when Byron, following the separation, relinquished his pose of gifted, indifferent amateur and directly involved himself in the negotiation of payment for the copyright to the third canto of *Childe Harold*. "With regard to price," he writes, "*I* fixed *none* but left it to Mr. Kinnaird—& Mr. Shelley & yourself to arrange—of course they would do their best—and as to yourself—I know you would make no difficulties. But I agree with Mr. Kinnaird perfectly that the concluding five hundred should be only conditional—and for my own sake I wish it to be added only in case of your selling a certain number—that number to be fixed by yourself—I hope this is fair" (*BLJ*, 5:105–6). Byron is not motivated by prudential considerations—say, the need to pay off debts. On the contrary, Byron's sale of the copyright he had previously given separates him from the debts of and to the past; as an acknowledgment of and investment in his poetic reputation it is a speculation on the future. According to customary business practice, the writer was not compensated for the product of his labor, a manuscript, nor did the bookseller return to the writer a share of his profits.[16] What was bought and sold was the copyright, a legal fiction that certified the right to reproduce an authorial name and to retain the profits from the sale of those texts that might appear under that sign. Murray abstained from making the adjustments against loss that Byron offered him—probably not because of an irresistible impulse of generosity but because he understood that the purchase of a copyright was an investment in the career that the name "Byron" described rather than a payment based on a judgment of the immediate market value of any individual work.

Coextensive with neither the author nor the publisher, copyright assigns a career to the name and the words that appear under the name which is independent of the life of either participant in the transaction, subject instead to the field of interests and forces that Byron knew as "the trade." It was because the trade did not operate according to an economy of fair compensation and did not regard the future as an inevitable continuation of the past that it could figure success from succession. In the mysterious craft of publishing, success was only marginally conditional on what things happen; instead the trade created the conditions that would determine what and how things would happen. The name "Murray" no more represented an individual than did the name "Byron"; like Byron it stood for a house; unlike Byron that house was not a crest, a prerogative, and an ancestral ruin, but a means and mode of production: of books and of the organ of their criticism, *The Quarterly Review*. The house of Murray was a literary circle, which from the start of Byron's involvement designed a consistent and efficient practice: first Gifford, editor of *The Quarterly,* would read the manuscript and pronounce on its fitness to Murray, who would, the recommended revisions having been made, then set the manuscript in type, at which time the proof was often corrected by Gifford; Murray would then print copies of the poetry for sale and criticism, a criticism never actually written by Gifford or Murray but one conducted in *The Quarterly* at their initiative and under their auspices (Marchand 1:419, 430; 2:556, 596, 654, 736). It is not necessary to attribute venal motives to Gifford or to reviewers like Scott in order to observe that the sequence here, an extraordinary publishing and publicizing machine, was ordered in such a way that the notion of critical independence was virtually meaningless. The sequence of interventions—transmissions, reproductions, revisions—represented a formula for the composition of a commercially successful publication first and of a poem only by the way. The Wordsworthian aspiration to create the taste by which one is to be appreciated has become the practical consequence of the publishing machine. In the first quarter of the nineteenth century the Murray circle described a speculative grammar according to which literary statements were made and recognized and by which a certain literary attitude, the Byronic, was institutionalized as a reliable formula for producing poems and profit.

Byron's career begins as a statement of that speculative grammar, a statement made possible by his separation from a network of natural attachments, what he calls in *Childe Harold III* the ties of "house and heart."[17] As the natural connections have been abstracted into legal associations conducted at great distance and mediated by briefs and attorneys, so is the natural poet abstracted into a man of letters whose relations with the public are channeled through the medium of his publisher. Once again, separation is not the same as divorce. Byron did not, could not break completely with wife, child, and country—he supplemented what he could no longer completely have with what he could not fully possess: nature with letters. Separation permits speculation, which feels like the promise of freedom—and will produce it, as long as freedom is construed as a distance from debts. "There is," Byron writes to Murray, "a great advantage in getting the water between a man and his embarrassments—for things and a little prudence insensibly reestablish themselves—and I have spent less money—and had more for it within the two years and a half since my absence from England—than I have ever done within the same time before—and my literary speculations allowed me to do it more easily— . . . out of England I have no debts whatever—" (*BLJ*, 6:65).

I have chosen to focus here on the speculative mode of Byron's career not only because it is medial but because "speculation" has implications that bear on the two most urgent problems a circumstantial history confronts. The first is the problem of the historical passage of time—that is, how to render time *as* a passage or series of passages, or periods, or phases, or stages, or whatever—to do so in good faith and to good effect when the deconstructive angel casts its shadow across the page, tracing the duplicity of every benchmark, inscribing an "always already" before every beginning. The second problem is a hermeneutical one. How does a circumstantial recombination of so-called literary texts—letters, journals, etc.—affect our reading of avowedly literary texts, the poetry that comes to us under the name of Byron? How can a circumstantial history engage the more than circumstantial inside of literature, the innerness that is still, by most accounts, not only the object of criticism but that which distinguishes literature from other forms of discourse? The latter problem especially bedevils any history of Byron, the sole member of what Macaulay aptly tagged an "exoteric lake school" (2:356). Writing of the *eso*teric lakers, Abrams, for example, could pass by, unalarmed, all apparent difficulties of accommodating history to interpretation. An insider's account of romanticism, *Natural Supernaturalism* took the shape that seemed designed by the spirit dwelling in its subject poems. It is no disparagement of Abrams's work to describe *Natural Supernaturalism* as inspired paraphrase, for Abrams's history aspires to give what Coleridge called "outness" to the life that inhabits the works and the period. Perhaps Abrams would impeach an exoteric history as not truly a *literary* history at all: at least his denomination of Byron as ironist presupposes that the poet can only be regarded as a legitimate subject for literary history if he is imagined as somehow esoteric.

"Speculation" directly engages the problems of time and interpretation. One can talk of a speculative *stage* in Byron's career because insofar as he is a speculator, reflecting *on* time, framing an image of the future by which he determines himself, he fabricates an identifiable if imaginary space, turns time into theater. And because speculation has both an entrepreneurial and a figurative logic, it promises to bridge the exo- and esoteric. Speculation denotes, according to the *OED*, a mentalistic orientation: "to engage in thought or reflection, esp. of a conjectural nature." Yet if it has theoretical, speculation also has practical dimensions: "to engage in the buying and selling of commodities . . . in order to profit by a rise or fall in their market value; to undertake, to take part or invest in, a business enterprise or transaction of a risky nature in the expectation of a considerable gain." Speculation is not a theory about making money; it is a practical way of turning a profit. But profit, of course, is always conjectural. Indeed, the ability to make money by speculation remarks on the theoretical status of the money that is made, its conjectural relation to real productivity or value.

In its mingling of theory and practice there is something uncanny about speculation, the kind of uncanniness that Coleridge tried to quash in the *Biographia Literaria* when he warned against violating "the sacred distinction between things and persons."[18] For Coleridge such a violation would have both universal ethical and epistemological implications and historically specific social and economic applications. The hybrid properties of speculation as well as its low place in high romanticism can be most economically indicated by referring to Coleridge's definition of the fancy in chapter 13 of the *Biographia*. Coleridge has described the personable secondary imagination as "essentially vital, even as all objects (*as objects*) are essentially fixed and dead." He goes on to say of the impersonable fancy that it "on the contrary, has no other counters to play with, but fixities and definites." Now since fancy is the *contrary* of the imagination, it cannot be "essentially vital."[19] And there can be no doubt that fixities and definites are "essentially fixed and dead." Where then does the "play" come from in this world of death? Wrong question. It lures us into the bogs and fens of theology. But if we rephrase the question and ask what supplies the opportunity for play, we can suggest an answer: in the "capacity" of fixities and definites to be counters—that is, in their capacity or liability to be not merely what they "essentially" are but also to be something else. As something else, counters may not be essentially vital but by the same token they are not definitely dead. Fixities and definites are deployed by fancy as counters to life *and* death in a fascinating liminal game—what game, with what goals and what moves, being the pretext for speculation.

It would have made it much easier to be convincing on this point had Coleridge written "Fancy, or speculation, has no other counters, or commodities, to play with but fixities and definites." But perhaps Coleridge was obliging enough in his insistence that fancy "must receive all its materials ready made from the law of association." Fancy neither sows nor reaps; it is unproductive. Fancy prospers solely by tactical interventions in the indefinite space between the fabrication of ready-mades and their use. By disregarding the inert objectivity of the object, by exploiting the play in essence, fancy finds a kind of life in an unimaginative game, in the same way that the speculator makes a kind of living from the manipulation of the ready-made as a commodity in the market. Speculation "is indeed no other than a mode of Memory emancipated from the order of time and space" (*Biographia* 1:202); its "vitality" depends on the supplemental properties of the object that make it liable to deployment as a commodity—the best word I know for that simulacrum which violates the distinction between things and persons, the bookseller's warehouse and the poet's soul.[20]

Had we been present at the moment of composition and read in manuscript these lines from stanza 6 of the third canto of *Childe Harold*, " 'Tis to create, and in creating live / A being more intense, that we endow / With form our fancy, gaining as we give / The life we image, even as I do now" (46–49)—had we been present, we ought to have been ready to wager that Byron would contract with Murray for the sale of the copyright. Those lines, conventionally taken as Byron's version of the therapeutic power of art, are as neat an epitome of speculation as appears in Byron's collected works. But, fortunately, as we were not there, we are spared all risk. The lines appeared to no eyes except under Murray's imprint, where they first come to life as an image of the "Fit speculation" (89) they propose.

"Gaining as we give / The life we image"—the lines are speculative not merely because they affirm that the life is acquired in a dynamic self-reflection of the "I" with its image but because they formulate the life so gained, so given, as conjectural. Life neither originates nor determines the process of reflection; it *tracks* reflection, surfaces as a variable, indeed nominal, byproduct of the speculative imaging.[21] The import of this formula can best be elucidated in comparison with another well-known passage, often characterized as a distillation of romantic reciprocity. Again from Coleridge, this time from "Dejection: An Ode": "Lady, we receive but what we give, / And in our life alone does Nature live." It could be debated where in the epistemological grounds of romantic knowledge to plant the vital source of this exchange between self and nature—whether to side with Abrams or Earl Wasserman or Paul de Man[22]—but regardless of what side one might take on the substance of Coleridge's faith, the grounds of the argument would remain the same: epistemological. The debate would continually turn on the issue of knowledge, its origin, direction, and end—all the while elaborating itself on the presumption of the priority of life, whatever its source. The whole Gothic facade of Coleridge's epistemological deductions in the *Biographia* conceals that presumption of life, wards off speculation. It is that presumption of life—aboriginally joyous, eclipsed by "abstruse research," and awaiting imaginative reclamation—that enables the idealist historian to believe he or she hears Coleridge's plaintive voice. Its resistance to that presumption makes Byron's poetry, even at its most oratorical or conversational, so voiceless.

The absence of any presumption of life also makes the Byronic speculation intrinsically successful. The blankness of life assures that the mere process of speculative reflection will succeed in enlivening, even if the life acquired is only a simulacrum, a staged version of that which the poet of "Dejection" supposes he has. Speculative success is not the same as dialectical triumph, however. Granted, it looks like dialectic. But it looks like dialectic as much as it looks like life. As speculative life is not truly life because it is from first to last anaclitic, incumbent on an image, so speculative exchange is not truly dialectical because there is no antithesis between the formal "I" and the formalized image—no antithesis, only a space. And not much of a space—about as much as there is between theory and practice in the word speculation itself, or between the biographical subject "Byron" and the image of the author, or between the writer and his English audience, which is the imaged life that sustains Byron's commerce.

The speculative space separating imager and imaged is inherently unstable, as is the profit of life which surfaces there. That instability is owed to a transience proper to the image as commodity, a transience that at once constitutes and undermines its recognizability and value. We gain as we give and only as we give: the commodity yields profit on investment, but successful venture capitalism demands a continual reinvestment in the image, which maps a string of new and improved images. Hence Byronic speculation is not only intrinsically successful, it is also extrinsically successive.[23] In *Childe Harold III* (the sequel to *Childe Harold II*, the eye for the hook of *Childe Harold IV*), one image of desire—fields and crags, warriors and philosophers—follows another, each an "advance" on the previous one, and each functioning according to a dynamic of speculation, which some, such as the image of Napoleon, also articulate.

The most glamorous aspect of Napoleon as Byron portrays him is his flagrant duality, the antithetical mixture of dust and deity. But the psychological image, though stimulating, is historically insignificant. The space between "conqueror and captive of the earth" (325) and the similarly conflicted figure of Childe Harold is insufficient to explain or dramatize satisfactorily the historical spectacle of Napoleon's singular career—too neat, the analogy is inert. Napoleon's duality or ambivalence may indicate who he is, but who he is is not materially different from who everyone else is. His character cannot explain the singular, historically contingent success of *this* character. The succession from the static image of an esoteric ambivalence to a dynamic image of reciprocal speculation charts a movement toward an engagement with the historical form of the historical character.

Napoleon speculated, we are informed, in "men's thoughts [which] were the steps which paved [his] throne, / *Their* admiration [his] best weapon shone" (364–65). Napoleon's strategy for political ascendance was to gain as he gave the life he imaged; the very fundament of this ascent was the image of public opinion that he created. Byron does not fault Napoleon for that speculation. One cannot criticize history, and, as for Byron Napoleon is the exemplary, all but the sole historical figure of his age, so speculation is the way history represents itself. Byron criticizes Napoleon for having forgotten the groundlessness of his triumph, having forgotten that the practical steps he took to the throne were on a theoretical ladder, that the height achieved was no real summit but the *image* of a height, as he himself was the image of a monarch to the public that gave him life:

Sager than in thy fortunes; for in them
Ambition steel'd thee on too far to show
That just habitual scorn which could contemn
Men and their thoughts; 'twas wise to feel, not so
To wear it ever on thy lip and brow,
And spurn the instruments thou wert to use
Till they were turn'd unto thine overthrow. . . . (352–58)

Napoleon fell because of his scorn; not, however, because of the scorn he felt—such feelings are irrelevant to history—but because of the scorn he showed.

Napoleon was victimized by what Byron calls, in his dispute with Murray over the staging of his historical dramas, a "cursed attempt at representation" (BLJ, 8:66), an attempt which is not the consequence of a character flaw in Napoleon but a corollary of his status as public person within a specific political context. It is possible to imagine that had Napoleon possessed the ring of Gyges, which endowed its wearer with invisibility, he might have been able to rule unseen and prevent the scornful semblance that led to his fall. But that myth of tyranny, which in all of its classical versions presumes that a monarch is in place and that Gyges is therefore already in a position to rule when he dons the amulet, does not conform to the political reality of nineteenth-century Europe, where there was no natural way for Napoleon to ascend, no monarch to hand him ring and kingdom, and where the public, which had already rent the veils that cloaked the mysterious sovereign, was in no state to be dictated to by a veiled, let alone invisible, monarch.[24] The same vacuum of authority that permitted Napoleonic speculation prescribed that Napoleon could only ascend by gaining as he gave the life he imaged for a public whose cynosure he became by repeated self-display.[25] Napoleon succeeded by transforming Europe into a stage for his astonishing improvisations, his gifted impersonation of a monarch. Yet he fell because after a long run of performances, even a talented, chameleon-like actor's face will eventually settle into a habitual expression; the luster decays, and the formerly enlivening image becomes a disposable icon. Napoleon's scorn froze the speculative dynamic, forcing the public to see its own servility—disastrous for a ruler whose fortune was hostage to opinion, whose theatrical encounters face to face with the French people had been the enabling pretexts for an imperial career.

Byron's critique of Napoleon's career makes it possible to imagine two kinds of imaging: one exploiting a differential counter, of no value in itself, that in its deployment acquires a temporary luster which propels the speculation in marketplace and poem; the other trusting to a persona modeled in and useful for face-to-face encounters, overinvested with cultic value, and hazarded in the political arena—a mask or image that initially stimulates, then fixes, and finally vitiates the enlivening play of speculation. Although he criticizes theatrical empowerment as intrinsically self-destructive (a critique he develops in his later historical drama *Marino Faliero* and *Sardanapalus*), Byron does not suppose that the life of politics, the power to mobilize and sway, could be acquired in any other way. By staging Napoleonic politics as merely a more mystified version of Byronic speculation, the poet significantly advances the Byronic career; that is, he rescues "Byron" and Byron's poetry from his adolescent hierarchy of action over poetry and from the zero-sum dualism of *"aut Caesar aut nihil"* (*BLJ*, 3:217). Byron's image of Napoleon adumbrates an unimaginable form of power—more radical, more pervasive, more *literal* than that accessible through the conventional representations of politics—a power in which reflection evades represention, albeit a power incapable of moving bodies or changing minds.

Adumbrates but scarcely realizes. Indeed, the speculative criticism of the iconic tendencies in the face-to-face encounter appears in a poem that begins with a wish for the face:

> Is thy face like thy mother's, my fair child,
> Ada, sole daughter of my house and heart?
> When last I saw the young blue eyes they smiled,
> And then we parted,—not as now we part,
> But with a hope.—(1–5)

Not only begins, but ends:

> My daughter! with thy name this song began
> My daughter! with thy name thus much shall end—
> I see thee not, I hear thee not, but none
> Can be so wrapt in thee; though art the friend
> To whom the shadows of far years extend:
> Albeit my brow thou never shouldst behold,
> My voice shall with thy future visions blend. . . . (1067–73)

This is nostalgia, certainly. But nostalgia has its uses. Here the statement and reiteration of a wish for a face-to-face encounter works to frame the succession of speculations within a mirroring reflection. Byronic nostalgia is nothing if not tactical: by facing those wishful moments, beginning and end, against each other like parentheses in specular complicity, the writer situates the undeveloping, indefinite succession of differential images (an oceanic or erotic drift) within a sentimentally human context. Not only is Byronic nostalgia indentifiable as such, these moments of nostalgia for the face-to-face are all that give this series of speculations an identity—an identity which is the figure of the author, whose face all but presents itself in these accents forlorn, whose life appears in the specular transaction between the beginning and end of the canto.

Although this is a nostalgia of and for Byron, we need not ascribe it to the poet—at least it does not have its source in the "I" which speculates with such sophistication in canto 3. The frame is adopted for what might be called, for convenience, extratextual reasons—extratextual because it demarcates the text from what is outside it. The brackets of nostalgia, which evoke the figure of the author and impose integrated form, constitute the text as book: an image fabricated, as the title page announces, by the commercial combination Murray/Byron; an icon designed to be recognized and purchased by the reading public. Mere successiveness must be *organized* in order for speculation to be successful. If the face-to-face encounter of Napoleon and his public represents a political space, the embodiment of the author in the organized book designates a social space suitable for the commerce between Byron and an eager public. Byron's speculations on Napoleon work like a lens to bring into focus the affiliations between the political and the social and to expose the congruence of the social and the commercial. By making book of Byron, consolidating the image within the covers of a specular reflection and making it available to an admiring public, Murray/Byron do succeed in turning Byron into the figure whom Pip called "the absolute monarch of words, [who] uses them, as Bonaparte did lives, for conquest."[26] Byron's public, like Napoleon's, could be relied on, in their vanity, to ignore the speculative stratagems that the text represents and to accept the book at face value—up to a point, as the writer of *Childe Harold III* knows. What he does not know is where that point is. He does not doubt, however, that the realms of rhyme are firmly situated in the precincts of the trade and that the approach to the point where the public will abandon the attitude that no longer reflects its desires is not fully subject to authorial control:

> I know the precise worth of popular applause—for few Scribblers have had more of it—and if I chose to swerve into their paths—I could retain it or resume it—or increase it—but I neither love ye—nor fear ye—and though I buy with ye—and sell with ye—and talk with ye—I will neither eat with ye—drink with ye—nor pray with ye. They made me without my search a species of popular Idol—they—without reason or judgement beyond the caprice of their Good pleasure—threw down the Image from its pedestal—It was not broken with the fall—and they would it seems again replace it—but they shall not. (*BLJ*, 6:106)

III

I must admit that the above extract from Byron's letters fails to illustrate neatly my preceding generalizations about knowledge and power. The writer of that letter seems much more certain of his powers and more confident of his ability to exercise them than the Byron whom I portrayed. There is not, I hope, a contradiction between my statement about speculation and Byron's, but there is, to coin a word, a paradiction. Byron remarks on speculation, its routine oscillation between idolatry and iconoclasm, as though he were outside of it—not exactly opposed, but certainly not a participant. This is a different character with a different diction from the one under contract to Murray: not a Murray/Byron but, as the series of phrases taken from act 1, scene 3 of *The Merchant of Venice* apprises us, a Byron/Shylock. The assertion of independence is a statement of that realignment, a move which contextualizes speculation—literally, because in aligning himself with the words of Shylock, Byron serves notice that the social space in which commerce occurs and idols are marketed is situated within a text, where the scapegoat survives all persecution, where the written outlasts all false representations, where the vitriol of the miserly Jew remains a constant paradiction to the cant of the idolatrous Gentile.

Among the corollaries of this paradiction four seem especially significant to an understanding of Byron's career. First, Byron's alignment with Shylock presupposes an unconventional reading of *The Merchant of Venice,* which preempts René Girard's discovery of the scapegoat mechanism in the play and inscribes the fate of Shylock in a thoroughly historical discourse.[27] To be exact, the words of Shylock that materialize in Byron's letter do not evoke, allude to, or have any association with a mimetic representation of a so-called historical action: they are history itself, an engaged text—now, at this writing, and only in writing. In that respect the letter is a refinement of the event-like character of the set piece on the battle of Waterloo and the career of Napoleon in *Childe Harold III.* A literally momentous occasion in English literature, it is the first instance that I know where the poem becomes the occasion for the confrontation of a world-historical event by a world-historical figure.[28] In the process, Byron-contemplating-the-ruins-of-Napoleon itself becomes a world-historical event. Or almost, since Byron only figuratively engages Napoleon. He sees him and interprets him through the eyes of Harold—a mediation by the image which is responsible for some of the more spectacular effects of the passage but also for its hollow theatricality. More authentically eventful if less grandiose, Byron-assuming-the-character-of-Shylock could never be mounted on the boards of Drury Lane. You could never stage this text. It is the drama it interprets, the history that it reads.

Second, Byron's realignment enacts his increasingly dominant theme of apostasy. Hardly exiled, Byron merely falls into the language of Shylock and with a casualness that belies the import of such a marginalization. For the traditional and desperately futile alliance of the aristocrat with the plebian against the tidal threat of the bourgeoisie is substituted an identification with the Jew. As a youthful lord poaching on his prospects, Byron lived off the parasitism of the London usurers. As a lapsed hero, Lord Byron returns to that parasitism, or, rather, refines that parasitism into a mutual empowerment. Shylock lives through Byron, returns as the repressed quotient in the systems of both monetary and literary exchange. As Shylock, Byron can speak back to the prince of publishing, the merchant of London, in a language recognizably his but one that is distanced and enlivened by the marks of the outcast and that is given critical force through the election of apostasy. The lesson is not the Coleridgean excuse that one must, in principle, fall, but that no fall is principled—"Apostasy's so fashionable, too" (*Don Juan*, "Dedication," stanza 17).

Third, the shift in context from the social/commercial to the textual is nothing more than a matter of circumstance: I can furnish only circumstantial evidence for it; and circumstances, not action or speculation, are its occasion. Byron happens to be in Venice, happens to have a copy of Shakespeare, happens to be provoked by Murray—no intention there, no ripening to expression; just a string of coincidences that issues in the coincidence of Byron/Shylock, this letter. To be fully circumstantial is to take a stand on what always surrounds one. Strange feat, to come to rest by and on a coincidence, a coincidence that is no place at all, nothing more than a siting in time.

Fourth, there are no quotation marks setting off the words of Shylock to identify them as belonging to *Shakespeare's* character. By taking Shakespeare's words as his own without citation Byron is guilty of plagiarism in letter and in spirit: at once appropriating the words of another and refusing to be original. This plagiarism rebuffs idolatry by its refusal to simulate life with the imaging marks of quotation (which would personify Shylock) and by declining to acknowledge that the poet or anyone else has any lawful interest in the life of his characters. To claim that the poet has would be to impute to him a base affiliation with his own personification of the mercantile spirit, Antonio, the Merchant of Venice. Although Antonio calculatingly sustains the pretense of giving Shylock a life in the island kingdom, the Jew actually has no genuine life or living. In the eyes of the Christian merchant Shylock is a blank counter to be idolized as sacred gold or profane scapegoat, whose value as profit or loss is entirely determined by the winds and waves of the market. Byron's plagiarism seals that absence of life by taking Shylock's words literally. By repeating those words without any image, even so much as is limned by inverted commas, he cuts them off from any source or imputation of life and thus from the possibility of any speculative play. Byron cannot, of course, keep *The Merchant of Venice* off the stage or abrogate the endless reenactments of the scapegoat ritual any more than he can stop Murray from selling copies of *The Corsair;* but he assures that the words of Shylock exceed the spurious "life" he is given by Shakespeare, by Antonio, by Portia, and by Murray. What remains of Shylock are only these letters, but at least these "relics" are beyond anyone's control.[29] By plagiarizing, Byron assigns to Shylock a thoroughly posthumous existence which, by coincidence, the plagiarist shares.

IV

Life has little left for my curiosity—there are few things in it of which I have not had a sight and a share—it would be silly to quarrel with my luck because it did not last. . . . I should not fall out with the past: and if I could but manage to arrange my pecuniary concerns in England—so as to pay my debts—& leave me what would be here a very fair income—though nothing remarkable at home—you might consider me as posthumous—I would never willingly dwell in that tight little island. (*BLJ*, 5:135–36)

"Life has little left for my curiosity." Not a suicide note, that assertion relinquishes a life that is nothing more nor less than a pretext for curiosity. Not a death wish nor, indeed, a wish of any kind, the assertion of posthumousness is the statement that the writer has taken a specific if marginal position that is on the edge of commerce, yet within the discourse of the career. He becomes fully a man of letters, resolving himself to the "living death" which Hazlitt described as the circumstance of the literary character (*Complete Works*, 4:135). For Hazlitt, as for Coleridge, however, it was enough to raise ominously the specter of death-in-life in order to cast opprobrium on careerism. The specter could be relied on to chase all God's authors back to the sacred precincts of a living life. But Byron, familiar of specters, was not to be cowed by sarcasm or superstition, by Murrayean ledgers or Coleridgean metaphysics. Only Byron among the Romantics set out to practice the man of letters's theoretical fate. Posthumousness ends speculation by realizing its implicit design, by sealing the absence of the author which is its prod and its lure. "No more—no more—Oh! never more" will Byron gain as he gives the life he images. Removed from life, whatever ink flows from the posthumous writer's pen is no longer under any influence from the quick or the dead. He does not revise. There is no turning back.

Notes

1. Thomas Babington Macaulay, "Moore's Life of Lord Byron," *Edinburgh Review,* June 1831, collected in *Critical, Historical and Miscellaneous Essays by Lord Macaulay,* 6 vols. in 3 (New York, 1860), 2:336–37.

2. M. H. Abrams, "Rationality and Imagination in Cultural History: A Reply to Wayne Booth," *Critical Inquiry* 2 (1976): 458–59.

3. Since this was written a study of Byron has appeared which does attempt to place Byron within his historical context, though without reference to romantic irony and with scarcely any attempt to engage the kind of issues that recent criticism of romanticism raises. Philip W. Martin's *Byron: a Poet before His Public* (Cambridge: Cambridge Univ. Press, 1982) offers many shrewd and stimulating perceptions of the way Byron's poetry responded to the pressure of his celebrity, but the work as a whole is marred by *its partiality:* it is both puzzlingly selective in its treatment of Byron's poems and committed to a patronizing view of Byron (owed to Paul West and W. W. Robson) as an intermittently cynical and desperate poet of no great distinction who happened to stumble into *Don Juan.* Martin's book is replete with irony, but it all belongs to the critic.

4. *Byron's Letters and Journals,* ed. Leslie A. Marchand, 12 vols. (Cambridge: Harvard Univ. Press, 1973–81), 9:47. Hereafter *BLJ.*

5. In the last few years there have appeared a number of distinguished books and articles on the idea and practice of the poetic career in Tudor and Stuart England. Those whose work has been most generally of use to me are Jonathan Goldberg, Stephen Greenblatt, Richard Helgerson, Arthur Marotti, and David L. Miller. . . . I want to stress that the issue at hand is the *poetic* career rather than, say, the career of a novelist like Fielding or Richardson or a man of letters proper like Hume or Johnson—each of which reflected an earlier demystification of the vocational myth than did poetry. Different occupations have different stories.

6. *Beginnings: Intention and Method* (Baltimore: The Johns Hopkins Univ. Press, 1978), 227.

7. *Natural Supernaturalism: Tradition and Revolution in Romantic Literature* (New York: Norton, 1971), 411–62. It is because of its insistence on a similar three-part pattern with overdetermined beginnings and endings as well as its faith that the life that gets into poetry "has passed through a refining poetic fire" that, despite its subtitle, I would consider Lawrence Lipking's elegant and suggestive *The Life of the Poet: Beginning and Ending Poetic Careers* to be, like Abrams's book, a study of the mythos of the vocation. For a study that successfully navigates the distinction I am trying to apply to Byron, see David L. Miller, "Spenser's Vocation, Spenser's Career," *ELH* 50 (Summer 1983): 197–232. Of especial interest is Spenser's association (in what Abrams would call a high romantic mode) of the vocation with the extension, continuation, or renewal of the cosmogony. Not only is Byron's repudiation of the vocational model signalled by his irreversible wreckage, but the beginning of the career that is the relic of that vocation, its only history, occurs not in the Spenserian fashion as an idealized, "self-constitutive internal replay of the hierogamy" (Miller, 200) but as the consequence of Byron's actual and final separation from his wife.

8. Byron, *Marino Faliero, Doge of Venice,* 1.2.597.

9. Among many testimonies by Murray: "It is impossible for you [Byron] to have a more purely attached friend than I am—My name is connected with your Fame" (Leslie A. Marchand, *Byron: A Biography,* 3 vols. [New York: Alfred A. Knopf, Inc., 1957], 3:1040). By insisting that "there are other and newer sins with which the author of *Don Juan* has stained himself—sins of a class, if possible, even more despicable than any he had before committed," the reviewer of *Don Juan* for *Blackwood's Magazine* (5 [August 1819]: 512–18) not only invoked the distinctively Byronic imagery of stain, mark, curse, etc., but also publicized what is in effect the poetics of Byron's satire at the moment he repudiated it (*Byron: The Critical Heritage,* ed. Andrew Rutherford [New York: Barnes and Noble, 1970], 169).

10. Subtitled *Memoir and Correspondence of the Late John Murray,* 2 vols. (London: John Murray, 1891).

11. Jeffrey, always interesting on Byron, most suggestively engages the poet's historical significance in the unsigned review of *The Corsair* and *The Bride of Abydos* (*Edinburgh Review* 23 [April 1814]: 198–229; in Rutherford, 53–64). Jeffrey's sense of Byron's imposing power emerges strongly in his review of *Childe Harold's Pilgrimage,* canto 3, where he lauds Byron's "force of diction, and inextinguishable energy of sentiment" and metaphorizes the poet as "a volcano in the heart of our land, and a cloud that hangs over our dwellings" (*Edinburgh Review* 27 [December 1816]; in Rutherford, 98 and 101). I would not want to deny that there is a great deal of condescension as well as complicity in that kind of maneuver (Jeffrey intends to impose on the public by dramatizing the way that Byron imposed on him) in Jeffrey's volcano metaphor (see Philip W. Martin, 55–57, for a discussion of Jeffrey's interest in Byron). Byron's sardonic abandonment of the volcano metaphor in his characterization of Lady Adeline in canto 13, stanza 36 of *Don Juan* ("As a Volcano holds the lava more / Within—*et caetera.* Shall I go on? No! / I hate to hunt down a tired metaphor: / So let the often used volcano go. / Poor thing!") testifies to his awareness of the cliché. I would only emphasize that the overt naturalization of imposition is circumstantial evidence of the fact of an imposition not yet natural.

12. Angus Fletcher, *The Prophetic Moment: An Essay on Spenser* (Chicago: Univ. of Chicago Press, 1971), 45–53. . . .

13. Marchand, 2:563.

14. *The Quarterly Review* 11 (July 1814): 428–57.

15. *ELH* 46.2 (Summer 1979), 193–221.

16. For the eighteenth-century background to the place of copyright in the dealings between booksellers and authors, see A. S. Collins, "Some Aspects of Copyright from 1700 to 1780," *The Library,* ser. 4, 7 (1926): 67–81. For Murray's transactions with Byron see Marchand, 1:288n, 424, 430, 2:654, 683n, 712, and *passim.*

17. *Lord Byron: The Complete Poetical Works,* ed. Jerome J. McGann, 2 vols, (Oxford: Oxford Univ. Press, 1980), 2, line 2. All references to *Childe Harold* are taken from this edition, and cited by line number.

18. Samuel Taylor Coleridge, *Biographia Literaria,* ed. John Shawcross, 2 vols. (Oxford: Oxford Univ. Press, 1907), 1:137.

19. This whether we take "contrary" here technically as expressing an absolute heterogeneity or whether we regard it as being loosely used to indicate a general notion of opposition. On the difference see Coleridge, *On the Constitution of the Church and State,* ed. John Colmer, vol. 10 of *The Collected Works of Samuel Taylor Coleridge,* ed. Kathleen Coburn (Princeton: Princeton Univ. Press, 1976), 24 and n.

20. The definitions of "commodity" in the *OED* veer from "a thing of use or advantage to mankind," to "an object of trade" to "a property of the person, etc., affected."

21. The operant authority regarding this mirroring would now be Jacques Lacan. Byron, had he been in a metaphysical mood, would likely have cited book 2 of David Hume's *A Treatise of Human Nature:* "[T]he minds of men are mirrors to one another, not only because they reflect each other's emotions, but also because these rays of passions, sentiments, and opinions, may be often reverberated, and may decay away by insensible degrees. Thus the pleasure which a rich man receives from his possessions, being thrown upon the beholder, causes a pleasure and esteem; which sentiments again being perceived and sympathized with, increase the pleasure of the possessor, and, being once more reflected, become a new foundation for pleasure and esteem in the beholder" (ed. A. D. Lindsay [1911; rept., two vols. in one, New York: Dutton, 1977], 2:83). If life is consciousness, consciousness is commerce and lasts until the luster of the reflected properties completely decays. If not Hume, perhaps Byron had in mind Shakespeare's *Troilus and Cressida,* 3.3.103–11. . . .

22. The sides are defined in Paul de Man's essay "The Rhetoric of Temporality," *Interpretations,* ed. Charles Singleton (Baltimore: The Johns Hopkins Univ. Press, 1969), 179–82.

23. The successiveness of speculation contributes to what might be called the logic of sequelization in Byron, evident in his poetry from first to last but present with almost irrational clarity in the sequence of the oriental romances from *The Giaour* to *Lara* and exploited with an almost uncanny finesse in *Don Juan.*

24. Marc Shell discusses the various versions of the tale of the ring of Gyges in *The Economy of Literature* (Baltimore: The Johns Hopkins Univ. Press, 1978), 14–30.

25. Even Hazlitt, who never recanted his admiration for Bonaparte, could in "On the Spirit of Monarchy" find no better way to distinguish between a ruler like Goerge II and Bonaparte than to contrast two kinds of acting styles: the pompous strutting of Young and the radical, heartfelt realism of Kean (*The Complete Works of William Hazlitt,* ed. P. P. Howe, 20 vols. [London: J. M. Dent, 1933], 19:256–57). One wonders whether Hazlitt is being willfully naive or abysmally ironic when, to indicate Kean's superiority, he remarks that he "has 'that within which passes shew,' " thereby endorsing Kean's authenticity with one of the more theatrical utterances of one of the more famous characters Kean was known for portraying. We cannot, of course, know the truth about Hazlitt (any more than we can know about Kean or Byron) when all the truth lies in the show of passing show. . . .

26. Marchand, 1:677. In 1822 circumstances dictated that Byron alter his name to Noel Byron. He subsequently signed most of his letters with the initials "N. B.," which, he noted,

not only served as an editorial convenience but were by coincidence the selfsame initials as Napoleon Bonaparte (Marchand, 3:971).

27. Girard's argument appears in " 'To Entrap the Wisest': A Reading of *The Merchant of Venice,*" *Literature and Society: Selected Papers from the English Institute, 1978,* ed. Edward W. Said (Baltimore: The Johns Hopkins Univ. Press, 1979), 100–119.

28. Cf., for example, Wordsworth's tortuously oblique engagement with the French Revolution in *The Prelude.* Even when Wordsworth does verge on the confrontation, it is precisely in the guise of the recluse, poet of the everyday. And when Wordsworth rises to the call of his genius, the consequences are more severe: the apocalypse of imagination eclipses not only nature but also, and especially, history. On this aspect of Wordsworth, see Alan Liu, "Wordsworth: The History in 'Imagination,' " *ELH* 51.3 (Fall 1984): 505–48.

29. I have put scare quotes around relics because relics are notoriously subject to fe-tishization, as Byron knew (see the evidence supplied by Marchand of his flirtations with Catholicism, whose "incense, pictures, statues, altars, relics, and the real presence, confession, absolution [provide] something sensible to grasp at") and as the fate of his corpse, which returned to England from Greece absent the lungs deposited in the church of San Spiridone, testified (Marchand 3:977–78, 1240–41). Byron aimed to avert such a fate for the writing he would leave behind.

Editor's Bibliographical Note

In a number of ways it is fair to say that this essay, expanded for inclusion in Christensen's forthcoming book on Byron (probably 1992), moves toward a new era of "biographical criti-cism" of the poet. But it is equally fair to say that this new approach is quite literally new, having nothing at all in common with the earlier lackluster nineteenth- and early twentieth-century tradition of biographizing Byron's poetry. Instead Christensen's approach is, as his title indi-cates, to study the shape and substance of a poetic career or vocation within, as he says, "a historical plot"—situating Byron's life/career/vocation, that is, in the social, political, and economic exigencies of his time. As such, his analysis here of "the speculative stage" of that career bears comparison only with the books he cites by Philip Martin (note 3) and Lawrence Lipking (note 7), even as Leslie A. Marchand's meticulously detailed three-volume *Byron: A Biography* (New York: Knopf, 1957) functions quietly but importantly in the background.

For all its fundamental incomparability, however, Christensen's work does intersect with the remarkable spate of books emerging from the prolific word-processor of Jerome J. Mc-Gann, beginning essentially with *"Don Juan" in Context* that inaugurates a major shift away from his earlier views in *Fiery Dust: Byron's Poetic Development* (Chicago and London: University of Chicago Press, 1968) and continuing through *The Romantic Ideology* (Chicago: University of Chicago Press, 1983) and especially *The Beauty of Inflections* (Oxford: Clarendon Press, 1985). Even more directly pertinent to Christensen's essay, however, is Kurt Heinzelman's fine essay earlier in this book, as well as his wider-ranging book, *The Economics of the Imagination* (Amherst: University of Massachusetts Press, 1980). See also Christensen's "Theorizing By-ron's Practice: The Performance of Lordship and the Poet's Career," *Studies in Romanticism* 27 (1988): 477–90. Useful here as well is Peter J. Manning, *Byron and His Fictions* (Detroit: Wayne State University Press, 1978), McGann's edited collection of essays, *Historical Studies and Literary Criticism* (Madison: University of Wisconsin Press, 1985)—particularly Cecil Y. Lang's long essay, "Narcissus Jilted: Byron, *Don Juan,* and the Biographical Imperative"—and the publications listed in the Editor's Bibliographical Notes to Gleckner's and Reiman's essays in this volume.

"Their She Condition":
Cross-Dressing and
the Politics of Gender in *Don Juan*

Susan J. Wolfson

I

Don Juan, like much Romantic writing, displays numerous demarcations of sexual difference. Indeed, there is a notable contradiction between the poem's social politics, which despite an aristocratic allegiance, tend to satirize prevailing ideologies, and its sexual politics, which often reflect a conventional masculinism.[1] Some have summoned issues of the latter to make categorical claims about Byron and his contemporaries. Questions of gender are certainly fundamental; evidence of Byron's—and many others'—sexism and patriarchal bias is clear and compelling. Yet I wish to revise some of the categories advanced in some recent feminist readings of English Romanticism by showing that Byron's sexual politics are neither persistent nor consistent. Even granting the notoriously adept ironies of *Don Juan,* its politics of sexual difference prove remarkably complex and unstable. At times they are governed by the general satirical perspective of the poem; at other times they clash with Byron's pronounced liberal politics; and at still others they appear scarcely fixed—even within their own frame of reference. Signs that seem clear markers of difference can become agents of sexual disorientation that break down, invert, and radically call into question the categories designed to discriminate "masculine" from "feminine."

This sense of dislocation is provoked in a variety of ways, but with particular agitation in instances of cross-dressing. Such agitation, not surprisingly, can generate a conservative counterreaction—a series of defensive maneuvers to reinscribe sexual orthodoxy. Even so, the energies released in such instances are central to Byron's writing, not only illuminating the codes that govern the behavior of men and women, but becoming a means of exploring new possibilities as well. The cross-dressings of *Don Juan* also, and undeniably, reflect a more private, and more privately coded, issue: Byron's homoeroticism. Louis Crompton's recent study, *Byron and Greek Love,* offers a lucid and powerful examination of Byron's literary and social behavior from this

ELH 54 (1987): 585–617. Reprinted by permission of the Johns Hopkins University Press.

perspective, especially in relation to Georgian and Regency homophobia. My essay concentrates on Byron's representations of heterosexual politics, which, sensitized by his homosexuality, turn personal experience outward into a critical reading of the discourses of sexual difference and sexual ideology that permeate his age.

II

Traditional distinctions of gender and corresponding habits of judgment are everywhere apparent in Byron's writing. A woman may be written off with the prescription of "a looking-glass and a few sugar plums . . . she will be satisfied."[2] If her gaze turns to man, he must guard against the peril to his security. "Love" in *Don Juan* is personified as a gallant male (9.44), but its female embodiments in the Sultana Gulbeyaz or the Empress Catherine are dangerous; and in Queen Elizabeth, love is so "ambiguous" in method and so incompatible with the exercise of political power, that she disgraces both "her Sex and Station" (9.81).[3] "Hatred," not coincidentally, is pure female treachery, a spidery woman with a "hundred arms and legs" (10.12). Even if "woman" in this poem escapes such extreme representations, it is only towards an unpredictable chaos of activity:

> What a strange thing is man! and what a stranger
> Is woman! What a whirlwind is her head,
> And what a whirlpool full of depth and danger
> Is all the rest about her! (9.64)

Man may be strange, but woman is both stranger than he and ultimately a stranger to him and his world. Thus, if as Peter Manning remarks, "Juan's education is his experience with women," *Don Juan* remains concerned about that economy, for female pedagogy, even when its curriculum is "that useful sort of knowledge . . . acquired in nature's good old college" (2.136), is of dubious value.[4] "'Tis pity learned virgins ever wed / With persons of no sort of education," the narrator muses, with Byron's line-break momentarily suggesting an even more radical solution to the summary lament, "Oh! ye lords of ladies intellectual, / Inform us truly, have they not hen-peck'd you all?" (1.22). This couplet may be Byron's most famous; it is significant that the point of its testy wit is the reduction of women's intellect to an instrument to torture a lord. When it is not so precise, women's learning is treated as an easily exposed pretension: "Men with their heads reflect on this and that— / But women with their hearts or heaven knows what!" (6.2). Their capacity for "sober reason" is so easily compromised that it is impossible, the narrator smirks, to know what "can signify the site / Of ladies' lucubrations" (11.33–34). Those subject to sharpest sarcasm are, predictably, "The

Blues"—a "tribe" whom even Juan ("who was a little superficial") can conquer, and with no more than a light continental style "Which lent his learned lucubrations pith, / And passed for arguments of good endurance" (11.50–52). Of the two orders of pretension, Juan's escapes derision because Byron allows him to recognize the hoax, indeed to participate in the self-parodies of his author, who could on occasion refer to "his masterpieces" as "his elucubrations."[5]

Byron shows his narrator preferring women who behave in accord with conventional models—for example, Haidée and Zoe nursing Juan "With food and raiment, and those soft attentions, / Which are (as I must own) of female growth" (2.123). Similarly, the Sultana Gulbeyaz is most affecting, to Juan and the narrator alike, when her "imperial, or imperious" manner (5.110) succumbs to the female heart, as when, for instance, she is moved to tears by Juan's own. If her rage at Juan's refusal to love on command reminds the narrator of King Lear's in intensity, he is struck by how "her thirst of blood was quench'd in tears," which he deems "the fault of her soft sex" and the conduit through which "her sex's shame broke in at last. . . . it flow'd in natural and fast." He is glad to note that on such occasions "she felt humbled," adding that "humiliation / Is sometimes good for people in her station" (5.136–37). For then, "nature teaches more than power can soil, / And, when a *strong* although a strange sensation, / Moves—female hearts are . . . genial soil / For kinder feelings, whatso'er their nation" (5.120). Byron's textual variants imply that tutelage by "nature" yields a political corrective as well: thus moved, Gulbeyaz not only "forgot her station," but may be addressed as a "Poor Girl."[6]

If tears mark the female here, they are still part of that world of woman's strangeness, and not always susceptible to certain interpretation. For what looks "natural" also has the effect of manipulating male sympathy, and we have just heard that women such as Gulbeyaz may "shed and use" tears "at their liking" (5.118). Tellingly, Juan finds that his resistance to sexual exploitation "Dissolved like snow before a woman crying" (5.141). By contrast, men's tears, the narrator is certain, are true "torture," agon rather than art: "A woman's tear-drop melts, a man's half sears, / Like molten lead, as if you thrust a pike in / His heart to force it out" (5.118). Men's tears reflect a wholly unsuspect emotion: when one of the shipwrecked crew "wept at length," the narrator assures us it was "not fears / That made his eyelids as a woman's be"; he weeps in pure pity for "a wife and children" (2.43).

The subject of tears is a synecdoche for the demarcations of gender that inflect the world of *Don Juan,* and one instance of how its narrator generates masculine self-definition by contraries and oppositions. These dynamics are typically represented as a contest between masculine and feminine will, in which female manipulation is represented as inimical to male independence and power. Significantly, the suspicion of calculation in Gulbeyaz's tears and their effect in mastering Juan's resistance recall the arts Donna Julia deploys to deflect interrogation by her husband, even as she conceals her lover in her bed. Byron's narrator, in solidarity with the cuckold, dons a voice of moral outrage at the whole gender. "Oh shame! / Oh sin! Oh sorrow! and Oh womankind! / How can you do such things and keep your fame, / Unless this world, and t'other too, be blind? / Nothing so dear as an unfilch'd good name!" (1.165). Byron, whose own name was tainted by sexual scandal, is perhaps a little irked by the female art of having it both ways. Thus of Lady Adeline, a later variation on Julia, he has his narrator remark, "whatso'er she wished, she acted right; / And whether coldness, pride, or virtue, dignify / A Woman, so she's good, what does it signify?" (14.57). Her security depends on remaining an opaque or perpetually intractable signifier to masculine intelligence, and her social power derives from such finesse: she acts the "amphibious sort of harlot, / 'Couleur de rose,' who's neither white nor scarlet," and who, with a "little genial sprinkling of hypocrisy," may become one of the "loveliest Oligarchs of our Gynocrasy" (12.62, 66). This is a rhyme Byron liked, for he summons it again to advise all who would "take the tone of their society" to "wear the newest mantle of hypocrisy, / On pain of much displeasing the Gynocrasy" (16.52). The hostility that sharpens the point of these pairings can be heard in Byron's self-congratulating claim to be neither surprised nor distressed on hearing of women's aversion to Don Juan: "they could not bear it because it took off the veil [of their] d[amne]d sentiment. . . . They hated the book because it showed and exposed their hypocrisy," he says, and he seems to have enjoyed provoking Teresa Guiccioli's dislike of "that ugly Don Juan."[7]

Yet if these numerous apostrophes to and declarations about arts of women, as well as the narrator's insistence on "their" hypocrisy, seem to divide the world of Don Juan securely along lines of gender, Byron's concentration tugs at a network of affiliations. Even to say "our Gynocrasy" implies a certain pride of identification. Indeed, in the stanza from Canto 12 quoted above, the third rhyme word, significantly, is "aristocracy"—as if Byron were signalling his awareness that women are culpable of nothing more than disclosing the master-trope of all social success. The play of rhyme itself is relevant, for if, as the narrator remarks with faint condescension, "There's nothing women love to dabble in / More . . . Than match-making in general: 'tis no sin" (15.31), Byron has him do so in matched words, a sign of his own love of match-making in the general society of language. There is an even more pronounced affinity of interest to challenge the supposition that hypocrisy is all "theirs": hypocrisy may be a moral fault, but it is also artful acting, and the narrator's confessed pleasure in performances both literary and social implicates him in a similar masquerade. It is interesting that Princess Caroline would apply the same term to Byron that his narrator applies to women: "He was all couleur de rose last evening."[8] These cross applications are not exactly "cross-dressing," but they indirectly participate—for the fashion, if not the material, is the same. Thus it is only half-sarcastically that Byron's narrator admits, "What I love in women is, they won't / Or can't do otherwise than lie, but do it / So well, the very truth seems falsehood to it"; their artifice is natural, and so their lies are true. And in a world where all pretenses to truth seem to veil the artifices of ideology, women's hypocrisy may, paradoxically, be the most honest behavior of all: "after all, what is a lie? 'Tis but / The truth in masquerade" (11.36–37). By Canto 16, in fact, Byron's narrator is praising his female muse as "The most sincere that ever dealt in fiction" (2), and reflecting this quality in the "mobility" of women such as Adeline who, in adapting to the performative requirements of any occasion, are not playing "false," but "true; for surely, they're sincerest, / Who are strongly acted on by what is nearest" (97).

Byron makes some attempt to distinguish the male poet and his muse from the behavior of such women, for mobility, his narrator says, is "A thing of temperament and not of art" (16.97), and a habit that may leave its possessor more "acted on" than acting—while his poem, presumably, is a thing of art alone. He implies that distinction elsewhere in his claims that it is "ladies' fancies" that are "rather transitory" (10.9), and "feminine Caprice" that inspires their "indecision, / Their never knowing their own mind two days" (6.119, 117). And of course, the poem's definitive figure of mobility is Lady Adeline. Even so, mobility is not the sure index of gender that tears are. Byron in fact added a note to the poem in Adeline's defense, as if to balance the masculine bias of Juan's external perspective on her "playing her grand role" (and thus prone to "doubt how much of Adeline was *real*" [16.96]) with a more sympathetic assessment: mobility is "an excessive susceptibility of immediate impressions," he explains, and "though sometimes apparently useful to the possessor, a most painful and unhappy attribute" (*CPW*, 5:769). This gloss seems more than sympathy; it has the sound of psychological self-pleading. Thus it is not surprising to hear from Thomas Moore that Byron "was fully aware not only of the abundance of this quality in his own nature, but of the danger in which it placed consistency and singleness of character" (*CPW*, 5:769). Lady Blessington comments that the "mobility of his nature is extraordinary, and makes him inconsistent in his actions as well as in his conversation"—a quality Hazlitt observes in *Don Juan* itself, summoning a term that suggests cross-dressing: the "great power" of this poem, he proposes, lies in Byron's ability to "turn round and *travestie* himself: the drollery is in the utter discontinuity of ideas and feelings."[9]

In Byron's experience, it seems clear, mobility is an epic renegade, loyal to no sex, itself showing mobility across gender lines. George M. Ridenour in fact discerns in Adeline's mobility "another version of that growing urbanity Byron has so praised in his hero himself: 'The art of living in all climes with ease' (15.11)," and he extends this art to include the narrator's acknowledged facility at playing "the *Improvvisatore*" "amidst life's infinite variety" (15.19–20).[10] This last allusion to the arts of Shakespeare's Cleopatra, which in their "infinite variety" defeat the attritions of "custom" (2.2.241), further perplexes discriminations of gender. Not only does Byron have his narrator apply the infinite variety of her art to his own general view of life, but it is worth recalling that Cleopatra's various repertoire includes the fun of cross-dressing: "I . . . put my tires and mantles on him, whilst / I wore his sword" (2.5.21–23).[11] With this borrowing, Byron fashions a kind of psychic cross-dressing for his narrator; not coincidentally, Byron's very language for "mobility" appears to have been converted from Madame de Staël's description of feminine consciousness in her popular novel, *Corinne*.[12]

As the issue of mobility suggests, *Don Juan* at times complicates the language of gender in ways that focus on the definition of self in gendered society, and may even expose the political investments of those definitions. Such preoccupation in Byron's poetry with "the social structures of its rhetoric," as Jerome J. McGann argues, works to reflect "the audience's character . . . back to itself so that it can 'reflect' upon that reflection in a critical and illuminating way."[13] That dynamic is especially active in the social and linguistic cross-dressings of *Don Juan,* for these figures not only concentrate the energies of Byron's satire, but compel our attention to those crucial discriminations through which the masculine and the feminine have been culturally defined, and through which men and women have been psychologically compelled and historically confined. Social cross-dressing includes both the "odd travesty" of Juan in the slave market "femininely all array'd" (5.74, 80) and "her frolic Grace—Fitz-Fulke" disguised as the ghost of the Black Friar (16.123); it also involves the less obvious but equally significant covering of Juan by female clothes—first by Julia, then by Haidée and Zoe. Linguistic cross-dressing materializes in transfers of verbal property, such as the narrator's calling himself "a male Mrs. Fry" (10.84), or Antonia's references to Juan as a "pretty gentleman" with a "half-girlish face" (1.170–71), corroborated by the narrator's descriptions of his hero as "a most beauteous Boy" (9.53), "feminine in feature" (8.52), who dances "like a flying Hour before Aurora, / In Guido's famous fresco" (14.40). These transfers also include the application of masculine-toned terms to women: the Sultan desires a "handsome paramour" (6.91); Empress Catherine is "handsome" and "fierce" (9.63)—her behavior "a kind of travesty" as one critic remarks, and so in the most fundamental sense, for "travesty" is a linguistic kin of "transvestite." (Suggestively, another reader discerns Catherine's origins in a male historical figure, the Ali Pasha, who implicitly feminized Byron by paying great attention to his beauty.)[14] An even more complex exchange of the properties of gender plays in the comment that Juan dances "Like swift Camilla" (14.39). The comparison may appear to feminize Juan, but it actually entertains a dizzying interchange of properties, for as a hunter and epic warrior, Camilla is associated with typically male pursuits.

The ambiguous swirl of Juan's sexual composition even spilled over into the extratextual realm of Regency society. As Byron knew, his hero—that slender, pretty "stripling of sixteen" (1.83)—was impersonated at a masquerade by Caroline Lamb (*BLJ,* 7:169), an early mistress who herself may have been a model for Juan. She was petite, epicene, and often described as resembling a young teenage boy: a famous set of portraits shows her in page's guise, a costume she enjoyed and on occasion adopted for discreet visits to Byron's apartment. Byron, for his part, sometimes disguised his female lovers in male attire to avoid gossip, once presenting one of these as "my brother Gordon"; as a result of such habits, some of the boys in Byron's circle were at times mistaken for girls in boys' clothes. Byron's own style of dress also played a part. In Italy he would often appear "holding a handkerchief, upon which his jewelled fingers lay embedded," so Leigh Hunt reports, adding that Byron trimmed and oiled his hair "with all the anxiety of a Sardanapalus. The visible character to which this effeminacy gave rise appears to have indicated itself as early as his travels in the Levant, where the Grand Signior is said to have taken him for a woman in disguise."[15] The composition of Juan's intersexual character, along with the poem's linguistic and social transvestism, is inhabited by these playful disguises and habits of dress, and all were undoubtedly energized by Byron's homoeroticism, which, in the repressive and punitive atmosphere of Regency England, could not risk exposure.[16]

The fictions of *Don Juan* serve Byron in part as an outlet for homoerotic material in disguise, but its cross-dressings accomplish something else as well, for they put his imagination in touch with heterosexual politics by animating a set of social signifiers that challenge conventional expectations and customary boundaries of demarcation. Some of these transfers and transgressions emerge as farce, but not exclusively, for Byron implicates them in deep (if not fully sustained) counterplots that perplex the terms "male" and "female"—both politically and psychologically construed—and thereby unsettle, even dismantle, the social structures to which gender has been assimilated. The result of these transsexual poetics is a qualified but potent redefinition of conventional sexual politics, for gender symbolism, as Natalie Zemon Davis remarks, "is always available to make statements about social experience and to reflect (or conceal) contradictions within it."[17] Thus the spectacle of Juan "femininely all array'd" in the slave market works to foreground female restriction and vulnerability, while the figures of women "masculinized" through social power or costume disguise emerge with the energy of self-direction and the force of sexual assertiveness. These transfers allow Byron to inscribe a language of cultural contradiction and personal self-division in which what has been habitually denied to one sex gets projected in terms of the other. And while the figures on both sides of these transfers are often made to seem absurd or anomalous, it is their very anomaly that makes palpable the ideology by which conventional codes are invested, maintained, and perpetuated.

It is fitting that *Don Juan,* an infamously impure poem assayed in terms of generic convention, should yield related transgressions of gender that may, in Jacques Derrida's words, test "identity and difference between the feminine and masculine." That test is a provocative one, for as Derrida notes, to cross the "line of demarcation," whether in terms of gender or genre, is to "risk impurity, anomaly or monstrosity."[18] To the extent Byron imports words such as "handsome" and "feminine" across conventional lines of demarcation, he speculates about such risks; but he also shies away from the full consequences by restabilizing these transgressions with plots of correction. For Julia's "handsome eyes"—like Austen's "handsome" Emma Woodhouse or Hemingway's "handsome" Margot Macomber—suggest theft or impropriety of character, and all three writers set their problematically self-possessed women into plots that conclude in their submission to male power and authority. Byron's tendency to conserve a traditional character within potentially subversive cross-dressing is also legible in the image of Kaled, who in *Lara* accompanies her lover disguised as his page. Kaled's hand seems "So femininely white it might bespeak / Another sex, when matched with that smooth cheek," even though "his garb, and something in his gaze, / More wild and high than woman's eye betrays; / A latent fierceness" (1.576–80). Byron underscores the tensions implicit in the convention of the disguised page (which in English literature is at least as old as Sidney's revised *Arcadia*) by having "his" behavior everywhere recall that of a wife or lover: "mute attention, and his care . . . guessed / Each wish, fulfilled it ere the tongue expressed" (556–57). Finally, as Lara dies, Kaled's emotions overwhelm restraint, and her true "sex confest": "Oh! never yet beneath / The breast of man such trusty love may breathe! / That trying moment hath at once reveal'd / The secret long and yet but half conceal'd" (2.513–17). Murray's edition of *Lara* gives a special prestige to the moment, in fact, by printing an engraving of the scene (see *CPW* 3, facing page 250). Byron's plots of correction and restoration not only counter but may even be compelled by the transfers he has entertained within them, for his experiments with the codes of gender are radical in their implications, and potentially chaotic in their social and psychological consequences.

The challenge such transvestite experiments pose to the integrity of social codes certainly alarmed that earlier legislator of propriety, Phillip Stubbes, who devotes a major part of his *Anatomy of Abuses* (1583) to dress. Stubbes is convinced that women who "weare apparel assigned onely to man" are ready "as wel [to] chaunge their sex, & put on the kinde of man . . . verely become men indeed." Not only social harmony but gender itself hangs in the balance, for "Our Apparrell was given us as a signe distinctive to discern betwixt sex and sex, & therefore one to weare the Apparel of another sex is to participate with the same, and to adulterate the veritie of his owne kinde."[19] Though lacking Stubbes's outrage, Byron reveals a compatible ambivalence about perverting the distinctiveness of the signifier—an ambivalence that grows increasingly acute when transgressions of the codes of gender surpass the play world of inversion (where binary oppositions still hold) to enter queasier realms of experience in which opposition is blurred or effaced altogether. These are occasions when the decree with which Derrida coyly begins "The Law of Genre"—"Genres are not to be mixed" (202)—is violated not just by transvestism, but by such "unnatural" embodiments of impurity and monstrosity as fops, epicenes, and eunuchs, figures Byron ascribes to "the *third* sex" (4.86). Here Byron is not that far out of step with Stubbes, who terms women who cross-dress *"Hermaphroditi,* that is, Monsters of bothe kindes, half women, half men" (73).

Byron's own touch is usually lighter: about applying feminine-gender pronouns to Juan's transvestism, his narrator explains, "I say *her,* because / The Gender still was Epicene, at least / In outward show, which is a saving clause" (6.58)—the term "epicene" referring both to neuter nouns and to theatrical characters of a somewhat amusing, somewhat disturbing, sexual ambiguity. But sometimes his point sharpens, as in the narrator's sneering at "the coxcombry of certain *She* Men" (14.31). And with other sorts of ambiguously gendered figures, there is an ideological issue. Baba, already degraded by race, is also made to embody the sexual degradation of the eunuch: he is "a black old neutral personage / Of the third sex" (5.26). Not coincidentally, Byron's favored means of abusing a political opponent is to degender him. The "emasculated" mind epitomized by the eunuch Eutropius is a despised *"It"* (Dedication 15; the pronoun had been "he" [*CPW,* 5.7]). The overstrained laureate Southey, "quite adry, Bob," is of a piece with the "intellectual eunuch Castlereagh" (Dedication 3; 11). The former figure is in fact stigmatized further by transvestite practice—"turncoat Southey"—and thus scorned for lacking both political and sexual integrity (11.56; see also *Vision of Judgment* 97); and the "turncoat" poet on Haidée's island is accompanied, significantly, by "dwarfs, dancing girls, black eunuchs" (3.78). Perhaps more worrisome than these easily apprehended outlaws of gendered society is the puzzling case of Lord Henry. Though a thoroughly masculine, "handsome man," who in love and war alike "preserved his perpendicular," there "was something wanting" on the whole, recalling "that undefinable *'Je ne sçais quoi'* " that turned Helen from the Spartan King Menelaus to the "inferior" "Dardan boy." Byron's narrator affects perplexity over this exception to the traditional codes of manly attractiveness, and imagines the answer may be known only to those "like wise Tiresias," who can prove "by turns the difference of the several sexes"—but who must in turn become an anomaly of nature, a monstrosity, an impurity, in order to assess and speak of that "difference" (14.71–73).

III

The condition of "something wanting" was normally ascribed in the dominant discourses of Byron's era to the female rather than the male, and the corresponding linguistic habits are evident enough in the culture of letters in which Byron came of age—even in writers of such opposite sexual politics as Alexander Pope and James Fordyce on the one side and Mary Wollstonecraft on the other. Pope's Epistle "To a Lady, of the Characters of Women" assumes, for instance, that "Most Women have no Characters at all" (2), and though it concludes, as the Argument promises, with a "Picture of an esteemable Woman, made up of the best kind of Contrarieties," Pope can describe that "best kind" only as an aesthetic enhancement of the male character: "Heav'n, when it strives to polish all it can / Its last best work, but forms a softer Man" (271–72).[20] Catherine Macaulay ponders this construction of the feminine in her *Letters on Education,* with a specific scrutiny of the linguistic conventions so incorporated:

> when we compliment the appearance of a more than ordinary energy in the female mind, we call it masculine; and hence it is, that Pope has elegantly said *a perfect woman's but a softer man.* And if we take in the consideration, that there can be but one rule of moral excellence for beings made of the same materials, organized after the same manner, and subjected to similar laws of Nature, we must either agree with Mr. Pope, or we must reverse the proposition, and say, that *a perfect man is a woman formed after a coarser mold.* The difference that actually does subsist between the sexes, is too flattering for men to be willingly imputed to accident, for what accident occasions, wisdom might correct.[21]

Both Pope's "Epistle" and Macaulay's critique of the ideology of masculine and feminine are potent points of reference for Wollstonecraft in *A Vindication of the Rights of Woman.* Yet her linguistic politics are inconsistent in ways that anticipate Byron's ambivalent plays with the conventions of gender in *Don Juan.* Sometimes her analysis is as sharp as Macaulay's, especially when the subject is Macaulay herself: "I will not call hers a masculine understanding," she insists, "because I admit not of such an arrogant assumption of reason."[22] But her Introduction, though its scrutiny of linguistic convention is as scrupulous as Macaulay's, reflects and perpetuates those conventions even as their application is called into question: "I have heard exclamations against masculine women. . . . If by this appellation men mean to inveigh against their ardour in hunting, shooting, and gaming, I shall most cordially join in the cry; but if it be against the imitation of manly virtues, or more properly speaking, the attainment of those talents and virtues, the exercise of which ennobles the human character, and which raise females in the scale of animal being . . . [may they] every day grow more and more masculine" (8). Wollstonecraft retains "masculine" as the nobler term, and in order to "render my sex more respectable members of society," she works a style that deliberately shuns "pretty feminine phrases, which the men condescendingly use to soften our slavish dependence." She spurns typically feminine dresses of thought—not only "pretty superlatives" but all "fabricating," "polish," and "dazzle"—to advance the "simple unadorned truth" of "masculine and respectable" conduct (9–11). In these sentences Wollstonecraft is at least self-conscious about the conventional language of gender, but elsewhere in *A Vindication* she seems to credit gendered terms by habit. Criticizing present codes of heroism, for instance, she complains that these favor "effeminacy" over "fortitude" (145). And she imagines "that the few extraordinary women who have rushed in eccentrical directions out of the orbit prescribed to their sex, were *male* spirits, confined by mistake in female frames" (35). Even of Macaulay, she implies gender is an obstacle to be overcome: "in her style of writing . . . no sex appears, for it is like the sense it conveys, strong and clear" (105). These usages, in effect, reinforce the orthodoxy of Fordyce's *Sermons to Young Women* (published the same year as *A Vindication,* 1792), which categorize as "masculine women" those who would share activities that are "properly the province of men"—"war, commerce, politics, exercises of strength and dexterity, abstract philosophy, and all the abstruser sciences."[23] Fittingly, though with a different stress, Mary Hays's memoir of Wollstonecraft would note the "high masculine tone" through which the "power and energy of thought" in *A Vindication* are conveyed.[24]

Don Juan at times perpetuates these linguistic and social conventions, but like Wollstonecraft, Byron intermittently calls attention to their codes in ways that provoke critical scrutiny. His attitudes are never of a piece, and often self-contradictory within the same stanza. This changefulness at once reflects the active power of his questioning of the "she condition," even as it suffers from the ambivalence afflicting those who would inaugurate or sympathize with such questions. Fluctuations of compassion and nervous scorn can be read in the very passage in which Byron has his narrator ponder the "she condition." He begins in tones of mock sympathy and blame, but within a few lines these become expressions of genuine sympathy:

> Alas! Worlds fall—and Woman, since she fell'd
> The World (as, since that history, less polite
> Than true, hath been a creed so strictly held)
> Has not yet given up the practice quite.
> Poor Thing of Usages! Coerc'd, compell'd,
> Victim when wrong, and martyr often when right,
> Condemn'd to child-bed . . . (14.23)

His sympathy modulates into a self-conscious contemplation of sexual politics and policy:

> who can penetrate
> The real sufferings of their she condition?
> Man's very sympathy with their estate
> Has much of selfishness and more suspicion.
> Their love, their virtue, beauty, education,
> But form good housekeepers, to breed a nation. (14.24)

Wollstonecraft herself could have written the next stanza:

> The gilding wears so soon from off her fetter,
>   That—but ask any woman if she'd choose
> (Take her at thirty, that *is*) to have been
> Female or male? a school-boy or a Queen? (14.25)

If Pope's Epistle assumes that "ev'ry Lady would be Queen for life" and shudders at the thought of "a whole Sex of Queens! / Pow'r all their end" (218–20), Byron's summary question guesses that any woman might prefer the lot of a schoolboy—the lowest of males—to that of a queen, the highest of females. But he allows the issue to diffuse as he returns his narrator to the more familiar ground of sexist mocking: " 'Petticoat Influence' is a great reproach, / Which even those who obey would fain be thought / To fly from, as from hungry pikes a roach" (14.26). Potential political commentary then evaporates into a digression on the "mystical sublimity" of the petticoat (14.26–27). Yet the evasion itself is revealing; the analogy of hungry pikes and their prey that Peter Manning remarks is indeed worth attention—not the least for renewing an earlier image of Englishwomen as unholy "fishers for men" (12.59).[25] Though the vehicle shifts, the tenor is the same: women are always the predators.

Despite the narrator's reversion to antifeminist bitterness, Byron's willingness to have him meditate on the "she condition" is a striking one, for it not only allows a male voice to confirm the validity of a woman's earlier lament—namely Julia's—but now invests that grievance with intersexual authority. Writing to Juan, Julia had complained that if

> Man's love is of man's life a thing apart,
> 'Tis woman's whole existence; man may range
> The court, camp, church, the vessel, and the mart,
>   Sword, gown, gain, glory, offer in exchange
> Pride, fame, ambition, to fill up his heart. . . .
> Man has all these resources, we but one,
> To love again, and be again undone. (1.194)

Not only does Byron's ventriloquy through Julia express a sympathetic understanding of the limits imposed on "woman's whole existence," but Julia's letter may actually have female authority—its voice inhabited by the language of both Jane Austen and (like the meditation on mobility) Madame de Staël.[26] Though still reflecting the terms of difference authorized by his culture, in his effort to address the "she condition," to hear and render its voices, Byron attempts a critical perspective, one that allows him to reveal and explore the ideological implications of those terms.[27]

That exploration is helped by Byron's capacity for owning what amounts to a "he" complicity in the "she condition": even as the narrator of *Don Juan* rails against marriage, Byron has him admit that not only do women invest "all" in love, but that "man, to man so oft unjust, / Is always so to women" (2.199–200). Byron himself informs an "incredulous" Lady Blessington that "men think of themselves alone, and regard the woman but as an object that administers to their selfish gratification, and who, when she ceases to have this power, is thought of no more, save as an obstruction in their path." His terms for assessing difference still inscribe a hierarchy: men enjoy the privilege of power, women the honor of a higher moral place: "women only know evil from having experienced it through men; whereas men have no criterion to judge of purity or goodness but woman"; "I have a much higher opinion of your sex than I have even now expressed," he adds (*Blessington,* 196)—a remark that his Italian mistress, Countess Teresa Guiccioli, underscored in her own copy of Blessington's *Conversations of Lord Byron.* These critiques reflect ideological myths of course, but their psychological reflex in Byron is revealingly self-critical. In the privacy of his journal he remarks: "There is something to me very softening in the presence of a woman,—some strange influence, even if one is not in love with them,—which I cannot at all account for, having no very high opinion of the sex. But yet,—I always feel in better humour with myself and every thing else, if there is a woman within ken" (*BLJ,* 3:246). Conventional polarities and traces of habitual opinion notwithstanding, one is struck by the implication that "the presence of a woman" seems necessary to Byron, both for his sense of self-completion and for his sense of integration with the world at large. He wants a heroine.

That psychological undercurrent to Byron's critique of the sexual politics that underwrite the "she condition" exerts a nervous force however—especially when that critique is articulated by cross-dressings, for these inversions and reversals not only erode male privilege, but inhabit plots in which such erosion is associated with images and threats of death. The dissolution of male power is apparent enough in the loss of male attire and the quasi-transvestism that ensues in Juan's romances with Julia and Haidée. Julia "half-smother'd" a naked Juan in her bedding to hide him from her husband's posse; it is a naked and half-dead Juan for whom "Haidée stripp'd her sables off" to make a couch—"and, that he might be more at ease, / And warm, in case by chance he should awake," she and Zoe "also gave a petticoat apiece" (2.133). Though not overtly transvestite, these coverings still compromise Juan's manhood, for each, while protective, also marks him as passive and dependent, the property of a woman's design. Significantly, after being discovered by Alfonso, Juan cannot recover his clothes, but must escape "naked" (188) into the night. That reduction is also suggested by the garments Juan, "naked" once again, receives from Haidée, for though these are men's, the apparel does not proclaim the man: the "breeches" in which she "dress'd him" are rather "spacious" (probably her father's) and more tellingly, she neglects to supply the real signifiers of male power—"turban, slippers, pistols, dirk" (2.160). With both Julia and Haidée, Juan remains a "boy" (Catherine too, we learn, "sometimes liked a boy," "slight and slim," preferring such "a boy to men much bigger" [9.47, 72]), and Byron underscores the corresponding impotence not only by confronting Juan with a genuine threat of death from the men betrayed by these affairs, but by masculinizing the women. Julia is given an uncommon bearing of "stature tall," complemented by a "brow / Bright with intelligence" and "handsome eyes" (1.60–61). Haidée's stature is "Even of the highest for a female mould . . . and in her air / There was a something which bespoke command" (2.116). The implicit maleness of this manner is confirmed when she confronts her father: protecting Juan, "Haidée threw herself her boy before"; "Stern as her sire" (Byron revises the adjective from "calm" [*CPW*, 5:216]), "She stood . . . tall beyond her sex . . . and with a fix'd eye scann'd / Her father's face. . . . How like they look'd! the expression was the same. . . . their features and / Their stature differing but in sex and years (4.42–45). Sexual difference is less remarkable than the display of common traits across gender lines, for Haidée and Lambro differ less from each other than both differ from the "boy" Juan—a term applied several times in this episode (2.144, 174; 4.19, 38).

All these inversions of socially prescribed character fuel a lethal economy, as if Byron worried that to indulge such transgressions were to tempt self-cancellation—a psychological updating of the well-known injunction of Deuteronomy dear to Stubbes and other chroniclers of abuses: "The woman shall not wear that which pertaineth unto a man, neither shall a man put on a woman's garment: for all that do so *are* abomination unto the LORD" (22:5). A feminized Juan always invites death into the poem, whether in the form of threats to his own life or to the lives of those implicated in his travesties. "Juan nearly died" (1.168) from affairs with Julia and Haidée, and they exact full wages: the passionate Julia is sentenced to life-in-death in a convent; Haidée's nurturing of Juan is allied with figures of death, and she herself dies.[28] The threat is nearly perpetual: when Gulbeyaz discovers her designs for Juan as odalisque usurped by his harem bedpartner, she issues a warrant for both their deaths, and Catherine's appetites all too soon reduce her "beauteous" favorite to "a condition / Which augured of the dead" (10.39). So, too, after his first sighting of the Black Friar's Ghost—itself a patent spectre of death—Juan and Fitz-Fulke look "pale" (16.31); the morning after discovering her within that "sable frock and dreary cowl" (16.123), Juan appears "wan and worn, with eyes that hardly brooked / The light"; Her Grace seems scarcely better—"pale and shivered" (17.14). Byron's "Memoranda" on the Murray manuscript scrap in fact reveals a suggestive linkage: "The Shade of the / Friar / The D[ea]th of J[uan]" (*CPW*, 5:761). All these presages and figures of death suggest that Byron senses fatal consequences when the law of gender is violated: the annihilation of self in both its social identity and psychological integrity.

In assessing Byron's apprehension of such consequences, it is useful to turn briefly to Keats, for his "feminine" flexibility of ego is often compared, for better or worse, to Byron's "masculine" force of self-definition. In commenting on Keats's "deficiency in masculine energy of style," Hazlitt, for one, cites Byron's racy violations of social propriety to sharpen his case.[29] Even to Keats, Byron's bold inscriptions of self—"Lord Byron cuts a figure," he says—are a felt contrast to his own "poetical Character," a "camelion" of "no self . . . no identity."[30] This chameleonism bears on the question of gender, for as Keats puts it, such self-effacement allows "as much delight in conceiving an Iago as an Imogen"—showing, in effect, ability to negate what some modern feminist critics call "masculine" self-assertion. Thus, sharing Hazlitt's sense of gender, Erica Jong, Adrienne Rich, and Margaret Homans all have perceived in Keats qualities they identify and value in women writers. Speculating that Keats's humble origins and poverty correspond to "certain aspects of women's experience as outsiders relative to the major literary tradition," Homans exempts him from classification with poets of the dominant masculine tradition, who typically construct "the strong self from . . . strong language." Rich, in the course of explaining the "female" ability to "lose all sense of her own ego" and exercise "tremendous powers of intuitive identification and sympathy with other people," cites Keats's term "Negative Capability." Jong summons the same term to declare that "feminism *means* empathy . . . akin to the quality Keats called 'negative capability'—that unique gift for projecting oneself into other states of consciousness."[31] And albeit with a different emphasis from Hazlitt's, there is an implied contrast to masculinism such as Byron's, whose poetry "simply exaggerates . . . societal experience" Homans says; "the men are even bolder, the ladies even more beautiful and passive, in Byron than in life" (8).

What is interesting is how slippery such distinctions become as soon as one applies any kind of pressure. The issues are not clearcut. *Don Juan* offers scant evidence of the sexual politics Homans describes—Byron in fact thought he was being "true to Nature in making the advances come from the females" (*Medwin,* 165). This may be sexism in a different form, but the difference is crucial, for the dynamics of power that seemed to Byron to be "natural" in English Regency Society run significantly counter to the politics feminists such as Homans ascribe to him: "I am easily governed by women," Byron confesses (*Medwin,* 216); and protesting *Blackwood's* charge that he treated women "harshly," he replies: "it may be so—but I have been their martyr. —My whole life has been sacrificed *to* them & *by* them" (*BLJ,* 6:257). Nor are Keats's sexual politics unproblematic. Like Byron in some moods, he condescends to "the generallity of women" as creatures "to whom I would rather give a Sugar Plum than my time"; he derides the bluestockings as do Byron and Hazlitt; and with a puerile fear of sexual self-discovery, he ridicules the "Man in love" (*KL,* 1:404; 2:187–88). His unassertive male ego, moreover, typically finds poetic correlatives not in figures of sexual equality, but in tales of young men dominated—sometimes fatally so—by powerful women: recall Venus and Adonis, Circe and Glaucus, Cynthia and Endymion, Moneta and the poet-dreamer, Lamia and Lycius, "Fanny" and her poet-lover. Indeed, such tales (as his letters show) are in many ways the reflex of a sexism that is hostile, adolescent, and more deeply entrenched than Byron's for want of the intimate friendships with women that complicate Byron's attitudes.

Nor is the much-credited flexibility of Keats's ego boundaries the clear mark of distinction that it is famed to be, for this quality has been noted of Byron as well, and with a striking similarity of metaphor: "Byron is a perfect chameleon," Lady Blessington reports; he takes "the colour of whatever touches him. He is conscious of this, and says it is owing to the extreme *mobilité* of his nature, which yields to present impressions." She is so perplexed with this "mass of heterogeneous evidence," in fact, that she finds it hard "to draw a just conclusion" of Byron's character (71–72). Keats's chameleonism bears a similar consequence—one elided by some feminist readers, but felt acutely by Keats himself: such easy projection into the other may in turn invite the "identity" of the "other" so "to press upon me," Keat says, "that, I am in a very little time an[ni]hilated . . . among Men" (*KL,* 1:387). That Byron's transvestite poetics intuit similar consequences is not remarkable; accommodation to masculinist social and political imperatives may be noted of many who wrote in early nineteenth-century England, including Austen and Wollstonecraft.[32] What is remarkable is the way *Don Juan* reveals the degree to which a poet whom contemporaries of both sexes (when they were not offended) found full of "manly" fun, and in whom modern feminists since Virginia Woolf have noted a "thoroughly masculine nature," can entertain the contradictions of male privilege in his historical circumstance and expose these in his artistic practice.[33]

IV

The two most extended episodes of transvestism in *Don Juan*—Juan's conscription as an odalisque and Fitz-Fulke's appropriation of a friar's habit—show Byron's effort to explore the arbitrariness of male privilege in an economy of sexual commodities. Both derive their energy from the inversion of that privilege, and both provoke Byron's ambivalence about the cost. Behind both, too, is Byron's participation in the institution of the "Cavalier Servente," the accepted escort and socially tolerated lover of a married woman. Byron could sometimes comment on the system in quasi-feminist terms, deeming Serventism a byproduct of the way Italian fathers treat their daughters as commodities to be sold "under the market price"—that "portion" of their assets "fixed by law for the dower." The successful bidder was often a man older than the father himself (Teresa Guiccioli's husband, for instance, was about three times her age). With "such a preposterous connexion," Byron exclaims, "no love on either side," extramarital romance was necessary, indeed inevitable (*Medwin*, 22). That is not the whole story, of course, for as Cavalier Servente to Teresa Guiccioli, Byron felt acutely the inversion of sexual privilege to which he was accustomed in England, an inversion that may have been doubly disturbing for bringing into prominence his intrinsic passivity with Regency women: in Venice "the *polygamy* is all on the female side. . . . it is a strange sensation," he remarks (*BLJ*, 6:226).

This wavering between defensiveness and feminist analysis in relation to Serventism thoroughly informs Juan's experience in the Turkish court. Here Byron partly redresses Venetian imbalances, for the polygamy is all on the male side: that Gulbeyaz is one of four wives and fifteen hundred concubines makes her purchase of Juan seem minor in comparison. Yet by placing Juan in women's clothes and in the role of a sex-slave, Byron does more than simply invert the cultural norm; he allows Juan's debasement to reflect in excess the customary status of women as objects of barter and trade in a male-centered economy. Behind Juan's shocked discovery at learning he is the property of a Sultana who asks only "Christian, canst thou love?" and who "conceived that phrase was quite enough to move" (5.116), one senses Byron's own discomfort at having actually become "a piece of female property" in his relationship with Teresa Guiccioli (*BLJ*, 7:28): "the system of *serventism* imposes a thousand times more restraint and slavery than marriage ever imposed," he laments to Lady Blessington (180). And he feels particularly taxed by the erosion of time and autonomy that his "defined duties" required (*BLJ*, 7:195). The mistress's word is "the only law which he obeys. / His is no sinecure. . . . Coach, servants, gondola, he goes to call, / And carries fan, and tippet, gloves, and shawl," the narrator of *Beppo* reports, describing the role of this "supernumerary slave" (the noun was originally "gentleman" [*CPW* 4:141]) in terms that tellingly figure such bondage as a species of transvestism: he "stays / Close to the lady as a part of dress" (40). As if to inflict his own lot on his hero, Byron considered submitting Juan to the "ridicules" of being "a Cavalier Servente in Italy" (*BLJ*, 8:78), a role he has him rehearse in Russia. And when he comments on his hero thus as "man-mistress to Catherine the Great" (*Medwin*, 165), he reveals his agitation about the radical cost of these inversions: degraded to sexual property, Juan has to be regendered.[34]

Juan had, of course, been something of an illicit or smuggled piece of property in his affairs with Julia and Haidée; but the spectacle of him as woman's property is particularly compelling "in his feminine disguise" (6.26) because Byron now makes his loss of power coincide with loss of male identity. The slave market itself is an omen, for in addition to being for sale, the "boy" Juan (5.13)—"an odd male" in more ways than one—gets paired with an "odd female" in an allotment in which everyone else is paired "Lady to lady . . . man to man" (4.91–92). Indeed this odd couple is linked only after the captors decide not to link Juan with one of the *"third* sex" (86), a castrato who inspires "some discussion and some doubt" if such a "soprano might be deem'd to be a male" (92). The precarious security of Juan's gender in the marketplace becomes yet more vulnerable when he is purchased by a eunuch and ordered to dress himself in "a suit / In which a Princess with great pleasure would / Array her limbs" (5.73). The narrator conspires in this travesty, not only by insisting on referring to Juan as "her"—"Her shape, her hair, her air, her every thing" (6.35; itself a parody of Shakespeare's Troilus on "fair Cressid": "Her eyes, her hair, her cheek, her gait, her voice" [1.1.54])—but also by teasing at Juan's latent affinities with the feminine odalisques "all clad alike" (5.99).[35] For in such company, Juan's difference is scarcely apparent: indeed "his youth and features favour'd the disguise" (5.115), and "no one doubted on the whole, that she / Was what her dress bespoke, a damsel fair, / And fresh, and 'beautiful exceedingly' " (6.36)— that last phrase further dressing Juan in Coleridge's phrase for Christabel's first sight of Geraldine.

Yet Byron's total treatment of Juan cross-dressed, though it exposes the politics of sexual property, ultimately contains its subversive impulses by subsuming them into renewed expressions of male power. That agenda is anticipated by Juan's steadfast adherence to the grounds of his identity: Byron allows him the dignity of protesting to his purchaser "I'm not a lady," and of worrying about his social reputation if "it e'er be told / That I unsexed my dress" (5.73, 75). It is only Baba's threat that he will be left with more unsexed than his dress if he does not cooperate that produces compliance, even as Juan declares his "soul loathes / the effeminate garb" (5.76). Juan's statements of resistance to the effeminate find an even stronger ally in Byron's narrative politics, which, as often happens with male transvestism in literary and theatrical tradition, give the occasion over to farce, yet another means of restabilizing the apparent sexual radicalism of Juan regendered.[36] The political implications of Juan's effeminate garb dissipate into a high-camp parody of the trappings of female subjection. Juan even has to be coached "to stint / That somewhat manly majesty of stride" (5.91). The Englishman who befriends him in the slave market sounds the cue as he favors Juan with a jesting version of Laertes' caution to Ophelia—"Keep your good name"—and Juan and the narrator merrily play along: "Nay," quoth the maid, "the Sultan's self shan't carry me, / Unless his highness promises to marry me" (5.84). And when the Sultan takes a shine to Juan's beauty, Juan shows how well he has learned to mimic feminine manners: "This compliment . . . made her blush and shake" (5.156). And quite beyond such campy playfulness, Byron actually reverses the seeming impotence of Juan's travesty by introducing another kind of potency: Juan discovers he is not so much an unsexed man as a newly powerful woman. "Juanna" immediately becomes the center of attention and rivalry in the harem; all the girls want "her" to share their beds. This turn of events affords Juan a novel indirection by which to find directions out, for as the only phallic woman in the harem, he discovers a world of sexual opportunity. Clothes make the man.[37]

Juan's success as a phallic woman is all the more significant for its relation to a set of psychological and cultural contexts that are particularly potent for Byron. The psychological matrix has been studied by Otto Fenichel, who argues that some forms of transvestism are the behavior of a man who fantasizes about being a woman with a penis. Elaborating this view, Robert J. Stoller claims that the male transvestite "does not question that he is male," nor is he "effeminate when not dressed as a woman"; the transvestite, in fact, "is constantly aware of the penis under his woman's clothes, and, when it is not dangerous to do so, gets great pleasure in revealing that he is a male-woman."[38] In *Don Juan* phallic womanhood is made to seem a lucky effect rather than the premise of Juan's transvestism, but Byron's letters suggest an impetus for such luck. The relevant issue is Stoller's proposal that the transvestite man senses "the biological and social 'inferiority' of women" and knows "that within himself there is a propensity toward being reduced to this 'inferior' state" (215)—a propensity Byron displays in Juan's "feminine" characteristics as well as in his affairs with Julia and Haidée. Both Fenichel and Stoller argue that the transvestite invents the fantasy of a "phallic woman" either to remedy his feminine tendencies, or to assert a superior presence in his relations with strong women. In fact, Stoller goes on to say, the "prototype" for this figure "has actually existed in his life—that is, the fiercely dangerous and powerful woman who has humiliated him as a child" (215), namely his mother, whom the male transvestite at once identifies with and supersedes. This analysis may seem to some to be the myth of a male-authored and male-centered psychoanalytic tradition, but it is for that very reason so appropriate in Byron's case, coinciding remarkably not only with Juan's mother, the tyrannical Donna Inez, but with Byron's picture of his own mother in his letters: "Mrs. Byron furiosa," a "tormentor whose *diabolical* disposition . . . seems to increase with age, and to acquire new force with Time" (*BLJ,* 1:93–94; 1:75). Byron's sense of his vulnerability is clear enough in his reports of her behavior and his own corresponding hostility: "I have never been so *scurrilously* and *violently* abused by any person, as by that woman, whom I think, I am to call mother" (1:66); "she flies into a fit of phrenzy upbraids me as if I was the most undutiful wretch in existence. . . . Am I to call this woman mother? Because by natures law she has authority over me, am I to be trampled upon in this manner?" (1:56).[39] Byron's fantasy of Juan-the-phallic-woman at once reclaims "authority" from "natures law" and redresses a psychic grievance by imagining, as Stoller puts it, the possibility of "a better woman than a biological female" (177).[40]

Because the biological female in Juan's case is a Sultana, Byron's promotion of Juan from odalisque to phallic woman invests transvestism with a political significance that exceeds the realm of specific psychic grievance.

Such potential is implicit in Stoller's incidental remark that "sanctioned transvestic behavior" is frequent "at carnival times, at masquerade parties" (186), behavior with which Byron was familiar, having attended "masquerades in the year of revelry *1814*" (*BLJ,* 9:168) and the Venice Carnival in 1818 and 1819. Even so sanctioned, the sexual inversions of the carnival, as Davis points out, were ambiguously productive. On the one hand, they could "clarify" the structure of hierarchical society in the very process of reversing it; these occasions offer a controlled "expression of, or a safety valve for, conflicts within the system" that operate, ultimately, to contain energy and reinforce assent. On the other hand, "festive and literary inversions of sex roles" could also excite "new ways of thinking about the system and reacting to it," and so "*undermine* as well as reinforce" assent to authority, and destabilize political structure—especially through "connections with everyday circumstances outside the privileged time of carnival and stage-play." Male transvestism, it turns out, is a particularly potent form of connection: aware that women were deemed susceptible to irrational behavior and so given some legal license for misbehavior, men resorted to transvestite cover, hiding behind the female dress when they wanted to challenge authority or engage in outright rebellion. "Donning female clothes . . . and adopting female titles" could even energize and "validate disobedient and riotous behavior by men." Davis notes a number of "transvestite riots" in Britain between the 1450s and the 1840s.[41] As a member of Parliament whose maiden speech passionately opposed the Frame-breaking bill (which specified the death penalty), and whose sarcastic "Ode to the Framers of the Frame Bill" was published (anonymously) a few days later in the *Morning Chronicle,* Byron knew about at least one such instance: the riot in April 1812 at Stockport, during which steam looms were smashed and a factory burned, led by "two men in women's clothes, calling themselves 'General Ludd's wives.' "[42] He may also have recalled that the Edinburgh Porteous Riots of 1736 featured men in women's clothes, led by one "Madge Wildfire." Certainly by the time he was writing cantos 5 and 6 of *Don Juan,* he knew Scott's representation of these riots in *The Heart of Midlothian* (1818), spearheaded by a "stout Amazon"—a term Byron applies to "bold and bloody" Catherine, that "modern Amazon" (9.70, 6.96).[43]

The figure of the phallic woman not only redeems the character of Juan in female garb, but reduces Gulbeyaz, the biological woman who would exercise "male" political and sexual power in this episode. For at the same time that Juan is newly empowered by his female attire, Byron's narrative abases the "imperious" woman by whom he had been abased: the episode ends with the Sultana's will subverted and her character refeminized. When we first meet her, she is an interesting "mixture . . . Of half-voluptuousness and half-command" (5.108), but the destiny of biology—"Her form had all the softness of her sex" (5.109)—prevails. Not only can she not command Juan, but having been outwitted by him and his harem bedpartner, she is reduced to a caricature of a woman scorned. Her culpability in commanding Juan's sexual service, moreover, is not something Byron cares to impose on the men in his poem who command women's bodies: in a later canto, he makes crude comedy out of geriatric rape. After the sack of Ismail, "six old damsels, each of seventy years, / Were all deflowered by different Grenadiers" (a couplet Mary Shelley refused to copy), and certain "buxom" widows who had not yet met the conquering army, we are told, were "heard to wonder in the din . . . 'Wherefore the ravishing did not begin!' " (8.130, 132).[44]

Nor surprisingly, such a heavy-handed restoration of male power does not settle the sexual politics of the poem. Byron renews the whole question with Fitz-Fulke's impersonation of the Black Friar, an episode that restages and makes more flexible the issues of transvestism and female appropriation of male property. In contrast to the Sultana's thwarted attempt to exercise male sexual prerogative, Fitz-Fulke's transvestism, even in the figure of a friar whose ghost is hostile to the sexual productivity of the House of Amundeville, is a relatively successful strategy. Byron may be recalling the chimerical behavior of Caroline Lamb, who sometimes visited him "in the disguise of a carman. My valet, who did not see through the masquerade, let her in," Byron recalls; when "she put off the man, and put on the woman . . . Imagine the scene" (*Medwin*, 216–17). Fitz-Fulke's disguise carries a similar force of surprise, giving her already aggressive sexuality an opportunity for bold initiative as she temporarily escapes conventional constraints on her behavior. Feminized men in *Don Juan* are typically objects of contempt or subjects for farce, but masculinized women are almost always figures of erotic desire, and Byron's characterization of English society makes it clear why some women might desire male prerogatives: women's whole existence is limited to gossip and social intrigue; marriage is the only game in town and an ummarried man the only game worth the pursuit; and for a woman to wield any kind of power is to risk men's derision as one of the scheming "Oligarchs of Gynocrasy" (12.66). Fitz-Fulke's cross-dressing releases her from these circumscriptions, affords an outlet for desire, and grants her a kind of "male" power of action within the existing social structure. Indeed, it aligns her with male power, for quite beyond her plotting against Juan, Byron allows the art signified by her disguise to operate as a witty deconstruction of the duplicitous political arts practiced by the men of that world—those "Historians, heroes, lawyers, priests" who put "truth in masquerade" (11.37), and whose example inspires the narrator to urge Juan to "Be hypocritical . . . be / Not what you *seem*" (11.86).

Fitz-Fulke's transvestite behavior draws even fuller energy and ideological significance in this respect from the highly popular institution of the masquerade, at which, Terry Castle reports, transvestism was not only frequent, but frequently suspected of encouraging "female sexual freedom, and beyond that, female emancipation generally." Indeed, in the world of the eighteenth-century English novel, Castle argues, the masquerade episode is "the symbolic theater of female power," for here women usurp "not only the costumes but the social and behavioral 'freedoms' of the opposite sex." As in Byron's transvestite episodes, there are conservative checks and balances: from the novelist's overall perspective, Castle suggests, the masquerade offers a way to indulge "the scenery of transgression while seeming to maintain didactic probity. The occasion may be condemned in conventional terms, yet its very representation permits the novelist, like the characters, to assume a different role."[45] Byron's version of such "probity" is typically not a matter of attitude, but an inference of those larger narrative patterns which "correct," or at least remain nervous about, the different roles played out in his episodes of transvestite transgression. Yet because Fitz-Fulke's disguise has less to do with the specific hypocrisies of the Gynocrasy than with the general ways of the world, her manipulations yield an ambiguously potent narrative. If, as Byron's narrator remarks, that "tender moonlight situation" in which she and Juan discover each other "enables Man to show his strength / Moral or physical," he remains coy both about who the "Man" is—the girlish Juan or the transvestite Fitz-Fulke?—and about what actions, and by whom, exemplify "moral or physical" strength. He merely remarks that this is an occasion on which his hero's "virtue" may have "triumphed—or, at length, / His vice." His "or" is not much help either, for insofar as virtue (in the Latin sense of manly power) may reveal itself in "strength / Moral or physical" (even if the bawdiness of "at length" favors physical vice), Byron's phrasing compounds rather than resolves the question. The issue is managed only by a provisional deferral, a decision to retract his narrator's power of speech: this "is more than I shall venture to describe;— / Unless some Beauty with a kiss should bribe" (17.12). That seduction is and remains merely potential, for the narrator soon becomes as silent as Juan himself, who is a thoroughly ambiguous signifier in the wake of his seduction: only his "face" can be called "virgin" and even that looks "as if he had combated" (17.13–14).

With the categories of virtue and vice, strength and weakness, activity and inactivity, male reticence and female determination, male coyness and female arts thus perplexed, Byron has his narrator "leave the thing a problem, like all things" (17.13).[46] If the "masculine tradition" is, as Homans remarks, typically manifested by "the masculine self dominat[ing] and internaliz[ing]" an otherness "identified as feminine," Byron's participation in such a tradition, as is his habit, is animated by critical self-consciousness: the sexual politics that inform Don Juan at once expose their ideological underpinnings and qualify the potential subversiveness of these exposures with strategies to contain the risks posed to male privilege.[47] The cross-dressings of Don Juan are thus significant not so much for showing the poem's male hero appropriating and internalizing female otherness (indeed, his very name implies a parody of that masculine tradition), as for provoking the poem's readers to attend to what happens—politically, socially and psychologically—when women and men are allowed, or forced, to adopt the external properties and prerogatives of the other. Byron's poem does not, finally, escape the roles fashioned and maintained by his culture, but it does explore the problems of living with and within those roles. And by doing so in the heightened forms of transvestite drama and verbal cross-dressing, Byron foregrounds the artifice that sustains much of what we determine to be "masculine" and "feminine"—a strategy at once cautious and bold, through which he engenders the world of *Don Juan* and generates its elaborate plays against the codes and laws of gender.

Notes

I wish to thank Ronald L. Levao and Peter J. Manning for especially helpful discussion at several stages of this project.

1. Leslie A. Marchand, in *Byron: A Biography* (3 vols., New York: Knopf, 1957), remarks that Byron "had always been most successful with girls below his social and intellectual level . . . who flattered his ego and looked up with awe at his title" (1:330). Similarly, Louis Crompton, in *Byron and Greek Love: Homophobia in 19th-Century England* (Berkeley: Univ. of California Press, 1985) suggests that Byron's favoring of the "pederastic" form of homosexuality over the "comrade" form corresponds to an overall sexual politics that "preferred aristocracies to democracy and hierarchies to egalitarianism" (239).

2. *Medwin's "Conversations of Lord Byron"*, ed. Ernest J. Lovell, Jr. (Princeton: Princeton Univ. Press, 1966), 73. Hereafter cited as *Medwin*.

3. Quotations of *Don Juan*, as well as of other poems, follow *Lord Byron: The Complete Poetical Works*, 5 vols., ed. Jerome J. McGann (Oxford: Clarendon Press, 1980–86). In the parenthetic references in my text, I note canto and stanza for *Don Juan*; for other poems, I give canto and line number; a number alone, unless the context of the paragraph suggests otherwise, designates stanza number. Citations of the edition itself hereafter are given as *CPW* with volume and page.

4. Peter J. Manning, *Byron and His Fictions* (Detroit: Wayne State Univ. Press, 1978) 180.

5. *His Very Self and Voice: Collected Conversations of Lord Byron,* ed. Ernest J. Lovell, Jr. (New York: Macmillan, 1954), 249.

6. See *CPW,* 5:279 and 5:284, respectively.

7. *His Very Self and Voice,* 452 and 299 respectively; compare *Byron's Letters and Journals,* 12 vols., ed. Leslie A. Marchand (Cambridge: Harvard Univ. Press, 1973–1982), 8:147–48. Cited hereafter *BLJ* by volume and page.

8. Marchand (note 1), 1:382.

9. *Lady Blessington's "Conversations of Lord Byron"*, ed. Ernest J. Lovell, Jr. (Princeton: Princeton Univ. Press, 1969), 47; hereafter cited as *Blessington*. Hazlitt, "Lord Byron," *The Spirit of The Age* (1825), reprinted in *The Complete Works of William Hazlitt,* ed. P. P. Howe, 21 vols. (London: J. M. Dent, 1930–34), 11:75. *Travestie* (Hazlitt's italics) abbreviates *transvestire* (the OED in fact gives the "odd travesty" of Juan in woman's garb as an instance of *travesty* meaning "alteration of dress"). Shelley is inclined to describe Byron's style in terms that play at a similar sense: of the same canto in which Byron makes Juan an odalisque, he writes, "the language in which the whole is clothed—a sort of chameleon under the changing sky of the spirit that kindles it" (*Letters 1818 to 1822,* ed. Roger Ingpen, 331; vol. 10 of *The Complete Works of Percy Bysshe Shelley,* 10 vols., ed. Roger Ingpen and Walter E. Peck [New York: Charles Scribner's Sons, 1926]).

10. George M. Ridenour, *The Style of Don Juan* (New Haven: Yale Univ. Press, 1960), 164–65.

11. My quotation follows the Arden edition of *Antony and Cleopatra*, ed. M. R. Ridley (Cambridge: Harvard Univ. Press, 1956).

12. Ridenour comments on the similarity, 165–66. See also Jerome J. McGann's discussion of "mobility" in *Don Juan* ("Byron, Mobility and the Poetics of Historical Ventriloquism," *Romanticism, Past and Present* 9 [1985]: 66–82—the terms of which bear on the question of gender, insofar as the poem does not confine this "psychological attribute and [its] social formation" to women such as Adeline, but "specifically calls attention to the relation of mobility to the structure of the artist's life" (69–71).

13. McGann, "Byron, Mobility," 69.

14. See Ridenour (140) for the remark about Catherine's "travesty," and Cecil Y. Lang for a discussion of Catherine and Juan as "masks" for Ali Pasha and Byron ("Narcissus Jilted: Byron, *Don Juan,* and the Biographical Imperative," *Historical Studies and Literary Criticism,* ed. Jerome J. McGann [Madison: Univ. of Wisconsin Press, 1985]: 143–79).

15. For the anecdotes, see *Medwin,* 67; Marchand (note 1), 1:156, note 5; Hunt, *Lord Byron and Some of His Contemporaries; With Recollections of the Author's Life, and of His Visit to Italy* (1828; reprinted, Philadelphia: Carey, Lea & Carey, 1828), 83. One reads Hunt's comments, of course, knowing that mutual insinuations of effeminacy were one medium through which mounting strains in the friendship of Hunt and Byron were exercised; see also 30, 69–70, 75, 77.

16. For a discussion of the constraints imposed on Byron's range of expression by the punishment of homosexuality as a capital crime in Regency England, see Crompton: "in societies where straightfoward representation of same-sex love was taboo" female transvestism afforded "homosexual writers a chance for surreptitious romance" (210). Crompton reads *Lara* in these terms, as well as the linguistic regendering evinced in Byron's "Thyrza" lyrics: their male subject—Byron's early love, the choirboy John Edleston—was disguised by feminine names and pronouns, also Byron's practice in his translations of Greek and Latin homoerotic lyrics (see 94, 105–6, 177–78). . . .

17. Natalie Zemon Davis, "Women on Top," *Society and Culture in Early Modern France* (Stanford: Stanford Univ. Press, 1975), 127.

18. Jacques Derrida, "La Loi du Genre" / "The Law of Genre," tr. Avital Ronell (*Glyph Textual Studies* 7 [Baltimore: Johns Hopkins Univ. Press, 1980]; 221, 203–4). Further citations appear parenthetically.

19. *Anatomy of the Abuses in England in Shakespeare's Youth, A.D. 1583* Part 1, The New Shakespeare Society Edition, ed. Frederick J. Furnivall (London: N. Trüber, 1877–79), 73. I have modernized typeface. See Laura Levine ("Men in Women's Clothing: Anti-theatricality and Effeminization from 1579 to 1642," *Criticism* 28 [1986]: 121–44) for a complementary discussion of "the fears of [men's] effeminization which dominate anti-theatrical tracts" of the English Renaissance, especially the fear that theatrical transvestism "could structurally transform men into women" (121–22). . . .

20. The parentheses give line numbers; quotations follow *Epistle 2* of *Epistles to Several Persons (Moral Essays),* vol. 3, part 2 of *Poems of Alexander Pope,* ed. F. W. Bateson; 6 vol. series ed. John Butt (New Haven: Yale Univ. Press, 1961). In *Alexander Pope* (New York and London: Basil Blackwell, 1985), Laura Brown discusses the "misogyny" of this Epistle in relation to its poetics of difference: women "serve to shore up the notion of a stable, morally determinate identity for men . . . by their eminently transparent, clearly despicable characterlessness" (101–7; I quote from 106).

21. Catherine (Graham) Macaulay, *Letters on Education, With Observations on Religious and Metaphysical Subjects* (London: C. Dilly, 1790), Part 1, Letter 22: 204.

22. Mary Wollstonecraft, *A Vindication of the Rights of Woman,* ed. Carol H. Poston (New York: Norton, 1975), 105. Further citations are given parenthetically.

23. 1.272; quoted by Ralph M. Wardle, *Mary Wollstonecraft: A Critical Biography* (Lawrence: Univ. of Kansas Press, 1951), 140–41.

24. Mary Hays, "Memoirs of Mary Wollstonecraft," *The Annual Necrology, 1791–8* (London: 1800): 422–23; reprinted in Poston (see note 22), 211–12.

25. Manning (note 4), 247.

26. Truman Guy Steffan and Willis W. Pratt, the editors of *Byron's Don Juan, A Variorum Edition* (4 vols., Austin: Univ. of Texas Press, 1957) cite *De L'influence des passions* (1976) and *Corinne, ou l'Italie* (1807), chapter 5 (1:45). McGann remarks that the same position "is memorably stated by Anne Elliot in Jane Austen's *Persuasion* . . . which [Byron's publisher] Murray published, and which he may very well have sent to Byron, not long before this passage was written" (*CPW*, 5:680).

27. Even *Blackwood's Edinburgh Magazine*, which charges Byron with "brutally outraging all the best feelings of female honour, affection, and confidence," admires Julia's "beautiful letter," printing stanzas 94–97, and regretting only the "style of contemptuous coldness" applied in stanza 98 to "the sufferings to which licentious love exposes" some women ("Remarks on Don Juan," vol. 5 [Aug. 1819]: 512–18; my quotations are from 512, 516–17; Donald Reiman thinks John Gibson Lockhart is the reviewer [*The Romantics Reviewed*, B:143]). Leigh Hunt's brief for Julia focuses on the social criticism implicit in the restriction of women by "custom." . . . ("*Don Juan. Cantos 1st and 2nd*," *Examiner* [13 Oct. 1819]:700–02; Reiman identifies the reviewer [B:1004]). Other readers are less sympathetic. . . . Even a modern reader, Bernard Blackstone, refused to hear any "compassionate sigh for poor woman" in Julia's letter, but finds it, instead, "a vampire threat to the whole structure of masculine, rational values painstakingly built up through the civilized centuries" (*Byron: A Survey* [London: Longman, 1975], 299–300). The sexual politics animated by this episode may help explain why, contrary to Byron's assumptions, some women *did* like the poem: "of all my works D[on] Juan is the most popular" in Paris, he reports to John Hunt, "especially amongst the women who send for it the more that it is abused" (April 9, 1823; *BLJ*, 10:146).

28. For a compelling reading of Haidée in these terms, see Manning: "enveloping protection becomes suffocation, and what were only undertones in Juan's affair with Julia become prominent" (186).

29. In his essay "On Effeminacy of Character" (1822) Hazlitt declares esteem for "a manly firmness and decision of character," and discusses Keats as a summary case of "effeminacy of style, in some degree corresponding to effeminacy of character" (*Table Talk: Opinions on Books, Men, Things*, 2 vols., [London: Henry Coburn, 1822] 2:199–216; I quote in order from 215, 212, 214–15). *Blackwood's* more pointedly—and suggestively for the terms of the issues I address—deems Keats's poetry "a species of emasculated pruriency . . . the product of some imaginative Eunuch's muse within the melancholy inspiration of the Haram" (vol. 19 [1826] Preface xxvi; J. R. MacGillivray identifies the reviewer as Lockhart's new successor, John Wilson: *Keats: A Bibliography and Reference Guide with an Essay on Keats' Reputation* [Canada: Univ. of Toronto Press, 1949], xliii. . . .

30. *The Letters of John Keats*, 2 vols., ed. Hyder E. Rollins (Cambridge: Harvard Univ. Press, 1958), 2:67 and 1:386–87, respectively; hereafter cited as *LK* by volume and page.

31. Margaret Homans, *Women Writers and Poetic Identity* (Princeton: Princeton Univ. Press, 1980), 240, notes 25 and 33, respectively. Adrienne Rich, "Three Conversations," *Adrienne Rich's Poetry: Texts of the Poems, the Poet on Her work, Reviews and Criticism*, ed. Barbara Charlesworth Gelpi and Albert Gelpi (New York: Norton, 1975), 115. Erica Jong, "Visionary Anger," *Ms.* 11, 1 (July 1973): 31. . . .

32. *A Vindication* urges that women be educated, not with an end to participating in public life, but primarily to become more rational wives and mothers, better able to manage the family and govern their children. All of Austen's mature novels, Sandra Gilbert and Susan Gubar argue, teach the same overt lesson. . . . (*The Madwoman in the Attic: The Woman Writer and the Nineteenth-Century Literary Imagination* [New Haven: Yale Univ. Press, 1979], 154 et passim).

33. Virginia Woolf, *A Writer's Diary*, ed. Leonard Woolf (New York: Harcourt Brace Jovanovich, 1954), 2–3.

34. The sexual ideology behind remarks such as this is so emphatic that it affects even a reader such as Cecil Lang (note 14), who is otherwise impressed by the "revolutionary" aspect of *Don Juan* "in transferring sexual aggression to the female figures"; Lang retains conventional terms of evaluation, speaking of aggressive women as "sexual predators," but crediting aggressive men with "an assertion of sexuality"; similarly, he describes Juan as Catherine's "male whore," as if the role were implicitly female and Juan something of a degenerate transvestite in such a position (152, 153, 158). The politics of this episode are discussed by Katherine Kernberger ("Power and Sex: The Implication of role reversal in Catherine's Russia," *The Byron Journal* 8 [1980]:49). . . .

35. My quotation follows the Arden edition of *Troilus and Cressida*, ed. Kenneth Palmer (New York and London: Methuen, 1981).

36. Contemporary reviews were divided over the evaluation of Julia's sexual aggressiveness, but were uniformly amused by Juan's adventures in the harem. . . .

37. This episode of transvestite opportunity may have been inspired by the resourcefulness of Byron's friend, Colonel Mackinnon: "Byron was much amused by Mackinnon's funny stories, one of which was later supposed to be the basis of *Don Juan*, V: Mackinnon disguised himself as a nun in order to enter a Lisbon convent" (*The Reminiscences of Captain {Rees Howell} Gronow*, [1862], 85–86, quoted in Lovell (note 5), 612 n. 39). The anecdote seems, in addition, to offer a fantasy continuation of Juan's aborted romance with Julia.

38. Otto Fenichel, "The Psychology of Transvestitism" (1930); reprinted in *The Collected Papers of Otto Fenichel*, First Series (New York: Norton, 1953) 1:167–80 (I refer to 169); Robert J. Stoller, *Sex and Gender: On the Development of Masculinity and Femininity* (New York: Science House, 1968), 176–77. . . .

39. For a perceptive discussion of Byron's relationship with his mother and its literary consequences, see Manning, 23–55 and 177–99.

40. Also referring to Stoller, Sandra M. Gilbert studies various "costume drama[s] of misrule" in modern literature with an aim to showing how "the hierarchical principle of an order based upon male dominance / female submission [gets] recovered from transvestite disorder" ("Costumes of the Mind: Transvestism as Metaphor in Modern Literature," *Writing and Sexual Difference*, ed. Elizabeth Abel [Chicago: Univ. of Chicago Press, 1982]: 193–219). Elaine Showalter, too, refers to Stoller in a witty and perceptive essay on how the figure of the "phallic woman" in the male feminism of the 1980s underwrites masculine power, usurping and in effect marginalizing the feminism it seems to endorse ("Critical Cross-Dressing: Male Feminists and The Woman of The Year," *Raritan* 3:2 [Fall 1983]: 130–149).

41. Davis (note 17), 130–31, 142–43, 147–50.

42. See E. P. Thompson, *The Making of the English Working Class* (London: Victor Gollancz, 1965), 567.

43. For Byron's references to Scott's novel, see *BLJ*, 9:87, 10:146, 11:46. The riots are represented in chapters 6 and 7.

44. Andrew Rutherford (while finding these stanzas "very funny") laments Byron's "abandonment of the standards of morality on which his satire has been based," for he frivolously refuses "to face the horror of mass rape, or even indeed of individual cases. Byron attacked Suvarov for callousness, for seeing men in the gross, but here he is himself prepared to think of women in the same way . . . to withhold in treating rape the moral sensitivity that he had shown in treating deaths in battle" (*Byron: A Critical Study* [Stanford: Stanford Univ. Press, 1961], 179).

45. I quote, in order, from "Eros and Liberty at the English Masquerade, 1710–90," *Eighteenth-Century Studies* 17 (1983–84): 164, and "The Carnivalization of Eighteenth-Century English Narrative," *PMLA* 99 (1984): 909, 912. . . .

46. If, as Castle argues, the masquerade episode has the effect of introducing "a curious

instability into the would-be orderly cosmos of the eighteenth-century English novel" ("Carni-valization," 904), the transvestite episodes of *Don Juan* reflect a world that presumes no such order, but is, as Anne K. Mellor puts it, "founded on abundant chaos; everything moves, changes it shape, becomes something different" (*English Romantic Irony* [Cambridge: Harvard Univ. Press, 1980], 42).

47. I quote Margaret Homans (note 31, p. 12) for a representative description of the masculine tradition.

Editor's Bibliographical Note

Other useful essays and books dealing with, broadly speaking, women (or the female) in Byron—in addition to Wolfson's citation of Manning's *Byron and His Fictions,* Katherine Kernberger's "Power and Sex" essay, and Lang's "Narcissus Jilted" essay—are, in chronological order: Gloria T. Hull, "The Byronic Heroine and Byron's *The Corsair,*" *Ariel* 9 (April 1978): 71–83; Charles J. Clancy, "Aurora Raby in *Don Juan:* A Byronic Heroine," *Keats-Shelley Journal* 28 (1979): 28–34; Joanna E. Rapf, "The Byronic Heroine: Incest and the Creative Process," *SEL* 21 (1981): 637–45 (a Jungian approach); Jenni Calder, "The Hero as Lover: Byron and Woman," in *Byron: Wrath and Rhyme,* ed. Alan Bold (London and Totowa: Vision Press and Barnes & Noble, 1983); 103–124; Marina Vitale, "The Domesticated Heroine in Byron's *Corsair* and William Hone's Prose Adaptation," *Literature & History* 10 (1984): 72–94; Anthony P. Vital, "Lord Byron's Embarrassment: Poetry and the Feminine," *Bulletin of Research in the Humanities* 86 (1983–85), 269–90; Caroline Franklin, "Haidée and Neuha: Byron's Heroines of the South," *Byron Journal* 18(1990):37–49. See also Bernard Beatty, *Byron's Don Juan* (Kent: Croom Helm, and Totowa, N.J.: Barnes & Noble, 1985), which argues the centrality of Aurora Raby to Byron's total conception of the "comedy" of *Don Juan.* Also relevant, for its wide-ranging essays as well as for its signaling a welcome increase in feminist approaches to, and discussions of, the feminine in, all of the romantic poets, is Anne K. Mellor's edited essay collection, *Romanticism and Feminism* (Bloomington: Indiana University Press, 1988), which includes Sonia Hofkosh, "The Writer's Ravishment: Women and the Romantic Authors—the Example of Byron" (93–114). See also Deborah A. Gutshera, " 'A Shape of Brightness': The Role of Women in Romantic Epic," *Philological Quarterly* 66 (1987): 87–108, and most recently, Jerome J. Mc-Gann's " 'My Brain is Feminine': Byron and the Poetry of Deception," in *Byron: Augustan and Romantic,* ed. Andrew Rutherford (New York: St. Martin's, 1990), 26–51, and Malcolm Kelsall's essay in the same volume, "Byron and the Romantic Heroine," 52–62.

Fiction's Limit
and Eden's Door

BERNARD BEATTY

If we take "the limits of fiction" as a problem, what kind of problem is it? We could insist that it is a literary problem, perhaps the defining literary problem, but then something seems to be left out. It is not long since that Bunyan was praised for his "realism" and Keats criticized, as poet and man, for that "escapism" which, allegedly, he would have overcome had not death overcome him. Who would not smile if these terms and these judgements were now to be advanced? Byron had at least as delicate a literary imagination as any of his contemporaries, but alternately bullied and protected it with something like the coarse affection shown to him by his matter-of-fact, yet slightly dotty, mother. From his mother's family and from his Scottish nurse Byron picked up an eminently rational frame of mind, contradicting passions, and a preoccupation with Adam's fall. If, as a poet, his characteristic stance is at the limits of fiction, this is bound up in his mind with the strange patterns of his own life and their relation to the archetypal pattern of the Fall. We could of course substitute "events" for "pattern" in both cases and Byron would not smile.

The importance of the Fall in Byron's thought and art has always been recognized.[1] It may seem that there is little point in reiterating its centrality. Twentieth-century interest in the use of myths in literature, however, and the subsequent, but in some ways contrary, concern with fictions and fictionality now begin to place Byron's conviction of the Fall in sharper perspective and help us to understand his own use of, and celebrated aversion from, literary fiction. First, I want to develop these ideas by contrasting Byron's practice with that of Coleridge in *The Ancient Mariner*. Subsequently, we will examine metamorphoses of the Fall in *Mazeppa*, *The Island* and the final cantos of *Don Juan*.

The Fall postulates the satisfactions of limitation in an enclosed garden, man's rejection of this archetypal home, and preference for the apparent unlimitation of exile, wandering, and homelessness. "Man" here means ge-

Reprinted from *Byron and The Limits of Fiction,* ed. Bernard Beatty and Vincent Newey (Liverpool: Liverpool University Press, 1988): 1–22, 24–25, 33–38, by permission of Liverpool University Press and Barnes & Noble Books.

nus but also signals typical masculine activity and understanding. Unlimitation in the Fall story is at once taboo, reward, and punishment. So it is throughout Byron's verse and, we may add, throughout his life.

The Byronic hero rather than the poet is at the centre of this concern. Dante, Tasso, and Byron himself may claim attention but do so because their acts of imagining involve their will as much as their fancy. Byron appears to be more interested in the boundaries crossed by the human will than were most of his contemporaries. For them, boundary crossing is usually an emblem of imagination's force and thus can never be finally repudiated. For Byron, boundary crossing remains a form of moral and metaphysical transgression. He is sympathetic to it, sometimes wholly so, but he declares and shows the punishment which is its consequence.

If we take the most obvious example of punished transgression in English Romanticism, Coleridge's *The Ancient Mariner,* it is easy to see why Byron admired the poem. It too appears as a version of the Fall. Coleridge juxtaposes the vocabularies of Christian redemption, forgiveness, love, and unity with Nature, against the inexplicable crime and apparently endless punishment of the Mariner, much as Byron does in *Manfred.* But whereas Byron makes us notice where these vocabularies are taken up or rejected, Coleridge blurs the boundaries between them. The Abbot, for instance, recognizes that Manfred's diagnosis of human life is founded on a sense of sin and thus proffers the intelligibility and force of the Christian cure: "And the commencement of atonement is / The sense of its necessity" (III.i.84–85). Manfred rejects this as explicitly as it is offered. Coleridge, however, contrives a Mariner who seems to be both fully redeemed and wholly condemned. We may prefer this and think Byron's request, in a different context, that Coleridge "would explain his Explanation" (Dedication to *Don Juan*) to be a trifle vulgar. But if we do so our poise probably depends upon taking punishment and redemption as self-cancelling polarities within imagination's other world where we might also find, similarly intense yet neutralized, "A sunny pleasure-dome with caves of ice." The imagination is enthralled rather than appalled by such transgressions, for it contemplates patterns rather than bears consequences. The last line of Byron's *Cain* suggests the difference.

Adah Peace be with him!
Cain   But with *me!*—[*Exeunt.*

The Ancient Mariner's pain is aestheticized and thus, like the Falls of Terni, "Horribly beautiful" (*Childe Harold* IV.72). Cain's fabled pain is unbearable and we recognize it as the foundation of adult life. Coleridge's myth is not a myth, for it does not explain anything. Instead the reader, like the Mariner himself, is mesmerized by the spectacle of past experience as spectacle. Byron's myth functions like its Biblical prototype; it leaves us with the consequences that it has explained. By "myth" here and in what follows I mean a communally appropriated story that is seen to engender and find repetition in human history. In this way, unlike a fiction, it is never simply its own terminus, nor, despite its openness to interpretation, is that the secret source of its fruitfulness and efficacy. Byron's *Cain* is a myth. Coleridge's *Ancient Mariner* is a fiction.

This distinction is a real one and we keep coming across it when we try to understand Byron and Coleridge together. But we have arrived at it too easily because not all the evidence fits. If we turn momentarily to classical literature's most celebrated myth of punished transgression, the myth of Prometheus, the picture looks a little different because Prometheus is a prototype artist as well as archetypal sufferer.

Prometheus (as mediated by what survives of Aeschylus's trilogy and therefore without the benign consequences which we think he intended) offers us the spectacle of pain. This pain, Carl Kerényi points out, has two elements: "on the one hand Prometheus' suffering, his punishments for taking the standpoint of man, and on the other hand his secret knowledge."[2] These two elements are signalled in Byron's "Prometheus" who suffers both "pity's recompense" and the result of what he can "foresee" but refuses to "tell" ("Prometheus," ll.29–30). He is thus a forerunner of Manfred who "champions human fears" (II.ii.205), has "this cautious feeling for another's pain" (II.i.80), craves and possesses forbidden knowledge. But he is also a forerunner of Byron's Dante and all other poets:

> For what is poesy but to create
> From overfeeling good or ill; and aim
> At an external life beyond our fate,
> And be the new Prometheus of new men,
> Bestowing fire from heaven, and then, too late,
> Finding the pleasure given repaid with pain,
> And vultures to the heart of the bestower,
> Who having lavished his high gift in vain,
> Lies chain'd to his lone rock by the sea-shore?[3]

We find the same insistence on the identity of suffering and creativity throughout Cantos III and IV of *Childe Harold*. Indeed, when Art does not immediately disclose this connection as it does in the Laocoon group, Byron goes out of his way to remind us that the serene dome of St. Peter's is "Christ's mighty shrine above his martyr's tomb!" (*Childe Harold* IV.153); or, more emphatically still, that the Apollo Belvedere's life of "beautiful disdain" must somehow proceed from the suffering of its creator:

> And if it be Prometheus stole from Heaven
> The fire which we endure, it was repaid
> By him to whom the energy was given
> Which this poetic marble hath array'd
> With an eternal glory—(*Childe Harold,* IV.163)

Byron insists that all Art is like this, indebted to Promethean fire as suffering as well as spark, and that we can therefore always detect the way it "breathes the flame with which 'twas wrought."

If then Byron is more concerned with what Kerényi calls "the moral suffering fundamental to human existence" (p. 93) than, say, Keats and Coleridge, for all their vocabulary of hearts "high sorrowful and cloyed" and "sadder and a wiser man," ever manage or mean to be, nevertheless Byron, too, seems to fuse suffering with imagination and thus escapes consequence and limitation on the wings of an obliging fiction. If we alter our perspective, however, we can find a way out of this much as Byron did himself. What happens to this fusion once it is established? In Byron's case it becomes itself an object of attention rather than simply triggering an aesthetic reaction in the reader. This needs explaining. In *The Ancient Mariner,* for example, we can never resolve the puzzle of the poem by the use of any one of the master-languages (religious, moral, psychological, philosophical) that the poem so fulsomely supplies. It is not hard to see why this is so. Coleridge's poem is a projection of his own nightmare of dejection. It proffers a "One Life" philosophy which he does not really believe, a religious release from the burden of his self which he has never experienced, a psychology whose origin and real character cannot be probed, and a moral which no one will ever carry out as a result of reading the poem. The horror is real enough but its causes and consequences are hidden, subordinated to its overwhelming realization. It is just this very blurring of agony, pastiche, theoretical knowledge, and unhoped hope which makes the poem what it is and not some other thing. But, and it is a very large Byronic "but," though Coleridge's poem makes something delightful out of these concealed limitations, it does not transcend them. Nor, unlike a myth, does it restore us to the immediacy which its own immediacy has displaced. Coleridge is careful to provoke the expectations of myth without allowing any myth to use, and thereby explain, him. We do not contemplate these problems aesthetically and morally because we do not recognize them as problems in the act of reading the poem. In this way, *The Ancient Mariner,* splendid as it is, always implies far more than it will ever yield.

Far other scene is Byron's field of fiction. Byron's poetry seeks to understand the ground of its own intensities as well as relishing them. It comes to the reader, therefore, as curtailer of the intensities which it stimulates, because it is simultaneously object and agent of attentiveness thus:

> 'Tis to create, and in creating live
> A being more intense, that we endow
> With form our fancy, gaining as we give
> The life we image, even as I do now.
> What am I? Nothing; but not so art thou,
> Soul of my thought! with whom I traverse earth,

Invisible but gazing, as I glow
Mix'd with thy spirit, blended with thy birth,
And feeling still with thee in my crush'd feelings' dearth. (*Childe Harold,* III.6)

Would Coleridge have recognized his own earlier enterprise in these terms? Certainly both poets write out of their "crush'd feelings' dearth," project themselves into wanderer figures that epitomize death-in-life as punishment but offer us the Promethean recompense of "A being more intense." In Byron's case, however, the self-conscious, explicit character of this offering refers us beyond itself to "the moral suffering fundamental to human existence," whereas Coleridge's apparent concern for religious and moral truth conceals the secret burden of aesthetic intensity which is all-sufficient provided that it passes unrecognized.

Perhaps this point needs to be re-stated—there is a sense in which this essay will not get beyond it—because it may appear as too confident a demolition of the moral case for Coleridge's art to which some remain attached, whilst, on the other hand, it may appear to take for granted the superiority of moral over aesthetic concerns which, though obvious to Byron ("in my mind, the highest of all poetry, is ethical poetry"),[4] is scarcely the shared postulate of today's desperate men. In any event, the borderline may be less distinguishable than the territories which it separates. We will need to track the consequences of the Fall carefully.

Adam's Fall is, in the first place for Byron, a story of punishment. Punishment is a limit which the past imposes on the experienced present and imagined future. Death, from one point of view, is the supreme punishment. It is a final limit on present and future imposed by Adam's past which, we must learn through this very claim, is our past also. From another point of view, there is a punishment beyond this, peculiarly interesting to Byron, which though limiting is limitless. The Fall inaugurates both the familiar boundaries of pain and death which we suffer from but continue to will and the latent possibility of endless limitation which may be dreaded but craved by those who can "champion human fears." Such endless suffering is Manfred's and the Mariner's prerogative. "I dwell in my despair— / And live— and live for ever" (*Manfred,* II.ii.149–50).

It is important here that although Cain, Manfred, Harold may have always been marked out for their "silent suffering and intense," they have, at some point, crossed a threshold. They have transgressed. Manfred, for instance, acknowledges this in a searing compound of grammatical and autobiographical tenses and in-tensity: "And to be thus, eternally but thus, / Having been otherwise!" (*Manfred,* I.ii.70–71). Harold, similarly, finds that suddenly "Worse than adversity the Childe befell" (I.4), and the change in Cain from intellectualized to actual desolation, as from a notion of death to the presence of a dead brother, is the point as well as the conclusion of the play.

What could terminate and thereby structure this unstructurable pain?

We could leave it as it is. *Childe Harold* and *Don Juan* are inherently unfinished. We could put Art's full stop at the point where it all begins. *Cain's*
final full stop and "Exeunt" work like this. We could terminate in death,
which *Manfred* very precisely does (and the majority of Byron's stories end in
death), or we could resurrect out of it into marriage, or something like it, as
Torquil, Mazeppa, and Juan manage to do. These three terminations—
Death, Hell, and Marriage—are staple in Byron's poetry and he loves to joke
about their interchangeability. They are the preferred destinations in Coleridge's verse too, but no one ever reaches them. Christabel may well have
been destined for marriage in Coleridge's head but his poem will never
consummate it. The wedding guest is barred from this ending also but he is
taken neither to death nor, quite, to hell, for the Ancient Mariner is an
embodiment of blessing as well as curse, wisdom as well as terror. Coleridge
directs us instead to repetition of the tale ("could I revive within me / Her
symphony and song") or the excuse of fragmentation with its *diabolus ex
machina* from Porlock. These are not so much devices of inanition as of
obfuscation. Coleridge takes our attention away from the change in the
Mariner, punished or redeemed, and redirects us to the change in the
wedding-guest and therefore to us as readers. This change is not itself an
object of attention; rather it is glossed (an appropriate word for *The Ancient
Mariner*) as wisdom ("sadder and wiser man") and morality ("he prayeth best
who loveth best"). It cannot be either of these in literal fact but the misdirec-
tion placates us into accepting the aesthetic residue as spiritual truth. This
"spiritual" meaning is that suffering intensity is worth having for its own
sake because it enlarges the imagination to know itself beyond good and evil.
In its present form, beyond Coleridge and Nietzsche, the print-out would be
something like this—*The Ancient Mariner*'s indeterminacy of meaning is
itself the self-conscious but disguised object of the poem's attention and its
deepest meaning. We could apply the same diagnosis to Byron's heroes but
not to the poems in which they are placed. If Manfred also knows himself to
be beyond good and evil, that is not the perspective of the chamois-hunter or
the Abbot, who are put in precisely to demonstrate but also to undermine
Manfred's claim. That is not why Coleridge put the hermit in *The Ancient
Mariner* or Keats included the beadsman in *The Eve of St. Agnes*. *The Ancient
Mariner*'s superiority to what the chamois-hunter and the Abbot represent is
unquestioned.

I have rounded on Coleridge here because so much twentieth-century
criticism of the Romantic Imagination has relied on Coleridge's authority for
allowing religious, moral, and psychological vocabularies to neutralize themselves within a fictional interplay as though something of import was going
on. Whatever *The Ancient Mariner* is concerned with (and it becomes less and
less decent to ask) we may be sure that it puts to one side anything so
vulgarly intractable as punishment. Unlike a myth, it does not function as
explanation but tantalizes us with its insolubility which, should we seek

further, will only refer us back to its provocatively concealed author. Grecian Urns have been known to behave in the same teasing (Keats's word) fashion.

In Byron's case, however, the limitation of punishment is disclosed rather than hidden by the shaping of the fiction. Conversely, where such limitation is not encountered, that too becomes part of the explicit design as well as the content. If for instance death, hell and marriage are clearly evident as Byron's end points, we should also insist on the public and recognizable character of the devices which bring us to these terminations. In a sense, as Brian Nellist argues so persuasively, Byron is always a lyric poet whose only purchase, even when he surveys vast tracts of space and history, is the immediacy of the present moment "where my steps seem echoes strangely loud."[5] But, just as throughout *Childe Harold* the great communal shapes of history, landscape, and architecture press in upon, offer release from, mediate, and express the charged yet vacant present ("And that one word were Lightning" [III.97]), so throughout Byron's verse the bleeding heart finds and bears its public pageant or makes a Roman holiday. Public trial or imprisonment, so obvious in *Parisina,* the Venetian plays, *The Prisoner of Chillon, The Lament of Tasso,* or the "Ode to Napoleon Buonaparte," fuse grief and pageant in this way. *The Vision of Judgment* is a kind of trial, too, in which George III finally escapes and Southey forever finds public chastisement. We are always interested in the final verdict and Byron never avoids it. Curse is a different but equally explicit form of judgement. Byron allows Dante and Marino Faliero to conclude their utterance in his poetry by a protracted curse. Byron shapes one himself to conclude *English Bards* and structure *The Curse of Minerva.* Most of Byron's fictions offer public guide-lines of this kind and show clearly who finds and who evades punishment.

The explicitness of all this has to do with the coincidence of the outer shape of Byron's fictions with the transgressions of will and heart which they chronicle, but even these inward territories are understood and traced out for us in a manner that belongs as much to "the moral suffering fundamental to human existence" as to lyric pattern. We can see this when we ask more precisely where Byron's concern with punishment finds it focus. If, unlike Coleridge, Byron really is interested in understanding punishment, that is to say finding its antecedents and consequences, it does not follow that he is convinced of its justice. He is always chary of punishing others, which is why, despite his curses and visions, he decided to withdraw *English Bards* from circulation and, unlike Southey, allows his political foe (George III) into heaven. Those who do suffer punishment within his work are, as often as not, objects of admiration. Imprisonment, for instance, is real enough but unjust in the case of Tasso, Jacopo Foscari, and Bonnivard, much as Byron's sympathies lie with Prometheus and only rarely does he acknowledge his transgression. Public executions (Marino Faliero, Hugo in *Parisina*) endorse the victims rather than the judges. Jacopo Foscari's is the one case, apart from Prometheus himself, of public torture, but we are not directed to Jacopo's physical pain so much as to Doge Foscari's suppressed and wholly interior suffering as he witnesses and supervises it. Jacopo's most intense and ethereal pain is caused by the idea of banishment. Byron is indeed not interested in physical pain as such in comparison with, say, Act I of Shelley's *Prometheus Unbound*. Nor is he ever interested in as plain a fable of punishment as Crabbe's *Peter Grimes*. He is interested in pain as consequential in some sense and, above all, in its recognition and acknowledgement by those who endure it. Why else should Byron's best poem on Napoleon have been released by his abdication and imprisonment? One stanza from "Ode to Napoleon Buonaparte" tells us instantly and takes us straight to Byron's peculiar territory:

> He who of old would rend the oak,
>   Dreamed not of the rebound;
> Chained by the trunk he vainly broke—
>   Alone—how looked he round?
> Thou, in the sternness of thy strength
> An equal deed hast done at length,
>   And darker fate hast found:
> He fell, the forest-prowlers' prey:
> But thou must eat thy heart away! (stanza 6)

The "He who" of the exemplum is, of course, Milo, whose hubris in rending the oak with his fist was punished by finding himself trapped within its "rebound." Byron's point is simpler and larger: "Alone—how looked he round?" Byron is only concerned with that instantaneous point of recognition, Cain's "But with *me!*," where outer look and hidden pang coalesce for ever in ghastly equipoise as they do in Michelangelo's great painting of "the damned before the Judgement-throne" (*Prophecy of Dante* IV.64).

Byron dated that point at which Napoleon has reached the limit of his fiction. Byron pinpoints his in "The Dream," but we may not altogether believe it: "a moment o'er his face / A tablet of unutterable thoughts / Was traced, and then it faded, as it came; . . . (ll.96–98). The same point is repeated (ll.149–55) a few lines and years later. In such passages, Byron engages and embarrasses us by the reflexive posing of his own private turmoil and by the open fictionalizing of autobiographical fact. The effect is similar to but not the same as Hardy's 1912 poems, for Hardy does not direct us to the stricken and inalienable remorse of his present experience, as Byron would, but to memory and colloquy with the dead. Hardy's predicament is separately picked out for us in a sequence of lyrics, but the pain that interests Byron, though paralysing, is the force that drives his poems along. It is in this sense that suffering and fiction unite not only at the boundaries (as in the stage sets of trial or imprisonment) but at the centre of Byron's poems. The most interesting case here is *Mazeppa*, which, since it is the only one of Byron's poems whose entire action is synonymous with punishment, may be briefly considered on its own.

Mazeppa should help us not only because of the self-consciously fictional treatment of the natural energies that are its focus but also because the poem, rarely seen in this way, nevertheless occupies a pivotal position in Byron's opus. We can see how the avoidance of punishment begins to oust punishment itself as Byron's major fictional theme in his non-dramatic poems. This has extra-fictional resonance since, not much earlier, Byron turned his great curse in *Childe Harold* (IV.131–37) into a proclamation of forgiveness that remains edged with threat[6] but seeks to move "In hearts all rocky now the late remorse of love." That wish remained fiction to the quite otherwise fact so far as Lady Byron's rocky heart, if not that of Ada and the reader of the poem, was concerned, but its positioning towards the end of *Childe Harold* as a counter to its record of the cycle of destruction that forms human history is part of Byron's moral strategy as well as of his fictional design. Byron's "look" at the end of this pilgrimage can no longer be mistaken for Harold's. In the case of Mazeppa, however, we do not see Mazeppa's "look" at all. This brings us close to *The Ancient Mariner,* which was, it seems probable, in Byron's mind when he wrote the poem. There are many passages that recall both this and *Christabel.*[7] Moreover, the central device of retelling a past tale of terror to a listener from a different world is common to both. We are caught up in the intensity and duration of Mazeppa's sudden punishment but, unlike the Mariner, what happens next can and does displace what precedes it just as it does throughout *Don Juan.* Mazeppa is not to be "eternally but thus" nor, and perhaps for the same reason, is his pain magnified by the consciousness of "Having been otherwise." For Mazeppa's punishment is, as everyone observes, a parallel and continuation of the wayward energies that engender it. In Coleridge's poem, sexuality is latent in the wedding framework, in the vision of Death in Life and, doubtless, in the ambivalent watersnakes but, like everything else in *The Ancient Mariner,* it cannot be greeted for what it is. In *Mazeppa,* the progress from sexual transgression via emblematic punishment (bound, naked, to a wild horse) to sexual resurrection ("The sparkle of her eye I caught, / Even with my first return of thought" [ll.808–09]) is as explicit as may be. For example, the lovers are bound by a "burning chain" (l.240) of "absorbing fire" (l.243), and Mazeppa's sudden understanding that Theresa will yield to him comes "Even as a flash of lightning there" (l.272). Exactly the same metaphor is continued into his punishment, where he is bound to the horse "as on the lightning's flash" (l.408). Similarly, the horses encountered by Mazeppa are "the wild, the free" (l.684) but the girl that later wakes him from his ordeal has "black eyes so wild and free" (l.812).

This sense of a sustained and identical energy throughout Mazeppa's progress is linked with the life of the poem itself, for the account of Mazeppa's experience comes to us as sharp, exhilarating, and yet dizzy, vague, and unfocussed. At the same time, the whole poem is framed by irony, for Charles XII is the silent, and finally sleeping, recipient of the narrative. As such he is in manifest contrast to the uncontrollable Mazeppa: "But all men are not born to reign, / Or o'er their passions, or as you / Thus o'er themselves and nations too" (ll.287–89). In another way, however, Charles resembles Mazeppa, for he too inhabits the rainbow of energy inscribed by his will. Here, Mazeppa's folly seems the more attractive of the two. Byron's deliberate confounding of animal energy and comic detachment as the foundation of his tale is a wonderful transformation of his source in Voltaire's life of the Swedish Alexander, which does not envisage Mazeppa telling his own tale to Charles and passes over the ride in a sentence. The composition of the last part of *Mazeppa* (end of September 1818) overlapped with the composition of *Don Juan* Canto I. Manuscripts of both poems were sent off together and the proofs were probably corrected together. It is, undoubtedly, closer in major respects to the mode of *Don Juan* than *Beppo*, for, like *Don Juan*, it depends upon conveying immediacy of life and sceptical detachment simultaneously. Where *The Ancient Mariner* gives us crime, penance, forgiveness, and hell in such a way that none of these can quite be meant, *Mazeppa* gives us both punishment and escape from punishment in a manner that confirms the validity of both. This can only be achieved by the self-conscious use of fictionality (tale-telling in *Mazeppa,* the narrator in *Don Juan*) but any self-conscious fiction is offering itself as an instance of the extra-fictional as well as heightening fictionality. We can see this most clearly in *The Island* and how, once again, it is bound up in Byron's mind with transgression, punishment, and escape, in myth and history.

Where Mazeppa is both the recipient of punishment and the one who evades it, these roles are quite separate in *The Island.* There is a magnificent section in Canto III which dramatizes this separation. It is worth quoting in full:

> Beside the jutting rock the few appeared,
> Like the last remnant of the red-deer's herd;
> Their eyes were feverish, and their aspect worn,
> But still the hunter's blood was on their horn.
> A little stream came tumbling from the height,
> And straggling into ocean as it might,
> Its bounding chrystal frolicked in the ray,
> And gushed from cliff to crag with saltless spray;
> Close on the wild, wide ocean, yet as pure
> And fresh as Innocence, and more secure,
> Its silver torrent glittered o'er the deep,
> As the shy chamois' eye o'erlooks the steep,
> While far below the vast and sullen swell
> Of ocean's alpine azure rose and fell.
> To this young spring they rushed,—all feelings first
> Absorbed in Passion's and in Nature's thirst,—

Drank as they do who drink their last, and threw
Their arms aside to revel in its dew;
Cooled their scorched throats, and washed the gory stains
From wounds whose only bandage might be chains;
Then, when their drought was quenched, looked sadly round,
As wondering how so many still were found
Alive and fetterless:—but silent all,
Each sought his fellow's eyes, as if to call
On him for language which his lips denied,
As though their voices with their cause had died. (III.59–84)

Ruskin paid eloquent tribute to the fidelity of Byron's imagination here.[8] If we cannot but be aware of innumerable sources for the symbolic conventions in play yet someone, Lord Byron, has also had occasion to look closely at a non-fictional stream in order to write like this. It is just this tantalizing juxtaposition of factual and symbolic detail which, here and elsewhere in Byron, is the poetry of the scene, much as, in the previous canto, he recalls how his first sight of the real but fabled landscape of Troy fused with his earliest memories of Scotland so that, amazingly, "Loch-na-gar with Ida looked o'er Troy . . ." (II.291).

In this almost operatic set-piece, experienced ("worn"), sick ("feverish"), and animal-like ("red-deer's herd") men rush to a stream of pure and innocent water which, in contrast to their hunted retreat, peeps out shyly on the world like "the shy chamois." They attempt to renew themselves and wipe away their "gory stains." However, their rush to the stream and the subsequent anxious inspecting of each others' looks ("But with *me*") after their unbaptizing immersion in it reveals their inability to receive what they seek. Contrast this with Byron's account of a more successful dialogue between Man and Nature in Canto II:

How often we forget all time, when lone,
Admiring Nature's universal throne,
Her woods—her wilds—her waters—the intense
Reply of *hers* to our intelligence! (II.382–85)

The "we" here includes the poet, reader, and extra-textual common humanity, but it is authorized fictionally by Torquil and Neuha's intense silent interrogation of one another and the surrounding landscape in the same section of the poem. This canto is the most obviously fictionalized in the poem. The island is placed in a deliberately mythical setting of song, dance, and festivity where "from the sepulchre we'll gather flowers" (II.21). The inhabitants of the island, though now introduced into the arts of war, prefer to spend their time simply gazing on Nature, receptive to her "intense Reply":

> And we will sit in Twilight's face, and see
> The sweet moon glancing through the Tooa tree, . . .
> Or climb the steep, and view the surf . . .
> How beautiful are these! how happy they,
> Who, from the toil and tumult of their lives,
> Steal to look down where nought but Ocean strives!
> (II.9–10, 12, 16–18)

This gazing outwards ("Who thinks of self when gazing on the sky?" [II.393]) is the opposite of the inner interrogation that fixes the dreadful look of Cain and all Byronic heroes. It is here marked on the brow of Fletcher Christian, who, like his ancestor, has tried to return to Paradise and has made and found death there:

> His light-brown locks, so graceful in their flow,
> Now rose like startled vipers o'er his brow.
> Still as a statue, with his lips comprest
> To stifle even the breath within his breast,
> Fast by the rock, all menacing, but mute,
> He stood; (III.89–94)

But where is the fictional reference here? If we begin with a mythical island, then Christian and his followers seem to be wretched historical outsiders. A Fletcher Christian certainly existed. His failure in the poem to return and stay on the island, his inability to renew his self, wash away "gory stains" in the "little stream" and become a gazer as the stream itself is (III.70), seems like Lycius's failure in Keats's poem to stay in the enchanted world of Lamia. But if the oppositions of Keats's poetry can no longer be thought of simply as Dream versus Reality since Keats's "reality" is as distorted and stylized as his "dream," this is far more true of Byron's poetry. Keats used myths and even, as in the "vale of soul-making," experienced the precocious pleasure of watching himself make one up. But Keats never allowed myths to use him. Keats insisted on his absence from his poems ("negative capability") in order to become their rifter ("load every rift with ore"), active in every nook and cranny of them. Byron, on the other hand, projects his self, his imaginings, and his historical/factual recall into verse so that these may appear as what they are and what he believed them to be, versions of archetypal stories, beyond his complete manipulation, which soothe, outrage, baffle, and clarify. In such a continuum, Byronic heroes, historical mutineers, paradisal islands, and South Seas' topography exist as sharply defined and yet interchangeable. We could never find a privileged point of reference which would enable us to read off where the fiction begins and ends. And yet Byron's island, impossible to classify as fiction or fact, bifurcates into its separate staple endings of comic marriage and tragic death whilst insisting that those who mistake fiction for fact (Christian) are punished for it or (Torquil) thrive only in such a fiction as *The Island*.

The commencement of this bifurcation occurs in the long section from Canto III already instanced. The mutineers are set between the oceans' "vast and sullen swell" and the "silver torrent" of the little stream. They have a few minutes of conscious pause before two sets of craft are to appear and take them to separate endings and worlds. One (Neuha's) is to rescue Torquil from punishment, the other (H. M. Navy) is to exact punishment from Christian and his two companions. In this space of time, they rush first, as we have seen, to the island's spring of life which offers momentary rather than eternal renewal and then each one of the four is presented in close-up. Torquil, one of the four, has to be presented as part of them. It is from the world of the mutineers that he is rescued and his transition from one world to another must be palpable. Yet he cannot wholly belong to them, for, in that case, Neuha could not reach the self-enclosed interiority of his being. Byron always manages these details with superb instinct and nonchalantly constructs our response. Here is how he does it:

> Some pace further Torquil leaned his head
> Against a bank, and spoke not, but he bled,—
> Not mortally:—his worst wound was within;
> His brow was pale, his blue eyes sunken in,
> And blood-drops, sprinkled o'er his yellow hair,
> Showed that his faintness came not from despair,
> But Nature's ebb. (III.97–103)

Three elements make up this representation, but their effect is controlled by the sequence in which they are presented. Torquil bleeds. The stream has not removed the "gory stains" of his mortality and his kinship with Cain. But yet "his worst wound was within." There is the clue to a deeper kinship still. Interior pain is the mark of all the mutineers. The bloodstain of his outer wound and the deeper pain within constitute Torquil's credentials as part of the group. But what is the character or cause of this "worst wound"? We are not told. It could, after all, be separation from Neuha. If Byron was writing about Lara or the Giaour or, more to the purpose, Christian, then this "worst wound" and its ramifications would be articulated at length. Instead of this, we move instantly to outer description and then to a new element which engineers a neat reversal in lines 101–3. It appears from this that the suggestion of inner pain is only a momentary and ambiguous one. Instead, we are directed to a pain which is simply part of "Nature's ebb," therefore curable and transient on Nature's island, rather than caused by that deathly fixity of will which the mariners bring to their paradise. The brevity of this description, too, in comparison with the next sixty lines which are devoted to the mental states of Torquil's companions, suggests the comparative simplicity of Torquil's pain. It is in him a temporary diminution of consciousness—"his blue eyes sunken in"—rather than the preternaturally acute consciousness of his companions. It is this awareness which is in sharp contrast to the relaxed "looks" and gazings of the islanders glimpsed at the beginning of Canto II. All four of these men are positioned at their limit. Their position by the jutting rock and, shortly, by a still more liminal rock which will be "their latest view of land" (IV.245) epitomizes their consciousness and, by presenting the limits of that consciousness to them, makes them recognize their own mental and moral territory for what it is.

Limits have two characteristics, as we may discover at any frontier post. In one way they maximize the character and status of the territory whose extent and appearance they announce. In another way, they are immediate transition points to unimaginably different territories. Of the four mutineers, three are to die into the limits which, alone, they now signify. One is to cross into a different world. If we stand back a little, we can see that *The Island* begins with Christian's transition, via transgression, from European history misnamed "the Bounty" to intended paradise but in fact to Hell (as he deems but we should, perhaps, not [I.164; IV.352]). It ends with Torquil's transition from kinship with his fellow Europeans, marked as Cain's heirs, to kinship with Neuha, Nature, and the Island. The mutineers cannot metamorphose themselves by drinking and bathing in the innocent torrent which the island permanently offers, but Torquil's plunge into the sea is a later baptism that functions. He finds himself immediately resurrected (IV.226) into a different dimension of time and space. Paradoxically, Torquil transcends limits by submitting and trusting himself to Neuha. He follows her as much child as lover. Christian, on the other hand, celebrates his petrification under the guise and boast of liberty: "For me, my lot is what I sought; to be, / In life or death, the fearless and the free" (III.163–64). In this he is more clearly presented as mistaken than any of his dark predecessors, not excluding Cain. Like Lara he is "A thing of dark imaginings" (*Lara,* I.317) but we fully understand Christian, as we do not Lara, and the island itself remains a place of bright imaginings which he can neither reach nor destroy. The Corsair is, however mysteriously, the cause of Medora's death on his island retreat. So, too, is that other returning pirate, Lambro, who transforms a bright island into a tomb for himself and his daughter in Canto IV of *Don Juan.* Christian's status is less assured than these for another reason also. He is presented as wholly superior to his three companions "Beside the jutting rock" in an extended image that could belong to Corsair, Lara, or Giaour:

> But Christian, of a higher order, stood
> Like an extinct volcano in his mood;
> Silent, and sad, and savage,—with the trace
> Of passion reckoning from his clouded face; (III.139–42)

As it happens, we can test and reject this simile for, unlike the Corsair's companions, who function simply as colourful film extras, we know exactly what it's like to be Ben Bunting and Jack Skyscrape and wait a few minutes before death with Christian. Ben Bunting passes the time by washing, wiping, and binding Torquil's wound, "then calmly lit his pipe" (III.106). He has always lived within the confines of practical life like this. His pipe-smoking is an indication of his relentless metaphysical inattention rather than of relaxation. He is an older version of Johnson in the middle cantos of *Don Juan,* but at once more ridiculous and more deadly. When we first encounter him in Canto II, he is festooned with weapons of all kinds ("our Europe's growth") and, though trouserless ("For even the mildest woods will have their thorn"), he retains his European decency (Neuha and the islanders are, like Mazeppa, naked) by a "somewhat scanty mat" which "served for inexpressibles and hat" (II.483). He is a grotesque example of the incongruity which is Christian's pain. He is a practical, charitable man, and a killer. He is Cain's comic, wandering heir, not at peace but accustomed to restlessness and pipe-smoking his way through it. He is a brilliant creation. The fourth mutineer, Jack Skyscrape, cannot hide his restlessness so readily. Byron pinpoints his disturbed occupancy of time:

> The fourth and last of this deserted group
> Walked up and down—at times would stand, then stoop
> To pick a pebble up—then let it drop—
> Then hurry as in haste—then quickly stop—
> Then cast his eyes on his companions—then
> Half whistle half a tune, and pause again—
> And then his former movements would redouble,
> With something between carelessness and trouble.
> This is a long description, but applies
> To scarce five minutes passed before the eyes;
> But yet *what* minutes! Moments like to these
> Rend men's lives into immortalities. (III.109–20)

Byron's comment on this undistinguished and slightly ridiculous figure aligns him with Manfred who is "Now furrowed o'er / With wrinkles, plough'd by moments, not by years" (I.ii.71–72) and also with Christian who, though "still as a statue," nevertheless betrays his agitation by "a slight beat of the foot" (III.94). Thus Christian's interior and his conscious predicament are virtually identical with those of his vulgar companions. The Abbott and the Chamois-hunter genuinely probe and, to some extent, understand Manfred, but he retains his mystery, superiority, and separate destiny. Christian cannot do this. More complex, more stylish perhaps, than his fellows, he is nevertheless of their kind, which means that we are of his kind too. There is no essential difference between the intolerable boredom and time-filling routines which any reader will recognize in Skyscrape and Bunting, or the inhabitants of Norman Abbey, and the intense ennui which is the foundation of the Byronic hero's claim to superiority.

Hence that remarkable scene where "the last remnant" of the mutineers rush to the young spring which is "as pure / And fresh as innocence," bathe their "gory stains" and cool their "scorched throats" and then look "sadly round" is not at all an advertisement for the romance world which it so thrillingly embodies. It is, we might say, a depiction in another mode of where *Don Juan* is written from. The last cantos of *Don Juan* coincide with the writing of *The Island*. Romance worlds and their "sober sad antitheses" (*Don Juan*, XIV.28) have been the staple ingredients of *Don Juan* but, alongside them at the end of his poem, Byron invokes a different vision and alters the limit of his fiction altogether.

The narrator of *Don Juan*, like the mutineers "Beside the jutting rock," lives in that fully understood space of time and consciousness which knows its immediate proximity to death, can mingle in but not be remade by untainted sources of life, and sees the world directly in front of him with sober clarity as his "latest view of land" but also as pure illusion. The narrator is both Christian ("aloof a little from the rest") and Everyman who has time to fill and needs distraction from death. He lives at this limit where, terrified, free, defiant, nonchalant, witty, he sets about constructing the unexpected and improvises an auld sang "with something between carelessness and trouble." He sits at night ("I sing by night"), thinking aloud and telling stories, poised between the inextinguishable stream and coming death. Torquil is to enter the first, Christian to find the other consummation, but the narrator of *Don Juan* knows them only as Cain knows death before he murders Abel.

Juan, of course, is the narrator's counterpart here as Torquil is Fletcher Christian's. Juan does not have Torquil's once for all resurrection to an unlimited world; rather, Byron presents him as experiencing a series of Mazeppa-like resurrections from apparent end-points. But what in that case happens to the notion of punishment in *Don Juan?*

The original Don Juan story is nothing other than a fable of punishment. Don Juan Tenorio's limitless will, and the repeated pattern of seductions which implements it, is countered by the unambiguous limitation of the Stone Guest's icy hand which summons Juan Tenorio to death and hell, leaving most of the other characters to *exeunt* to the wedding bells Christabel never hears. Byron's *Don Juan* begins by spectacularly reversing this pattern. His Juan seeks resting places with women rather than escape from them, his will is subject to theirs. At the end of the poem, the interruption of Canto XVII implies the narrator's death (what else could stop him talking?), but Juan is left unlimited though drawn to marriage with Aurora.

Similarly, Don Juan Tenorio imposes his will on circumstances, and this shapes the pattern of the original play much as trial or imprisonment shapes many of Byron's fictions. Byron's Don Juan, however, never seeks to impose himself on circumstances, and the apparent randomness of his adventures clearly parallels the unpredictable mode of Byron's poem.

This simple pattern and apparent unlimitation is not the whole pattern. Byron's Juan, like Tirso da Molina's, leaves behind him Julia, Haidée, Lambro, drowned sailors, and slaughtered combatants in the siege. All these find limitation, almost punishment. Their immobility is a foil for Juan's invariable renewal, yet, as the poem proceeds, it seems also to threaten and taint that renewal.

We could see the pattern differently. Some readers have wanted to stress Juan's fall from innocence. Byron himself makes the point explicitly (*Don Juan* X.23) and through the symbolic presence of Leila and Aurora. If, as we predict in Canto XIII,[9] Don Juan was to revive the neglected theme of love in the poem by becoming the minion of Lady Adeline, then we would have to regard Juan as incapable of subsequent resurrection. But he does not do so and Aurora Raby, far from being simply a symbolic counterpart to Juan's tainted innocence like Leila, becomes the object of his attention, bearer of new meaning in the poem, and an occasion for a transition to limitlessness as startling and more substantial than that epitomized in Torquil's dive. For Aurora is "pure / And fresh as innocence" like the little stream on *The Island,* but she knows all that Christian knows. . . .

In the first place, Aurora's sadness is quite distinct from Manfred's or Christian's:

> Early in years, and yet more infantine
>   In figure, she had something of sublime
> In eyes which sadly shone, as Seraphs' shine.
>   All Youth—but with an aspect beyond Time:
> Radiant and grave—as pitying Man's decline;
>   Mournful—but mournful of another's crime,
> She looked as if she sat by Eden's door,
>   And grieved for those who could return no more. (XV.45)

That is an extraordinary position for anyone to be placed within Byron's poetry or outside it.[10] She sits "by Eden's door." She does not herself grieve like Manfred or rail like Cain and Christian at her exclusion from Eden. Nor does she represent, as Neuha does, Imagination's hope of re-entry to a natural paradise. Neuha, mythical, "naiad of the deep," plucks Torquil from the punishment intrinsic to human history, but Aurora sits and does not intervene, much like the angels in Blake's "Night"; she sits, knows, and mourns the crime and punishment of those who can return to Paradise no more. Despite this knowledge, she remains "All Youth," her eyes are "sublime," and she has an aspect "beyond Time." She is thus positioned by the archetypal limit (Eden's shut door) but is in touch with unlimited reality. Juan, who so soon after his expulsion from Haidée's Eden could not "altogether call the past to mind" (IV.75), moves towards this grave radiance, a fiction so retentive of an actual history, and is then galvanized by the shocks of religious fear (Black Friar) and sudden sexual arousal (blonde Duchess) which are its cruder, concomitant, and almost interchangeable bestowals.

. . . .

Aurora draws sustenance from the ruined history of her ancestors, imaged in Norman Abbey itself and, though "a flower," has the indestructible radiance of a gem (XV.58). Like the ghost, whose disinheritance she shares, she is an emblem of unattended punishment in the Amundeville's Vanity Fair but she is, too, a Romance heroine and a new Eve who, alone in Byron's verse, fuses dark knowledge and the "bounding chrystal" of the mutineers' unreachable stream on Toobonai. She annihilates the split between cherub and seraph, love and knowledge, which withers Manfred and is the apparent structure, offered only to be superseded, of *Don Juan*. Byron's life and work is a meditation upon and witness, conscious and inadvertent, to the Fall. Most of the time, like Job, he is demolishing the comforters but, like the Book of Job, his poetry is itself a tale of comfort. Aurora recapitulates the long-absent Harold as well as lost Haidée, but, and this is the truth to which we have not yet grown accustomed, Conrad, Lara, Harold *et al.* pay deformed witness to the Aurora which they will become.

A circle, said Byron, makes "A holiness appealing to all hearts" (*Childe Harold* IV.147). It does so because it is limited and limitless. Our expanding universe pays new tribute to this concept much as Byron in St. Peter's finds his mind "Expanded by the genius of the spot" (*ibid.*, 155). If we were to put our arms around the unlimited, as Aurora's "depth of feeling" embraces boundless thoughts and space, then this circle and this holiness would be ours too. All Byron's poetry is concerned with this sublimity and this limitation. He is always in some sense a religious poet. His rage for justice and his preternatural sense of immediate given life make it impossible for him to be anything else. Aurora Raby is not an accidental construct of his art, she is generated out of the whole of it as no other of his characters is. T. S. Eliot was quite right. She *is* "the most serious character of his invention." She is, and is fully understood as being, the limit of his fiction.

This point could be put in many ways. It is open to qualification. If it is resisted altogether, however, we are not following Byron's thought through and will misinterpret its earlier direction.

Aurora exists in two dimensions. She is an invented fiction within a fiction but she seems also to exist outside it. A. B. England, who writes extremely well about Byron but is without metaphysical inclination and is thus a neutral witness, comments: "Aurora is a fictional character that he has himself created but . . . he establishes the illusion that she possesses a life independent of his mind, a life of which he is not entirely the master."[11] How can this be so? The easiest way would be for Aurora to be a historical character like Byron's Catherine the Great, but she is not. The processes involved in reading the last sentence postulate an immediate and easy reference to history and fiction as distinct territories peopled respectively by existences and essences. In so far as Byron emerges as Byron within and without *Don Juan,* conducting us through his partly historical fiction and thus not wholly a fictive device within it (the narrator or "Byron"), then *Don Juan* itself preserves the familiar demarcations of history and fiction. Fictionalists may react with horror to this, but there must be at least some sense in which writing the poem is recognizably Byron's act[12] just as much as his stylized but actual intervention into Greek politics. The recipients of both (Greeks and common readers) encounter Byron who, though present as stereotype and contained within what appears, is acknowledged in that presence as coming from elsewhere.

Yet Aurora too seems to come from elsewhere. Her origin is mysterious. She is an orphan brought up in a song of Innocence by "guardians good and kind" (XV.44). She gazes upon Juan and upon the activity within the Abbey as a contemplative outsider who remains in touch with "worlds beyond this perplexing waste." Yet it is precisely this "perplexing waste" beyond Eden's door that is the object of her unillusioned attention.

It has sometimes been suggested that Mr. Jaggers in *Great Expectations,* who, it turns out, knows all the characters in the book, and Iago, who is in a way the author of *Othello*'s plot and remains in some unreachable mode of continuance after its conclusion, are mysterious counters to the creative intelligence. They have, as it were, emerged from the other side of the fiction which claims to contain them and, instead, dispute control of it with the author. Aurora is like this but she is a contemplative and not an active presence. Her intelligence is seraphic not destructive. Nor is she simply an essence, for "worlds beyond this world's perplexing waste / Had more of her existence." If we ask, a little incredulously, "where does she come from then?" the answer must be that the whole of *Don Juan* (and much of *Childe Harold*) is concerned with hinting, articulating, and showing the nowhere and the nothingness which remain represented in the life and thought which spring unmediated from them. If this is lapsing into metaphysics more than Byron would tolerate for long, it is so only in manner. Byron is more metaphysical than I am. Aurora is there because Byron very fairly and perspicuously agrees "that what is, is" (*Don Juan,* XI.5). Critics such as R. F. Gleckner and Brian Wilkie,[13] who get this far but omit Aurora, tell us that Byron was a nihilist. Indeed, as we have seen, we encounter in Aurora the nihilism of her predecessors (Lara, Manfred, Cain) but she wears a smile which, like that of Buddha,[14] denotes plenitude.

The satirical observation of a historical society and the death into life clowning of Byron's blonde duchess, which terminate *Don Juan,* are enabled by and held within the religious circle of that smile. If such a circle is fiction's limit then the myth of the Fall, which is the presiding fiction of limitation for Byron's poetry, is, finally, neither fiction nor limitation.

Notes

1. G. Wilson Knight, G. M. Ridenour, E. D. Hirsch, Bernard Blackstone, and R. F. Gleckner are amongst the major modern critics to insist on this emphasis, but of course it has always been noted.

2. *Prometheus,* trans. R. Manheim (London, 1963), p. 93.

3. *The Prophecy of Dante,* IV.11–19. Byron offers a parodic version of poetic inspiration as Promethean suffering in *The Blues,* II.131–42.

4. *Byron's Letters and Journals,* ed. R. E. Prothero (London, 1898–1901), V, 554.

5. *Childe Harold,* IV.142 [Ed. note: Nellist's essay is entitled "Lyric Presence in Byron from the Tales to *Don Juan,*" *Fiction's Limit,* 39–77.]

6. Byron later projected a similar redirection of a curse onto his Dante: "Great God! / Take these thoughts from me—to thy hands I yield / My many wrongs, . . . (*Prophecy,* I.118–20: but see the whole passage).

7. McGann lists these in *Complete Poetical Works,* IV, 494.

8. "Fiction, Fair and Foul," *The Works of John Ruskin,* ed. E. T. Cook and A. Wedderburn (London, 1908), XXXIV, 333: "Now, I beg, with such authority as an old workman may take concerning his trade, having also looked at a waterfall or two in my time, and not unfrequently at a wave, to assure the reader that here *is* entirely first-rate literary work. Though Lucifer himself had written it, the thing is itself good, and not only so, but unsurpassably good, the closing lines being probably the best concerning the sea yet written by the race of the sea-kings."

9. We are told in prospect that something "Occurred" at the end of Canto XII (85), and as we meet Lady Adeline in the second stanza of the next canto we are bound to imagine that she is its occasion.

10. Lamartine, for instance, in "L'homme" positions man by Eden's door:

> Tout mortel est semblable à l'exilé d'Éden:
> Lorsque Dieu l'eut banni du céleste jardin,
> Mesurant d'un regard les fatales limites,
> Il s'assit en pleurant aux portes interdites. (ll.81–84)

Byron may accept the diagnosis but his heroes won't submit to it; and Aurora, who indeed "s'assit en pleurant aux portes interdites," does so on behalf of "another's crime." Lamartine gives us the myth straight but does not quite accept it. Byron dramatizes it less straightforwardly but, far more than Lamartine, seems concerned with its truth rather than its piquancy.

11. *Byron's Don Juan and Eighteenth-Century Literature* (London, 1975), p. 169.

12. The arguments of E. D. Hirsch in *The Aims of Interpretation* (Chicago, 1976) on this point seem to me unanswerable.

13. Brian Wilkie, *Romantic Poets and Epic Tradition* (Madison and Milwaukee, 1965), pp. 188–226; R. F. Gleckner, *Byron and the Ruins of Paradise* (Baltimore, 1967), passim.

14. *The Island* gives, as we would expect, a more overtly erotic basis for this kind of smile: see II.374–81.

Editor's Bibliographical Note

Given the exigencies of space in a volume such as this, as well as the number of essays included herein that deal at some length with *Don Juan,* regrettably I have had to truncate that portion of Beatty's essay devoted to *Don Juan.* While I believe I have preserved the core of his argument, which speaks eloquently to his essay's title, the reader is encouraged to consult Beatty's original. That volume includes as well essays by Brian Nellist (see note 5 above),

Marilyn Butler (on *The Giaour*), J. Drummond (on *Beppo*), David Seed (on Byron's prose vampire fragment and his verse narratives), Vincent Newey (on "authoring the self" in the last two cantos of *Childe Harold*), Geoffrey Ward (largely on *Childe Harold* and, to a lesser extent, *Don Juan*), F. M. Doherty (on Byron's "sense of the dramatic"), and Philip Davis (fascinatingly on Byron's idea of "night" and another look at the Fall in his work). Most important, the reader should turn from Beatty's essay to his *Byron's "Don Juan"* (Kent: Croom Helm, and Totowa, N.J.: Barnes & Noble, 1985) for its elaborate and compelling argument for Aurora Raby's centrality to *all* of *Don Juan,* not merely the so-called English cantos where she is actually on stage.

Since this essay ranges rather more widely through Byron's canon than a number of others in this collection, I take this opportunity to cite a number of works of especial pertinence to the study of those poems other than *Don Juan* that Beatty deals with at some length. The critical work on *Mazeppa* and *The Island* is rather astonishingly slim, almost all of it in books that are already familiar to the reader of these bibliographical notes, particularly those by Joseph, Gleckner, McGann (*Fiery Dust*), Cooke (*The Blind Man*), Marshall, Rutherford, and Manning. On *Mazeppa* see also the bibliographical note to Cooke's essay in this collection. In addition to commentary on it in several of the books just referred to, *The Island* has received a few other valuable treatments: Robert D. Hume, "*The Island* and the Evolution of Byron's 'Tales,' " and E. D. Hirsch, "Byron and the Terrestrial Paradise," both in *From Sensibility to Romanticism,* ed. F. W. Hilles and H. Bloom (New York: Oxford University Press, 1965); Paul D. Fleck, "Romance in Byron's *The Island,*" in *Byron: A Symposium,* ed. John D. Jump; and Angus Calder, " 'The Island': Scotland, Greece and Romantic Savagery," in his edited collection *Byron and Scotland* (Totowa, N.J.: Barnes & Noble, 1989). Less useful is Arthur D. Kahn, "The Pastoral Byron: Arcadia in 'The Island,' " *Arcadia* 8 (1973): 274–83.

Related in different ways to Beatty's concentration on the Fall trope in terms of "punishment" are Bernard Blackstone, "Guilt and Retribution in Byron's Sea Poems," *Review of English Literature* 2(1961):58–69, and especially Frederick Garber's contention that *Don Juan* is about "recovery" as well as fall in chapter 10 of *Self, Text, and Romantic Irony* (Princeton: Princeton University Press, 1988). Needless to say, the whole matter of guilt has taken up more critical verbiage than it may, finally, be worth, but the matter of punishment as Beatty sees that idea has occupied some of Byron's best critics, albeit without their focusing upon it so sharply. Most of those discussions are found, as in Blackstone's essay, in discussions of Byron's so-called Turkish or Oriental tales (particularly but not exclusively *The Giaour* and *Parisina*), of *The Prisoner of Chillon, Manfred,* and *Cain,* and of *Marino Faliero* and *The Two Foscari* (again not to the exclusion of Byron's other plays).

Given Beatty's at least passing reference to Byron's tales other than *Mazeppa* and *The Island,* as well as to several of his plays, this seems an appropriate place to compensate in some measure for the absence in this volume of an essay on those tales and an essay on the dramas. The former are dealt with in some detail in the books cited elsewhere by Marshall, Joseph, McGann (*Fiery Dust*), Gleckner, Manning, and Garber, but it is only recently that we have a book devoted exclusively to them, Daniel P. Watkins' *Social Relations in Byron's Eastern Tales* (Rutherford, N.J.: Fairleigh Dickinson University Press, 1987). Other works that contribute valuably to our sense of precisely what the tales are and do include, chronologically, Carl Lefevre, "Lord Byron's Fiery Convert of Revenge," *Studies in Philology* 49 (1952):468–87; W. Paul Elledge, *Byron and the Dynamics of Metaphor* (Nashville: Vanderbilt University Press, 1968); Peter B. Wilson, " 'Galvanism upon Mutton': Byron's Conjuring Trick in *The Giaour,*" *Keats-Shelley Journal* 24 (1975):118–27; Blackstone's quirky and virtually unclassifiable *Byron: A Survey* (London: Longman, 1975); Manning's "Tales and Politics: *The Corsair, Lara,* and *The White Doe of Rylstone*" and "The Hone-ing of Byron's *Corsair,*" the former in *Byron: Poetry and Politics,* ed. E. Stürzl and J. Hogg (1981), the latter in *Textual Criticism and Literary Interpretation,* ed. Jerome J. McGann (Chicago: Chicago University Press, 1985).

Although there have been several books devoted to the plays, notably Samuel Chew's pioneering work, *The Dramas of Lord Byron* (Baltimore: Johns Hopkins Press, 1915), and John W. Ehrstine's *The Metaphysics of Byron: A Reading of the Plays* (The Hague: Mouton, 1976), in my judgment they are less critically incisive and insightful than the following: E. D. H. Johnson, "A Political Interpretation of Byron's *Marino Faliero*," *Modern Language Quarterly* 3 (1942): 417–25; Michael Cooke, "The Restoration Ethos of Byron's Classical Plays," *PMLA* 79 (1964): 569–78; Murray Roston, "The Bible Romanticized: Byron's *Cain* and *Heaven and Earth*," in his *Biblical Drama in England: From the Middle Ages to the Present Day* (Evanston: Northwestern University Press, 1968), 198–215; Jerome McGann, "Byronic Drama in Two Venetian Plays," *Modern Philology* 66 (1968): 30–44; Truman G. Steffan's elaborate edition and commentary, *Lord Byron's "Cain"* (Austin: University of Texas Press, 1968); Charles E. Robinson, "The Devil as Doppelganger in *The Deformed Transformed*," *Bulletin of the New York Public Library* 76 (1970): 177–202; William Ruddick, "Lord Byron's Historical Tragedies," in *Essays on Nineteenth-Century British Theater* (London: Methuen, 1971), 83–94; Terry Otten, "Byron's *Cain* and *Werner*," in his *The Deserted Stage: The Search for Dramatic Form in Nineteenth-Century England* (Athens, Ohio: Ohio University Press, 1972), 41–75; Thomas L. Ashton, "The Censorship of Byron's *Marino Faliero*," *Huntington Library Quarterly* 36 (1972): 27–44, and "Marino Faliero: Byron's 'Poetry of Politics,' " *Studies in Romanticism* 13 (1974): 1–13; Anne Barton, " 'A Light to Lesson Ages': Byron's Political Plays," in *Byron: A Symposium,* ed. John Jump (London: Macmillan, 1976), 138–62; Daniel P. Watkins, "Violence, Class Consciousness, and Ideology in Byron's History Plays," *ELH* 48 (1981): 799–816, "The Ideological Dimensions of Byron's *The Deformed Transformed*," *Criticism* 25 (1983): 27–39, and "Politics and Religion in Byron's *Heaven and Earth*," *Byron Journal* 11 (1983): 30–39; Thomas J. Corr, "Byron's *Werner:* The Burden of Knowledge," *Studies in Romanticism* 24 (1985): 375–98; and Lynn Byrd, "Old Myths for the New Age: Byron's *Sardanapalus*," in *History and Myth,* ed. S. C. Behrendt (Detroit: Wayne State University Press, 1990), 149–87. Also worth consulting is M. S. Kushwaha, *Byron and the Dramatic Form* (Salzburg: University of Salzburg, 1980).

Continuing *Manfred*

FREDERICK GARBER

In his *Byron: A Survey* (London: Longman, 1975) Bernard Blackstone points out some of the ways in which the beginnings of the four cantos of *Harold* relate to each other. The movement toward canto 4's comments on "the beings of the mind" recalls the movement in canto 3 toward "the soul's haunted cell." At that same point in canto 2 Harold plays Hamlet with a skull in view, a series of reflections echoing a similar sequence at just that point in canto 1. Blackstone is surely correct in his sense of the rhythms of repetition in Byron's poem, but those rhythms go much deeper and take in a far larger sweep of the canon and its concerns than the instances to which he refers. Indeed, those rhythms are so crucial to Byron's understanding of the way the world works (and the way the self works in the world) that they will occupy us, in one way or another, for the rest of this study. Yet they have already caught our attention: the echoes and mirrors of self that appear from the early *Harold* on are instances of those rhythms at work. Their movements grow more vigorous as the canon develops and as Byron comes to see the full extent of the rhythms' significance.

They appear with particular vigor at the beginning of the third canto of *Harold,* which sets out an intricate interplay of disjunction and repetition, continuity and separation, endings and beginnings. Yet there is a sense in which that interplay began before the canto's beginning, because it starts out by stretching back to the conclusion of the previous canto to make one of its major points. This is a crucial and timely experiment in undoing beginnings and endings. It carries on the line of experiments with closure seen in *The Giaour* and other texts, all of them testings that lead eventually to the mode of *Don Juan.* In the last stanza of the second canto the narrator addresses "vain days": "full reckless may ye flow, / Since Time hath reft whate'er my soul enjoy'd" (2.98.7–9). Time is the maker of disjunctions, the fashioner of those snappings-off which this and the previous canto dwelt on from their earliest points. But the epigraph that begins the third canto has other comments to make about time and its workings, and they flatly contradict those which ended the previous canto: "Afin que cette application vous forcât à penser à autre chose. Il n'y a en vérité de remède que celui-là et le temps."

From *Self, Text, and Romantic Irony: The Example of Byron,* © 1988 by Princeton University Press. Reprinted by permission.

Those lines are taken from a letter of Frederick the Great to D'Alembert. The latter having lost a friend, the king proposed "quelque problème bien difficile à résoudre" as a way of diverting D'Alembert's mind (McGann, 2:76). Only such diversions, and time itself, are sufficient remedies. Time, then, is all that it was *not* just a few lines (and one canto) earlier: it is the undoer of disjunctions, the fashioner of those plasterings-over which, one has to hope, will follow in the subsequent cantos. The interplay of this and the previous comment is brief, incisive, and unsettling. It reneges on what it gives with a celerity matched only by the speed with which it gives (or seems to give) things back again. We are left with a handful of ironies and an awareness of what Byron has come to see of the perplexities of continuity. By linking the second and third cantos the echoes assert and reinforce the continuity of the entire poem. But by flatly contradicting what the earlier stanza said about the relations of time and disjunction, the echoes create the very disjunction they deny. And there is more of such play at hand. As though to assert that matters of repetition are to be found in every corner, that there are mirrors on every wall and that this world is made up of walls, Byron puts those matters into the makeup of the mode in which he discusses them. He does at the beginning of the third canto what he did at the beginning of the first, proffering, through an epigraph, a set of instructions for reading what is to follow. Thus, the mode through which he introduces the question of continuity contains an echo of an earlier gesture. That is, it acts out what it asserts. An introduction so intense, so dense and self-regarding, has the proper force and weight for what is to be so important an issue: difference and continuity are grounded deep within the canto, not only sketching the shapes of repetition but questioning, at times, whether repetition is fully, genuinely, possible.

Canto 3 was published by itself on 18 November 1816, some four and a half years after cantos 1 and 2. No reader having the new volume in hand could be expected to notice the play of ends and beginnings that the prefatory quote introduces, and he would therefore have to receive his precise instructions for reading from other sources. Byron supplies them so liberally at the beginning of the canto that they come on like an onslaught. That sort of continuity which stems from the relations of parent and child turns up just after the epigraph from Frederick; and yet part of that linkage is questioned even as it is expressed, the speaker wondering whether his child's face is like that of her mother, whether it repeats or stops the pattern. Whatever the case, there is certainly no continuity in what he is doing now: when he and his child last parted they did so "not as we now part, / But with a hope" (3.1.3–4). Nor is there an unimpeded linkage in what he is now about to do: the uncertainty of a beginning—"I depart, / Whither I know not" (3.1.7–8)—is matched by the uncertainty of endings and beginnings accomplished by the epigraph.

At this point in the text there are, it seems, only shifting grounds to stand on. Endings and beginnings are as hard to pin down as the junctures in the sea on which the narrator now sets out (the sea the aptest image for all the shiftiness he describes, the aptest place imaginable to tell of more of the same). His voice now clearly quasi-Byronic, he speaks in the first stanza about his setting sail from home, though, as he says, "the hour's gone by, / When Albion's lessening shores could grieve or glad mine eye" (3.1.8–9). Those lines are a bold and open echo of Harold's departure from England at the beginning of canto 1. Perhaps, because of their boldness, the echo is apparent to many readers; yet this time it is the quasi-Byronic figure who is doing these things and not the melancholy Harold. If he echoes what Harold did he links up with his hero's earliest acts; yet since it is *he* who now does the departing and not his desolate hero, the continuity between the cantos is partly qualified, that is to say, partly dissolved into disjunction and difference. Still, even with that disjunction we can see a continuity among three selves. One is the self of the fictive hero, the second the self of the narrator (who shares characteristics with Byron but is, unlike Byron, a voice from inside the fiction, himself a fiction). The third is the self of George Gordon Lord Byron, who has a daughter named Ada and, as everyone knows, has written some melancholy poems and has left his wife and his country. In the second and third stanzas that interplay continues and affirms the continuity of selves, the third stanza in particular reminding the reader of "One, / The wandering outlaw of his own dark mind," whom the voice sang of in his own "youth's summer" (3.3.1–2). Yet Byron is much too canny to leave it at only the continuity of his canon and the selves attached to it. The second stanza repeated, in a manner not to be mistaken, the beginning of *Lycidas:* "Once more upon the waters! yet once more!" so patently echoes the first line of Milton's monody about death by water ("Yet once more, o ye laurels, and once more") that Byron's canto takes on another sort of life and other sorts of continuities. The literary life of these cantos is profoundly intertextual, reaching back through a slew of beginnings. If any is fully definitive— stopping at Milton or Spenser will in no way end their play—he never points it out.

By the time one gets through the third stanza, the questioning of continuity that appeared so strongly in the first is likely to be a dim memory at best. It is therefore time to unsettle complacency, and the fourth stanza does just that. His young days of passion having unstrung the self as instrument (his "heart and harp"), he may not be able to continue his acts and his canon: "it may be, that in vain / I would essay as I have sung to sing" (3.4.3–4); and yet he holds on to this "dreary strain," hoping to continue a linkage with the old so that it will "fling / forgetfulness around me" (3.4.7–8). The irony is at its brightest, fiercest, funniest at this point: he wants to hold on to the old so that he can break with the old, to remember so that he can forget. The celerity of his reneging is as startling as the flash of wit that brings it about. His giving and partial retaking echo the counterpart play of wit we saw in the epigraph. The paradox in stanza 4 is as precise, incisive, and unsettling as its predecessor, as effective in unloosing conclusions. By November 1816, these matters of sequence and fracture, beginnings and endings that do not quite do all we expect them to do, had become obsessive. We are less than two years away from the earliest cantos of *Juan* and the mode in which those matters found their finest, most fluent form.

They take the form they do in this canto and the quizzical fourth stanza because he is setting about on a search for ways to dull parts of the self. The paradox of the fourth stanza continues in the fifth as he tells why thought moves into the "lone caves" of the self, those caves an updated version of the well-stocked larder of the self seen in the earlier cantos. Here they enclose a content composed of "airy images, and shapes which dwell / Still unimpair'd, though old, in the soul's haunted cell" (3.5.8–9). The paradox continues, as does the play of continuity and disjunction, because he is still seeking to fling forgetfulness around him, to break off the hold of the past by using elements from the past—this time old but unimpaired shapes that will figure in texts. It is usual to see these stanzas as showing how art becomes diversion, compensation, a patch for pain. And yet what the speaker seeks is much more complex than that, more respectful of art than that.

It as though he cannot bear the thought of the vacancy that would occur if he were to thoroughly blot out the past. He turns, for his own reasons, to doing what Harold did with Sappho's landscape and what Manfred was to do all over his own: people the vacancy that is left. He tells in the fourteenth stanza of the Chaldean who "could watch the stars, / Till he had peopled them with beings bright / As their own beams; and earth, and earth-born jars, / And human frailties, were forgotten quite" (3.14.1–4). Perhaps he populates places because, if they stay vacant, the old figures will return. Perhaps he does so because the self craves places where it can extend itself, keep on with its acts and encounters, and if the old places no longer work then new ones will have to be made. All of these reasons are plausible, and there are more. The craving for a continuity of being that was figured at the beginning of the canto in the remedies life brings and in the linking with those we have borne appears here too. Here there are other beings we have made, no Ada this time, in whom our blood goes on, but those of the fancy, which continue our thoughts and feelings. In order to unmake parts of this selfhood, to fracture links with the past, he sets out to make new selves to inhabit his texts. Not only will those figures people the vacant spaces in the enclosure of self, but they will establish new continuities to replace the old that have been blotted out. "Gaining as we give / The life we image" (3.6.3–4), we increase the range of our selfhood by drawing on the larder the selfhood holds in some of its strata. To dip into that larder is in fact to stock other strata with more than they had before. And we also set up links with that which has newly come out of us, for not only do we gain additional life but we go where that new life goes:

> What am I? Nothing; but not so art thou,
> Soul of my thought! with whom I traverse earth,
> Invisible but gazing, as I glow
> Mix'd with thy spirit, blended with thy birth,
> And feeling still with thee in my crush'd feeling's dearth.
>
> (3.6.5–9)

Ending and beginning occur in the same act. Peopling blots and bears, unmakes and makes, all in a single gesture. It is becoming more and more difficult to speak of beginnings and endings with the ease and confidence we are used to, given the evidence we have seen of the uncertainties of each, of their refusal to stay put and rounded out. They too, it now seems clear, seek continuities for themselves.

And the speaker seeks even more, what he has done not nearly enough to quench his compulsion for continuity—a compulsion that, we are now beginning to suspect, owes as much to fear of disjunction as to the positive effects of linkage. In stanza 6 he joyed in being mixed with the spirit of his creations, blended with their birth. That mixing and blending will appear once again in the famous stanzas on nature, which continue with passionate intensity the questions worked out in the introductory stanzas. Indeed, they so patently continue the earlier stanzas that they take much of their life from what those stanzas were working out and from the instructions they offer for reading. In stanzas 5 and 6 the self stretches itself to go forth and traverse earth with its creations. Yet the self does not lose itself fully in its creations but holds on to its separate awareness of the world and its separate awareness of itself, "invisible but gazing." We have to note this careful balance because we cannot read stanzas 72–74 as though the dissolution they discuss, and which he says occasionally happens, is anything like total. "I live not in myself, but I become / Portion of that around me (3.72.1–2) . . . And thus I am absorb'd, and this is life" (3.73.1). The sort of dissolution depicted in 72 and 73 prefigures the most desirable sort of all, the dissolving of the "carnal life." The latter is tested in 74, where what would be left after the unmaking of carnality would be pure mind, "free / From what it hates in this degraded form" (3.74.1–2). What he seeks in 72 and 73, and predicts in 74, is precisely what he says he achieves with his creations: it is a carefully crafted balance in which the self foregoes none of its autonomy (we are looking forward to Manfred's compulsions), in which the self is in no sense unmade, its integrity in no sense qualified. Indeed, it would be more integral than ever since the self in such a state is purely itself, in a wonderfully satisfying way both absorbed and self-sustaining. There is much of that careful balance even in the testing of the final state seen in stanzas 72 and 73, where his relation to the things of this world is seen to be the same as his relations to his own creations. Even at his most intensely Shelleyan, as in stanza 93, he never could say to the night or the tempest "Be thou me." That would tip the oxymoronic balance of integrity and dissolution too far to the side that unmakes. All of his careful delineation shows that it is in the chance of such tipping that the ultimate danger lies.

The play of peopling and continuity goes on to the end of the canto . . . [where] the speaker returns to specifics on how our creations continue ourselves. Once again he speaks of Ada: "Albeit my brow thou never should'st behold, / My voice shall with thy future visions blend, / And reach into thy heart" (3.115.6–8). There is ample impurity of self here, much of the turmoil that Rousseau's ideal beings began to feel only when their actions clustered into stories: "The child of love,—though born in bitterness, / And nurtured in convulsion,—of thy sire / These were the elements,—and thine no less" (3.118.1–3). All he can hope is that the fire will be more tempered in Ada than it has been in him. Here too there are continuities, but of a sort that bear a taint foreign to Rousseau in his movements of vision and to the speaker of stanza 90 who has known the feeling infinite that purifies from self. Continuity may not, after all, be fully pure, clean, and without stain.

And in fact these concluding remarks reveal another line of argument that has been at work in the canto, a subtext that comes to the surface at moments in the canto's progress and undoes with incisive precision what the text has been bodying forth about matters of continuity. The interplay of fracture and sequence at the beginning of the canto gave us our instructions for reading. We have to follow those instructions carefully to gather the *entire* meaning of those movements in the canto.

"I live not in myself, but I become / Portion of that around me": that gesture has all sorts of special tones attached to it, but it is not the only mode of the self's potential unmaking that the canto has broached. Earlier in the canto another mode of melding in which we blend into our surroundings was carefully spelled out, different in quality than this, put in a tone that is far less fine. Further, those earlier comments showed another way in which we can become what stanza 72 calls "a link reluctant in a fleshly chain." Stanza 28 carries the warriors of Waterloo from last night's dance to today's grave, a meeting of man and earth in which each dissolves into the other: "The thunder-clouds close o'er it, which when rent / The earth is covered thick with other clay, / Which her own clay shall cover, heaped and pent, / Rider and horse,—friend, foe,—in one red burial blent!" (3.28.6–9). "And thus I am absorb'd," he was to say in stanza 73; and thus were they, their fleshy, fleshly selves, absorbed into the great arithmetic accomplished by Waterloo. Of such encounters of kinds of clay is the earth's continuity made; and that sort of continuity does its part in creating another sort, the rolling around of the seasons. The quasi-Byronic voice goes on to speak of his distant relation, "young, gallant Howard," and of how the narrator, standing on the field at Waterloo, saw the field revive around him "with fruits and fertile promise, and the Spring / Come forth her work of gladness to contrive" (3.30.6–7). The mouldering mentioned in stanza 27 and the blending of clays in stanza

28 have their part in this new greenness, the "next verdure" of stanza 27. These earlier stanzas play off against the later, Shelleyan sort to create a bitterly ironical pattern of absorption and continuity; and it is a pattern whose components—the modes of continuity—are so different in tone, quality, and accomplishment that, whatever their ironical likenesses, they create an aporia that can never be bridged over. After all, the thousands who were added to Waterloo's clay most likely knew nothing of Shelleyan linkages with "the sky, the peak, the heaving plain / Of ocean, or the stars" (3.72.8–9). There is nothing said in the Waterloo stanzas about the joys beyond carnality.

The self's ironical arithmetic continues in the next two stanzas, but with other functions now at play. The addition of bodies like Howard's to the clay at Waterloo in fact created elsewhere a division, a fracture of sequence. The death of Howard and each of the thousands "a ghastly gap did make / In his own kind and kindred," the contrary to the blended clay that their deaths created (3.31.2–3). Death, it seems, adds, subtracts, and divides.

The result is to create in the survivors the same desire seen in the narrator at the beginning of the canto, a wish for forgetfulness. The survivors seek to match the gap in kind and kindred with another gap, a blank of consciousness, a fracture of continuity to counter the thoughts of the ironic continuity that Waterloo brought about. Mourning but persevering they go on in the same way as "the hull drives on, though mast and sail be torn" (3.32.3). Stanza 32 describes the state of the survivors in terms used to describe survivors in Byron's canon from Harold on. "The ruin'd wall" that "stands when its wind-worn battlements are gone" is a figure applying as much to the voice that begins this canto and to the Manfred who was to be described in terms of a burned-out wreck of a star as to those who have kept on going after the gaps caused by slaughter. (Robert Gleckner's comments on the increasing universality of the voice in the later cantos are pertinent at this point.[2]) Sometimes, of course, the images for this state seem to come too easily: "And thus the heart will break, yet brokenly live on" is, by itself, too tawdry a figure with which to speak of the consequences of gaps. And yet the figure is flaccid only for a moment and only in part. "Break" and "brokenly" are echoed straight away in the first line of the following stanza ("even as a broken mirror"), an echo leading into a rich and crucial image about a thousand vibrating echoes. That image sets up a series of complex ironies whose play echoes and reverberates to the deepest levels of the canto. The gaps and fractures in kind and kindred cause the self to collapse into fragments:

> Even as a broken mirror, which the glass
> In every fragment multiplies; and makes
> A thousand images of one that was,
> The same, and still the more, the more it breaks;
> And thus the heart will do which not forsakes,
> Living in shattered guise, and still, and cold,

> And bloodless, with its sleepless sorrow aches,
> Yet withers on till all without is old,
> Shewing no visible sign, for such things are untold. (3.33)

The result is a sardonic parody of homeopathy: the fractures in kind and kindred cause fractures in the selves that remain. This unmaking of the self into a thousand images of itself is the most ironical version in the canto (and in fact in Byron's canon) of the peopling we perform when we are frightened by vacancy.

And yet this incessant fracturing of self is curiously ineffectual. However often it occurs, however many fragments it makes, it is a breaking of what we are that cannot undo what we are: "the same, and still the more, the more it breaks." The doubling and duplicity of self seen in earlier texts like *The Giaour* is carried on in a painful multiplicity, as though we were pierced by the shards that make the thousand reflections. To suffer, in this canon, is to be forever in the mirror stage. Once again we have come to an aporia: these assertions about the self cannot be reconciled with the assertions in the same stanzas on the self's at-homeness in the world, its rapturous continuities, its radical oneness with itself. Once again these sets of stanzas cannot be comfortably reconciled in substance, thrust, or tone. . . .

The Prisoner of Chillon was written about . . . June 27–28 [1816], and it bears all sorts of relations not only to *The Dream* but to the third canto of *Harold* and other contemporary poems.[3] Those relations are so curious, not only in their content but their tone, that they add qualities to the context that complicate the whole considerably. But the poem is, in itself, quite a complicated business. Samuel Chew has argued that it was popular because "such thought as it was charged with was free from uncomfortable questionings in the domain of religion and morals."[4] Yet that point about its freedom from questionings is so far from being the case that it turns the truth quite around, especially when we consider the prefatory sonnet which, as Chew himself noticed, is quite out of spirit with the poem.[5] When the two are taken together they result in a number of "uncomfortable questionings," not least of comforting readings of Byron's poems of the time. And their mode of being together, whatever its qualities of dissonance, is itself quite consonant with the canon's built-in tendencies. Being out of spirit is not unrelatedness but a special sort of relation. . . . That sort is characteristically Byronic.

The "Sonnet on Chillon," added to the beginning of the whole after Byron learned more about Bonivard, continues the practice of prefatory instruments that proved so significant earlier in the canon. In this case, however, it takes the potential for irony in such conjunctions and works the potential in such a way that (as at the end of *Harold* 2 and the beginning of *Harold* 3) conjunction and disjunction come into being together, each created by the context, each intensifying the other. And yet those contraries are implicit not only in the conjunction but in the movement of the sonnet itself, though their import comes out most fully when sonnet and poem are taken together. The first line of the sonnet tells of "the chainless Mind" (McGann, 4:3), a concept taken, in most readings, as the point of the poem's import. "My mind to me a kingdom is" of course lies behind the phrase. No enforced linkages are at play, nothing that ties the mind to anything but itself. Self has no true home except within its own confines, no place in which it is inscribed except where it wants to be. Yet there are difficulties within the sonnet, potentials for contradiction that, though never pursued within it, set the stage for the undoing of the sonnet's ostensible thrust:

> Chillon! thy prison is a holy place,
>   And thy sad floor an altar—for 'twas trod,
> Until his very steps have left a trace
>   Worn, as if thy cold pavement were a sod,
> By Bonnivard!—May none those marks efface!
>   For they appeal from tyranny to God. (9–14)

Self is so fully inscribed into this place that the floor of the dungeon becomes the site of a trace of Bonivard. Self turns its context into a text, a place of profoundest linkage between engraver and engraved. Mind (Bonivard's and all free ones), memory (ours of Bonivard and his like), and place (the dungeon and mind-as-place) come together into a system that lives as much by subterranean paradox as by unqualified declamation.

The play of those ironies and contradictions pervades the following poem through all its interstices, surface and depth, act and emotion, theme and variation. Among those ironies is the insistence that inscribing will be mutual, that there will be a sardonic justice in this matter of engraving:

> And in each pillar there is a ring,
> And in each ring there is a chain;
> That iron is a cankering thing,
> For in these limbs its teeth remain,
> With marks that will not wear away,
> Till I have done with this new day. (36–41)

As he inscribes himself into his dungeon so do the instruments of the dungeon inscribe themselves into him, his flesh their text. Here too, though the roles have shifted, engraver and engraved cannot undo themselves from each other, whatever he may do to the literal chains that bind. Self and dungeon have a relation much like that which Delacroix saw in Byron, antagonists drawn together to make an oxymoronic whole, each stuck with (into) the other just as the Giaour is stuck with Hassan, carrying his enemy around with him though they have long since literally unlinked. And this is by no means the only instance of such practices in the poem. *Chillon* is very clearly taken by those long-standing obsessions with junction and disjunction, wholeness and fragmentation, self and context and their continuities, which, at this time of *Harold* 3, *The Dream,* and *Manfred,* had come to a point of crisis. *Chillon* itself contributes a particular twist to the crisis, its ironies based, in part, on the duplicity engendered by the sonnet—what are, in effect, its misleading instructions for reading. Yet we are misled on another level if we argue or assume that there is *only* absolute disjunction between sonnet and poem (just as we would be wrong to argue for such final fracturing between Harold and the Other in "To Inez" or between the Giaour and Hassan, not to speak of other sets we have inspected). The play of likeness and otherness, continuity and separation, turns into an intricate mixture of seeing and nonseeing, absence (of a sort) and presence (of a sort), which makes *The Prisoner of Chillon* a difficult business to fix, to say that it is conclusively one thing or another. Most events within it turn into multivalent symbols of a terrible state of being where scission and sequence struggle for ultimate primacy.

Neither wins, of course, nor could either be well pleased at the various turns of events. Byron builds those turns on the little he heard about Bonivard and the much he added to it—the matter of family, for example. There was nothing concerning family in what Byron heard about Bonivard, and the fact that he adds to the story a pair of imprisoned siblings shows that his interests are far less in the assertions of the sonnet than in the question of relation—here put in its most basic form—and its deep potential for fissure. He toys with sentiment about relation at various points in the poem, the toying signaled and initiated by the blunt echo of Wordsworth ("We were seven—who now are one") and carried on with the bird that comes and goes, leaving Bonivard bleaker than before. But relation at these levels of sentiment matters less, finally, than an existential sort that threatens to undo him. Here is stanza three:

> They chained us each to a column stone,
> And we were three—yet, each alone,
> We could not move a single pace,
> We could not see each other's face,
> But with that place and livid light
> That made us strangers in our sight;
> And thus together—yet apart,
> Fettered in hand, but pined in heart,
> 'Twas still some solace in the dearth
> Of the pure elements of earth,
> To hearken to each other's speech,
> And each turn comforter to each,
> With some new hope, or legend old,
> Or song heroically bold;
> But even these at length grew cold.

> Our voices took a dreary tone,
> An echo of the dungeon stone,
> A grating sound—not full and free
> As they of yore were wont to be:
> It might be fancy—but to me
> They never sounded like our own. (48–68)

They are grouped yet singled out; together yet apart; unable to see each other yet "strangers in our sight." There is nothing firm to fix on in this place of aporia, nothing that does not bring along its dark and undoing twin; nothing, that is, except sound. In the bitterest irony of all, their voices come to be inscribed with the sounds of the place that enfolds them, so that the dungeon not only engraves itself into the prisoners' flesh but into the sounds of their voices as well: "Our voices took a dreary tone, / An echo of the dungeon stone, / A grating sound not full and free, / As they of yore were wont to be." Poe would have understood this meeting of self, place, and text, where each becomes the other in the only absolute certainty that the dungeon will permit.

It will not even permit irrevocable chaining; nor, scariest of all, will it permit the continued certainty of the self's existential location, that which should always remain, whatever else they take from him. In stanza 8 the last link with his "fading race" falls asunder with the death of his younger brother. In a parallel whose ironies pursue him for some time, he breaks his literal chain at just that point and rushes to his brother's corpse. In stanza 9 he loses touch with light and then with darkness (a state of total lack, impossible to conceive), and slips into an emptiness that has swallowed time and place, leaving him tied but tied to nothing, again beyond all logic: "vacancy absorbing space, / And fixedness—without a place" (243–44). Whatever it may seem, this is not to be considered a return to primal chaos, which, by its very nature, always ferments with possibility. There is here, in echoes of Coleridge's *Ancient Mariner,* only the opposite of possibility, the inertia of that which has been moved so deeply that it can no longer move, of that which cannot rot (for rotting is too active) but simply sits: "silence and stirless breath / Which neither was of life nor death; / A sea of stagnant idleness, / Blind, boundless, mute, and motionless!" Any relation this condition takes to the fertility of chaos has to be parodic. Any awakening of the sort that happens with "the carol of a bird" has therefore to be equally parodic, a play on acts of rebirth. No wonder that the awakening leaves him not only alone but with another echo of Wordsworth that turns the screws even tighter: "Lone—as the corse within its shroud, / Lone—as a solitary cloud, / A single cloud on a sunny day, / While all the rest of heaven is clear" (293–96). Toward the end he manages to find a sort of fixedness, "a second home," in this place of spiders and mice. He also finds the sort of linkage that the term "communion" holds: "My very chains and I grew friends, / So much a long communion tends / To make us what we are" (391–93). Part of the space where acts of connection occur is once again filled in, enough to patch over some of the fractures but never enough to negate that aporia which pervades every level of the poem and leaves it beyond ultimate resolution.

That final patching of connection serves also to give to Bonivard what Harold was never able to achieve, a viable tie to place. But what a tie and what a place! This shows nothing like a solution to Harold's ongoing task as a turner of the world's pages, nothing like the awakening achieved by Fougeret de Monbron, nothing of the happy prison Stendhal was to offer as an ironical optimum condition.[6] Stendhal, indeed, as attuned to Byron's ironies as any one of his time, showed Julien Sorel to be happy in a special, unparalleled way but to have achieved such ultimate happiness by the gift of his life. Fabrice del Dongo fared somewhat better but ends with little of what he had in his paradisiacal prison. Of all Byron's heroes only Tasso is as closely tied to place as Bonivard, rooted in a way that Harold never was in the cantos we have about him. But that is clearly no answer either. The solution may well have to be a special place for the self that is no literal place at all. What we saw of the sad engraving in which prison and place become each other's text, making a kind of text a kind of place for the self to be, was, in fact, a very good guess at where the ultimate answer could lie. Here too the necessity of *Juan* was to grow more apparent.

Yet this does not exhaust the canonic ironies (the ironies the canon engenders about itself) to which *The Prisoner of Chillon* contributes. The third canto of *Harold* was still very fresh in Byron's mind when he wrote *Chillon*, and one of that canto's central passages takes, in retrospect, all sorts of sardonic tones when seen (reseen) in the light of the linkages in *Chillon*:

> I can see
> Nothing to loathe in nature, save to be
> A link reluctant in a fleshly chain,
> Class'd among creatures, when the soul can flee,
> And with the sky, the peak, the heaving plain
> Of ocean, or the stars, mingle, and not in vain. (3.72.4–9)

The communion that ends *Chillon* is an earthy, pathetic substitute for the mingling Harold's narrator calls for in his ecstatic, Shelleyan moments. As happens so often in Byron the passages speak to each other in a way that uneases them both. But there is more. Bonivard was not a reluctant but a willing link in the fleshly chain that tied him to his brothers. The snapping of that link through his younger brother's death (paralleled by the snapping of the literal ties that bind) gets Bonivard a version of what *Harold*'s narrator wanted; here too an earthy, pathetic surrogate for the narrator's chief desire. This canon has a way of realizing desire in a most undesirable manner, engendering its own private scandals. *Manfred* was Byron's next major step, and it took such bitter realizations into a deep cul-de-sac and one of the canon's major crises.

The canon cannot, it seems, cease from commenting on itself, worrying how what it is fits in with where it has been. Such regular self-pondering shows the subdued but active presence of a subterranean pattern of continuing self-adjustment. It is, indeed, a kind of mapping, one of many simultaneous acts the canon performs as it goes along. Take, for example, *Manfred,* act 3, scene 3, the scene that ended the original version of the drama. Several of Manfred's retainers are hanging about the tower while Manfred is within it, pursuing whatever it is he does in his long vigils. Manuel, the oldest retainer, recalls Sigismund, Manfred's father and a figure as unlike his son in personality as any could be:

> I speak not
> Of features or of form, but mind and habits:
> Count Sigismund was proud,—but gay and free,—
> A warrior and a reveller; he dwelt not
> With books and solitude, nor made the night
> A gloomy vigil, but a festal time,
> Merrier than day; he did not walk the rocks
> And forests like a wolf, nor turn aside
> From men and their delights. (3.3.17–25)[7]

This is an echo out of two pasts, that of the family and that of the canon. The description takes us back to the first stanzas of the earliest *Harold,* before Harold turned "aside / From men and their delights." Everything before that turn in Harold's mode of being is a species of prehistory. The turn was, at once, a gesture of self-enclosing (of self within its own contours) and of self-loosening (of self from manifold ties). Its end result is in this text, which has taken a moment, in the third scene of the last act, to go back into history and locate itself precisely. These moments of self-locating are often pointers to conditions of crisis. When the text locates itself within the context of the canon it comes to see itself more clearly, work out with greater precision the import of its point of crisis. The fact that the drama once ended here (the tower suddenly, strangely, bursts into flame and Manfred is carried out dying) shows the unusual importance of the scene. All the more reason, then, for its need to place itself in the canon.

The search for greater precision continues in what follows these lines. The thrust of Manuel's careful distinction between father and son, establishing nonresemblance, is countered with subtle force by the rest of his speech, where he speaks of intense resemblance. He tells of another person related to Manfred by blood; one who, we have already learned, is exactly like him in features and form and who, unlike his father, shares his thoughts and habits.

She is, we are told, "the sole companion of his wanderings / And watchings" (3.3.43–44). We have come, once again, on a basic set of Byron's mind: "A" (here, Manfred's relation to Sigismund) cannot be fully understood until we have examined "B" (here, his relation to Astarte). Each needs a knowledge of the other in order to know itself more precisely and therefore to be fully itself. The emphasis falls on "fully." What we see at work in this passage is a very important segment of the self's search for integrity, for an unbreakable wholeness that would do for every purpose. It is the play of identity and difference that contributes most to the precision and thus, eventually, to the fullness. By this time Byron had become remarkably skilled at working resemblance and nonresemblance. He uses it here, as often elsewhere, as a rhetorical tool that not only manages the movement of ideas but echoes, in the handling of the text, the way in which the self meets and makes its world and itself. Manfred is set between Sigismund on the one hand and Astarte on the other, partaking in the blood of each, quite possibly even partaking in the features of each: Manuel's comment—"I speak not / Of features or of form"—could mean that father and son are similar in those aspects. Manfred differs from Sigismund in habits exactly as much as he matches Astarte.

Put another way, a way that will lead us into the deepest structures in the drama, the relation of Sigismund and Manfred is a diachronic one, that of Manfred and Astarte a synchronic one. It is as though time were pressuring Manfred into greater and greater resemblance with those who are important to him, that increase in resemblance creating an increase in pressure: the more time the more likeness, the more likeness the more intensity, the more intensity the more likelihood that all will come undone. The implicit temporal thrust of Manuel's final speech opens dimensions in the drama that were not there before. Coming as it does in what was to be the final scene, the speech seems designed not only to open out another perspective and a greater comprehension but to fuse that moment of insight with the ultimate catastrophe, the final, fiery undoing. Thus, the early version of the drama puts the play of distinction and likeness even closer to the center of focus than the later version does. What was added in the later version (the last meeting of Manfred and the abbot) brings in another sort of perspective, one that focuses on will and the self's autonomy; and yet that perspective turns out to be not entirely different after all, for it is, in part, closely related to the emphases of the earlier version. Indeed, an important aspect is frankly derived from those earlier emphases. Manfred's denial of the spirits' dominance and his echo of Milton's Satan assert that the self has sole power in making a time and place for itself:

> The mind which is immortal makes itself
> Requital for its good or evil thoughts—
> Is its own origin of ill and end—
> And its own place and time. (3.4.129–32)

The echo is a pointed rejoinder to the import of Manuel's speech, his emphasis on the pressure that time knows how to exert on the self's acts and integrity. Manfred could not have heard the speech, but what happens at the endings, the old one and the new, shows that—whatever else is said—this permeating pressure cannot be put behind without some final comment. It calls for a rebuttal just as arrogant as itself, just as insistent as it is on its own ultimate power. The accuracy of the rejoinder will be discussed in subsequent chapters.

Manfred became a collecting point for most of the major matters that had been driving Byron's canon. Only *Juan* is more significant in that regard. *Cain* approaches *Manfred* in importance as a place where so much comes together, but *Cain* is finally less crucial, in part because of its timing. *Manfred* takes those earlier concerns into that terminal softness where ripeness ends and decay begins. *Harold* 4 follows right after but, whatever its considerable qualities, it is not the thesaurus that *Manfred* is. And it is by virtue of that status, by bringing it all together onto the field of its discourse, that *Manfred* shows more clearly than any Byronic text of its time why something had to be done, why things could go no further. In this and subsequent chapters we shall be looking at more of its preoccupations.

We began this chapter with comments on one of them, the rhythms of repetition. Of course those rhythms take one of their forms in the play of likeness and unlikeness that we have been following from the point where Harold thought of Sappho and encountered his somber *semblable* in "To Inez." *Manfred* takes those rhythms to a pitch that only *Juan* was to surpass. Byron seems to have wanted to seek out the purest case, distilled to essential elements, and test it to see what outcome it would bring.

To begin with there are the numerous self-images studded throughout the drama, most designated to put echoes of Manfred into the world outside of himself, most quite heavy handed. To take two from the drama's first scene, Manfred, in addressing the spirits, speaks of the birthplace of his power as "a star condemned, / The burning wreck of a demolish'd world, / A wandering hell in the eternal space" (1.1.44–46). The seventh spirit tells Manfred that the star that rules his destiny "became / A wandering mass of shapeless flame, / A pathless comet, and a curse, / The menace of the universe" (1.1.116–19). Since the star the spirit refers to is surely the one from which Manfred drew his power, the spirit is telling him nothing he did not already know, including the blunt implication that Manfred is as the star is. Such images, vitiated by their crudeness, matter less in themselves than in what they show of Manfred and the question of relation. Further, the images point out the importance of the rhythms of repetition to the question of relation; how, in at least this case, the images turn those rhythms into a mocking commentary on the self's at-homeness in the world. Where Manfred's predecessors read the text of the world in what was (whether they knew it or not) a search for a way home, Manfred, in an essential sense, never leaves home at all. Wherever he looks in his world he finds himself mirrored, either in the heavens with the star, or in the Alps with its "blasted pines" and its deadly rocks that destroy only the innocent. Working busily beneath all this is another echo from Milton's Satan ("Which way I fly is Hell, myself am Hell"). More important, however, is the dreadful continuity of self and place, the ironical linkage of consciousness and the world in which the world becomes a text in which we read only of ourselves. Even the chamois hunter becomes, for Manfred, mainly an image of all that he is not (see 2.1.63–73). At one level this is a parody of third-rate narcissism. At another, however, it takes the theme of linkage and continuity implicit in every narcissism and infuses it with ironies appropriate to Byron's canon. Poolgazing and stargazing play off against each other, both acts the same, the emotions tied to the acts radically different. Narcissus's desire for connection and Manfred's for its opposite are enfolded in the same image, the same flexible and bitter myth finding room for both.

And yet the myth is so flexible that—as the rest of the drama shows— it manages to contain, at one and the same time and all for Manfred alone, not only repulsion but desire, not only a quest for a final untying but also a compulsion for continuity with the figure of Astarte, a need that drove him once and drives him still. He is made to taste and feel every aspect of the myth, to apply its every contour to himself alone. Where the stars and the Alps lead him to wish for separation, Astarte led and leads him still toward the sort of linkage that Narcissus himself desired and, to his cost, got. In its original form that continuity was natural. Manfred is, we hear, related to Astarte by blood, the specifics never in doubt though never unequivocally put. The continuity grows subtler and more refined (and at the same time more intense, pushing him deeper into the cul-de-sac) when it comes to person and mind. Manfred tells the Witch of the Alps that Astarte was exactly like him in lineaments: "her eyes, / Her hair, her features, all, to the very tone / Even of her voice, they said were like to mine" (2.2.105–107). And, he continues, she was also his like in mind: "She had the same lone thoughts and wanderings, / The quest of hidden knowledge, and a mind / To comprehend the universe" (2.2.109–111). What we come to learn about both brings them closer to a kind of fusion, to a classic sort of narcissim where self and what it stares at are perfectly alike. But Manfred and Astarte never get to that point of absolute likeness, and in never quite doing so they take this text back through the canon and all those elaborate instances of that image of ourselves which is not entirely ourselves. The passage in which Manfred describes their likeness also carefully spells out difference. She is not his precise counterpart but a tenderer version, the lineaments the same "but softened all, and tempered into beauty," her powers ("pity, and smiles, and tears") gentler than his own. The tenderness she had, he had only for her. The humility she had, he never had. And then the passage ends with a pair of potent statements that have no obvious connection to each other but seem to have one in Manfred's mind: "Her faults were mine—her virtues were her own— / I loved her, and destroyed her!" (2.2.116–17).

It is in passages like these that *Manfred* shows itself to be a surfacing of the implicit, designed to help the mind decide where it should go from there. In this case it is a question of the self's ties to the world. With both Astarte and the stars the same act occurs, a multiplying of self that keeps the self complete. The relation to Astarte adds special possibilities. Through it he can break out of the circle of self, resisting a suffocating entrapment of the sort to which Harold was prey. To extend the self beyond its borders toward an Astarte who is not exactly oneself offers obeisance to the need to ward off solipsism, promising a partaking of the world that grants what seems to be the most satisfying completeness. One achieves spiritual health by a crafty movement of self in which one carries much of its content out beyond its edges. One leaves the circle in a way that is almost a not-leaving. If *Manfred* is a point of collection it is also the site of an experiment. It is an especially clever quizzing of possibility because it appears to satisfy every demand.

Such practices, both with the stars and Astarte, continue that special creativity we have seen often before, the peopling of vacancy. I take the specific phrase from the chamois hunter's remarks to Manfred ("which makes thee people vacancy" [2.1.32]), though similar phrases occurred earlier. They were to occur just after *Manfred* at the beginning of *Harold* 4, as follows: "For us repeopled were the solitary shore" (4.4.9); "Such is the refuge of our youth and age, / The first from Hope, the last from Vacancy; / And this worn feeling peoples many a page" (4.6.1–3); "I can repeople with the past" (4.19.1). That last sort is the particular bent of the early Harold, continued into the later. It is Manfred's bent as well. Of course not every image that Manfred works out in his world is a self-image: the peopling also occurs with the seven spirits and the Witch of the Alps, all of whom Manfred brings up, none of whom is (in some cases to his agony) at all like himself. But most important of all are those images that repeat the self. The text signals their importance not only by stressing the stars in the first scene but in what Manfred says to the spirit of Astarte when she has been raised up before him:

> And I would hear yet once before I perish
> The voice which was my music—Speak to me!
> For I have call'd on thee in the still night,
> Startled the slumbering birds from the hush'd boughs,
> And woke the mountain wolves, and made the caves
> Acquainted with thy vainly echoed name,
> Which answered me—many things answered me—
> Spirits and men—but thou wert silent all.
> Yet speak to me! I have outwatch'd the stars,
> And gazed o'er heaven in vain in search of thee.
> Speak to me! I have wandered o'er the earth,
> And never found thy likeness. (2.4.134–45)

The voice he wants to hear is—we have already heard him tell the Witch of the Alps—exactly like his own. In seeking for her likeness he is seeking his own, almost. Peopling as he prefers to practice it should be (almost but not quite) an act of self-making, (almost but not quite) a composition which is self-composition. The "almost" is, of course, the safety valve. The question is whether "almost" is able to do that job.

In fact it is not. Going back to that curious pair of statements at the end of his description of Astarte to the Witch of the Alps ("Her faults were mine—her virtues were her own— / I loved her, and destroyed her!"), we can only conclude that, whatever the attempt at distancing involved in "almost," the faults in which they shared finally did Astarte in. This means that, though Manfred says he destroyed her she must have been part of her own unmaking, participant to the degree that she shared in their dangerous faults. Astarte was done in by those rhythms of repetition with which Manfred had sought to enlarge the active territory of the self. Aspects of their continuity had undone the continuity, recoiling upon themselves and fracturing the wholeness he is now so painfully reseeking.[8]

Such, then, was the essence of the testing that Byron pondered, the questions that were brought, in this text, to their utmost clarity. They were never put forth so clearly because Manfred and Astarte are paragons, the intensest of a kind. Consider the way in which their relation reaches a purity and refinement that have never been seen before. The pairing of Manfred and Astarte promised the self's absolute completeness and it gave them exactly that in a gift fraught with irony, a gift that picks up all the sly and subliminal ironies of the canon's previous pairings and brings them to their bitter pitch. The gift offers all that they asked and more: they were indeed autonomous, absolutely so, for just as they needed only themselves to reach the intensest sort of love, so did they need only themselves to destroy their union. They did not in fact need to leave the perimeters of what finally proves to be (despite the attempt in the "almost" to keep them slightly apart) only an extended circle of self. To commit incest means that one keeps within the family. But Manfred and Astarte carry the narrowing even further, taking it to its finest point, for theirs is *narcissistic* incest, a sort that reduces to its smallest reach the distance one needs to go to get outside of the self. If what one reaches for is the exactest cast of oneself, then one has hardly to reach at all.

Taken from a different perspective, this is another way of looking at the narrowing cul-de-sac that informs the drama: as the extent one needs to reach outside in order to complete the self grows smaller and smaller, the walls close in more tightly, the pressure on the self increasing until it becomes nearly unbearable. With only a single step the cul-de-sac will reach its narrowest point, the place of the dead end and ultimate entrapment. Manfred has only to say that his mind is its own source of reward and punishment because it is its own place, its own maker of heaven and hell; to say, that is, that we never need to go beyond the confines of the self in order to be at home in the world, to be fully in the world. And he says exactly that in the final version of the text. This was one of the major reasons for adding the new material at the end. Byron saw the cul-de-sac developing and knew that he needed only a single degree of centripetence to take it to its conclusion. The logic of his conception of Manfred's situation is precise, inexorable, and brilliant. The self can go no further in the direction Manfred takes it than Manfred actually goes. At the dead end there is only himself, those closed-in walls and that bitter kingdom of the mind in which he is lord and subject and, he argues, his own destroyer.

He is his own consumer as well. What we see at play in this drama is an especially telling instance of a familiar Byronic gesture, an act of consciousness that seeks to save consciousness from itself. Manfred's reaching for Astarte is an implicit recognition that the self by itself is subject to serious threats; yet in practicing what is, in effect, a lust for self, Manfred tries to have it both ways and ends with having it no way at all. Astarte is destroyed by the faults they share, Manfred by those and also the others he privately owns. An attempt at self-completion becomes an act of self-consumption, and it seems to do so inevitably; no other roadway is open. Of course that condition cannot be accepted; not, that is, if self and canon are to do more than stare at the impasse. Self-making and text-making, always intimately linked, will have to grow even closer than that. Indeed, we may have to come to think of them as essentially the same gesture in order to work this problem out. If that solution to the problem sounds suspiciously like part of the problem—the solution partaking in that narcissism which helps to do Manfred in—then that bit of homeopathy is yet another irony in a canon that seems to relish them; that, in fact, had better relish them since it finds them wherever it goes.

Notes

1. [Ed. note: Parenthetical references are to *Byron: The Complete Poetical Works,* ed. Jerome J. McGann (New York: Oxford University Press, 1980–86) by canto, stanza, and line numbers. "McGann" followed by volume and page numbers refers to other materials in this edition.]

2. *Byron and the Ruins of Paradise* (Baltimore: Johns Hopkins University Press, 1967), 251.

3. McGann, 4:3–16. Unless otherwise specified, all references following quotations from *The Prisoner of Chillon* are to line.

4. *Childe Harold's Pilgrimage and other Romantic Poems* (New York: Odyssey Press, 1936), 301.

5. Blackstone (*Byron: A Survey,* p. 126) seems almost alone in seeing a congruence between the prefatory sonnet and the poem. The most persuasive argument against congruence is in Marshall, *Structure of Byron's Major Poems* (Philadelphia: University of Pennsylvania Press, 1962), 82–96. Marshall's study is, along with that of Rutherford (*Byron: A Critical Study*

(Edinburgh: Oliver & Boyd, 1961), 66–75), among the best readings of the poem. Gleckner (*Ruins of Paradise,* 191) and most other modern critics argue against a positive interpretation of the poem as a "tribute to the unconquerable nature of the human mind." See also Cooke, *The Blind Man Traces the Circle* (Princeton: Princeton University Press, 1969), 87. Leslie Marchand (*Byron: A Biography* [New York: Knopf], 2.632) supports the older, positive reading of the poem.

6. See Victor Brombert, *La Prison Romantique* (Paris: José Corti, 1975), and also my *Autonomy of the Self from Richardson to Huysmans* (Princeton: Princeton University Press, 1982).

7. All references following quotations from *Manfred* are to act, scene, and line.

8. On the seeking of unity in the play see W. P. Elledge, *Byron and the Dynamics of Metaphor* (Nashville: Vanderbilt University Press, 1968), 91, and also Marshall, *Structure of Byron's Major Poems* (Philadelphia: University of Pennsylvania Press, 1962), 100.

Editor's Bibliographical Note

As Frederick L. Beaty remarks in his review of of Garber's book, "During the past two decades [he] has become a leading exponent of the consciousness of self as a major Romantic concern" (*Keats-Shelley Journal* 38 [1989]: 165)—not to mention, of course, his major contribution via the Byron book to the vigorously ongoing discussion/debate over romantic irony. Other important participants in this debate are Ingrid Strohschneider-Kohrs, *Die romantische Ironie in Theorie und Gestaltung* (Tubingen: Max Neimeyer, 1960); Ernst Behler, *Klassische Ironie, romantische Ironie, tragische Ironie* (Darmstadt: Wissenschaftliche Buchgesellschaft, 1972), part of which is available in English as "Techniques of Irony in Light of Romantic Theory," *Rice University Studies* 57 (Fall 1971): 1–17; Stuart Sperry, "Toward a Definition of Romantic Irony in English Literature," in *Romantic and Modern: Revaluations of Literary Tradition,* ed. George Bornstein (Pittsburgh: University of Pittsburgh Press, 1977), 1–28; Michael G. Cooke, *Acts of Inclusion: Studies Bearing on an Elementary Theory of Romanticism* (New Haven: Yale University Press, 1979); Anne K. Mellor, *English Romantic Irony* (Cambridge: Harvard University Press, 1980); and Lilian Furst, *Fictions of Romantic Irony* (Cambridge: Harvard University Press, 1984). Although neither treats Byron, I would also include here David Simpson, *Irony and Authority in Romantic Poetry* (Totowa, N.J.: Rowan & Littlefield, 1979), and Tilottama Rajan, *Dark Interpreter: The Discourse of Romanticism* (Ithaca: Cornell University Press, 1980).

For other treatments of *Childe Harold's Pilgrimage* see the bibliographical note to McGann's essay earlier in this volume. Once again, as is the case with *Childe Harold,* all major critical books on Byron (especially those cited repeatedly in my bibliographical notes) deal in some to great detail with *Manfred,* though commentary on *The Prisoner of Chillon* is surprisingly less plentiful. In addition to those books I would note here the following as very useful on one or the other of these major poems: Bertrand Evans, "Manfred's Remorse and Dramatic Tradition," *PMLA* 62 (1947): 752–73; Edwin M. Everett, "Lord Byron's Lakist Interlude," *Studies in Philology* 55 (1958): 62–75 (on *Prisoner*); K. McCormick Luke, "Lord Byron's *Manfred:* A Study of Alienation Within," *University of Toronto Quarterly* 40 (1970): 15–26; Edward Engelberg, "The Price of Consciousness: Goethe's *Faust* and Byron's *Manfred,*" in *The Unknown Distance: From Consciousness to Conscience, Goethe to Camus* (Cambridge: Harvard University Press, 1972), 40–57; John Clubbe, " 'The New Prometheus of New Men': Byron's 1816 Poems and *Manfred,*" in *Nineteenth-Century Literary Perspectives,* ed. Clyde de L. Ryals et al. (Durham: Duke University Press, 1974); David Eggenschweiler, "The Tragic and Comic Rhythms of *Manfred,*" *Studies in Romanticism* 13 (1974): 63–77; Stuart M. Sperry, "Byron and the Meaning of *Manfred,*" *Criticism* 16 (1974): 189–202; James B. Twitchell, "The Supernatural Structure of Byron's *Manfred,*" *Studies in English Literature* 15 (1974): 601–14; Leslie Brisman, "Byron: Troubled Stream from a Pure Source," *ELH* 42 (1975): 623–50 (on *Lara,*

Manfred, Cain); Gerald C. Ward, "Nature and Narrative in Byron's 'The Prisoner of Chillon,' " *Keats-Shelley Journal* 24 (1975): 108–17; Daniel M. McVeigh, "Manfred's Curse," *Studies in English Literature* 22 (1982): 601–12; Vincent Newey, "Byron's 'Prisoner of Chillon': The Poetry of Being and the Poetry of Belief," *Keats-Shelley Memorial Bulletin* 35 (1984): 54–70. I should also add George M. Ridenour's splendid essay on "Byron in 1816: Four Poems from Diodati," in *From Sensibility to Romanticism,* ed. F. W. Hilles and H. Bloom (London and New York: Oxford University Press, 1965), 453–65, which, though not on the major poems of 1816, is a revealing analysis of Byron's mind, as it were, in that crucial year Garber also addresses. And, finally, see also Andrew M. Cooper, "Chains, Pains, and Tentative Gains: The Byronic Prometheus in the Summer of 1816," *Studies in Romanticism* 27 (1988): 529–50.

[The Poetry of Byron's Italian Years]

Donald H. Reiman

The poems and poetic dramas that flowed from Byron's fertile pen following 1818 exhibit certain common elements. First, rejecting the dim archetypes (psychological and/or literary) that had peopled so many of his poems from *The Giaour* through *Manfred,* Byron drew almost all of his plots from historical sources or from the works of others. After *Childe Harold,* IV, Byron first published anonymously *Beppo* (treated later in this essay) and began *Don Juan.* His next published volume contains *Mazeppa* and "Ode to Venice" (1819), the former based directly on Voltaire's life of King Charles XII of Sweden[1] and the latter raising the same kind of topographical-historical reflections that fill *Childe Harold.* Then come *Marino Faliero* (accompanied by "The Prophecy of Dante") based on historical sources (1820), and *Sardanapalus, The Two Foscari,* and *Cain,* issued together in 1821—the first based on mythologies embedded in classical histories, the second on genuine Venetian history, and the third on Biblical tradition. Besides two satires—*The Blues* (a lively but slim farrago reflecting Byron's continuing animus towards William Sotheby and his coterie)[2] and *The Age of Bronze* (an attack upon the Holy Alliance and British foreign policy, on the occasion of the Congress of the Allied Sovereigns in 1822)[3]—Byron wrote two complete dramas, *Heaven and Earth* (a "mystery play" in the manner of *Cain* but developed imaginatively from a brief text in Genesis)[4] and *Werner* (which follows the plot of *Kruitzner,* a novel by Harriet and Sophia Lee),[5] and the fragmentary drama entitled *The Deformed Transformed* (deriving from both the Faust legend and a novel by Joshua Pickersgill),[6] and finally *The Island: or, Christian and His Comrades* (based on the story of the mutineers from the "Bounty").[7]

Whereas in *Manfred* Byron had explored the Faust legend in mythic terms, in *The Deformed Transformed* he ties it to history. Arnold and the devil (here given the name Caesar that, in its various forms, including Kaiser and Czar, signified the autocratic dynasties of Europe) are involved with the army of Charles V, the pious Catholic Emperor who commited the ultimate act of imperial excess by sacking Rome in 1527 over a political dispute with the Pope. Thus Byron transforms a legend of individual hubris into a judgment on the hierarchical European political system.

Reprinted from *Intervals of Inspiration: The Skeptical Tradition and the Psychology of Romanticism* (Greenwood, Fla.: Penkevill Pub. Co., 1988), as edited by the author and with his permission.

All these later dramas and tales explore interrelations between the Byronic protagonist and the outer, objective world. Byron resisted the speculative hopes of other Romantics that the human will might reliably echo the divine will. On the other hand, he was too skeptical to make up new gods, to place moral values in the fate of species rather than of individuals, or to trust his fate to a collective unconscious or racial memory. He saw both Nature and human society as magnifying mirrors that revealed to the individual the state and potentialities of his own soul. Nature, society and other individuals were not trustworthy guides, but rather landmarks to indicate dangerous shoals toward which the self might be moving. To put Byron's position metaphorically, we can imagine many individuals facing backwards in small boats, rowing in a dim twilight across a large lake toward goals they glimpse only fleetingly when they turn around; while proceeding, they take their bearings from natural objects, the lights of towns and houses, and the progress of other rowers who seem to have chosen the same destination. Byron attributes no teleological values to natural objects, which cannot communicate with him; and other travelers have no special authority to chart his course. But by calling out when they encounter rocks or other obstacles, people can warn one another of dangers on the voyage. Thus, accurate reporting of experience is the chief didactic value that Byron attributes to literature. Rather than attempting to set goals for others, Byron describes his own psychic pilgrimages and records the obstacles he encounters on the way.

In the dramas and tales Byron wrote in Italy, he coalesces the tale of his own journey with the stories of historical figures or characters drawn from the fictions of others. By so doing, he declares the commonality of the mortal journey. No longer does he assume that he is different from men and women of other social conditions or other times and places; he is, by nature, neither better nor worse than they. (The idea that all human hearts speak a universal language is a lesson that may have been reinforced by Shelley and by their reading of Wordsworth and Rousseau during the summer of 1816.) But Byron's doubts about the moral efficacy of even this didacticism are reflected in his unchanging distrust of certain kinds of sentimental fiction, such as Madame de Staël's *Corinne* (as an antidote for which, he lent Teresa Guiccioli a copy of *Adolphe* by Benjamin Constant, de Staël's disillusioned lover).[8] Byron feared that such authors, to make their own lives appear more enviable than they really were, suppressed information about the emotional rocks on which their barks had nearly foundered, thereby threatening with disaster those who emulated them. Thus candor—honesty about experience— becomes for Byron the primary virtue, while "cant" and theoretical extrapolations from experience—flights of imagination beyond the experiential evidence—become the cardinal sins. To avoid such cant, Byron renewed his interest in history and sought to sift fact from myth in treating the stories of the Venetian doges Faliero and Foscaro; he based the scenes of storm and shipwreck and the events in the lifeboat in Canto II of *Don Juan* closely on published accounts of actual shipwrecks, most of them written by survivors, and in his later years he asked that Murray send him chiefly histories and books of fact, rather than poetry and fiction.

Byron's distrust of the imagination was not, as some have argued, a renunciation of the values espoused by the other Romantics.[9] None of the Romantic writers gave unqualified credence to his own imagination, much less to anyone else's, though some poets—notably Wordsworth, Shelley, and Keats—invoked it to authorize explorations beyond the bounds of what their skeptical bias told them were the limits of trustworthy experience. Byron also used the imagination in this way, "guessing at truth" when he could not testify to it; the difference between Byron and most of his contemporaries is that the other Romantics did not always sign-post as clearly as he did when they were speculating beyond their experience and when they were not. Whenever Byron spreads his wings for imaginative flight, he portrays himself both taking off from a solid base of experience and landing there again. Shelley uses the same technique (a variant of the traditional uses of the dream-vision) in "Lines written among the Euganean Hills," "Ode to Liberty," and some other poems, but Shelley employs his skepticism to suggest that—though he cannot *know* that his imaginative visions are valid—they are as likely to be accurate as are conclusions drawn from mere reason and sensory evidence. Byron, believing in exactly the same *possibility,* chooses to protect himself and his readers by underlining the negative side of the same proposition: the imaginative flights are just as likely to be *false.* When Shelley and Byron look at the same tumbler, Shelley exults that it is half full, while Byron regrets that it is half empty. The two value the contents equally.

Byron's stress on the value of experiential knowledge over flights of imagination explains and justifies his declared preference for the poetry of George Crabbe over that of his other contemporaries and for that of Pope and the Augustans over all of them. Pope declared his intention to avoid the presumption of pretending "to scan" God; and his attention to "the proper study of mankind"—the vagaries of human behavior—was exactly what the mature Byron came to see as the role of creative literature. Byron's conscious motivation, particularly in his later works, was not merely to save himself by expelling the outlaws of his own dark mind but, in Shelley's words, to "beacon the rocks on which high hearts are wreckt": to provide warnings to others of the nature of these dark passions and to identify as well the objective values that can help to tame them—the saving "other," the polar star that enables the lost boatman to find his way to port.

Finally, Byron's view of the function of literature demanded a concomitant simplicity of language that would be accessible to a broad spectrum of readers. Just as Byron was the only one of the Romantics who developed meaningful friendships with lords and fencing masters, bankers and boxers, guardsmen and gondoliers, so he was the only one among them who successfully communicated through his poetry with men and women of all social classes. He neither invented, nor drew from recondite authors, nor imported from Germany a private vocabulary, nor invented an intricate private symbolism, as did Blake, Coleridge, Wordsworth, Shelley and Keats. McGann has compared Byron's use of everyday words and concepts and his use of historical contexts to convey part of his meaning to the work of Wittgenstein and his followers who are called "ordinary language philosophers."[10] But the most significant defense to date of Byron's style is Manning's essay, "*Don Juan* and Byron's Imperceptiveness to the English Word," which demonstrates how—and, in part, why—Byron rejected the symbolist tendencies inherent in the poetry of his contemporaries. Byron writes from "a poetics based not on the word but on words: that is, not on the charge granted the individual word (whether through special diction . . . or by an aura of numinous presence), but on the relationship between words in themselves unremarkable. . . . a discourse based on absence, one that never offers the consolations of climax or comprehensiveness, never holds forth the promise of an order suddenly made manifest."[11]

"Never" is a dangerous word to use about Byron. I find, in fact, throughout *Don Juan* as well as Byron's more "Romantic" poems many individual passages that, in themselves, offer "the consolations of climax or comprehensiveness": Donna Julia's farewell letter; the moments of moral decision shown by Juan during the storm, in the lifeboat, in saving Leila at Ismail; the idyllic love of Juan and Haidée; the purity of Aurora Raby. These and other imaginative moments, often characterized by such loaded words as "love," "innocence," "natural," "pure," "courage," or "honest," provide the same sort of value-statements (or "pseudo-statements") that are to be found in other Romantic poems. But Byron always returns his characters and their loaded words to larger contexts in human life and discourses in which such values appear, at best, transitory, at worst, illusory, and in all cases limited. For the early Wordsworth (or for Keats in *Endymion*), such "spots of time" are experienced *passively,* imposed by uncertain but probably divine activity, a search for the meaning of which can give value to the meaningless waste of surrounding time; for Byron, such value-moments usually result from the moral or emotional *activity* of the participants, and the individual's task is to train himself to increase their frequency by making more and better moral choices and by purifying his emotions to respond more lovingly and less viciously to the people and situations he encounters in the flux of life.[12]

Beppo, written in September and October 1817 and published anonymously in February 1818, presents the first fruits of Byron's poetic maturity. Here Byron follows Pope's example by examining the values of a social system from a detached perspective. The plot of *Beppo* follows not only an ostensibly true story, but also parallels several other situations Byron had observed or been told about since his arrival in Italy. The factual plot and characters thereby provide valid insight into human nature under the influence of particular customs and circumstances. The narrator's asides contrast the pomposity and cant of Regency London's society with the natural *joie de vivre* of Venetian society, which is unencumbered by both the pseudo-intellectuality and the narrow moralism of London's blue-stockings (Lady Byron and her ilk). Byron sympathizes with Italian manners and mores, which he rates as much more sensible and practical than those he left behind him in England.

Byron's audience is the British society who have exiled him, and he satirically undercuts their values to vindicate his own. Yet, as a stranger and sojourner, he can also view Italian society as an "other" to counteract the English prudery and snobbishness that still cling to his own character. Byron exploits, to a degree, the comic possibilities provided by his readers' (and his own) distance from Italian mores, treating Laura, her *cavaliere servente* the Count, and her husband Beppo with comic detachment. But all things associated with England, from its "cloudy climate" to its "chilly women" (stanza 49), are treated satirically—being in need of definite improvement, though Byron has few illusions about the chances of reforming either. But by juxtaposing English limitations with the more humane and joyful climate and manners of Italy, Byron hopes at least to knock out of the British some of their sense of superiority and condescension toward customs differing from their own.

Beppo was inspired by the first half of John Hookham Frere's parody that represents the attempts of two tradesmen, "William and Robert Whistlecraft," to compete with educated aristocrats by undertaking an epic poem on a chivalric theme. In *Beppo* Byron not only reprimands Frere's implied snobbishness by noting how the Venetian nobility (far more ancient and historically significant than Frere's and Byron's Norman families) mix freely and happily with the bourgeoisie and even with the lower classes, but he also adopts the digressive, freely associative style at which Frere had poked fun as a failing of uneducated poets. Byron's success in mixing literary styles (as had major Italian poets) becomes, among other things, a critical judgment on British snobbishness and exclusivity.

In writing *The Vision of Judgment, Suggested by the Composition So Entitled by the Author of "Wat Tyler"* [i.e., Robert Southey], Byron faced the opposite problem.[13] Instead of playing off his poem against one by a personal friend like Frere, a man of Byron's own social class with whom he shared some social prejudices, he was replying directly to a poem by a personal enemy of lower social origins, whose character as well as values—religious, political, and literary—he despised. Reversing the procedure of *Beppo,* Byron in *The Vision of Judgment* directed his satire, not against British society in general, but against particular individuals, and he portrays both Southey and himself as central figures in the action of the poem.

Editors and critics had always been aware of the obvious attacks on Southey, and some had suggested that Byron himself might be figured in the character of Satan. (In the preface of his *A Vision of Judgment* Southey had attacked Byron and the "Satanic School of Poetry"). Stuart Peterfreund has argued convincingly not only that all the major characters in Byron's *The Vision of Judgment* are based on individuals but that the poem's inquiry into the character and conduct of King George III is set as a debate in the House of Lords.[14] In this reading, Michael is identifiable with Lord Eldon, the Lord Chancellor, who both presided at the trial of Queen Caroline and had ruled against Southey's efforts to suppress the publication of *Wat Tyler*. St. Peter is based on the Earl of Harrowby, President of the Council, who supported Catholic Emancipation, and Asmodeus, the devil who rushes in from outside the chamber with Robert Southey, is William Smith, a liberal M. P., who had brought Southey's *Wat Tyler* and his subsequent apostasy into a House-of-Commons debate in 1817.[15] Peterfreund also demonstrates parallels between passages in the poem that support Satan's case against George III and passages in Byron's 1812 speeches in the House of Lords.[16]

These discoveries do not change our understanding of the main elements of *The Vision of Judgment*—the satire on Southey as poet and turncoat, the moral judgment on King George III, and the forbearing tone in which both the narrator and the character of Satan in the poem confess to their own limitations and in which George III is allowed at the end to slip quietly into Heaven unmolested. But the personal parallels provide a dimension of specificity and historical reality to the situation that adds both to our aesthetic delight in the author's ingenuity and to our understanding of Byron's success in fulfilling one of his primary ambitions: "Throughout his life Byron strove to become a 'historical figure,' and to make that figure identical with the dreams of his own very personal imaginations."[17] Byron here again separates himself from all of the other Romantics. For he made a conscious effort to experience enough of life to make his public actions as well as his inner life the subject-matter of his art. But we ought not lose sight of Byron's larger concern—the need for the truth of human experience rather than for literary wish-fulfillment. To add to his own knowledge, Byron struggled throughout his life to broaden himself by stretching out to every experience that presented itself to him.

By the time he settled down with Teresa Guiccioli in 1820, Byron had become a man much like Prince Hal: he had "sounded the very base-string of humility" and could "drink with any tinker in his own language" and yet seriously longed for an occasion to "salve / The long-grown wounds of [his] intemperance" in some historically significant movement. In 1820 at Ravenna, Byron joined the liberal Italian gentry of Romagna in the Carbonari movement; but their hopes were crushed with the defeat of the Neapolitan constitutionalists (March 1821), and the Counts Ruggero and Pietro Gamba, father and brother of Byron's beloved, were driven into exile from one Italian duchy and principality to another. At last, urged on by the idealistic Pietro Gamba and by more self-interested friends on the Greek Committee in

London, Byron devoted himself to the cause of Greek independence and became one of many Western martyrs in that lengthy and bloody war.[18] That action marked Byron as a more vital historical personage than any other European writer of his era. Place names and postage stamps of Greece are slender reminders of the popular appeal he exerted on liberal noblemen in Italy, Greece, Poland, and Russia throughout the revolutionary movements of the nineteenth century. And if this inspiration were his only claim to fame, it would still distinguish him from the other Romantic writers who, being more contemplative and less active, appeal so strongly to the denizens of cloudy academe.

Had Byron written only the poems and dramas that we have discussed and enumerated thus far—that is, everything except the sixteen-plus cantos of *Don Juan* (1818–23)—he would still rank as one of the six great English Romantic poets. The quantity of his poetry and his impact on the history of British and European literature, thought, and history would doubtless maintain his place in courses in English and European Romanticism, as well as a popularity among several types of non-academic readers of poetry. His brilliant letters, as we have recently witnessed, win him a still broader audience. But when ranking Byron as a literary figure on the basis of aesthetic criteria quite distinct from quantitative or sociological ones, *Don Juan* weighs more heavily in the balance than all his other works combined. Great as some of them are, they would only make him the *equal* of Wordsworth and Shelley. *Don Juan,* in my opinion, elevates Byron as the greatest of the British Romantics. I base this judgment partly on the traditional hierarchy of forms, which has since the time of Aristotle accorded epic poetry the highest rank. *Don Juan* is the great European epic of the nineteenth century.[19]

Don Juan fulfills all the principal criteria for an epic poem enumerated in both the most perceptive studies of the genre and the best account of its fate among the English Romantic poets, Brian Wilkie's *Romantic Poets and Epic Tradition.*[20] More significantly, *Don Juan* fulfills the role of a *great* epic poem in the sense in which Shelley in *A Defence of Poetry* declared Dante's *Commedia* to be an epic: it is a "bridge thrown over the stream of time," and Byron is the fourth epic poet by the criteria Shelley used to name Homer, Dante, and Milton as the three earlier ones. The poetry of Byron, like their masterworks, "bore a defined and intelligible relation to the knowledge and sentiment and religion and political conditions of the age in which he lived, and of the ages which followed it: developing itself in correspondence with their development." In *A Defence of Poetry,* Shelley distinguishes epic from drama, which he describes not as a *bridge* from the past age to the future, but as "a prismatic and many-sided *mirror,* which collects the brightest rays of human nature and divides and reproduces them from the simplicity of these elemental forms." His account of the history of literature notes that "in periods of the decay of social life, the drama sympathises with that decay." Obviously, he felt that in just such transitional periods, when the old order waned, giving place to new, the great epics were written. Shakespeare grew up and flourished at the culmination of Renaissance Christian-humanism, before its synthesis had begun to dissolve in a renewal of rationalism; Milton wrote his epic amid the intellectual currents that carried Western civilization from the Renaissance exploration of ancient verities toward the Enlightenment spirit of rational inquiry; he utilized the epic form to synthesize a new world-view from recent modes of thought and older mythic structures. Though Shelley was too close to *Don Juan* and too fully immersed in Byron's age to be aware of the fact, Byron also stood between two intellectual eras: having been raised in the Enlightenment (with its cocksureness about the powers of rational systems), he contributed to a renewed awareness of the irrational powers haunting the human psyche that would eventually find their expositors in Darwin, Marx, Nietzsche, and Freud. By the time Byron wrote *Don Juan*, he was prepared to delineate the encounter between a rationalistic concept of human nature and the irrationalities of human experience.

As McGann demonstrates in *"Don Juan" in Context*, the action of the poem is relentlessly unteleological and often fortuitous, the force of random circumstance interacting with—and often overpowering—imaginative ideals that served as focus for purely Romantic narratives, as well as the providential teleology that governs epics like *The Aeneid, Jerusalem Delivered,* and *Paradise Lost*. In *Don Juan* Byron also reintroduces aspects of the mode of the "Primary Epic," as C. S. Lewis defines it in his *Preface to Paradise Lost;* specifically, *Don Juan*, like *The Iliad, The Odyssey,* and *Beowulf* (but unlike the epics of Vergil, Dante, Tasso, Milton, or Camoëns), is without "a heroic story and cares nothing about 'a great national subject.' . . . Heroism and tragedy there are in plenty, therefore good stories in plenty; but no 'large design that brings the world out of the good to ill.' The total effect is not a pattern but a kaleidoscope."[21] Unconsciously, perhaps Lewis alludes to *Don Juan*, which he may have known is often described by a word that Byron was the first to use in poetry—a "kaleidoscope." Lewis goes on to clarify his point in this striking example:

> In Homer, its [Primary Epic's] greatness lies in the human and personal tragedy built up against this background of meaningless flux. It is all the more tragic because there hangs over the heroic world a certain futility. "And here I sit in Troy," says Achilles to Priam, "afflicting you and your children." Not "protecting Greece," not even "winning glory," not called by any vocation to afflict Priam, but just doing it because that is the way things come about. . . . Perhaps this was in Goethe's mind when he said, "The lesson of the *Iliad* is that on this earth we must enact Hell." (page 31)

If Goethe saw *The Iliad* in the terms Lewis describes, so might Byron or Shelley. Thus Byron's use of the subject-matter of the Primary Epic may have been not only precedented but calculated, even though he lacked the temerity to broach the comparison.

Lewis describes the language of the Primary Epic as "a Poetic Diction; that is, a language which is familiar because it is used in every part of every poem, but unfamiliar because it is not used outside of poetry" (pp. 21–22). This combination was necessary, says Lewis, because the audience to whom the poetry was read aloud had to be able to grasp the meaning instantly but would expect the poet to rise above everyday speech. The language of *Don Juan*, of course, opposes this ideal in both respects, for Byron not only employs common, everyday language that is anything but specifically "poetic," but he also employs strange words from various languages, as well as English slang and neologisms.[22] It should be remembered, however, that the epic poetic diction had carried over directly from Primary Epic into the great Secondary Epics like *Paradise Lost* and that Byron (who wrote for readers rather than auditors) had to distinguish the focus and vision of his epic from those of traditional epics by finding or creating a language as apparently chaotic and unpredictable as the moral nature of the treacherous world through which his hero navigates. What I have said of the language may be said also of the standard epic conventions—the address to the Muse, the opening of the story *in medias res,* the epic similes, the detailed descriptions (e.g., of the shield of Achilles), the catalogues, etc.—each of which Byron rejects or subverts. These conventions, like the poetic diction, were carried over from Primary to Secondary Epic without alteration and had become elements or accompaniments of the High Style; and one of Byron's means of justly distinguishing his epic purpose from that of Vergil or Milton was to disrupt or reverse the significance of their conventions in his work.

To understand fully the relationship of Byron's narrative method in *Don Juan* to that of the Homeric Primary Epics, we must turn from C. S. Lewis to another master scholar, Erich Auerbach. In "Odysseus' Scar," the first essay of *Mimesis,* Auerbach explains clearly and precisely that "Homer . . . knows no background. What he narrates is for the time being the only present, and fills both the stage and the reader's mind completely."[23] Auerbach also, in discussing a correspondence between Goethe and Schiller in 1797 on the nature of "the retarding element" and the episodic structure of the Homeric poems, quotes Schiller as saying that Homer gives us " 'simply the quiet existence and operation of things in accordance with their natures'; Homer's goal is 'already present in every point of his progress.' " When Auerbach concludes that "the true cause of the impression of 'retardation' appears to me to lie . . . in the need of the Homeric style to leave nothing which it mentions half in darkness and unexternalized" (p. 3), he delivers an oblique but recognizable account of Byron's narrative mode in *Don Juan*.

To take a cluster of examples almost at random from Byron's poem, let us look briefly at the opening of the second published unit (Cantos III–V). After his "Hail, Muse! *et cetera*" and a "digression" on the nature of love and marriage (III. stanzas 2–12, in which, incidentally, Byron associates himself with his epic predecessors Dante and Milton even in his marital difficulties), Byron describes Lambro and his return in a passage (III. stanzas 12–61) that contains a pointed allusion (III. 23) to the parallels and differences between his return home and that of Odysseus to Ithaca. During this passage there is much detailed description of Lambro's character, emotions, and activities (recent and habitual) which we may accept as germane to the subsequent action, but as Lambro begins to glimpse the signs of holiday on his island, Byron further retards his narrative to describe "a troop of Grecian girls" dancing, the feast, "children round a snow-white ram," "a dwarf buffoon," and several other people and things that never reappear or affect the subsequent action. After Lambro has queried the ignorant revellers concerning his own and his daughter's fates, he enters the house—only to have the action retarded once more by several stanzas that examine in greater detail his character and feelings—and when Lambro finally "stood within his hall," Byron again suspends the action for fully seventy-five stanzas (III. st. 61–111, IV. 1–34), besides the lyric on "The Isles of Greece," before Lambro confronts the lovers. Within this long "retardation" are passages that may be considered reflective and/or satirical (such as the detailed description of the trimming Poet Laureate), but other sections seem to serve no other function than to describe the physical details of one particular moment held in stasis before the narration resumes.

Byron, of course, could not produce "naive" poetry in the Homeric vein. His education, encompassing not only "Ossian's" Homeric vision of human passions and random experience but also the Enlightenment dreams of rational orderliness in human society, provided him with the choice between these incompatible ways of presenting human experience. But his habit of keeping his eye fixed on a variety of "others," rather than imposing on the outer world a pattern derived from his own desires, enabled him to approximate the mode of the Homeric Primary Epic, keeping every (or almost every) character, object, place, and event that he mentions fully in the foreground, with an importance (as long as it occupies the stage) equal to every other person, object, place, or event, existent or fictional. Such a blurring of the traditional hierarchies of "important" or "momentous" or "significant" people, places, and things is a natural outgrowth of the British empirical tradition in psychology and epistemology. If every human was, in effect, the prisoner of his own mind, then as Earl Wasserman points out in his analysis of *Tristram Shandy,* "meaning had become a function of each person's private, subjective concerns, which alone remained as an interpretive organization."[24] For most of the Romantics (as for Uncle Toby), awareness of this subjectivity challenged them to create private, personal hierarchies according to their own beliefs or experiences. They rode their own personal hobbyhorses that they might not be trampled by another man's. But Byron, unwilling to play god by reordering the world he never made, chose to embody in *Don Juan* the ultimate skepticism by presenting every object and every idea as equally present, equally real, and equally important—the real-life objects of his indifference and his scorn, as well as the ideals of his devotion.

Those who find unconvincing my suggestions for the reasons behind Byron's style in *Don Juan* must confront the style itself. *Mimesis* shows us how Homer's narrative method corresponds to the capriciousness that C. S. Lewis sensed in the moral universe of *The Iliad* and *The Odyssey;* the poet brings all facts into the foreground, giving the shield of Achilles or the scar on Odysseus's knee a narrative interest equal to that accorded to the wrath of Achilles or the slaughter of Penelope's suitors. Employing a modern version of the same technique, Byron's digressive narrative weighs equally the fates of nations and the stylistic and moral peccadillos of the Lake Poets, and he describes and narrates in similar detail and with equal gusto an idyllic scene of young love, cannibalism among the survivors of shipwreck, and the persons and history of a group of opera singers who appear only to disappear from the life of his hero.

The randomness of *Don Juan,* along with the structural anomaly of this epic that lacks a traditional beginning, middle, or end, links the poem with the thought and literature of the past seventy years, during which period the orthodox teleological systems deriving from German Romantic idealism (including the Marxist dialectic) have taken hard knocks from the recalcitrant facts of history and personal experience, as well as from the anti-systems of thinkers from Kierkegaard to Wittgenstein. Byron's skepticism, rooted in the thought of Montaigne, Voltaire, Hume, and others who demolished earlier Panglossian systems (only to rouse a new generation of system-builders from their dogmatic slumbers into equally categorical alertness), allows him to reflect or to anticipate all modes of thought from the Enlightenment to Existentialism.

Byron's religious upbringing imposed on him an uncomfortable awareness of God, even when his own beliefs and behavior failed to conform to doctrinal Christianity. Thus Byron, with *Don Juan,* builds a bridge between the litigious religious temper of post-Reformation Europe and the restless, non-doctrinal individualized god-seeking in modern secular society. Byron, through *Don Juan,* takes seriously the material facts of human existence, including such elementary physiological drives as hunger and the sexual instincts, thereby subverting ideologies of the political and moral Right and Left that attempt to avoid or ignore these elements of mundane existence. At the same time, he shows Juan and other characters transcending merely animalistic behavior through the quirky strength of a reverent humanism that refuses to allow their ideals of conduct to be completely overridden by merely material considerations. Thus Byron, through *Don Juan,* upholds traditional, humanistic idealisms against later analytical scientism.

As a scion of the old feudal aristocracy who personally held many of the ideals of the French Revolution, Byron in *Don Juan* also bridges the gap between the hierarchical orders of past societies (depicted and upheld with varying emphases by Homer, Dante, and Milton) and modern egalitarian ideals. Each character in *Don Juan* is judged on his moral characteristics alone, whether fate has cast him in the role of Lambro, a pirate, or the Czarina Catherine the Great; Daniel Boone, a private citizen, and George Washington, the chief of state, carry equal weight as ideal inhabitants of a commonwealth. (This blend of aristocratic and egalitarian ideals, by the way, is the moral and thematic thread that makes so effective Byron's blend of the Horatian and Juvenalian styles in his satirical passages.) One could, in like manner, go through the other ideals depicted in Byron's poem, and find that they bear "a defined and intelligible relation to the knowledge and sentiment" of the age out of which he grew and that which his poems both anticipated and helped create.[25] The personal physical courage that Juan exhibits (during the shipwreck, at the siege of Ismail, and in the face of the armed highwaymen) combines, for example, both with his tenderness as a lover and as the protector of helpless innocents (and with his disgust at useless carnage) to link the macho knight-errantry of the past with the pacific ideals of loving, sacrificial heroism which have been voiced (if not widely exemplified) in our own time.

Byron's refusal to portray only part of human experience—the earthly beatitude of Juan and Haidée or the horrors of the fall of Ismail—stands as a sign both of the poem's epic inclusiveness and of the skepticism that informs Byron's vision of the human condition. *Don Juan* thus fulfills the conditions of modern skeptical epic.[26] In that capacity, it not only recreates the nature of the epic itself (in many ways demonstrated by Wilkie and suggested by McGann), but also—as great epics do—provides us with an encyclopedic work that delineates the ideals and attitudes that have dissolved during the past one hundred and fifty years, just as Cicero's dialogues and Montaigne's essays, to a lesser degree, portray the plethora of dogmatic arguments and opinions from which those earlier Skeptics strove to liberate their contemporaries.

Byron's greatness as a poet lies in his comprehensive vision and in his ability to touch so many chords in the depths of human life. Other writers were more learned men, more systematic thinkers, or even more careful artists, but Byron, because he early turned to the outside world to counteract his own deepseated feelings of inadequacy, was able to embody the spirit of the Romantic questioning in accessible symbols, discourse, and narration that reach men and women of all social and intellectual levels. This ability was not shared by other major poets of the period. We need not subscribe to the egalitarian aesthetics of Tolstoy's "What is Art?" to recognize that all the very greatest poets—Homer, Aeschylus, Sophocles, Euripides, Dante, Shakespeare, Molière—exhibit such a universality as *one* of their salient characteristics. Once the meaning of their works has been transmitted to any audience, the power of the moral and emotional forces that their intellects have probed can electrify men and women of all ages and conditions. That is why their works are repeatedly being rewritten, translated, and modernized with greater success than is attained by the original works of the very writers who translate or modernize them.[27]

Byron has been called a "negative Romantic," whose irony undercuts all values.[28] But only those who see dogmatism as the goal of philosophy should find Byron lacking in values. The moral actions of Don Juan and many of Byron's other poetic characters—like Byron's own willingness in England, Italy, and Greece to commit himself fully and intelligently to causes he thought just—provide models of responsible action that ought to satisfy the moral sensitivity of existentialists of every theistic and atheistic denomination. His values are neither dogmatic nor elitist—and this last negative may explain why he has not been given his due by elitist critics, who seem to feel that the intellectual life is compromised whenever someone can read and enjoy a poem without their guidance.

To be relevant in the Romantic period, a major poet had to be, to one extent or another, a Skeptic just as surely as in Dante's time and place he had to be a Christian. Without skepticism in some form, the intellectual climate dictated that the poet would either sink under the dead weight of an outworn Anglican orthodoxy or else chain his conscience to one of the anti-humanist alternative orthodoxies then current—either sectarian fideisms (Calvinist or Wesleyan) or a variety of the pervasive rationalist utilitarianism that survived the failure of the French Revolution to evolve later under varying conditions into Positivism, Marxism, or democratic Liberalism.

Both Shelley and Byron maintained a skepticism during their mature years. But whereas Shelley did so to preserve freedom to assert the self—to liberate his desire for immortality from the necessitarian doctrines of his early mentors—Byron maintained his skepticism as a two-edged weapon, one side to keep at bay the would-be gods of the phenomenal world—the relative ideals longing to be absolutized—and the other edge to trim the luxuriant growth of his own ego-centered aspirations. In Byron's hands skepticism helped a humanist give due respect both to tradition and the great achievements of the past and to the concepts of historical development and progress, without bowing the knee to either Baal. It enabled him to maintain self-respect without converting it to solipsistic self-worship. Thus balanced and stabilized, Byron's great poetic genius produced a body of poetry that marks the culmination of the skeptical tradition in the English Romantic period.

Notes

1. See Hubert F. Babinski, *The Mazeppa Legend in European Romanticism* (New York: Columbia Univ. Press, 1974).
2. Written on 6 August 1821; published in the third issue of *The Liberal,* April 1823.

3. Written December 1822–January 1823; published 1823.

4. Written October 1821; published in the second number of *The Liberal*, January 1823.

5. Byron wrote *Werner* in December 1821–January 1822 (though he had originally begun a play based on *Kruitzner* in 1815); it was published as a volume by John Murray in November 1822.

6. Written ca. May–June 1822; published in the first issue of *The Liberal*, October 1822.

7. Written January–February 1823; published in June 1823 by John Hunt.

8. See *Byron's Letters and Journals*, ed. Leslie A. Marchand (Cambridge: Harvard University Press, 1977), VII, 161–163; *Shelley and his Circle*, VII, ed. Reiman (Cambridge: Harvard University Press, 1986), 59–61.

9. See especially Edward E. Bostetter, *The Romantic Ventriloquists* (Seattle: Univ. of Washington Press, 1963) and Jerome J. McGann, *"Don Juan" in Context* (Chicago: Univ. of Chicago Press, 1976).

10. See McGann, *"Don Juan" in Context*, pp. ix–x; in Chapter V, *"Don Juan:* Style," McGann emphasizes the more traditional ideas of classical rhetoric on the interplay of the high, low, and middle styles, as well as the contrast in tone between Juvenalian and Horatian satire. On this subject, see also Frederick L. Beaty's excellent article, "Byron's Imitations of Juvenal and Persius," *SiR*, 15 (1976), 333–355.

11. Manning, *SiR*, 18 (1979), 208. [Ed. note: Also appears in this volume.]

12. Shelley's value-system, though based on the valorization of a few quasi-mystical experiences such as that recorded in "Hymn to Intellectual Beauty," is much closer to Byron's. In fact, Shelley probably influenced Byron's thinking by urging the exercise of free moral choices to validate the rest of life.

13. The poem was begun in May 1821, completed in October 1821, and published in the first number of *The Liberal*, October 1822.

14. Peterfreund, "The Politics of 'Neutral Space' in Byron's *Vision of Judgment*," *MLQ*, 40 (1979), 275–291. In Byron's day the House of Lords was the appropriate place for judging a peer or a royal personage. The debate on a bill judging the conduct of Queen Caroline had occupied the attention of all Englishmen through much of 1820; earlier, William, fifth Lord Byron, had stood trial in the House of Lords for killing William Chaworth in their fateful duel. See Byron's poem "The Duel," written at Venice on 29 December 1818.

15. There is room for further exploration of Byron's allusions in the poem. For example, St. Peter's reference to exchanging places with Cerberus and Satan's reply on trying "to coax *our* Cerberus up to Heaven" (stanza 1) are two of Byron's many hits at Canning, whom he considered two-faced and who was in the House of Commons rather than the House of Lords ("Heaven").

16. See Peterfreund, pp. 287–288.

17. Jerome J. McGann, *Fiery Dust: Byron's Poetic Development* (Chicago and London: University of Chicago Press, 1968), p. 27.

18. See Harold Nicholson, *Byron: The Last Journey* (London: Constable, 1924; new ed., 1948). For Byron's integrity among the moral ambiguities of the War for Greek Independence, see William St. Clair, *That Greece Might Still Be Free: The Philhellenes in the War of Independence* (London: Oxford Univ. Press, 1972). For the continuing influence of Byron's example, see *Byron's Political and Cultural Influence in Nineteenth-Century Europe*, ed. Paul Graham Trueblood (Atlantic Highlands, N. J.: Humanities Press, 1981).

19. Besides the *Variorum Edition* of Steffan and Pratt, the most important books devoted entirely to *Don Juan* include (in chronological order) those by Paul Graham Trueblood (1945), Elizabeth French Boyd (1945), George M. Ridenour (1960), and McGann (1976). [For these and other studies of *Don Juan*, see the introduction to this volume and the bibliographical notes passim.]

20. Madison: Univ. of Wisconsin Press, 1965. I refer specifically to Wilkie's excellent first chapter, "The Romantics and the Paradox of the Epic."

21. Lewis, *A Preface to Paradise Lost* (1942; rpt. London: Oxford Univ. Press, 1960), pp. 29–30.

22. Though Byron thought that attempted imitations of Shakespearean and Elizabethan language in British drama had debased the style (and he therefore eschewed it in *Marino Faliero* and his other dramas to revivify English dramatic writing through the use of Continental models), in *Don Juan* he employs far more echoes and direct quotations from Shakespeare than from any other writer. Obviously Shakespeare's vital, colloquial language aided Byron's efforts to break with the Latinate formality of British epic diction.

23. *Mimesis: The Representation of Reality in Western Literature,* trans. Willard Trask (1953; rpt. New York: Anchor Books, 1957), pp. 2–3.

24. Wasserman, *The Subtler Language* (Baltimore: The Johns Hopkins Univ. Press, 1958), p. 170.

25. Byron's ideas often anticipate not only those of the next generation but even those of their great-great-grandchildren: Referring to beauty in African women, Byron says that "black is fair" (XII. lx, lxi); he also predicts that technology deriving from the scientific discoveries of such men as Newton will soon carry men to the moon (X. ii). As the notes in the Variorum *Don Juan* attest, these opinions were not idle speculations but convictions based on Byron's profound understanding of human nature.

26. In *Byron and Joyce through Homer: "Don Juan" and "Ulysses"* (New York: Columbia Univ. Press, 1981), Hermione de Almeida argues convincingly that James Joyce's *Ulysses,* which she relates to Byron's *Don Juan,* is the epic of the twentieth century and bridges the chasm separating the Victorian extension and transformation of the Romantic impulse from the Modernist era.

27. Among a host of possible examples, I shall cite George Chapman's translations of Homer; Leigh Hunt's *The Story of Rimini; A.* W. Schlegel's Shakespearean translations; Eugene O'Neill's *Mourning Becomes Electra;* the translations of Dante by Henry Francis Cary, John Ciardi, and Dorothy Sayers; Richard Wilbur's brilliant translations of Molière; and the Arthur Laurents-Stephen Sondheim adaptation of *Romeo and Juliet* into *West Side Story.* Not all adaptations or translations successfully transmit the works of great writers, but one sign of imaginative greatness and universality is the capacity of a work to interest and inspire even after it had been mutilated by really inferior adapters and translators. The stage history of Shakespeare's works provides more than enough examples to illustrate what we might call the "Venus de Milo phenomenon."

28. Morse Peckham, "Toward a Theory of Romanticism: II. Reconsiderations," *SiR,* 1 (1961), 1–8.

Editor's Bibliographical Note

Reiman's comments on the poems and plays of Byron's Italian years should be compared with those in the books and articles listed in the Editor's Bibliographical Notes to the essays earlier in this volume by Ridenour, McGann, Gleckner, Beatty, and Garber, as well as the excerpt from McGann's *Beauty of Inflections* that follows. Reiman's more wide-ranging and vigorous discussion of *Don Juan* as "the great European epic of the nineteenth century" revives a major and complex issue that has been debated almost ad nausem ever since the poem's publication, though addressed less often in the last decade or so. Some purchase on the contours of that debate may be gained from the following key critical studies: Ridenour's 1960 *The Style of "Don Juan"* (New Haven: Yale University Press), particularly (but certainly not exclusively) his fourth chapter, entitled "My Poem's Epic"; Alvin Kernan's long essay on *Don Juan* in his

The Plot of Satire (New Haven: Yale University Press, 1965), still the most masterly exposition of the competing claims of epic, comic, and satire (or some combination of these) to characterize the poem adequately; Brian Wilkie's 1965 *Romantic Poets and Epic Tradition* (see Reiman's note 20); McGann's *"Don Juan" in Context* (1976; see Reiman's note 9); the 1977 *Studies in Romanticism* symposium (see the bibliographical note to Ridenour's essay earlier in this collection), the final section of which is by Reiman and is included in the portion of his book, *Intervals of Inspiration,* reprinted above; and Hermione de Almeida's *Byron and Joyce through Homer: "Don Juan" and "Ulysses"* (N. Y.: Columbia University Press, 1981).

There are, of course, numerous other analyses of *Don Juan* as an epic of *some* sort, but I can think of only two that take us much beyond those just listed, neither of which directly addresses the *idea* of epic in *Don Juan* but both of which display an acute sense of its "epic" dimensions: Bernard Beatty's *Byron's Don Juan* (Kent: Croom Helm, 1985), which subsumes Byron's "epicness" into an even more inclusive and chameleonlike term, "comedy," and Malcolm Kelsall's 50-page chapter entitled "There Is No Alternative: *Don Juan*" in his *Byron's Politics* (Sussex and Totowa: Harvester Press and Barnes & Noble, 1987), which also abjures the term epic while arguing that *"Don Juan,* if finished, would be *The Dunciad* of political liberty" (p. 146). Also worthy of note is Stuart Curran's brief discussion of *Don Juan* as exemplifying "composite order" in his *Poetic Form and British Romanticism* (Oxford: Oxford University Press, 1986) as well as his en passant judgment that "Byron's witty claims for its epic stature are now, in general, seriously weighed" (p. 191) and his implicit "correction" of Wilkie's definition of romantic epic in chapter 7.

The critical literature on skepticism is predictably considerable and immensely varied; in the romantic period most of the commentary is directed to elucidating Shelley's thought and poetry. Most notable in this regard, though hardly alone, are C. E. Pulos, *The Deep Truth: A Study of Shelley's Scepticism* (1954) and Lloyd Abbey, *Destroyer and Preserver: Shelley's Poetic Skepticism* (1979), both Lincoln: University of Nebraska Press, and Terence Hoagwood, *Skepticism and Ideology: Shelley's Political Prose and Its Philosophical Context from Bacon to Marx* (Iowa City: University of Iowa Press, 1988), the most thoroughly philosophy-oriented book on Shelley to date. On Byron specifically, we have the relatively conventional and less than satisfying *Byron as Skeptic and Believer* by Edward W. Marjarum (Princeton: Princeton University Press, 1938) but also the far more incisive book by Michael Cooke, *The Blind Man Traces the Circle: On the Patterns and Philosophy of Byron's Poetry* (Princeton: Princeton University Press, 1969), particularly the chapter derived from his earlier essay, "The Limits of Skepticism: The Byronic Affirmation," *Keats-Shelley Journal* 17 (1968): 97–111. See also David J. Leigh, S. J., "*Infelix Culpa:* Poetry and the Skeptic's Faith in *Don Juan,*" *Keats-Shelley Journal* 28 (1979): 120–38, and Andrew M. Cooper, "Shipwreck and Skepticism: *Don Juan* Canto II," *Keats-Shelley Journal* 32 (1983): 63–80.

One should compare Reiman's implicit "placing" of Byron in the English romantic movement with the similar periodic contextualization sketched out by Jerome McGann, in response to George Ridenour, in the *Studies in Romanticism* symposium cited in the first paragraph of this note, to which Reiman also contributed. The argument about Byron's "place" goes back, of course, much further than that—certainly to Arthur O. Lovejoy's famous (or infamous) essay "On the Discrimination of Romanticisms," *PMLA* 39 (1924): 229–53 and its innumerable "responses," perhaps most notably Morse Peckham's 1951 attempt, as he put it, to "reconcile" Lovejoy's position and with that taken by René Wellek in his two-part "The Concept of Romanticism," *Comparative Literature* 1 (1949): 1–23, 147–72, and Peckham's relegating Byron to an exemplar of "negative romanticism" (for Peckham's argument see "Toward a Theory of Romanticism," *PMLA* 66 [1951]: 5–23, and *Studies in Romanticism* 1 [1961]: 1–8). It is beyond the parameters of this volume to even summarize all the crosscurrents of the debate, but some of its key ingredients, at least up through the early 1960s may be found in my *Romanticism: Points of View,* rev. ed. (Detroit: Wayne State University Press, 1975).

Needless to say, much more water has gone over the dam since then, some muddy, some clear, though Peckham's position vis-à-vis Byron perhaps rather oddly resurfaces in M. H. Abrams's influential *Natural Supernaturalism: Tradition and Revolution in Romantic Literature* (N. Y.: Norton, 1971), where Byron is omitted altogether on the grounds that "in his greatest work he speaks with an ironic counter-voice and deliberately opens a satirical perspective on the vatic stance of his Romantic contemporaries" (p. 13).

It is in both contexts, then—the publication of McGann's *"Don Juan" in Context* and Abrams's striking exclusion of Byron from what Bloom called "the visionary company"—that the *SIR* symposium re-raises the question of what "romanticism" is, especially McGann's sketching out, in response to Ridenour, a position vis-à-vis the internal coherence of romanticism that appears more fully argued in his later *The Romantic Ideology* (Chicago: Chicago University Press, 1983). Among the other most interesting and provocative recent contributions to the discussion (aside from the circling and eddying of definitions and redefinitions of romantic irony, bibliographical notes on which accompany Garber's essay in this volume) are Stuart Curran's argument that poetic form "is a significant key" to the character of British romantic poetry, *Poetic Form and British Romanticism* (N. Y. and Oxford: Oxford University Press, 1986), Marilyn Butler's revisionist *Romantics, Rebels and Reactionaries: English Literature and Its Background, 1760–1830* (London: Oxford University Press, 1981), Thomas McFarland's *Romanticism and the Forms of Ruin: Wordsworth, Coleridge, and the Modalities of Fragmentation* (Princeton: Princeton University Press, 1981), and, just prior to all of these, Michael G. Cooke's *Acts of Inclusion: Studies Bearing on an Elementary Theory of Romanticism* (New Haven: Yale University Press, 1979), which contains an important chapter on "Byron's *Don Juan:* The Obsession and Self-Discipline of Spontaneity."

Finally, in his concentration on Byron's years and poems of his exile, particularly those of 1818 to his death, Reiman takes up, if briefly, a number of poems that are only minimally dealt with elsewhere in this volume—most notably the plays, *Beppo,* and *The Vision of Judgment.* The plays I have addressed under Byron's politics in the bibliographical note to Beatty's essay earlier in this volume, and *The Vision of Judgment* in the bibliographical note to Gleckner's essay. For *Beppo,* see particularly Truman G. Steffan's seminal essay, "The Devil a Bit of Our *Beppo,*" *Philological Quarterly* 32 (1953): 154–71; Lindsay Waters, "Pulci and the Poetry of Byron: *Domestische Muse,*" *Adam: International Review* 1 (1983): 34–48; Peter G. Vassallo, *Byron: The Italian Literary Influence* (New York: St. Martin's, 1984); W. Paul Elledge, "Divorce Italian Style: Byron's *Beppo,*" *Modern Language Quarterly* 46 (1985): 29–47; and Jerome McGann's " 'Mixed Company': Byron's *Beppo* and the Italian Medley," in *Shelley and His Circle,* vol. 7, ed. Donald H. Reiman (Cambridge: Harvard University Press, 1986).

The Book of Byron
and the Book of a World

JEROME J. MCGANN

Byron wrote about himself, we all know, just as we all know that his books, like God's human creatures, are all made in his image and likeness. This quality of his work is apparent from the very beginning. His first book, *Fugitive Pieces,* was privately printed in 1806 for an audience of friends and acquaintances who were privy to its local references and biographical connections—many of which were connections with themselves. *Hours of Idleness,* his first published work, appeared the following year, and it sought to extend the range of Byron's intimacies to a somewhat larger book purchasing audience. In *Hours of Idleness* Byron projected himself before his English audience as a recognizable figure whom, he trusted, they would be happy to take to their breasts. In *Hours of Idleness* the English world at large met, for the first time, not the Man but the Lord of Feeling, a carefully constructed self-image that was fashioned to launch him on his public career. This was not conceived, at the time, as a literary career.[1]

Byron succeeded in his effort, though not precisely as he had expected. Certain hostile reviews—most notoriously, Brougham's in the highly visible and influential *Edinburgh Review*—interruped Byron's initial, unruffled expectations. Had he reflected more critically on the hostile reception that *Fugitive Pieces* had provoked in certain narrow quarters of its local (Southwell) society, he might have anticipated some trouble for his next book.[2] But he did not, apparently, and seems only to have realized later that he was destined to be both the darling and the demon of his age.

The attack on *Hours of Idleness* was another opportunity for Byron to produce yet a third Book of Himself: this time, *English Bards and Scotch Reviewers,* the fiery counter-attack on his persecutors and the culture that supported such beings (*CPW,* 1:398–99). If it is true that Byron was "born for opposition," this book revealed that fact, for the first time unmistakably.

And so it went on. In 1809 Byron left benighted England to chew over the high rhetoric of his last book, and he plunged into Europe and the Levant, where his next productions began to accumulate their materials in

Reprinted from *The Beauty of Inflections,* © Jerome J. McGann 1985, by permission of Oxford University Press and the author.

the much larger context of European affairs. He wrote a continuation, or sequel, to *English Bards and Scotch Reviewers* called *Hints from Horace,* which was not published in his lifetime, and he composed the first two cantos of that unsurpassed act of literary self-creation, *Childe Harold's Pilgrimage. A Romaunt (CPW,* 1:426–27, 2:268–71).

This book is worth pausing over—not the poem, but the book.[3] It is a handsome and rather expensive (30s.) quarto volume beautifully printed on heavy paper. It comprises four distinct parts: (1) the title poem in two cantos (pp. iii–109); (2) the extensive notes to these cantos (pp. 111–61); (3) a section headed "Poems" that included fourteen short pieces (pp. 163–200); (4) an appendix containing bibliographical materials, translations, Romaic transcriptions, and one facsimile MS, all having to do with the current state of the literary culture of modern Greece (pp. 201–[27]). Its publisher conceived its audience to be a wealthy one, people interested in travel books and topographical poems, people with a classical education and with a taste for antiquarian lore and the philosophical musings of a young English lord. As it turned out, all of England and Europe were to be snared by this book's imaginations. It went through a dozen (cheaper) editions in three years and established all of the principal features of that imaginative (but not imaginary) world-historical figure known as Byron. Later circumstances would only provide the public with slightly different perspectives on this figure.

The book of *Childe Harold* published in 1812 picks up the autobiographical myth that Byron had left *in medias res* when he left England in 1809.[4] The notes specifically recall the controversy surrounding *English Bards and Scotch Reviewers,* the section of "Poems" is so arranged as to mirror the personal tale narrated through the title poem, and the latter presents a dramatic picture of a young lord who leaves his local home and friends, as well as his country, in a condition of psychic and cultural alienation. Simply, he is disgusted with himself and the world as he has thus far seen it. He finds, when he flees to other lands and in particular to the fabulous Levantine seat of western culture, that his own personal anomie, experienced in the tight little island of Britain, mirrors the condition of Europe (or, in Byron's startling and important variation on this ancient topos, that Europe and the entire world mirrors *his* personal condition). Thus does Byron force himself—and the individual person through himself—to the center of attention. What his book says is not simply that we should deplore the condition of western culture in this critical time, but that we should deplore it because its debasement has poisoned its chief, indeed, its only, value: the individual human life. In particular, Byron's life.

Byron inserts his personal history into the latest phase of the European crisis that began in 1789. The outbreak of the Peninsular War in 1809 initiated the last act in the drama of the Napoleonic Wars, which would end in the defeat of Napoleon and the restoration of the European monarchies under the hegemony of England. In *Childe Harold* (1812) Byron's itinerary takes him first to the very heart of the Peninsular events, where his initial mood of disgust at his English existence acquires its European dimensions. When he moves to the East and the dominions of the Turkish Empire, including Greece, his cynicism is confirmed: Greece, the very symbol of the west's highest ideals and self-conceptions, lies in thrall not merely to the military rule of the Porte but to the contest of self-serving political interests of the English, French, and Russians.

This is the context that explains Byron's peculiar appendix, with its heterogeneous body of Romaic materials. *Childe Harold* (1812) is obsessed with the idea of the renewal of human culture in the west at a moment of its deepest darkness. This means for Byron the renewal of the value of the individual person, and the renewal of Greece as an independent political entity becomes Byron's "objective correlative" for this idea. *Childe Harold* (1812) is thus, on the one hand, a critique of present European society and politics and, on the other, a pronouncement of the crucial need throughout Europe for the independence of Greece. As Byron would later say: "There is *no* freedom—even for *Masters*—in the midst of slaves."[5] The question of Greece thus becomes for Byron a way of focusing the central questions that bear upon the present European epoch. The Europeans normally date this epoch from 1789, and rightly so, but in this book (as well as in his next two books, *The Giaour* and *The Bride of Abydos*), Byron argues that the conflict of European self-interests can be best and most clearly understood in terms of the recent history of Greece, whose abortive efforts for independence in the late eighteenth century were either neglected by the European powers or actively betrayed.

Thus, in *Childe Harold* (1812) Byron enlarged his personal myth, which he had already begun to develop in his earlier books, by inserting it into the wider context of the European political theatre as it appeared to him in 1809–1812. The central ideological focus of the entire myth involves the question of personal and political freedom in the oppressive and contradictory circumstances that Byron observed in the world of his experience. More than anything else this book says that the most personal and intimate aspects of an individual's life are closely involved with, and affected by, the social and political context in which the individual is placed. Byron goes further to say that such a context is more complex and extensive than one ordinarily thinks, that each person is more deeply affected by (as it were) invisible people, places, and events than we customarily imagine. Ali Pacha and his Albanians may appear far removed from England and the Napoleonic Wars, but to the perspicacious European they will have more than a merely exotic interest. Similarly, Byron's rather ostentatious use of antiquarian and classical materials is not merely a clumsy display of learning and artistic pedantry. On the contrary, Byron invokes the classical world and the later history of Europe's investment in that world because this complex ideological and political network impinges directly upon current European affairs and hence on the experience of each single person living in Europe. A powerful and illuminating irony runs through Byron's flight from contemporary England and Europe and his pursuit of ancient Greek ideals:

> Of the ancient Greeks we know more than enough; at least the younger men of Europe devote much of their time to the study of Greek writers and history, which would be more usefully spent in mastering their own. Of the moderns, we are perhaps more neglectful than they deserve; and while every man of any pretensions to learning is tiring out his youth, and often his age, in the study of the language and of the harangues of the Athenian demogogues in favour of freedom, the real or supposed descendants of these sturdy republicans are left to the actual tyranny of their masters. . . . (p. 143)

Byron's proposal in his book is to look at England, Europe, and Greece, not as these political entities appear in their ideological self-representations, but "as they are" (p. 144) in fact. The reality reveals an Islam and a modern Greece very different from what they are commonly represented to be in English and European commentaries; it also reveals the hypocritical fault lines that run through the high-minded and Greek-derived ideologies of liberty to which the major European powers give lip-service. In Byron's book, the image of the young European gentleman acquiring a classical education is contradictory and deeply satiric. Such a person's mind is filled with self-congratulating and self-deluding ideas that permit him to identify with the dream of ancient Greece even as they also allow him to remain blind to certain important actualities: that the Russians "have twice . . . deceived and abandoned" the Greeks; that the French seek "the deliverance of continental Greece" as part of their policy for "the subjugation of the rest of Europe"; and that the English, in addition to the pursuit of their economic self-interests, profess to seek the freedom of Greece even as they subjugate the rights of "our Irish Helots" (p. 161) and "Catholic brethren" (p. 143).

In Byron's books—*Childe Harold* (1812) is merely prototypical in this respect—the variety of materials often conveys an image of heterogeneity, but in fact this image is no more than the sign of intrinsic connections that are not normally perceived, of connections between "opposite and discordant" matters that only *appear* to be separated but that are in fact fundamentally related. The soon-to-be-published Oriental Tales are not merely a set of exotic adventure stories. They constitute a series of symbolic historical and political meditations on current European ideology and politics in the context of the relations between East and West after the breakup of the Roman Empire and the emergence of Islam.[6] That later readers and critics have often taken Byron's Levantine materials as a sign of a (presumptively shallow) poetic interest in local color and oriental ornamentation merely testifies to a failure of critical intelligence and historical consciousness. Byron was deeply interested in these social and political questions and he used his poetry to probe their meaning and their roots. Later criticism has too often translated *its* disinterest into a myth of the intellectual poverty of Byron's verse.

Byron's skill at manipulating his publications produced some of the strangest and most interesting books of poetry ever printed in England. *The Giaour* may stand as one example out of many.[7] Like the other tales that were soon to follow, this poem is a political allegory told from the point of view of those "younger men of Europe" whom Byron described in the notes to *Childe Harold* (1812). The subject of the poem, at the plot level, is the state of modern Greece around 1780. At the narrative level, the poem is a contemporary (1809–13) meditation on the meaning of the European (and especially the English) understanding of Levantine politics between 1780 and 1813. The poem's story (its plot level) is a nihilistic tragedy in which all parties are involved and destroyed. The meditation on the story is carried most dramatically in the introductory 167 lines, which appear as the "original" work of the poem's redactor (Byron himself), as well as in the poem's "Advertisement" and its many prose notes, also represented in *The Giaour* as the "original" work of the editor/redactor Byron. The entire significance of this excellent work does not appear unless one responds to the interplay between the poem's two "levels." Briefly, the "original" work of the editor/redactor comprises a set of deeply contradictory materials: on the one hand, a complete romantic sympathy with the characters and events as well as an absorption in the heroic ideology that they exhibit; on the other, a mordant series of comical remarks on Eastern mores and commonplace European ideas about such matters. This radical split in the poem's attitude at its meditative level reflects back upon, and interprets, the European understanding of the Levant between 1780 and 1813. The interpretation that Byron produces is a critical one: the European understanding is self-deluded and helpless, and Byron's own exposure of this failed understanding is represented as the one-eyed man's vision in the kingdom of the blind. The comedy of the poem's notes, apparently so urbane, is in fact a flinching away, the laughter, spoken of in *Don Juan,* that serves to hold back weeping and bleaker realities.

All of Byron's works, and especially his published books, exhibit intersections of these kinds. Thus, his bibliography is more than a scholar's guide and resource, it is as well a graphic display of his life in books and of the extension of his life through books. The piracies, the huge number of translations, the numerous printings all attest and perpetuate the poetic explorations of reality that he initially set in motion. And it is the "books," rather than the "poems" (or least of all the "texts"), that draw attention to the central quality of Byron's poetical work; for when we study the works through their material existences we are helped to see and understand the social and historical ground that defines their human meanings.

Nowhere is this fact about Byron's work more clear than in the case of his masterwork, *Don Juan.* We respond to its name as if it were one thing, as indeed it is; but it is also, like the world it expresses and represents, incredibly various and polyglottal. Readers have of course always responded to that variety, but we must do so even as we also bear in mind that the variety is of a determinate and specifiable sort. *Don Juan* is, formally, a romantic fragment poem comprising six authorized and published volumes, along with a body of material that was not published until after Byron's death, at different times and with various justifications. The first two volumes were published by John Murray in a certain way, and the next four volumes were published by John Hunt in a very different way. Important aspects of the meaning of the poem are bound up with these interesting events in the work's publication history.[8]

Most important to see is that when Byron began publishing the poem with John Hunt he was released from certain constraints that he had to struggle against when he was publishing with the conservative house of Murray. *Don Juan*'s (rejected) preface and (suppressed) dedication emphasize the political and social critique that is finally so fundamental to the poem.[9] But Murray and his allies forced Byron to revise the published version of the first five cantos so as to *de*-emphasize this aspect of the epic. As a consequence, the original cantos 1–5 (the first two published volumes of the poem) preserve the poem's social and political critique as a peripheral and subsidiary matter, an incidental topic that seems to appear and disappear in the poem in a random way. The suppressed dedication was not published until 1832, and the rejected preface did not appear until 1901.

With the appearance of cantos 6–8, published by Hunt, the situation changes radically. These cantos are introduced with a prose preface where the social and political issues are finally raised to a great, even to a dominant, position; and the poetic materials as well undergo a shift in emphasis toward more explicitly social and political matters. This change in the poem has been recognized for some time and critics have described the differences between the earlier and the later cantos in various (often useful) ways. What has not been seen, however, is the structural change brought about in the poem as a whole when Byron began his epic "again" (as it were) with cantos 6–8 and John Hunt.

We can begin to see what is involved here by looking briefly at the original preface to cantos 1–2. Byron never completed this preface, which descends to us in his fragmentary draft MS. Nevertheless, what he did complete gives us some interesting information about Byron's initial conception of his work. In the course of satirizing Wordsworth, Byron tells his readers that "the following epic Narrative" is to be regarded as the work of a certain "Story-teller" who is living, and delivering his narrative, at a certain place and time: specifically, "in a village in the Sierra Morena on the road between Monasterio and Seville" sometime during the Peninsular War (the reference to the village in the Sierra Morena is autobiographical and specifies the date as 1809). As for the narrator himself, "The Reader is . . . requested to suppose him . . . either an Englishman settled in Spain—or a Spaniard who had travelled in England—perhaps one of the Liberals who have subsequently been so liberally rewarded by Ferdinand of grateful memory—for his restoration" (*DJV*, 2:4–5). This passage establishes a second point of view on the events treated in the poem: that is, one subsequent to 1814 and the early years of the period of European restoration following the fall of Napoleon. As it turns out, the reader inevitably places this historical vantage point at that moment of contemporaneity that attaches to the poem's date of composition and/or publication (in this case, 1818–19).

Byron finally dropped his preface with its specific historical perspectives, and he did not fully exploit the structural advantages of his poem's double perspectivism until he began to reconceive the project of *Don Juan* in 1822–23. Before considering that act of reconception, however, we should reflect upon the double historical perspective in terms of which the work was initially conceived and set in motion. Like the later cantos, cantos 1–5 organize their materials in two dialectically functioning historical frames of reference: on the one hand, the frame of the poem's plot or "story," which contains the narrated events of Juan's life; and, on the other hand, the frame of the poem's narrating voice, which comprises Byron speaking to his world between 1818 and 1824 via the six published volumes of *Don Juan*. Byron's rejected and incomplete preface to cantos 1–2 reminds us that he initially had some idea of using the plot level and the narrative level to comment on each other and that he thought of Juan's life in specific historical terms. As it turned out, he rejected the idea of setting the poem's narrative frame in the complicated way suggested by the initial preface, where it is unclear whether the narrator speaks from the vantage of 1809 or 1818, or both. In cantos 1–5 Byron also neglected to specify clearly the historical frame in which Juan's career is placed. When he published cantos 6–8 with John Hunt, however, he finally let his contemporary readers see very clearly the exact relation between the history of Juan's career and the history of the poem's narrator, Byron *in propria persona*.

We can date Byron's reconception of his epic fairly exactly: in January and February 1822, which is the period when Byron resumed his composition of *Don Juan* (he left off his poem when he finished canto 5 at the end of 1820). Byron wrote to Murray on 16 February 1821 (*BLJ*, 8.78) and outlined a projected plot for Juan's adventures. This outline, however, only corresponds in a loose and general way to the episodes of the poem that he was soon to write and hence shows that Byron had not yet fixed on a definite plan. Byron first articulated this plan to Medwin between December 1821 and March 1822:

> I left him [Juan] in the seraglio. There I shall make one of the favourites, a
> Sultana . . . fall in love with him, and carry him off from Constantinople. . . .
> Well, they make good their escape to Russia; where, if Juan's passion cools, and I
> don't know what to do with the lady, I shall make her die of the plague. . . . As

our hero can't do without a mistress, he shall next become man-mistress to Catherine the Great. . . . I shall . . . send him, when he is *hors de combat,* to England as her ambassador. In his suite he shall have a girl whom he shall have rescued during one of his northern campaigns, who shall be in love with him, and he not with her. . . . I shall next draw a town and country life at home. . . . He shall get into all sorts of scrapes, and at length end his career in France. Poor Juan shall be guillotined in the French Revolution! What do you think of my plot? It shall have twenty-four books too. . . .[10]

This scheme corresponds fairly closely to the poem as we now have it, and it holds to the general plan that Byron gave to Murray at the beginning of 1821 (though not to the particular details of the episodes). The most important episode missing from Byron's outline is the siege of Ismail, though it is clear from this and Byron's immediately preceding discussion that he planned to send Juan into war. But in the first few months of 1822 Byron seems not yet to have decided on the Ismail episode, as he had not yet worked out how to separate Juan and Gulbeyaz. These decisions would be made in the next few months. The idea of having Juan die on the guillotine in the French Revolution was certainly fundamental to the plot of the poem from the earliest stages of its conception as a plotted sequence.

The preface to cantos 6–8, written in September 1822, calls attention, on the one hand, to the historical immediacy of the poem as it is Byron's act of discourse with his world and, on the other, to the specific (past) historical nexus in which Byron's story of Juan's career is imbedded. The second part of the preface is a bitter diatribe against Castlereagh, who had recently taken his own life, against the present condition of Europe under the restored thrones and their allied policies, and against those like Southey who were at once supporters of these institutions and detractors of Byron's recent work. The opening sentences of the preface, on the other hand, tell us that the material in cantos 7 and 8 is based upon an actual event: the siege of Ismail by the Russians in November–December 1790. The latter was the chief episode in the (latest) Russo-Turkish War, which had been renewed in 1787. The preface tells the reader, in other words, that Juan's career in Byron's poem is unfolding within real historical time, and—specifically—that we are to map his career in terms of specific places, dates, and events. When Juan goes to Catherine's court after the siege of Ismail, the date is early 1791. Shortly afterwards he goes to England.

Clearly, then, Byron's projected scheme for the plot of Juan's career was actually being implemented when Byron renewed the poem's composition at the beginning of 1822. That he was preparing Juan for a trip to Paris and death on the guillotine in 1793 at the end of the poem is borne out by the fulfillment of the other details that he gave to Medwin, as well as by the chronology of Juan's exploits established in the siege of Ismail episode.[11] We should note that this precise dating of Juan's life in the poem accommodates itself to the events of cantos 1–6. Byron had not, before the preface to cantos 6–8, forced his audience to read the events of cantos 1–6 within a specific historical frame of reference. After the preface, however, those events are drawn into the poem's newly defined historical scheme. Juan's life in Byron's poem begins in Seville just as the French Revolution has broken out, or is about to break out. His life will end at the end of Byron's poem, and the date for him will be 1793.

Lacking the precise historical frame that Byron established for his poem in 1822, Juan's career would appear episodic, the verse equivalent of the fictional careers of characters in Smollett, Sterne, and Fielding.[12] The exact historical placement changes the situation dramatically. Juan at first appears to move through Byron's poem in a picaresque fashion, but as the poem develops and his life is brought into ever-closer relations with the great and epochal events shaking Europe in the early 1790s, the reader begins to glimpse an order, or perhaps a fate, that was not at first evident or even suspected. Having Juan die in the Reign of Terror at the end of Byron's poem is a daring conception: on the one hand, it seems a surprising, even an arbitrary, end for Byron's inoffensive hero, but, on the other, it calls attention to a hidden constellation of forces drawing together far-flung and apparently unrelated people and events. History proceeds "according to the mighty working" of forces that gather up the odd and the disparate, and historical explanation, in Byron, proceeds according to the mighty working of a poem that *reveals* these odd and unapparent connections.

Not least of all does it reveal the connections that hold between the pan-European world of 1787–93 and its counterpart in 1818–24. The revolutionary epoch in which Juan's career begins and ends is explicitly examined from the vantage of the period of Europe's restoration. Juxtaposing these two worlds allows each to comment on the other. More crucially for the poem, however, the juxtaposition gives Byron the opportunity to expose certain congruences between these periods and to suggest that the second period is a variant repetition of the first. These congruences are established via the third historical frame that gives a structure to *Don Juan:* the period in which the Book of Byron was initially composed, and more especially the central years of that period, 1809 to 1817/18.

The congruences appear most dramatically as a series of related and repeating sequences of gain and loss, rise and fall, triumph and disaster. Juan's career illustrates this pattern both in its particular episodes and in the larger scheme that Byron projected for his hero. Adversative forces of various kinds interrupt and thwart Juan's plans and hopes. Some of these are represented as his responsibility while others originate in external circumstances over which he can have no control. In both cases, the pattern of an early promise that later fails or is betrayed appears in Juan's life as well as in the course of the French Revolution. Juan's life follows the moral arc of the revolution even as his career follows its early chronological development. But what is most important, so far as Byron's poem is concerned, is that both of these sequences recur in the next generation. The second phase of the revolution is dominated by the rise and fall of Napoleon, whose professed aim (at any rate) was to establish the revolution on a secure European footing. The consequence of his career was, on the contrary, the final defeat of the revolution's historic agenda. This repetition, in Napoleon's life, of the historical course of the early years of the revolution appears in Byron's poem through its autobiographical analogue: the meteoric rise and subsequent fall of Lord Byron, a series of events that we—following Byron—associate with the years 1809–1817/18. In Byron's and Napoleon's careers the reader of *Don Juan* observes, once again, the pattern established in Juan's life and in the course of the early revolution.

Following his self-exile from England in 1816 Byron meditated on the meaning of this pattern in his life and on its relation to similar patterns in past and contemporary history. The most important of these meditations comes down to us as *Childe Harold's Pilgrimage,* canto 4, which Byron completed shortly before he began *Don Juan.* Here Byron decides that all history, when judged by meliorist or revolutionary standards, is a story of disaster and unsuccess. What he also decides, however, is that against this fatal and repeating story may be, and has been, placed the deed of the opposing mind and will, the individual voice which, while it recognizes the evil pattern, refuses to accept or assent to it.

> Yet, Freedom! yet thy banner, torn, but flying,
>   Streams like the thunder-storm *against* the wind;
> The trumpet voice, though broken now and dying,
>   The loudest still the tempest leaves behind. (*CHP* 4, stanza 98)

> Yet let us ponder boldly—'tis a base
>   Abandonment of reason to resign
> Our right of thought—our last and only place
>   Of refuge. . . . (*CHP* 4, stanza 127)

These attitudes establish the ground on which *Don Juan* comes to judge the patterns of historical repetition. Byron begins the poem from the vantage of 1818, a point in European history when time appears to have rolled back upon itself. Thirty years have passed, yet the enormous upheavals that marked those years seem to have returned the European world virtually to the same political position that it occupied in 1788. Furthermore, Byron observes in this period a series of repetitions that suggest that the cycle of revolutionary disappointment is a general pattern that is found in many historical periods and is replicated for the individual as well as for society. In terms of the narrator's historical frame (1818–24), *Don Juan* is yet another revolutionary undertaking begun in a period of darkness. As such, the bleak patterns of repetition over which the Byron of 1818–24 will brood—the pattern of Juan's career and the early phase of the revolution, the pattern of Byron's career and the Napoleonic wars—threaten the narrative project of 1818–24 with a fearful end.

Byron begins *Don Juan* already knowing that individual and social history, from a revolutionary point of view, always follows a curve of disappointment or disaster. In this sense (but only in this sense) the poem is "nihilistic." In every other respect the poem is a great work of hope, for it insists that projects of change and renewal must continue to be raised up despite the fact of absolute adversity. The Byron who set *Don Juan* in motion understands that the eye begins to see only in a dark time, and—more crucially—that there never is a time that is or was not dark. Those who seek not merely to understand the world, but to change it, strive toward an ideal of human life that will have to be "anywhere out of the world." This is the strife of *Don Juan*'s hope, the deed of its mind—the fact of its books. The poem begins its quest for renewal under its own prophecy of failure, and it seeks to persuade its readers that one begins in this way simply because there is no other place *to* begin, that the renewal arrives with the event, not in the end. For in the end you lose, always.

Thus Byron begins his poem in 1818 by calling for a new hero to take the place of all the failed heroes of the past and, in particular, of all the failed heroes of the preceding revolutionary epoch. Byron catalogues their names in canto 1 only to toss them aside in favor of "our friend, Don Juan," whose history he purposes to tell. As we have seen, however, and as every reader of the poem has always recognized, that fictive history recollects and alludes, at every point, to the actual history of Lord Byron, who is the poem's true "hero" and central figure. Juan's progress from Seville to the Levant, and thence via Russia to England and (prospectively) to Paris and his death, is shadowed by the actual career of Byron. In fact, Juan's career is no more than a displaced re-presentation of Byron's, a coded fiction through which the reader may glimpse the friends, enemies, and the incidents of Byron's life, as well as the patterns and epochs of that life. The English cantos, at the level of the poem's plot, should be located in the summer and early autumn of 1791; at the level of the poem's recollective autobiographical structure, as everyone knows, these cantos reflect Byron's life in England during his Years of Fame.

When Byron reinitiated his *Don Juan* project at the beginning of 1822, therefore, he did so with two objects clearly in his mind. The first of these involved structural matters: specifying a precise chronology for Juan's life in the poem. This move entailed, as a consequence, a dramatic refocusing of the poem's materials. Because of the move readers would be better able to see the tripartite organization of the poem's historical vision. *Don Juan* examines the period 1789–1824 in terms of its three dominant phases: the early years of the French Revolution (the poem's displaced fiction); the epoch of the Napoleonic Wars (viewed through Byron's analogous and contemporary experience of those years); and the epoch of the European restoration (dramatically fashioned and presented at the poem's immediate narrative level).

Byron's second object, which is related to the first, aimed to reassert in an unmistakable way the socio-political character of his work. When he began *Don Juan* he spoke of it as "bitter in politics" (*BLJ*, 6:76–77), but as he struggled to get Murray to publish his cantos he was gradually led to de-emphasize both the bitterness and the politics. The de-emphasis appeared in the published work itself—the removal of the dedication, the decision not to print the Wellington stanzas in canto 3, and so forth—as well as in Byron's letters back to England in which he raised his defense of the poem against his publisher's and his friends' objections.[13] During 1819–21 these letters take a conciliating and mollifying line. Byron tried to get his poem accepted by assuring his friends that it was actually a harmless thing, an elaborate *jeu d'esprit* conceived more in a comic than a satiric mode, "to giggle and make giggle" (*BLJ*, 6:67, 208). In 1822 the structural changes are accompanied by an uncompromising and candid political stance. In his resumed poem, he told Moore in July 1822, he meant to "throw away the scabbard" and make open ideological war with the new reactionary spirit of the age (*BLJ*, 9:191). By December he was equally clear on the subject in a letter to Murray: *Don Juan* "is intended [as] a *satire* on *abuses* of the present *states* of Society" (*BLJ*, 10:68). Cantos 5–8, issued by the liberal Hunt rather than the conservative Murray, are prefaced with Byron's prose declaration of mental war, and the next volume—cantos 9–11—begins with the diatribe against war and Wellington which Byron, in 1819, had withdrawn from canto 3.

Byron's purposes with his poem, then, are accompanied by important changes in his aesthetic and political consciousness. Not the least of these was his new and clearer understanding of the *wholeness* of the period 1789–1824, of the intimate relations that held between the three major phases of this period, and of the connections between people and events that might appear, at first, to have little to do with each other. No episode in the poem reveals more clearly Byron's increased understanding of these historical repetitions and relations than the Siege of Ismail, the episode in which Byron initially focused the historical and political restructuring of his epic.

The siege is, at least in part, what it appears to be: a satire on war and its violence. Byron was not a pacifist, however. He supported patriotic struggles and wars of liberation, and he eventually went to serve in the Greek effort to break free of the Turkish Empire. We have to specify, therefore, the ground of Byron's satire. This ground begins to emerge when we reflect upon Byron's chief source for his details. He used the account in Marquis Gabriel de Castelnau's *Essai sur l'Histoire ancienne et moderne de la nouvelle Russie* (3 vols., Paris, 1800).[14] The ideology of this book is reactionary and monarchist, and its narrative of the siege is largely based on the first-hand details supplied to Castelnau from the diary of Armand Emmanuel du Plessis, Duc de Richelieu

(1767–1822). Byron mentions Castelnau's *Essai* in the preface to cantos 6–8, where he also speaks of the Duc de Richelieu as "a young volunteer in the Russian service, and afterwards the founder and benefactor of Odessa" (*DJV*, 3:3). The irony and satire implicit in these remarks arises from Byron's negative approach to Castelnau's glorifying account of the siege, as well as from his ironic sense of the young Richelieu's benefactions.

Reading Castelnau, Byron saw that many of the officers in Catherine's army at the siege of Ismail were "distinguished strangers" (canto 7, line 254), a wickedly oblique phrase calling attention to the fact that these men, like the young Duc de Richelieu, were emigrés from France and the revolution. Richelieu and the other distinguished strangers are not patriots fighting for their country, they are military adventurers. That Byron intended this line of attack on the French emigrés at Ismail is perfectly plain from the letter to Moore in which he said that his new cantos (the siege cantos, that is) constitute an attack upon "those butchers in large business, your mercenary soldiery" (*BLJ*, 9:191). Lying behind the satire of this battle and the entire Russian episode in the poem is the idea, commonly found in liberal thought of the period, that monarchists like Richelieu have no other business in life except to fight in wars (any wars will do) and intrigue at court. The fact that Juan's rescue of Leila is based upon an actual incident in Richelieu's life only underscores Byron's mordant comments on the indiscriminate militarism of aristocratic ideology:

> If here and there some transient trait of pity
>   Was shown, and some more noble heart broke through
> Its bloody bond, and saved perhaps some pretty
>   Child, or an aged, helpless man or two—
> What's this in one annihilated city? (8, stanza 124)

These lines, and the larger passage from which they are drawn, cut back against Castelnau's account of the war and the supposed "noble heart" of the young duke. The man celebrated by reactionaries like Castelnau as "the founder and benefactor of Odessa" is as well one of those who destroyed a city in which he had no personal or political interest whatsoever, who fled his own country at a moment of crisis, and who later—after the fall of Napoleon—returned to France to become minister for foreign affairs in the restored monarchy. [15]

Richelieu merely epitomizes what Byron wishes to attack in his narrative of the siege and in the Russian cantos generally: the character of monarchist regimes. He is even more important in Byron's poem, however, as a focus for the political filiations that connect, on the one hand, such apparently separated events as the siege of Ismail and the events in France in 1789–90 and, on the other, the strange twists and eventualities of European history between 1789 and 1818. Richelieu and the other distinguished strangers do not find their way into Catherine's army merely by chance, nor is it chance that brings him back, at the Bourbon restoration, to serve as an important functionary in the reactionary alliance. Neither is it chance that leads Byron in 1822 to expose this pattern of relations through his narrative of the siege. Byron was well aware, at least since 1809, of the imperialist stake that various European powers had in Balkan and Levantine affairs. The narrative of the siege of Ismail forces the reader to recall to mind that network of political and economic interests, as well as to see that the power and self-interests of the monarchies have not been broken by the revolutionary and Napoleonic years. When Byron looks at the siege from the vantage of the restoration, then, he integrates it into the pattern of pan-European affairs of 1789–93 (that is to say, the event is integrated into the order and fate of Juan's fictional-historical career), and he also uses it to comment upon current European conditions. In effect, Byron's employment of his sources involves him in a massive critical-revolutionary reinterpretation of the history of Europe from the outbreak of the French Revolution to the early years of the restoration.

Thus, in 1822 Byron transforms *Don Juan* into a book of the European world, a comprehensive survey and explanation of the principal phases of the epoch 1789–1824. The period is dominated by repetitions, by the violence that has accompanied them, and by the ignorance and indifferences that have abetted these repetitions and their violences. Against these things Byron sets the project of *Don Juan,* which is itself finally recognized to be involved in, to be a part of, the epoch and its repetitions. *Don Juan* becomes a book of the European world by becoming, finally, the Book of Byron, an integrated meditation and commentary upon his own life as it is and was and continues to be a revelation of the meaning of his age.

Don Juan is the Book of Byron because he is its hero, because the poem gives the reader a history of 1789–1824 that is set and framed, at all points, in terms of Byron's history. Juan's fictional movements retraverse actual places and scenes that Byron once passed through, and their details recollect persons and events in his past. In addition, the digressive narration often ruminates Byron's career to comment on and finally to judge it. In short, the poem repeatedly gives the reader views of Byron's past life in the coded sequence of its fictional level as well as in the memorial sequence of its narrative level. All this is widely recognized, as is the related fact that the history of an entire epoch is to be glimpsed in the reflective details of the poem.

Less apparent is the significance of the narrative as it is an *immediate* rather than a recollective event. Cantos 1–5 constitute the fictional level and the narrative level through two volumes of verse issued by John Murray in 1819 and 1821, and the remaining cantos constitute themselves through the four succeeding volumes issued by Hunt in 1823 and 1824. In addition, however, the last four volumes reconstitute what was originally printed in the first two volumes (a) by forcing the reader to place the whole of the fictional level in a specified historical frame of reference, and (b) by making this important interpretive shift a part of the poem's developing structure, a part of its own self-criticism. Byron begins the Hunt volumes of his poem, cantos 6–16, with a preface announcing his ideological purposes and describing the key elements in the historical restructuring of the poem. Cantos 6–16 then carry out these changes of direction and thereby force cantos 1–5 to accommodate the changes. The structural accommodations we have already discussed. The ideological changes appear as a more comprehensive understanding of the subjects taken up by the project of *Don Juan*. Most noticeable here is Byron's effort to present a totalized interpretation and critique of his age: to compel his readers to understand how the several phases of the period 1789–1824 hang together and to persuade them that his critical-revolutionary reading of the period is the correct one. Related to this polemic is the poem's vision of self-judgment, its critical-revolutionary reading of the limits and blindnesses of cantos 1–5. Byron's revisionary turn on the first five cantos is not, of course, a repudiation of them. Though an act of self-criticism, the change of direction in cantos 6–16 assumes—indeed, it demonstrates—a dialectical continuity with its objects of criticism. The advances and the retreats of cantos 1–5, their boldness and timidity, accumulate a set of dynamic contradictions that eventually generate cantos 6–16.

In this way *Don Juan* represents not merely a comprehensive interpretation of the period 1789–1824 but a comprehensive critical interpretation that incorporates its own acts of consciousness in its critique as part of a developing and changing act of interpretation. All readers have recognized this quality of the poem's digressive and shifting style, but it is important to see that this stylistic feature is grounded in the work's ideological structure. Even more important to see, however, is that the ground of this ideological structure is not in some definable form of critical interpretation that we may educe from the work. Rather, it lies in the act of the poem, the social and historical deeds of its consciousness that appear to us, most immediately, as a set of specific acts of publication. Of course, the fragmentary character of the work has heretofore obscured somewhat the comprehensiveness of its historical argument. Scholarship helps to bring that argument into sharper focus, to lift it from the sphere of a reader's intuition into a more explicit and defined frame of reference.

Late in the poem Byron says of himself that like his own work *Don Juan* he is "Changeable too—yet somehow '*Idem semper*' " (17, stanza 11). Readers have not found it easy to say what exactly in the poem is "changeable" and what exactly stands resistant to change. I think we can now make an attempt to isolate these factors. What changes in the poem are its ideas; these are continually subjected to qualification, revision, even repudiation. What remains the same is the perpetual dialectic of the individual mind in its social world, the active deed of its committed intelligence. Fichte called this ground of permanence "Tat," Schopenhauer "Wille." These are of course nothing more than conceptual markers for an act of social consciousness that can only be *carried out* in words but that cannot be defined in them. The act of the poem's mind, then, is an understanding that changes and brings about change. In *Don Juan*—to adapt a contemporary formulation of a fragment from Herakleitos—"What does not change / is the will to change."[16]

Notes

1. For a discussion of these matters see my *Fiery Dust: Byron's Poetic Development* (Chicago: University of Chicago Press, 1968), chap. 1, and *Lord Byron: Complete Poetical Works*, ed. Jerome J. McGann (Oxford: Clarendon Press, 1980–) 1:360–63. The latter work is hereafter referred to as *CPW*.

2. See poems 24, 25, 28, in *CPW* 1.

3. For complete bibliographical details see *Byron's Works: Poetry*, ed. E. H. Coleridge (London: John Murray, 1901–1904) 7:180–84 and T. J. Wise, *Byron: A Bibliography . . .* (London: n.p., 1932–33) 1:50–54. The history of the book's publication is discussed in the *CPW*, 2:268–69. The prose quotations below from *Childe Harold's Pilgrimage. A Romaunt* are taken from the first edition, and page numbers are given in the text.

4. For a more detailed discussion of the context and meaning of the poem see *CPW*, 2, and *Fiery Dust*, part 2. The poem is hereafter parenthetically cited as *CHP*, plus canto and stanza numbers.

5. See *Byron's Letters and Journals*, ed. Leslie A. Marchand (Cambridge, Mass.: Harvard University Press. 1973–82) 9:41; hereafter referred to as *BLJ*.

6. See the commentaries to the Oriental Tales in *CPW*, 3.

7. *CPW*, 3:406–415. For an excellent discussion of the political aspects of two of the books of Byron's tales see Peter Manning, "Tales and Politics: *The Corsair, Lara,* and *The White Doe of Rylstone*," in *Byron. Poetry and Politics . . .* , ed. E. A. Stürzl and James Hogg (Salzburg: Institut für Englische Sprache und Literatur, 1981), pp. 204–30.

8. For a discussion of the history of the poem's publication see *Don Juan: A Variorum Edition*, ed. T. G. Steffan and W. W. Pratt (Austin, Tex.: University of Texas Press, 1958) 1:25–52 *passim* (hereafter cited as *DJV*).

9. See *DJV*, 2:3–20 and 4:4–15. The preface is placed at the beginning of the text of *Don Juan* in *DJV* as well as its sequel, the Penguin modernized edition. Leslie A. Marchand's school edition also places it at the poem's beginning. Such a placement is seriously misleading, however, for Byron not only left this preface in an uncompleted state, he discarded it.

10. *Medwin's Conversations of Lord Byron*, ed. Ernest J. Lovell Jr. (Princeton, N. J.: Princeton University Press, 1966), pp. 164–5.

11. Some of Byron's marginal jottings in canto 14 schematize two of the poem's future episodes, including the death of Juan. These marginalia appear on a scrap of MS (not known to the *DJV* editors) now in the Murray archives. The notations occur on a MS carrying a variant version of lines 479–80.

12. Critics have frequently drawn attention to *Don Juan's* parallels with eighteenth-century picaresque novels. See Elizabeth Boyd, *Byron's "Don Juan"* (1945; rpt. New York: Humanities Press, 1958), esp. chaps. 4–7; Andras Horn, *Byron's 'Don Juan' and the 18th Century Novel*, Swiss Studies in English, No. 51. (Bern: Frank Verlag, 1962), and A. B. England, *Byron's Don Juan and Eighteenth Century Literature* (Lewisburg, Pa.: Bucknell University Press, 1975), esp. chap. 3.

13. See *DJV*, 1:13–24; Samuel C. Chew, *Byron in England* (London: John Murray, 1924),

chap. 4; and J. J. McGann, *Don Juan in Context* (Chicago: University of Chicago Press, 1976), pp. 51–67.

14. See Boyd, *Byron's "Don Juan,"* pp. 148–50 and Nina Diakonova, "The Russian Episode in Byron's 'Don Juan,' " *The Ariel* 3 (1972): 51–57.

15. Byron's critique of the contemporary world of the restoration operates as well in his treatment of "Suwarrow" in the Russian cantos. For a good discussion see Philip W. Martin, *Byron: A Poet Before His Public* (Cambridge: Cambridge University Press, 1982), pp. 213–17.

16. This is Charles Olson's translation of Herakleitos, frag. 23, which appears as the first line of Olson's poem "The Kingfishers."

Editor's Bibliographical Note

Although his *Social Values and Poetic Acts: A Historical Judgment of Literary Work* (Cambridge: Harvard University Press, 1988) and *Towards a Literature of Knowledge* (Chicago: University of Chicago Press, 1989), with its chapter on "Lord Byron's Twin Opposite of Truth," postdate *The Beauty of Inflections,* it is fair to say, I believe, that this essay is the culmination of McGann's careerlong engagement (since *Fiery Dust* in 1968) with Byron—critically, ideologically, historically, socially, politically, economically, even psychologically (however much this last is not Freudian or Jungian or any other recognizable formulated approach). Two other essays by McGann representing, as he noted in a letter to me of 27 October 1989, "quite a different way of thinking about Byron for [him]" are: "Byron and the Truth in Masquerade" (forthcoming) and " 'My Brain Is Feminine': Byron and the Poetry of Deception," in *Byron: Augustan and Romantic,* ed. Andrew Rutherford (New York: St. Martin's, 1990), 26–51. As intriguing as these post-1985 pieces are, and however "different" their ways of "thinking about Byron," *The Beauty of Inflections* is in some sense McGann's "Book of McGann"—or, if that is outrageous, at least the "Book of McGann's Byron." For all the recent critical lumps his four-book project has received—from *The Romantic Ideology* through *The Beauty of Inflections* to the two books cited in the first sentence above—Clifford Siskin, in his probing and astute review of *Social Values* (*Journal of English and Germanic Philology* 89 [1990]: 234–37), is correct about regarding McGann's work as "positioned at the key intersections of contemporary critical debate: history, textuality, social and political action" (p. 237).

There are few if any analogues to this achievement in Byron studies, but I will cite a few pertinent impingements on or extensions of some of the salient points of this essay: on the *Hours of Idleness* poems, Kurt Heinzelman's and Jerome Christensen's essays in this collection; on the tales, Daniel P. Watkins' different, yet complementary *Social Relations in Byron's Eastern Tales* (Rutherford: Fairleigh Dickinson University Press, 1987); on the economics and politics of Byron's relationship to his publishers, Peter Manning's "Tales and Politics: *The Corsair, Lara,* and *The White Doe of Rylstone,*" in *Byron: Poetry and Politics,* ed. E. A. Stürzl and J. Hogg (Salzburg: Universität Salzburg Institut für Anglistik und Amerikanistik, 1981), 204–34, and William H. Marshall's *Byron, Shelley, Hunt, and "The Liberal"* (Philadelphia: University of Pennsylvania Press, 1960); and on the political scene in England and on the Continent Malcolm Kelsall's *Byron's Politics* (Sussex and Totowa: Harvester Press and Barnes & Noble, 1987), especially chapter 1, which lays out Byron's "world" in admirable and telling detail (if with significant differences in its analysis of Byron's interrelationship with the events of Europe circa 1788 to 1818–24), chapter 3 entitled "Harold in Italy: The Politics of Classical History," and chapter 6, "There Is No Alternative: *Don Juan.*" For whatever it is worth, Kelsall ignores McGann's critical/historical work.

Impinging on McGann's analysis of, broadly speaking, Byron and politics are the following, which describe a recent rising tide of, again broadly speaking, sociopolitical criticism on Byron. By far the best study to date, other than Kelsall's, is Carl Woodring's pioneering and thorough survey, *Politics in English Romantic Poetry* (Cambridge: Harvard University Press, 1970), 148–229, both entirely superseding the older standard studies: Dora N. Raymond, *The Political Career of Lord Byron* (London: Allen and Unwin, 1924), and Crane Brinton, *The Political Ideas of the English Romanticists* (London: Oxford University Press, 1926), 147–95. Both also generally go beyond most of the essays in Stürzl's and Hogg's *Byron: Poetry and Politics* collection cited in the previous paragraph. Prior to Woodring and Kelsall, certainly the most important contributions to the subject are four essays by David V. Erdman: "Lord Byron and The Genteel Reformers," *PMLA* 56 (1941): 1065–94; "Lord Byron as Rinaldo," *PMLA* 57 (1942): 189–231; "Byron and Revolt in England," *Science and Society* 11 (1947): 234–48; and "Byron and 'the New Force of the People,' " *Keats-Shelley Journal* 11 (1962): 47–64.

To all of the above I would add Carl Lefevre, "Lord Byron's Fiery Convert of Revenge," *Studies in Philology* 49 (1952): 468–87; E. E. Bostetter, "Byron and the Politics of Paradise," *PMLA* 75 (1960), reprinted in his *The Romantic Ventriloquists* (Seattle: University of Washington Press, 1963), 241–301; Michael Robertson, "The Byron of *Don Juan* as Whig Aristocrat," *Texas Studies in Language and Literature* 17 (1976): 709–24; Paul G. Trueblood, ed., *Byron's Political and Cultural Influence in Nineteenth-Century Europe* (Atlantic Highlands, N. J.: Humanities Press, 1981), especially William Ruddick's essay, "Byron and England: The Persistence of Byron's Political Ideas" (although the volume also includes essays on Byron and France, Germany, Greece, Italy, Poland, Portugal, Russia, Spain, Switzerland, and Europe as a whole); Daniel P. Watkins, "Byron and the Politics of Revolution," *Keats-Shelley Journal* 34 (1985): 95–130; and Angus Calder, ed., *Byron and Scotland: Radical or Dandy?* (Totowa, N. J.: Barnes & Noble, 1989), particularly David Craig's "Byron the Radical" and Andrew Noble's "Byron: Radical, Scottish Aristocrat." See also Michael Foot's very different but interesting tour de force, *The Politics of Paradise: A Vindication of Byron* (London: William Collins, 1988), and Christina M. Root's "History as Character: Byron and the Myth of Napoleon," in *History and Myth*, ed. S. C. Behrendt (Detroit: Wayne State University Press, 1990), 149–65.

Finally, McGann's powerful argument that *Don Juan* "is the Book of Byron because he is its hero, because the poem gives the reader a history of 1789–1824 that is set and framed, at all points, in terms of Byron's history," implicitly raises the question of how the letters and journals may, or may not, be regarded as, if not *the* book of Byron, *a* book of Byron. Extraordinarily enough, critical commentary and analysis of them are disappointingly rare. Leslie A. Marchand's introduction to his magnificent edition of the *Letters and Journals* (Cambridge: Harvard University Press, 1973–82), vol. 1, 1–23, is graceful, perspicuous, unabashedly appreciative, and without obtrusive thesis other than remarking on the letters' "healthy and good-humored cynicism combined with a general benevolence toward human frailty" and on the journals' "exuberance" and "clear candour of their statement of what came uppermost to his active mind" (pp. 18, 23). A more provocative reading of the letters and journals—though not particularly focused on Byron's sociopolitical side—is Frederick W. Shilstone's chapter entitled " 'Pardon Ye Egotism': The Dialogue between Soul and Self in the Letters, Journals and Conversations" in his *Byron and the Myth of Tradition* (Lincoln: University of Nebraska Press, 1988), an essay I had hoped to include in this volume but was unable to because of its length.

Other interesting if not compelling efforts at analyzing this rather wondrous prose "kaleidoscope" (one of Byron's terms for *Don Juan*, but equally applicable to the letters and journals) are Charles Keith, "Byron's Letters," *Queen's Quarterly* 3 (Winter 1946–47): 468–77; Jacques Barzun, "Introduction: Byron and the Byronic in History," in his *Selected Letters of Lord Byron* (New York: Farrar, Straus, Young, 1953): vii–xli; John D. Jump, "Byron's Prose," in *Byron: A Symposium*, ed. Jump (London: Macmillan, 1975), 16–34, and his "Reflections on Byron's Prose," *The Byron Journal* 3 (1975): 46–56; Nina Diakonova, "Byron's Prose and Byron's Poetry," *Studies in English Literature* 16 (1976): 547–61; and L. J. Findlay, " 'Perpetual Activity' in Byron's Prose," *Byron Journal* 12 (1984): 31–47. To these should be added the numerous reviews by eminent Byron scholars of Marchand's 12-volume edition of the letters and journals. Also well worth consulting is *Byron's Bulldog: The Letters of John Cam Hobhouse to Lord Byron,* ed. Peter W. Graham (Columbus: Ohio State University Press, 1984) and the more narrowly focused but nonetheless fascinating "decoding" of some of Byron's correspondence (and that of his closest friends) in Louis Crompton, *Byron and Greek Love: Homophobia in 19th-Century England* (London: Faber; Berkeley: University of California Press, 1985). Important cautions with respect to the complex difficulties in determining when and where the "real" Byron speaks "straight"—particularly in his variously "recorded" conversations—may be found in Ernest J. Lovell's introductions to *His Very Self and Voice: Collected Conversations of Lord Byron* (N. Y.: Macmillan, 1954) ix–xl, and to *Lady Blessington's Conversations of Lord Byron* (Princeton: Princeton University Press, 1969), 3–114.

Index

♦